BANQUET AT DELMONICO'S

BANQUET AT DELMONICO'S

Great Minds, the Gilded Age, and
the Triumph of Evolution in America

· ·

BARRY WERTH

RANDOM HOUSE · NEW YORK

Published in the United States by Random House, an imprint of The Random House Publishing Group, a division of Random House, Inc., New York.

RANDOM HOUSE and colophon are registered trademarks of Random House, Inc.

LIBRARY OF CONGRESS CATALOGING-IN-PUBLICATION DATA

Werth, Barry.
Banquet at Delmonico's: great minds, the Gilded Age, and the triumph of evolution in America / Barry Werth.
p. cm.
Includes bibliographical references and index.
ISBN 978-1-4000-6778-7 (alk. paper)
eBook ISBN 978-1-5883-6798-3
1. Social Darwinism—United States—History—19th century. 2. Human evolution—Social aspects—United States—History—19th century. 3. Social change—United States—History—19th century. 4. Spencer, Herbert, 1820–1903—Influence. 5. Dinners and dining—New York (State)—New York—History—19th century. 6. Delmonico's Restaurant (New York, N.Y.)—History—19th century. 7. Intellectuals—United States—Biography. 8. United States—Intellectual life—19th century. 9. United States—Social conditions—1865–1918. 10. United States—Social life and customs—1865–1918. I. Title.
HM631.W47 2009
303.40973'09034—dc22   2008016567

Printed in the United States of America on acid-free paper

www.atrandom.com

9 8 7 6 5 4 3 2 1

FIRST EDITION

Book design by Simon M. Sullivan

To Kathy

CONTENTS

INTRODUCTION

THE CIVIL WAR THRUST AMERICA into the modern world. When the first shots were fired in 1861, we were an unsettled country composed mostly of farm families and independent local industries and institutions, a young patchwork race, overwhelmingly Christian. We would kill 620,000 of our own—almost two percent of the population—to preserve our idea of ourselves as a united, God-fearing, freedom-loving people. By the time it was done we were hurtling toward becoming a world power. Yet as Lincoln pointed out in his immortal first phrase commemorating the battle of Gettysburg—where more than fifty thousand died in three days of fighting—the nation in the bloody summer of 1863 was just eighty-seven years old; old enough for its people to have conquered the continental lands and set up institutions to rule them, but on the cusp of another, even more colossal challenge: *Now what?*

What were we to become, and to think? After decades of struggling over slavery, a revolution in natural science, and an upheaval in the moral role of men and women in society—then the crisis of the terrible war itself—churches and colleges were convulsed over the old truths about the hand of God in human affairs, and about the nature of reason and sin. New York had taken over as the power center of finance, information, and business, and the Republicans controlled the national government, including most urgently how to treat the vanquished South and West. Charles Darwin's *The Origin of Species,* published two years before the war began, was read and obsessed over by scientists and theologians, but it was a biology book, and the country in its upheaval paid it only scant attention.

Traditional theology crumbled nearly to dust in the new postwar age. Many people craved an alternate system of beliefs—new principles to live and prosper by in the changing world, a creed—but Darwin, an English country gentleman, was a naturalist, not a philosopher. He had done more than anyone else to demonstrate the laws of change in nature, but during the war and for years afterward he publicly avoided the question of what evolution said about human behavior and society, and about right and wrong. It was Herbert Spencer, another Englishman and architect of the new system of science and reason, who first undertook that challenge. Spencer—a fearless and encyclopedic thinker and libertarian political theorist who privately was tortured, lonely, and consumed with his own frailties—set out nearly a decade before the war to explain the universality of evolution not only in nature but in man, society, behavior, morals, history, and ideas; that is, in the entire living world.

In 1851, in his first major work of political philosophy, Spencer proposed what he called the Law of Equal Freedom: "Every man is free to do that which he wills, provided he infringes not the equal freedom of any other man." This was the ethical stance from which all Spencer's social prescriptions proceeded. Earlier liberals had recognized liberty as the key to life in society, but Spencer alone made equal freedom a general law of nature, the social equivalent of gravity. And in the years after the war, as the nation boomed and anything seemed possible to the rising classes, his philosophy uplifted those who used it to justify and explain everything from their own success in life, to why the North defeated the South, to why some races dominate others, to why the government shouldn't help the needy or interfere with trade; ultimately, to why America was destined to become the world's preeminent society. Evolution elevated superiority to a natural imperative, a mark of fitness, and across the spectrum of ideas, thinkers looking both back through history and ahead to the future found Spencer irresistible.

His adherents extended wide power and influence. Carl Schurz, the country's most powerful independent political figure, adapted Spencer's Law of Equal Freedom to government; straddling the party divide, he helped thwart an early stab at imperialism, pressed the Republicans and President Grant to confront rampant corruption in their ranks, and reformed the management of the West, both of the land and of the Indians. The Brooklyn clergyman Henry Ward Beecher, storied equally for his progressive oratory and his scandalous personal life, used the most acclaimed pulpit in America to preach the gospel of evolution; that is, that it was God's way to build better men and sort the worthy from the wretched. At Yale, Professor William Graham Sumner, a former minister, crusaded to bring economics and sociology under the Law of Equal Freedom by blending Christian virtue with the belief that unfettered competition is both natural and crucial for survival, while paleontologist Othniel Charles Marsh, discoverer of many of the great dinosaurs and of the first fossils to confirm evolutionary theory, transformed organized science by campaigning for and applying Darwin's and Spencer's ideas. Steel tycoon Andrew Carnegie exalted Spencer as a prophet of peace. Popular philosopher and historian John Fiske found in Spencer's writing a basis for asserting that God's destiny for America was to lead the world.

Most Americans still believed that sinners rotted in hell and tried to act accordingly, yet within a decade and a half after the war, Spencer influenced nearly every area of modern thought: science, ethics, sociology, anthropology, political theory, philosophy, psychology, metaphysics, economics, and religion. Darwin, who always hoped to see America, suffered from a range of chronic ailments that kept him from ever making the voyage. By the time Spencer, who expanded evolution into a far-reaching cosmology, visited the United States in 1882, he was hailed nearly as a conqueror. His three-month tour was a kind of victory lap for those mostly Republican men of science, religion, business, and government—his proselytizers—who in a few short decades had plugged Darwinism into the main circuitry of the industrial age. His visit climaxed in a grand farewell banquet at Manhattan's finest and most venerable restaurant, Delmonico's.

PRINCIPAL CHARACTERS

(in order of appearance)

HERBERT SPENCER
Influential British popular philosopher who adapted the theory of evolution to the study of human society, history, psychology, and ethics. Father of social Darwinism and archdefender of individual liberty and laissez-faire capitalism. Inventor of the phrase "survival of the fittest."

EDWARD LIVINGSTON YOUMANS
Leading writer, lecturer, editor, and scientific popularizer, whose evangelical crusade on behalf of Victorian science—Spencer in particular—evoked comparisons with John the Baptist. Founding editor and publisher of *The Popular Science Monthly*.

JOHN FISKE
Ecstatic Faustian Harvard-based lecturer and author whose cosmic philosophy bridged science and theology, and who electrified audiences with his lectures on America's divine destiny as the world's crowning race. Ardent disciple of Spencer.

LOUIS AGASSIZ
Swiss-born naturalist at Harvard, the most renowned and influential scientist in mid-nineteenth-century America. An avid anti-Darwinian whose views on separate creations among humans put him in league with the American School of Anthropology, which supported white supremacy and slavery.

Asa Gray

Harvard botany professor and orthodox Christian who, as Darwin's strongest and most vocal scientific ally in the United States, sought to mediate between science and religion on the question of design in the natural world. Agassiz's chief rival and antagonist.

Charles Darwin

British naturalist and codiscoverer of the theory of evolution through natural selection, whose "big book on species" in 1859 revolutionized nineteenth-century science, religion, society, and morality. Father of modern biology.

Thomas Henry Huxley

Influential British physician/naturalist—self-anointed as "Darwin's bulldog"—whose 1876 tour of the United States galvanized American science and scandalized creationists. Coiner of the term "agnosticism."

Henry Ward Beecher

"The most famous man in America," the country's leading liberal Christian minister, brother of abolitionist author Harriet Beecher Stowe, who said of Spencer's works, "They have been meat and bread to me," and whose adultery trial became the greatest social drama of the century.

Victoria Woodhull

America's first woman candidate for president. Spiritualist, women's rights advocate, first woman (along with her sister) on Wall Street, publisher, she exposed Beecher's alleged infidelity.

Carl Schurz

Transplanted German revolutionary; a Union general in the Civil War. As the nation's most prominent political independent, became a senior statesman and reformer, serving as senator from Missouri, interior secretary, and intimate adviser to President Rutherford Hayes. Famous for saying, "Our country right or wrong. When right, to be kept right; when wrong, to be put right." Devout follower of Spencer.

Andrew Carnegie

Rising titan of the business world and avatar of the Age of Steel; later, world's richest man, leading anti-imperialist crusader, and educational philanthropist. Rivaled Youmans and Fiske as Spencer's most prominent American follower.

Charles Hodge

Orthodox Princeton theologian with a passion for the natural sciences. Believed Darwinism led logically to atheism because it denied intelligence (the argument from design) in the material world.

William Graham Sumner

Episcopal rector turned Yale professor of political economy who provoked the marquee academic freedom battle of the century by teaching Spencer's works to undergraduates. America's foremost social Darwinist.

Othniel Charles (O. C.) Marsh

Yale paleontologist whose discoveries in the American West were pronounced by Huxley to be the strongest physical evidence in support of evolutionary theory. Discoverer of giant dinosaurs including *Tyrannosaurus* and *Apatosaurus*. The country's leading scientific spokesman after Agassiz's demise.

William Evarts

Powerful Boston-born lawyer, statesman, and orator. Defended Beecher at his adultery trial, President Andrew Johnson against impeachment, and the Republican Party in the contested 1876 presidential election; served as U.S. attorney general and secretary of state and New York senator. Touted Spencer as the smartest man in the world.

PROLOGUE

> *The ultimate result of shielding men from the effects of their folly is to fill the world with fools.*
>
> —Herbert Spencer

After nearly three months in America, the English philosopher Herbert Spencer arose alone in his room at the Windsor Hotel in a fitful state. Always an intolerably poor sleeper, he dragged himself to the mirror, exhausted and out of sorts. Gaunt and angular, Spencer wore thick side-whiskers, his massive overarching crown was all but bald, and light locks of gray hair enswirled his ears. He guarded his time and privacy as if his life depended on it, yet pressures now intruded from all sides. All he hoped was to survive the next few days of crippling social obligations and board the White Star steamship *Germanic* for the voyage home. The whole expedition, he believed, had been unwise, a grievous blunder—"another step downwards towards invalid life" he should not have undertaken.

Little had gone right from the beginning, despite exaggerated efforts by his friends to shield him, at age sixty-two, from the public clamor generated by his first American visit. Here, unlike in Britain, Spencer was the most celebrated thinker of the day; many of the most influential men in politics, law, industry, scholarship, and religion revered him and exalted his social and scientific doctrines. Probably no other man of ideas had ever enjoyed such a vogue. But Spencer had seldom felt weaker or less sure of himself. Since to say no was impossible, he had agreed to the unavoidable necessity of a farewell dinner in his honor. "The prospect before me was sufficiently alarming," he would recall. "An occasion on which perhaps more than any other in my life I ought to have been in good condition, bodily and mental, came when I was in a condition worse than I had been in six-and-twenty years."

Spencer had booked the trip in January after much hesitation, yielding to the mild but persistent urging of his irreplaceable friend and promoter, the American publisher Edward Livingston Youmans. Spencer took great pains never to do more than he ought to, while Youmans never ceased doing more than he should, immolating himself in work on Spencer's behalf. Six months earlier, Spencer hinted in a letter that he was entertaining the thought of a visit, and Youmans at once took up the cause of selling him on the idea. "Our fifty million people will soon be a hundred million," he replied, "and they are developing a continent at a rate which must be seen to be understood." Anticipating Spencer's need for rest and distraction, Youmans sought to tempt him further by offering to arrange a salmon fishing trip to Canada. Spencer declined, having heard that the place was infested with flies and mosquitoes. "I like to take my pleasure neat," he wrote back. "If the drawbacks are considerable, I would rather not have it at all."

Spencer had likewise turned down a lucrative lecture tour. "I absolutely decline to make myself a show," he explained adamantly.

What I do while with you I mean to make entirely subordinate to relaxation and amusement; and I shall resist positively anything which in any considerable way entails on me responsibilities or considerable excitements. I suppose you have long ago discovered that I have a faculty of saying No, and that when I say No I mean No.

Foreign notables, especially those from mother England, could anticipate major crowds and front page headlines across America, but Youmans knew Spencer too well to allow him to be run after by the public and the press. For months, newspapers heralded his visit, even as they dampened expectations. "Being one of the great thinkers of the day," *The Washington Post* warned, "he comes here not to exhibit himself [and] he is not available for tea parties. . . . We must remember that he will not only see us, but see through us." Such forbidding obstinacy had its rewards: Spencer would see America on his own terms or not at all—yet only, it would turn out, at the price of yielding to Youmans's suggestion in a subsequent letter that he submit to a public dinner with at least some of those who hungered to see *him*. "To decline," he wrote Youmans in June, two months before setting out on the Cunarder *Servia* from Liverpool, "would be awkward."

Now in his room at the Windsor, Spencer cursed his decision to agree to the banquet: "Would that my boasted ability to say 'No' had been more fully justified!" Almost from the start, he had suffered the wear, tear, and aggravations of travel. Spencer prided himself, and was known, as an obsessively critical thinker: the class of Americans who considered him one of the great men and giant intellects of history—an Aristotle, a Newton—thought that his genius stemmed precisely from this thorough, exacting, and unconventional turn of mind. But when he arranged passage he had accepted the common wisdom that berths were best amidships because the pitching motion was least there, only to discover on retiring for the night—an elaborate ritual, according to a friend, in which he soaked his head with brine, covered his wet hair with a flannel nightcap, then donned a waterproof cap to keep the moisture from evaporating— the shrieks of the *Servia*'s fog whistle just overhead. "A horrible night from the noises," he wrote in his diary. When Youmans came on board off Staten Island to greet him, he found Spencer "in so low a nervous state that the excitement of ordinary conversation was too much for him."

Youmans managed to dodge several reporters in transporting Spencer to his residence on West Sixteenth Street, but Spencer dared not expose himself to the expectations of being a houseguest, and he and his companion, a lifelong friend named Edward Lott, quietly checked in to a hotel. "Am astonished by the grandeur of New York," he noted in his diary, commenting that London had nothing to compare with Fifth Avenue. He originally hoped to travel as far west as Chicago, swinging up through the Adirondacks, Niagara Falls, Montreal, and the Great Lakes before looping back through Washington, Baltimore, Philadelphia, and on through New York to New England. After taking a steamer up the Hudson, he tried briefly to go incognito, ducking into one hotel as "Mr. Edward Lott and friend" until the host and some of the guests recognized him and he had to abandon the ruse as useless. In Saratoga, Youmans arranged for him to stay at the fifteen-hundred-room United States Hotel, said to be the largest in the world, but the dining room was so vast and multitudinous that the opulence was lost on him.

Spencer, who had found himself alternately bored and distressed at sea, soon discovered overland travel, even in the more domesticated regions of the wide-open continent, equally challenging to his shattered nerves. And so less than three weeks into his tour, he forswore the grueling train ride to Chicago and reluctantly opted to see Cleveland and Pittsburgh instead. The latter boasted of being the smokiest town in the world, but on the *Servia*'s tender at Liverpool, he'd been handed a letter of introduction by a fellow passenger, the financier and industrialist Andrew Carnegie, whose iron and steel mills there had made him a millionaire. Spencer normally avoided talking with people he didn't know and resisted conventional niceties on principle. But he dined throughout the voyage with Carnegie, who more than any other American businessman advertised Spencer's creed of unfettered competition and individualism and who revered Spencer as a prophet, and he now accepted Carnegie's offer to tour his works and travel with him by private rail coach to his summer cottage in the Alleghenies. "The repulsiveness of Pittsburgh," he explained, "led me to break through my resolution always to stop at an hotel."

In Washington, he toured the White House. To his relief, President Chester Arthur was at home in New York, where he spent more time than he did in the nation's capital. In Baltimore, he reflected on the startled reaction of the hotel staff—"negro and half-caste"—to his grumbling assertiveness against their peremptory authority. "Avoidance of draught, attainment of light, or other reason, often led me to reject the choice made for me, where no claims of other guests were in question," he wrote. "Evidently the waiters were unused to this: for Americans commonly make no demurs either to the bedrooms assigned to them by the clerk at the bureau, or the tables they are motioned to by the head waiter." In Philadelphia, where six years earlier the nation had celebrated its centennial with a triumphal display of industry and technology, he marveled at the vast Baldwin engine works, where a complete locomotive engine was turned out each day.

Reporters tailed him in every city he visited, clamoring for interviews.

Lott rebuffed them, explaining that Spencer was too unwell to submit to questions; and so they derived what details they could from railway agents, porters, hotel clerks, and Spencer's hosts. One paper reported that he subsisted entirely on dry toast and sardines; another that he toted around a bag of hops that he put under his pillow as a soporific. As reports spread that his health was so poor and his irritation at traveling so great that he had curtailed his itinerary and was considering an early return to England, a few publications speculated that his disappointment would cause him to blame the bustle of American life. Most Eastern papers were sympathetic, remarking on his eminence and accomplishments, but in the South and West a few played up his insomnia, demanding habits, and disagreeable nature—even his bachelorhood. "The great Spencer, now in America, is unmarried," the New Orleans *Picayune* commented. "It is to be hoped that Mr. Spencer's ice cream bills while he is with us will not frighten him away from the girls." The St. Louis *Post-Dispatch* advised him to go west, to cure his dyspepsia and "find out what America was really like."

Upon returning to New York after seven weeks, Spencer confessed to Youmans his annoyance at the poor publicity. The Louisville *Courier-Journal*, noting that his ill health prevented him from lecturing, quoted him as calling the British playwright and aesthete Oscar Wilde, then in the midst of his own nearly yearlong triumphal American lecture tour, "an outlandish person who attempts to reconcile idiocy with art." Spencer fumed that the comment was "purely fictitious." "I remarked," he later would write, "that it would be almost worth while to have an interview for the purpose of contradicting these false statements." Ever poised to make the best of the occasion, Youmans offered to carry out the questioning himself, and the next morning he invited Spencer to share his impressions of America. Youmans distributed the interview the same day to papers in New York and Chicago, which ran it verbatim with the explanation that it had been conducted by "an intimate friend."

Youmans quizzed Spencer just as Spencer would himself, as a scientific observer, albeit one biased by patriotism. "Has what you have seen," Youmans began, "answered your expectations?"

"It has far exceeded them," Spencer said, seeking to correct the negative impression of the secondhand stories. "The extent, wealth, and magnificence of your cities, have altogether astonished me."

"I suppose you recognize in these results the great benefit of free institutions?"

"Ah," Spencer replied, "now comes one of the inconveniences of interviewing." On so little time and data, Spencer resisted offering a definite opinion, but he replied that "though free institutions have been partly the cause, I think they have not been the chief cause." Spencer, even more than his contemporary Charles Darwin, was identified in America with the doctrine of evolution, which Darwin theorized explained the emergence of all living species, including man, but which Spencer had spent the past thirty years extending beyond nature to history, society, politics, economics, philosophy, psychology, and morals. His laboratory encompassed all human experience, and no scholar in any field of study could now ignore him. In his view, America had evolved quickly based on its good fortune and determination, but had not evolved as far as it could, or should. Noting the widespread acceptance of corruption, graft, and "wire-pullers," he thought he detected a "lack of certain moral sentiments." He called this failure to reckon with public malfeasance "the root of the evil."

Pursuing the point, Youmans questioned whether that meant Americans lacked a sufficient sense of public duty. Esteemed guests as a rule avoid offending their hosts, but Spencer, a devout nonconformist, considered unvarnished honesty both a social necessity and proof of his personal independence and creativity. Despite being thin-skinned about criticism, he felt forever obligated to say what he thought.

"Well, that is one way of putting it," Spencer replied.

> But there is a more specific way. . . . That is what I mean by
> character. It is this easygoing readiness to permit small trespasses,
> because it would be troublesome or profitless or unpopular to oppose,
> which leads to the acquiescence in wrong and the decay of free
> institutions. . . . As one of your early statesmen said, "The price of
> liberty is eternal vigilance." But it is far less against aggressions
> upon national liberty that this vigilance is required than against the
> insidious growth of domestic interferences with personal liberty.

Whether with imperious waiters or political bosses, American passivity in the face of authority kept the country from meeting its full promise.

"The republican form of government is the highest form of government," he went on, "but because of this it requires the highest type of human nature—nowhere at present existing. We have not grown up to it, nor have you."

"Must I, then, understand you to think unfavorably of our future?" Youmans asked.

Spencer theorized that everything in the world, from molecules to societies, went through a process of change in form from simple and homogeneous to complex and diverse. The struggle for survival dictated which forms flourished and which ones failed. "It may, I think, be reasonably held that, both because of its size and the heterogeneity of its components, the American nation will be a long time in evolving its ultimate form, but that its ultimate form will be high," he concluded.

> One great result is, I think, tolerably clear. From biological truths it is to be inferred that the eventual mixture of the allied varieties of the Aryan race forming the population will produce a finer type of man than has hitherto existed, and a type of man more plastic, more adaptable, and more capable of undergoing the modifications needful for complete social life. I think that, whatever difficulties they may have to surmount, and whatever tribulations they may have to pass through, the Americans may reasonably look forward to a time when they will have produced a civilization grander than any the world has known.

AFTER A DAY in Central Park, two excursions to Brooklyn, sundry hours at the Century Club, and a couple of nights at the theater, Spencer felt refreshed, and his optimism impelled him on to New England, home of his spiritual forebears. Unitarians, transcendentalists, and scientists had paved his way by breaking up the old orthodoxies, and many of them, especially at Harvard and among the men of letters around Boston, had subscribed early and enthusiastically to his work.

In New Haven, he visited Othniel Charles Marsh, the blunt, baronial Yale paleontologist who co-pioneered the study of prehistoric remains out west during the final years of the conquest of the Indians. Independently wealthy, Marsh financed his own expeditions, unearthing fossilized skeletons of giant dinosaurs and flightless birds with teeth and a succession of horse species receding back millions of years, and exhibiting them at his Peabody Museum, now a premier stop for those in search of evolutionary evidence. After viewing Marsh's "marvelous fossil mammals," Spencer lunched at the bachelor professor's hilltop mansion, an overstuffed eighteen-room Victorian brownstone with an enclosed porch overlooking hills breasted with sparkling autumn foliage and with a high octagonal reception hall that Marsh called his "wigwam." Mementos and treasures from Marsh's adventures crammed the room; stuffed birds, a peace pipe from Sioux chief Red Cloud, a Mormon bible from Brigham Young, paintings, Japanese and Chinese enamelware and bronzes, a frontier pistol, a scalp.

Spencer and Lott traveled on to Newport to relax and sightsee, then to Boston, arriving on October 28, less than two weeks before the banquet in New York. Since Spencer's comments in the papers, Youmans had been deluged with urgent appeals from prominent men eager to attend, but the hall he had chosen seated no more than two hundred, and he was determined to make the event not only a testimonial gala to honor Spencer, but an occasion for setting forth the doctrine of evolution in America. Six pleasant and beneficial days at the shore had made Spencer almost jovial, and on his first evening in Boston he dined at the Saturday Club, the Olympian weekly dinner society founded by Emerson, Longfellow, and others. Spencer read the work of few other authors, but he was a penetrating student of Emerson, who after presiding over club dinners for nearly thirty years had died in February, leaving his friend Dr. Oliver Wendell Holmes at the head of the table. Spencer was also an admirer of Holmes, a medical pioneer, popular poet, and renowned Brahmin opinion maker. "It was pleasant to meet, in company with others less known, one whose writings had given me so much pleasure," Spencer would recall.

Among Bostonians, his most ardent champion and deepest interpreter was the freelance philosopher and historian John Fiske, who through his involvements at Harvard did much what Marsh did at Yale: help make evolution respectable to traditional Christians. Both on the lecture platform and in books, Fiske popularized Spencer's system of evolution chiefly through his ability to reconcile it with orthodox religious beliefs and apply it to America's sense of promise as a great nation and aspiring world power. Trained as a lawyer, Fiske had discovered natural selection as an undergraduate in 1860 on reading Darwin's *The Origin of Species,* and he had recently enjoyed sudden great success and begun to make his first real money, as a historian of the early American period. Employing evolutionary theory, he elucidated the clash between civilization and savagery that resulted in the development of the nation's advanced political institutions. His most popular lecture, "Manifest Destiny of the English Race," explored how America's rise reflected divine will.

Fiske lived in a clamorous household with his wife and six children, including four sons, the youngest of whom was christened Herbert Huxley after Spencer and Thomas Henry Huxley, evolution's master proselytizer in England and champion of both Spencer and Darwin. Seated in a comfortable easy chair in front of an open wood fire in Fiske's cluttered library, Spencer noted with annoyance his young friend's cuckoo clock, another apparent American willingness to submit to intrusion. "Doesn't it disturb you, Fiske, to have so many books and things all about you, and this little monitor to remind you of the passing time? I couldn't work at all under such conditions." Spencer kept his own books behind curtains, needing to relieve his mind of all possible distractions: Fiske told him he enjoyed the stimulation, at times finding it inspirational. As they talked, Spencer admitted that his visit to America *had* broadened his understanding of the social and political problems the country faced—especially the mixing of races.

Here was the question of questions for the new sciences of society and politics. The speed, scale, and complexity of recent immigration in America was unprecedented in human history. After seeing various nationalities—Irish, German, Italian, Negroes, and others—intermingling with the dominant English race in New York, Spencer now wondered about the effect of this mixing under a democratic form of government on the future of the American people and, through them, the world. The immediate effect, he warned Fiske, would inevitably be to lower the standard of intelligence, of virtue, in the electorate, furthering bossism and civic corruption. Spencer opposed expanding governmental powers on the grounds that it thwarted the natural discipline wielded by life's harsh challenges in weeding out the unfit, and thereby weakened the population, and in England he strongly opposed public education and sanitation, believing such "reforms" only fostered a spirit of dependence and undermined the class order that girded the nation.

Fiske believed America faced a higher evolutionary challenge. As society became more heterogeneous, it also required an ever increasing development in the power of the state to bring people together and integrate their activities. Such integrating power was "particularly noticeable in the provisions for public education, sanitation, and transportation; and for the protection of the public from unjust demands of capitalistic combinations and labor organizations, as well as the protection of the country from individual or capitalistic exploitation," he explained. Spencer held the proper sphere of government to be enforcing contracts and keeping people from harming each other, but that was about all. Still, he conceded Fiske's point, urging him to study how America's staggering increase in wealth influenced political corruption, and to guard against the insidious growth of special privileges for the few.

At lunch, Spencer was inquisitive, importuning Fiske's children about their interests. When a plate of raised biscuits was passed to him, he asked: "Fiske, do tell me, are these *buckwheat cakes?*" However self-involved, Spencer also was companionable when relaxed, and others, even children, could be charmed by the guilelessness of his intellect. In England, he sometimes "borrowed" the sons and daughters of friends, submitting them for several weeks to an experimental regimen of hot baths instead of cold ones, thick flannel clothing, increased exercise, and animal products at four daily meals, which seemed to improve their health, temperament, and behavior. Their mothers appear to have welcomed the arrangement.

Fiske took Spencer for a walking tour of Harvard, where they paid a courtesy call on the botanist Asa Gray. As Fiske was to Spencer, the spare, patriarchal, lushly bearded Gray was to Darwin—not just a friend, ally, and proxy, but an important scholar of deep religious faith who had spent the last two decades helping to define and defend a Christian evolutionism. Spencer "saw something" of Gray's magnificent herbarium, but neglected to visit the more wondrous Museum of Comparative Zoology, founded by the naturalist Louis Agassiz, Gray's erstwhile rival and foil who during the war years and for almost a decade afterward, up to his death, led the nation's antievolutionary crusade.

Lott wanted to see a typical New England village, and so the following day the party traipsed to Lexington and Concord, in the western suburbs. They visited Emerson's house, spending an hour with his widow, son, and daughter, and Spencer asked to be taken to the cemetery, to pay his respects. "The grave-heap was undistinguished by any monument," he later wrote. " 'Sleepy Hollow' is so beautiful and poetical a spot as to make one almost wish to die at Concord for the purpose of being buried there."

Late in returning from the graveyard, Spencer feared they were in danger of missing the train back to Boston. One of the benefits of his preoccupation with his health and iron determination not to overextend himself was a varied regimen of exercise—racquets, tennis, fishing, hiking—and he was in far better physical shape than, say, Youmans, who regularly broke down from overwork. Now, though, "there occurred a disaster," Spencer wrote. He "thoughtlessly" ran some distance at full speed to catch the departing train. The effort was too much for him. Less than a week before his scheduled return to New York, he suffered a sleepless night "so wretched as to prompt the immediate resolution to leave Boston and its excitements." Hastily writing his regrets to Holmes, with whom he was to dine, he decided to return at once to Newport, where he hoped that the off-season quiet and sea air would restore him.

Sequestered, Spencer at first improved, so much so that he still hoped he might have a few days' strength to enjoy New York before going home. He'd been invited to spend Saturday with the renowned Brooklyn preacher and orator Rev. Henry Ward Beecher. The most controversial and appetitive minister in America, Beecher also was an evolutionist— a "cordial Christian Darwinist," he called himself—and he had promised, knowing neither Spencer nor his mood, an entire day of lavish entertaining, gushing in a note to Youmans on November 2:

> I will ride with him, talk with him, be silent with him, eat with him, or do anything but commit suicide with him. We dine at one o'clock. If he will, he shall have oysters and lobsters, beef or mutton, game or fish, or all of them: tea, coffee, or wine—and if the latter, I will give him better port than New York can produce; or he shall have Madeira, or sherry, or claret or champagne; or if the British blood calls for beer, he should have that—English ale, brown stout of the finest, German beer, lager beer; and such is my wish to please him that I will give him *cold water*. He shall have all of these, or, if, he prefer, he shall have none of them. . . . I have a complete set of his works, and he may read *them* if he likes. . . . Of course you are expected to come also. . . .

But after two more sleepless nights, despite taking increasing amounts of morphia, Spencer worried he could no more endure lunch or a carriage ride or a conversation than he could the thought of standing up and speaking at the banquet. "I went wrong again at Boston," he wrote Youmans from Newport on November 4, after considering Beecher's invitation,

> and my head has been quite as much disordered as at any time since my arrival. I stay here until Wednesday, because it is *absolutely* needful to shun all excitements save that of the dinner itself. I must peremptorily decline committing myself to anything else. I am sorry to disappoint you; but even as it is I look forward with some alarm to the state of brain with which I shall start on my return voyage.

As the next night's banquet loomed, Spencer departed Newport by train for New York on November 8. "Five days did a little, but only a little, towards mitigating the mischief," he recalled. Youmans, having seen "how serious an invalid" Spencer was upon first arriving in the city in August, feared the worst. Spencer's chief concern was to recover enough strength to endure the return voyage to England, but Youmans needed him first to mount the dais in the ornately paneled function hall at Delmonico's restaurant and, after a twelve-course dinner, and the provision of an equal number of wines, speak with enough vitality to reward the audience for its faith and adoration. Marsh, Fiske, Beecher, and Holmes were set to deliver testimonials linking evolution to the highest interests of humanity. The enthusiastic German American orator, politician, journalist, and Civil War general Carl Schurz, the most acclaimed foreign-born figure in the country, would speak on the connection between evolution and international harmony. Yale economist William Graham Sumner, whose determination to teach Spencer's book on sociology ignited the era's premier battle over academic freedom and unleashed a surge of secularism at Christian colleges, would address America's need for a new science of society. Former secretary of state and attorney general William Evarts, for whom Spencer was the smartest man alive, would preside. Elite politicians, jurists, publishers, religious leaders, scholars, and industrialists including Carnegie would lean in eagerly from their seats to hear what he had to tell them.

Spent and curdling in his room at the Windsor, Spencer doubted he could go on. At the defining, triumphal moment of his life's journey, the peak of his influence, he was once again anxious, dilapidated, and frail— a ringing irony in that for thirty years he had expounded on how nature favored the strong and fit. But that was Spencer. He regarded his nervous condition as the result of his inability to stop himself from overdoing it, even when all he had done was to try futilely to rest and distract himself sufficiently to have a clear head for a few precious hours.

"Wretched night; no sleep at all; kept in room all day," he wrote in his diary. "Great fear I should collapse."

BANQUET AT DELMONICO'S

CHAPTER ONE

CAMBRIDGE, 1871

Eleven years earlier

> *What a set of men you have in Cambridge. Both our*
> *universities put together cannot furnish the like. Why*
> *there is Agassiz—he counts for three.*
>
> —CHARLES DARWIN to
> HENRY WADSWORTH LONGFELLOW, 1868

EVEN AFTER HE WAS OUSTED as the premier naturalist of his age and the most celebrated man of science in America—even as he suffered, at age sixty-two, a cerebral hemorrhage that first paralyzed him, then required him to take to his bed for most of a year, forbidden by his doctors to smoke his beloved cigars or even to think, either of which they predicted might kill him—Harvard professor Louis Agassiz never stopped spinning grand plans or forging ahead with them. Preternaturally ambitious, a large, vibrant man of murderous industry, deft political skill, and outsize charm, Agassiz identified himself as no less than a reflection of the universe, mirroring its magnificence through his ability to observe and explain the natural world. He also considered himself the herald of the rapid advance of knowledge in America, his adopted land—an intellectual high priest for a rising, if still uncertain, world power. And so, though it had been a year since he'd been all but marginalized on campus following the selection of a new president, Agassiz remained baldly optimistic about the future.

How could he not? Other than the risks to his health brought on by overwork with each new venture, fortune seemed to favor his every step.

The son of a strong-willed assistant pastor to the Protestant congregation of a lakeside village in French-speaking Switzerland who married well, he was his parents' fifth child but the first to survive infancy, and as a student he displayed a rare surplus of talent, energy, imagination, fearlessness, and determination. At twenty-nine, an intrepid adventurer studying glaciers in the Alps, he descended alone at one point 120 feet into a crystal-blue abyss, and mounted at another a massive section of the earth's crust that had vaulted upward to almost fourteen thousand feet. He was the first scientist to propose that a prehistoric ice age had gripped the earth, and that extinct giant tropical quadrupeds such as mastodons had been wiped out by a worldwide Siberian freeze. "Their reign was over," he announced. "A sudden intense winter, that was also to last for ages, fell upon our globe."

In an early triumph of paleontology, Agassiz conducted a comprehensive study of every fossil fish in every major collection on the Continent, establishing himself as a tireless investigator and winning him favor with two of Europe's most influential naturalists, who delighted in opening doors for him. His bonhomie and good luck were inexhaustible: when his first wife, upset over his obsessive work habits and troubled finances, left him (she later died of tuberculosis), he took off to lecture in America, where Harvard promptly created a scientific school for him and where he married the daughter of a wealthy lawyer, a pillar of New England society.

Yet what most distinguished Agassiz's career was his superiority at getting others—not just important individuals and adoring audiences, but institutions and, ultimately, governments—to adopt his outlook and objectives. Less than a decade after he arrived in America in 1846, outsiders began referring to the famous Saturday Club as "Agassiz's Club." During the Civil War, he and his so-called Scientific Lazzaroni, a close network self-mockingly named for Florentine beggars, created a national scientific enterprise with themselves in charge, soliciting Congress to found the National Academy of Sciences. Dominated by Agassiz and his allies, it would serve as an equivalent of the French Academy, providing government subsidies, publications, and other spurs to selected research.

Agassiz's faith in special creation informed his worldview. He believed the Almighty made species separately and successively, dismissing evolutionary theory as "folly." If species descended from other species through slight modification, as Darwin himself was forced to acknowledge, there ought to be fossil remains of "innumerable transitional forms," yet no scientist had ever found one. Agassiz believed that his discovery of the Ice Age amply explained the disappearance of some older extinct species and the emergence of more recent ones, and that in nature there existed specific "zoological provinces" with distinct plants and animals and "varieties" of men, also created separately. In other words, humans were all one species, but races from different zones did not share a common ancestry. He interpreted the history of man by the same logic he applied to the origin of plants and animals, and though such reasoning had become harder and harder to defend, he remained the nation's foremost creationist and intellectual critic of Darwin and Spencer.

During the worst of his illness, Agassiz despaired of ever working again. All around him his celebrated friends seemed to be faring little or no better, sundered by age and grief. "The year ends with a club dinner," his neighbor Longfellow wrote dismally in his journal on December 31. "Agassiz was not well enough to be there. But Emerson and Holmes of the older set were, and so I was not quite alone." Headlong change during and since the war had overtaken everything, especially America's old guards and ideas. Longfellow, once a glamorous figure in Cambridge with his flowing hair, flowered waistcoats, and yellow gloves, had published his most important poems twenty years earlier. In 1861 his wife was sealing packages of their children's curls with matches and wax when they burst into flame, killing her. Longfellow suffered severe burns to his own face and hands as he tried to save her, and with shaving painful and difficult, grew a biblical beard. Deeply withdrawn, he spent much of his last decade in Europe, translating Dante.

"It is time to be old, / To take in sail," wrote Emerson, still physically vigorous but with his own fiery mind lost, more and more, to senility.

Agassiz would not take in sail. As his health returned through the early winter, he grew restless and impatient. He raised public and private subscriptions for the one project at Harvard he still controlled, the Museum of Comparative Zoology, which his son, Alexander, an accomplished naturalist in his own right, had managed in his absence. Then, in mid-February, he received a letter from Benjamin Peirce, a Harvard mathematician, astronomer, and fellow Lazzarono who served as superintendent of the U.S. Coast Survey, which for more than two decades had put its resources at Agassiz's disposal for research in marine biology.

"Now, my dear friend, I have a very serious proposition for you," Peirce wrote. "I am going to send a new iron surveying steamer round to California in the course of the summer. She will probably start at the end of June. Would you go in her, and do deep-sea dredging all the way round?"

Here lay a route out of Agassiz's morass: his growing isolation at Harvard, his need to do original research to resume a place at the forefront of postwar science, his craving for a change of atmosphere after a year as a shut-in, the yawning imperative—shared by all scientists—of new experiments, new technologies, new data, new worlds to examine. Indeed: a future. That the journey would take him down the east coast of South America, up the west, and through the Galápagos Islands—virtually the same voyage taken by Charles Darwin aboard HMS *Beagle* four decades earlier—went unsaid, but could not fail to ignite his spirit and ambitions. Assuredly the one person in America who could slow the juggernaut of liberal science, Agassiz relished having a last chance to again dominate the fray.

"My darling Ben," he wrote back at once, "I am overjoyed by the prospect your letter opens before me. Of course I will go . . . as I feel there never was, and is not likely soon again to be, such an opportunity for promoting the cause of science generally, and that of natural history in particular."

As AGASSIZ'S NEMESIS in Cambridge, in the councils of organized research, and in the debate over the mysteries of the natural world, Asa Gray seemed conspicuously ill suited—not overmatched intellectually, for Gray possessed an exceptional mind, but in his relative lack of social connections, financial support, and charisma, endowments Agassiz enjoyed wielding against rivals. A few years Agassiz's junior, Gray first trained as a physician in upstate New York during the boom years after the opening of the Erie Canal. Without formal education in botany, he collected and traded in and elucidated the structural relations of plant species so prodigiously that four years before Agassiz's arrival in Cambridge he was called to Harvard to teach plant biology—a smooth-faced, wiry, kinetic figure who, at 135 pounds, half-sprinted around campus and up stairs, seeming more student than professor.

Gray's work was a model of carefully observed science without prejudice, even though he himself was an orthodox Presbyterian and dutiful follower of the Nicene Creed, the most widely utilized brief statement of Christian faith: *"We believe in one God, the Father, the Almighty, maker of heaven and earth, of all that is, seen and unseen. We believe in one Lord, Jesus Christ, the only Son of God. . . ."* An indifferent teacher, Gray grimly tolerated his students: the labors of attending to their needs while developing and managing an herbarium of more than two hundred thousand specimens exhausted him, and his own original research and writing often languished.

What Gray had, besides uncommon intellectual ferocity and a zest for scientific combat equal to Agassiz's, was his abiding, conflicted—and now famous—relationship with Darwin. During the twenty-five years after his voyage when Darwin developed his theory of natural evolution in reclusion and secrecy, the first American he told of it was Gray, and only then with crippling apprehension. Darwin, a painfully modest, cordial-to-a-fault English country gentleman, judged the risks of revealing such heterodox thinking prematurely, without ample proof, to be monumental, disastrous—"like confessing a murder." "I daresay I said that I thought you would utterly despise me," he told Gray in 1857, two years before circumstances forced him to publish his masterwork, *The Origin of Species,* "when I told you what views I had arrived at."

By taking Gray into his confidence, Darwin ensured that Gray became his American gatekeeper, and Gray worked skillfully to guarantee that Darwin's books were well published and widely disseminated, and that his ideas received a fair hearing in intellectual circles—despite disapproving of many of their implications. It was the publication of *Origin,* which Darwin called "one long argument" for the view that new species develop gradually through random variations that help some organisms survive better than others, that had driven Gray twelve years earlier to confront Agassiz, then at the height of his power and fame. Agassiz defined a species as "a thought of God"—permanent, immutable, and designed specifically as part of a divine plan. Christian faith notwithstanding, Gray was too much of an empiricist to accept Agassiz's metaphysical biology, and so even as he realized somewhat bitterly in recent years how far he and Darwin were from agreeing on the subject of intelligent design in nature, he stood staunchly by him as Darwin's man in the New World, his first friend, collaborator, proxy, and shield. Gray longed to retire from Harvard so he could write and pursue his own research, but as Darwin became one of the world's most famous and controversial men, his name synonymous with an intellectual cataclysm, he was not readily let go.

"My Dear Gray," Darwin wrote from his country haven near the village of Downe in Kent, twenty miles from London, days before Peirce invited Agassiz to go abroad. He apologized as always for adding to Gray's burdens. "*If you can,* will you send the enclosed to anyone who has charge of Laura Bridgeman [*sic*] & beg for an answer." As a near-invalid who seldom left his home and gardens except to seek seaside rest cures or visit close colleagues and family members in London, Darwin relied utterly on his scientific friends to assist his investigations. Laura Bridgman was something of a national treasure, a Victorian version of Helen Keller, whom she later would inspire. Though blind and deaf, she had been educated through sign language, and Darwin had read in *Smithsonian Contributions to Knowledge,* the new museum's Lazzaroni-inspired journal for touting American science, that when astonished, she raised both her hands with her fingers extended and pressed her open palms toward the person causing her amazement. Since she couldn't acquire expressions through imitation, Darwin theorized that such movements were traceable to animal behaviors. "I should very much like to know how this is," he asked Gray.

Darwin had long avoided publishing his ideas on human evolution, letting Huxley and others speculate before him on the effects of natural selection and the universal linkages between people and animals. But by 1867, eight years after *Origin* and following two years of crushing illness—vomiting, nausea, eczema, and an "accursed stomach" that for months on end left him sleepless and all but unable to work—he decided he could wait no longer. His "man-essay," as he had described it to Gray, had grown into two parts. The first, due to be published at the end of the month, addressed the conjoined questions of whether man, like any other species, descended from earlier forms; the manner of human development; and, most explosively, for this had been his urgent agenda since he first recorded his thoughts on evolution in secret notebooks thirty-five years earlier, "the value of the differences between the so-called races of man"—the race question. A follow-up book—a rare sudden respite from his health problems was now letting him surge ahead, writing four hundred pages in three months, and adding, for the first time, photographs—would address the similarities in feelings and expression between humans and animals. Hence his interest in Laura Bridgman.

Darwin informed Gray that he had finished work on the first volume—*The Descent of Man, and Selection in Relation to Sex,* now at the printer's—and would soon send him a copy. "Parts, as to the moral sense, will I daresay aggravate you," he wrote, "and if I hear from you I shall probably receive a few stabs from your polished stiletto of a pen."

Polite jests aside, Darwin and Gray had long since argued themselves into a stalemate on many fronts. Darwin had confessed to Gray a year earlier that he was having great difficulty explaining the animal underpinnings of civilized behavior—the "moral sense"—and he dreaded another onslaught of scalding criticism, public and private, from Gray and others. Many people might be prepared for Darwin to claim that man physically descended from apes, as Huxley and several other widely respected naturalists had already done, through the process of natural selection—"survival of the fittest," to use Spencer's phrase. But how did one explain a mechanism for discerning right from wrong? Good from evil? Righteousness from sin? What animal ancestry, he knew he'd be asked, could possibly account for such virtues as a love of justice, or of Jesus?

All these added up to the "highest and most interesting problem for the naturalist," which Darwin now sought to answer. He had come to attribute morality to a combination of three evolutionary forces: instinctive sympathy born (as in many other species, notably dogs and monkeys) of family and tribal ties in the struggle for survival; habit ingrained by social behavior; and education. At the same time, natural science contained for Darwin, who grew up in a world of deep-seated antiroyalist and anti-Anglican leanings, a political thrust. Nothing so appalled him as blind Christian acceptance of the immorality and sufferings of genocide and slavery—nothing except the use of science to justify that indifference. Loath to offend a pious wife and friends like Gray, he withheld from making direct attacks on religion in his new work, seeking instead to show only how such creeds might have evolved. "How so many absurd rules of conduct, as well as so many absurd religious beliefs, have originated, we do not know," he wrote in *Descent,*

> but it is worthy of remark that a belief constantly inculcated during the early years of life, whilst the brain is impressible, appears to acquire almost the nature of an instinct; and the very nature of an instinct is that it is followed independently of reason.

Darwin had made up his mind about racial origins during his voyage, where he first encountered the "shocking barbarity" of slavery in Brazil, then primitive "savages" in Tierra del Fuego, but only now felt confident enough in his research to publish his theory. Two views of racial descent recently competed in Western thought, neither egalitarian. People either believed all humans descended from a single stock (monogenism), and that while the entire species had degraded since Creation, some races, usually those in hot climates, degraded more than others; or else that the races were created separately and hierarchically, with distinct and unequal endowments (polygenism). Either way, whites had no difficulty deeming themselves intellectually and morally superior. Darwin, though he shared in the general self-congratulation, held the radical notion that racial distinctions were fundamentally cosmetic: that features such as skin color and hair texture were simply caused by sexual selection—different beauty standards and mating preferences among different groups. However disturbing the notion to contemporary Western sensibilities, he believed that all mankind was one species. As he now predicted confidently in *Descent*, "when the principles of evolution are generally accepted, as they surely will be before long, the dispute between the monogenists and the polygenists will die a silent and unobserved death."

As Gray realized, Darwin intended *Descent* to smash both the science and the morality of the polygenists, most notably Agassiz, a culture hero alike to abolitionist Yankee intellectuals and Southern "niggerologists," who justified slavery upon the alleged God-given inherent inferiority of Negroes. Agassiz discerned eight separately created human types—Caucasian, Arctic, Mongol, American Indian, Negro, Hottentot, Malay, and Australian—which he ranked in intelligence according to cranial capacity. He disputed the doctrine of the unity of man—which was supported, oddly, both by evolutionary logic and by the Holy Scriptures—as "contrary to all the modern results of science."

After receiving his copy of *The Descent of Man*, Gray apologized in his return letter for having had only time to read Darwin's preface and conclusion, and he promised not to examine the parts that might offend him until "I can get a good pull at it." Checking around about Laura Bridgman, he'd discovered that her doctor was in "San Domingo, one of those Commissioners to see what sort of fellow citizens those tropical blacks will make," and he vowed to keep after him. A month later, in mid-April, Gray wrote Darwin again:

Almost thou persuadest me to have been "a hairy quadruped,
of arboreal habits, furnished with a tail and pointed ears" &c.

I have been besought to write notices of the book, but I decline.
You don't know how distracted I am in these days—doing the work
of Professor, gardener, builder, financier and whatnot all at once.

But I must not let this mail pass without sending you the little I
could get as to Laura Bridgman. . . . I got the queries out to the
woman who now has personal charge of Laura [which] brought me
the enclosed—which I think I should not much rely on. When Dr.
Howe is on hand, some day, I will see if I can get anything authentic
and particular,—not, I fear in time for you.

"THINGS ARE GOING here furiously," Edward Livingston Youmans told
Herbert Spencer, writing a week later from New York. As Gray was
Darwin's man in America, Youmans was Spencer's, but incomparably
more so; not an overextended academic, but a tireless lecturer, writer,
editor, and impresario whose singular mission was to promote Victorian science—Spencer in particular—not only to scientists but to the
education-obsessed working masses. It had been Spencer who in 1851 introduced the phrase "survival of the fittest," which even Darwin now employed in place of "natural selection" in the latest edition of *Origin*. "I
have never known anything like it," Youmans went on:

> Ten thousand *Descent of Man* have been printed and I guess they are
> nearly all gone. . . . The progress of liberal thought is remarkable.
> Everyone is asking for explanations. The clergy are in a flutter.
> McCosh told them not to worry, as whatever might be discovered he
> would find design in it and put God behind it. Twenty-five clergymen
> in Brooklyn sent for me to meet them on a Saturday night and tell
> them what they should do to be saved. I told them they would find
> the way of life in Biology and in the *Descent of Man*. They said "very
> good" and asked me to come again at the next meeting of the clerical
> club, to which I went and was again handsomely resoluted.

That the Reverend James McCosh, the president of the College of
New Jersey (later Princeton) and a native Scot who'd become the semi-
official voice of American Presbyterianism, could reconcile human evo-

lution and Christianity with little moral or intellectual fallout was not unusual: many on both sides of the divide between natural science and natural theology, like Gray, saw evidence of each in the other and worked to
accommodate fact to faith, and vice versa. Spencer, who had beaten Darwin to publication with similar theories yet received far less notice, re-
acted less equably. He would breeze over these months in his memoir,
recalling decades later that they "furnish no incidents calling for mention," writing instead about having played billiards every afternoon and
"chattings" with old friends at the Athenaeum Club, where he'd recently
been elected. In truth, Spencer felt the stab of Darwin's new upheaval
keenly, and he strove hard to downplay and disguise his feelings.

Youmans's excitement jarred him, reviving Spencer's bitter experience
in making public his own views on the evolution of mind and behavior, in
1855, in his second book, *The Principles of Psychology*. Self-published after
he failed to interest publishers in the project, selling just 200 of 750
copies, thrashed by all but two critics as atheistic and impenetrable, "cod-
liver oil" for the general reader (as he later conceded), the book had
plunged him, at age thirty-four, into a nervous collapse from which sixteen years later he continued to suffer nightly bouts of dire sleeplessness
and a pathological inability to work more than a few hours a day.
Spencer's father was a quarrelsome, iconoclastic schoolteacher who was
cold and impersonal with his only son, and Spencer grew up believing
"that if he were to give free reins to his feelings he would be cruel," his biographer Mark Francis observed. Lacking warmth and personality, he
contrived to cloak his emotions with good-natured, if strained, cordiality.
Now, dictating revisions to an amanuensis, he quietly scrambled to update the earlier volume and return to print with a new edition. "My Dear
Youmans," he wrote in return, on June 3,

> I inclose a brief article just out. I wrote it partly as a quiet way of
> setting opinion right on the matter. Since the publication of Darwin's
> Descent of Man there has been a great sensation about the theory of
> the development of mind—essays in the magazines on Darwinism
> and Religion, Darwinism and Morals, Philosophy and Darwinism,
> all having reference to the question of mental evolution, and all
> proceeding on the supposition that it is Darwin's hypothesis. And
> no one says a word in rectification, and as Darwin himself has not

indicated the fact that the Principles of Psychology was published five years before the Origin of Species, I am obliged to gently indicate it myself.

Spencer proposed to Youmans that a similar published explanation "might not be amiss in America," where, owing chiefly to Youmans's self-sacrificing zeal, Spencer enjoyed a growing vogue far in excess of his standing in Europe. He and Darwin, albeit intellectual allies, were far from friends, and great gulfs separated their thinking. Many naturalists and philosophers before them had theorized that life evolved, but without identifying the mechanism by which the process worked. While Darwin and Spencer agreed on the fundamental idea that evolution resulted from the struggle to survive, they held radically different views on how it functioned and what it meant, especially regarding the tendency toward advancement. "For Darwin, evolution was directionless and morally neutral," scientific historian Steven Shapin writes, "but for Spencer evolution was *going somewhere:* natural change was progressive, and it was good." The forces behind Darwinian evolution were random, mindless, blind, but for Spencer survival of the fittest also meant survival of the best, suggesting a cosmic value system. Progress wasn't accidental; it was imperative, even programmed.

Believing the universe to be inherently moral, Spencer could not have found a more devoted apostle than Youmans. Son of a pious mechanic, he showed an early enthusiasm for science that was all but extinguished when an infection ravaged his eyesight as a teen. Blind on and off for nearly twenty years, Youmans despaired as a young man that he was destined for "an eternity of tripled, yea quadrupled misery"—the dark, lonely life of a shut-in. It was science—and Spencer's theory of an ever-improving cosmos—that rescued him. Youmans invented a device that enabled him to write, and with the help of his sister, Catherine, who read to him and conducted his experiments, he completed a medical degree, wrote a bestselling textbook on chemistry, and traveled widely as a popular lecturer on the lyceum circuit, handily translating abstruse science into ordinary language. At five foot ten and 190 pounds with a clear complexion, soft curly brown hair, and exorbitant side-whiskers, and peering narrowly through thick oval wire-rimmed glasses, Youmans was a riveting public speaker, his voice booming and hands windmilling so emphatically that on a night in Faribault, Minnesota, the "amplitude of his excited gyrations . . . exceeded the rather narrow bounds of the platform," Fiske recalled. "Twice he slipped to the floor."

In 1856, after seeing a review of Spencer's *Principles of Psychology*, Youmans sent to England for the book, read it, and—three years before Darwin's *Origin*—pledged himself to a life of promoting and marketing the concept of evolution. This meant, by and large, sponsoring Spencer while tirelessly disseminating his work. By 1860, five years after his breakdown, Spencer was nearing the pitch of despair. Undeterred by the failure of *Principles*, he had decided to examine and unify through evolution the whole range of human history and thought—"Synthetic Philosophy," he called it—but he was lonely, anxious, disappointed, and depressed. The sole survivor of his parents' ten children, unmarried, a former civil engineer and writer and subeditor at *The Economist* who moved among rented quarters supported by a modest family inheritance, he envisioned producing a systematic nine-volume account of evolution in philosophy, biology, sociology, ethics, and politics. Taking morphia to sleep to little avail, he spent his days circulating a brief prospectus outlining the project. He hoped to raise enough money to support himself through the agency of friends and admirers including novelist George Eliot, who loved him, once telling him "If you become attached to someone else, then I must die," and Huxley, who invited him into England's scientific clerisy, the X-Club, a national force equivalent to the Saturday Club and the Lazzaroni combined.

Youmans saw Spencer's circular and contacted him the next day to offer his aid in procuring American subscriptions. A forerunner of the modern agent/impresario, he secured Spencer a New York publisher, Appleton and Co.; pressed for—and won—royalties on a par with native authors' at a time when most American houses ignored international copyrights; churned out scores of reviews and notices with publication of each new volume, which he placed in newspapers and magazines across the country; pressed other reviewers into service; helped Spencer organize and popularize his most arcane thoughts; and cultivated literary clubs, college professors, editors, ministers, politicians, tycoons, and labor councils. In 1865, when Spencer doubted he could afford to go on with the project, Youmans made up his mind to raise subscriptions with the express purpose of getting Spencer out of debt, delivering in person $7,000 in American railroad stocks and the best gold watch he could buy, a testimonial from Spencer's admirers in this country. Despite relapses of failing eyesight and crippling rheumatism, he continued to lecture on Spencer's behalf, dragging himself around the Midwest in unheated trains to proselytize in town after town where often, he would recall, he encountered "a protracted meeting in full blast at every church in town except the Episcopal, and a general feeling of pious rage at my appearance on the scene."

Now, Youmans received Spencer's reply in midocean. Youmans was traveling to Europe to promote a grand new venture that he hoped would erase the stain and failure of his own last enterprise, a weekly paper of culture and science, *Appleton's Journal,* which he edited. After having promised the public a serious forum for research, he quickly had been forced to scale the magazine back when the publisher demanded fewer pieces on new ideas and more on social comings and goings and the arts. Undeterred, he hoped to induce Europe's leading scientists to contribute small volumes, written for the general public, to a series to be published simultaneously in several countries and languages—a set of gospels for the new scientific age. Determined to remain abroad until he signed up masters in each field and publishers in several capitals, he was grimly uncertain of his prospects: "very much in my own mind," as he wrote his mother. Away from his wife, Kate, celebrating his fiftieth birthday alone on board, Youmans reported that although the sea was calm and the passengers agreeable, the passage was only "tolerable. Meals could be enjoyed but for the horrible, sickening ship smells."

YOUMANS FOUND LONDON to be no better; overcrowded, teeming, foulsmelling, the savage hub of empire. Hiring a cab by the hour, he visited "about a dozen places of all sorts, high and low," but found no vacancies, finally taking a room no bigger than his stateroom. "It is close and suffocating, and I have had a hard time in it," he wrote to his sister. Unable to sleep but a couple of hours, his strained eyes burning and uncomfortable, he ventured out the next morning to meet with Spencer feeling "much used up."

"Spencer is looking very well," he reported to her the next day; "plays billiards a great deal; disciplines himself to amusement." If Spencer, who more than any of his contemporaries sought to take in all knowledge and understanding in pursuit of an encompassing, systematic philosophy, had a blind spot, this was it: he refused to admit to himself how well off he was, never taking into account his own privilege. Blaming his breakdown and insomnia on overwork, he pursued idleness and leisure with the same puritanical zeal with which Youmans sought out punishing labor. Nearly finished with his reissued *Psychology*, he described for Youmans his next endeavor, a large book codifying a new science of society. Undaunted, Youmans urged him to consider writing an abbreviated volume for his proposed "International Scientific Series," as he now called it. "Spencer's side projects on the sociology are amazingly interesting," he told Catherine. "He is afraid of their being stolen and is being shady, but he will show them to me."

Racing around London throughout the summer, Youmans found genial support for his series, but also mounting obstacles. Many of the authors he called on had been engaged to write for *Appleton's Journal*, disappointingly, or were committed to other publishers. All were overly busy with their own work. More than a few doubted he could succeed. Youmans persisted, gaining endorsements from Spencer, Huxley, and others, as well as an unsolicited pledge from Darwin to have the idea brought up at the British Association for the Advancement of Science. Gleefully he told Catherine about having lunch with Darwin and his wife, Emma. "They were all curiosity about America," he wrote:

> I told them about my lecturing the Brooklyn clergymen on evolution. "What!" said he, "clergy of different denominations all together? How they would fight if you should get them together here!" They were greatly amused with a spiritualistic paper they had received from Chicago, which stated that if it were known that God were dead Beecher would be unanimously elected by the American people to fill his place.

Even more than McCosh, it was Beecher who Youmans believed might lead American clergy to accept the doctrine of evolution, as Darwin seemed to appreciate. Beecher was, as Sinclair Lewis would write, "the archbishop of American liberal Protestantism." He had sold female slaves from the pulpit to gain their freedom and helped finance John

Brown's attempted insurrection in Kansas—Brown's rifles were called "Beecher Bibles." In 1864, four months before President Lincoln would choose Beecher to consecrate the end of the Civil War with prayers at Fort Sumter, South Carolina, Beecher had told Youmans in a letter: "Stir them up—subsoil the people with Spencer, Huxley and [Irish natural philosopher and physicist John] Tyndall. I've got them all, and go in for them all. If the trellis of old philosophies is falling down, take it away and let us have a better. We can train the vines of faith on the new one just as well."

Now, though, Youmans was blocked. He couldn't ask Darwin, Huxley, Spencer, and others "to go in on the enterprise, but I must make them as available as possible to get other men." Leveraging commitments, like building a house of cards, called for delicacy and patience, and privately he was anxious and out of sorts. "I prayed that this cup might pass from me," he wrote Catherine, "but the world's scientific salvation required that I drink it to the dregs."

Before leaving for the Continent, Youmans dined with the botanist Sir Joseph Hooker, the first recognized man of science to risk his reputation by publicly supporting Darwin. It was Hooker, director of the world-famous Royal Botanical Gardens of Kew, who had introduced Darwin to Asa Gray. Weeks earlier, at Spencer's urging, Hooker had invited Youmans to Kew, where they now discussed at length not the international series but Youmans's decision to endow Spencer. Hooker recently had tried to do the same for Gray, but the deal soured when Gray "gave the money to Harvard instead," he explained. "You did better for Spencer," he told Youmans.

Your work told where it should: Spencer is the mighty thinker among us. And what a splendid talker. He talks right at you like a book, and his language is so fluent and adaptive! He is all right now. The recognition of his genius is now complete. What a lucky thing it was that he failed in getting a consulate or some other public appointment when he began his Philosophy. . . . No man can do great original work and be hampered by the cares of a position. The thing is impossible. The work must have the whole man. That is why I have tried to get Gray free in America. You Americans don't know how much of a man Gray is. But he is hampered with students' work, and is not able to keep an assistant.

IN MID-NOVEMBER, Beecher, the fifty-nine-year-old pastor of Plymouth Church of the Pilgrims in thriving Brooklyn Heights, received a note from thirty-three-year-old Victoria Woodhull, celebrated copublisher of *Woodhull & Claflin's Weekly,* which advanced among other causes women's suffrage, shoetop-length skirts, spirit contact with the dead, free love, vegetarianism, and licensed prostitution. Some months earlier a vague, menacing statement had appeared in her newspaper:

> Civilization is festering to the bursting point in our great cities and notably in Brooklyn. . . . At this very moment, awful and Herculean efforts are being made to suppress the most terrific scandal which has ever astounded and convulsed any community. . . . We have the inventory of discarded husbands and wives and lovers, with dates, circumstances and establishments.

Since then Beecher had resisted Woodhull's efforts to meet with him. Men of God, like politicians, grow accustomed to accusations of infidelity, but Beecher, an antislavery and women's rights paragon, feared that Woodhull could destroy him. More than a year earlier his parishioner Elizabeth Tilton had confessed to her husband, Theodore, a popular newspaper editor, poet, reformer, and devoted friend and follower of Beecher's, that she and Beecher had been sexually intimate. Rumors of the charge coincided with Woodhull's sensational rise to national prominence. Betrothed to an alcoholic with whom she bore a profoundly retarded son at age fifteen, she had eked out a living in the years before the war operating séances, telling fortunes, and peddling patent medicines and abortifacients before finally divorcing him, marrying an anarchist, and moving with both of them (her first husband was now infirm) to New York City. With her sister, Tennessee Claflin, she soon came under the wing of railroad and shipping mogul Cornelius Vanderbilt, who established them as the first female brokers on Wall Street, where in six months they made enough money to enter the rising mainstream of Manhattan society, establish their weekly, and launch Woodhull into politics.

A businesswoman, Woodhull wore tailored, mannish jackets, skirts that ended above the ankle, and colored neckties, trappings that downplayed her passions and rage at society, though only slightly. She was dark-eyed, surprisingly elegant considering her history, and slimmer than her sister, whom Vanderbilt, an illiterate transportation genius with a wife and thirteen children, liked to call "my little sparrow" as he cooed to her and bounced her on his knee in his office.

In January, after deciding to run for president of the United States, Woodhull catapulted herself to the top of the fractured women's rights movement by becoming the first woman to address a committee of Congress. She told lawmakers that the recently adopted Fifteenth Amendment, which extended the right to vote to all citizens regardless of "race, color, or previous condition of servitude," compelled them to take the next and final step of granting suffrage "without regard to sex." Woodhull's suspect past, unconventional home life, rapid rise, and radical views—she believed the fight for equality began not with the ballot but in the bedroom, and that Victorian marriage laws making divorce all but impossible rendered women, in effect, slaves of their husbands—scandalized traditional feminists, none more than Beecher's own sisters, two of whom, including Harriet, attacked her relentlessly in print.

Then, over a chess game, Theodore Tilton told Elizabeth Cady Stanton, a matriarch of the suffrage movement, about his wife's secret affair, and she repeated the story to Woodhull and to Beecher's younger sister Isabella, who in a notable act of family rebellion embraced Woodhull as a "prophetess" and called her "my queen." Thus Woodhull's veiled statements in the *Weekly*. While Beecher's other sisters branded her as depraved and immoral in the pages of Beecher's newspaper, *The Christian Union*, Woodhull possessed compelling evidence that Beecher practiced the very doctrine she espoused—free love—walled within a citadel of Victorian hypocrisy. Theodore Tilton, meanwhile, became Woodhull's acolyte and, most likely, lover, publishing a campaign biography of her so fawning and uncritical of her claims as a spirit medium in touch with the ancient Greek orator Demosthenes that Julia Ward Howe, author of "The Battle Hymn of the Republic," sneered: "Such a book is a tomb from which no author again rises."

Now, in her letter to Beecher, Woodhull shed her gloves: "You doubtless know that it is in my power to strike back, and in ways more disastrous than anything that can come to me," she wrote,

> but I do not desire to do this. I simply desire justice from those from whom I have a right to expect it; and a reasonable course on your part

will assist me to it. . . . I repeat that I must have an interview tomorrow, since I am to speak tomorrow evening at Steinway Hall and what I shall or shall not say will depend on the result of the interview.

This time Beecher agreed to the meeting. A fleshy, carnal man swathed in fine suits and capes, who jiggled opals in his pocket and wore his long hair behind his ears, he enjoyed life's pleasures, however guiltily. His wife, Eunice, did not. At the heart of Victorian sexual morality lay Victorian marriage, with its double standard for adulterers, and it was standard gossip that "Beecher preaches to seven or eight of his mistresses every Sunday evening." As Darwin illustrated in *Descent*, monogamy, though socially imposed, was not man's original design, and among primitive cultures, as among most primates, "polygamy is almost universally followed by the leading men in every tribe." As Beecher and Woodhull spoke privately late in the afternoon of the nineteenth, she later recalled, he confessed that he shared her view of matrimony.

"Marriage is the grave of love," Beecher told her. "I have never married a couple that I did not feel condemned."

Woodhull challenged him to preach that conviction. "I should preach to empty seats," he replied; his wealthy congregants would reject such radical ideas. "Milk for babies, meat for strong men."

Woodhull pressed him. She wanted him to introduce her at Steinway Hall, where she planned for the first time to go beyond the issue of voting rights to a full call for basic changes in the structure of society. She traced all social ills—crime, drinking, poverty, abortion, disease—to bad marriages, and she believed freedom for women would be achieved only when women could obtain divorces without being shamed and vilified by society. Beecher himself had almost lost his pulpit to those in his congregation who denounced him for sanctioning bigamy, after he chose to perform a deathbed marriage for a terminally ill man and a divorced woman whose life was being destroyed by her drunken, abusive ex-husband. The only way Woodhull thought she could ensure a fair hearing was if Beecher preceded her to the rostrum. Finally, when all her arguments failed to persuade him, she confronted Beecher with the inevitability that word of the Tilton scandal would soon leak out. She would do it herself if need be. "The only safety you have," Woodhull warned, "is in coming out as soon as possible as an advocate of social freedom and thus palliate, if you cannot completely justify, your practices, by founding them at least on principle. Your introduction of me would bridge the way."

Beecher pleaded with her. "I shall sink through the floor," he moaned. He "got up on the sofa on his knees beside me," Woodhull later reported, "and taking my face in between his hands, while the tears streamed down his cheeks, he begged me to let him off." Whether Woodhull exaggerated his reaction, appearing onstage with her surely would have raised grave questions, especially among Beecher's sisters and their friends. And Beecher sought to avoid encouraging Tilton, who was drinking heavily and openly criticizing him to powerful church members and outside friends. He anticipated that Tilton would use any sign of cooperation against him.

Disgusted by what she considered his cowardice, Woodhull prepared to leave, telling the preacher: "Mr. Beecher, if I am compelled to go on that platform alone, I shall begin by telling the audience why I am alone and why you are not with me."

THE NEXT NIGHT, November 20, a driving rainstorm soaked Manhattan. Sodden ten-foot red-and-gold banners reading *Freedom!* twisted in the lashing wind above the stiff-hatted heads of three thousand men and women who funneled into the grand auditorium on Union Square to hear Woodhull lecture on "The Principles of Social Freedom." Beecher remained in Brooklyn, leaving Theodore Tilton to introduce her.

"The basis of society is the relation of the sexes," Woodhull declared, reading from a prepared speech. "There is no escaping the fact that the principle by which the *male* citizens of these United States assume to rule the *female* citizens is *not* that of self-government but that of despotism. . . . Our government is based on the proposition that all men and women are born free and equal and entitled to certain inalienable rights. . . . What we, who demand social freedom, ask is simply that the government of this country shall be administered in accordance with the spirit of this proposition."

Here was the evolutionary imperative applied to sex and politics alike. Much as with race relations, sexual relations in America collided with essential national ideology—that is, freedom and equality for all, as inscribed in the Constitution. If mankind was monogenic, and if nature's universal drive was survival and improvement of the species, was it not the job of governments to combat whatever repressed nature and sanctioned inequality? Woodhull, though never an affirmed Darwinian, grasped the root connection between biological evolution and social progress. As a spirit medium in long contact with suffering souls, she believed optimistically that humanity would eventually evolve to higher spiritual, moral, and political states. Two months earlier she had been elected president of the American Association of Spiritualists, which professed as many as four million, mostly female, adherents, in a country of forty million.

"My brothers and sisters," Woodhull continued. "You are all aware that my private life has been pictured to the public by the press of the country with the intent to make people believe me to be a very bad woman." As Woodhull went on to describe how divorce and property laws codified man's rule over woman, and how laws can't regulate love, the hall erupted, half cheers, half hisses. Challenged by the baying crowd, she departed from her text. "I can see no moral difference," she said,

> between a woman who marries and lives with a man because he can provide for her wants and the woman who is not married but who is provided for at the same price. . . . The sexual relation must be rescued from this *insidious* form of *slavery*. Women must rise from their position as *ministers* to the *passions of men* to be their equals. Their entire system of education must be changed. They must be trained like men, [to be] independent individuals, and not mere appendages or adjuncts of men, forming but one member of society. They must be companions of men from choice, never from necessity.

"*Yes!*" Woodhull declared finally, amid deafening cries of "*Whore!*" and "*Shame!*" that all but drowned out her confession. "*I am a free lover!* I have an inalienable, constitutional and natural right to love whom I may, to love for as long or as short a period as I can, to change that love every day if I please! And with that right neither you nor any law have any right to interfere."

The speech lasted two hours. Amid the uproar in the days ahead—the

New York *Herald* called it "the most astonishing doctrine ever listened to by an audience of Americans" and castigated the Steinway crowd for allowing her to finish—Woodhull became instantly scandalous while Tilton, serially cuckolded, deserted by the public, and verging on bankruptcy, was ruined. Meanwhile, Beecher kept his silence. Having skirted the wreckage by refusing Woodhull's gambit, he returned, tired and unfocused, to work, preaching to packed crowds at the Plymouth Church in Brooklyn Heights, churning out sermons and prayers, and researching a much-awaited two-volume novelistic biography of Jesus called *The Life of Christ*. His friends urged him to go on a pilgrimage to the Holy Land, to get away and work on his book, but Beecher couldn't resist being at the center of events, and so he remained in Brooklyn. Though the church board pressed hard to investigate Tilton's accusations, he ignored their pleas.

"DROVE OVER TO the Navy Yard in the afternoon with my girls to see the little steamer [the *Hassler*] in which Agassiz is going round the Cape," Longfellow wrote in his journal on November 26.

Delays in assembling the fifty-person exploring party and fitting the ship with equipment for dredging and sounding what Agassiz called the "deepest abysses of the sea" had postponed departure by several months, and though his health wavered, Agassiz hastened to complete final preparations before winter hit New England. When young Darwin, after first training to be a doctor like his father until he realized he couldn't bear to practice medicine, then studying, with no particular religious conviction, to become a clergyman so as to provide respectable cover for his passion for nature, shipped out on HMS *Beagle,* he signed on primarily to serve as an educated companion for the imperious captain of a creaking, 98-foot, three-masted wooden sailing ship with a crew of ninety men doing mostly coastal surveys—a floating jail, his father called it. But the *Hassler,* a 370-ton double-hulled steel oceanographic vessel with powerful new two-cylinder engines, had been fully optimized to serve Agassiz's quest, making it capable of hauling sea life with ropes and winches from depths of more than 4,200 feet, and preserving tens of thousands of specimens until they could be returned to Harvard for study. Like his last expedition five years earlier to Brazil, where he claimed to have found evidence of glaciers deep in the interior, the trip was trumpeted as a historic national enterprise, attracting money, publicity, and students, to whom Agassiz planned to lecture on the universality of God's "plan" all the way around.

Publicly, Agassiz's confidence in himself and his worldview was never higher. On the eve of his departure he wrote a letter to Peirce, widely reprinted, promising that his trip would yield momentous discoveries about the origins of the earth and its earliest inhabitants—discoveries that would confirm and expand on his earlier work. Evolutionists and nonevolutionists alike believed that the ocean depths held fossil forms of ancient sea life that resembled modern organisms. Agassiz predicted as a matter of certainty that the *Hassler* would haul up varieties closely resembling those found in the earliest geological periods, when shallow seas covered the earth, thus demonstrating that species were created of a piece and distributed wholesale, by God, once and for all. He also predicted he would find evidence of massive glacial activity at the southern tip of South America, adding to the picture of a universal ice age. He told Peirce:

> If there is, as I believe to be the case, a plan according to which the
> affinities among animals and the order of their succession in time
> were determined from the beginning . . . in other words, if this world
> of ours is the work of intelligence, and not merely the product of
> force and matter, the human mind . . . may reach the unknown.

By now, Agassiz also realized the stakes. This trip would be his last legacy, both as a scientist and as the main architect of America's scientific enterprise. When he had first come out forcefully against Darwin more than a decade earlier, his record of trailblazing discoveries and his reputation as an arbiter of rigorous research gave him instant standing and credibility, not only among the adoring intelligentsia and general public but also among other naturalists. He still knew more than anyone else about ancient life-forms and the fossil realm. Yet his empire building, public heroics, and preference for amassing natural treasures over testing his theories through experimentation increasingly estranged him from those now pushing the field ahead. As Agassiz knew, he was no longer working anywhere near the forefront. Many of his peers scoffed at his recent science, especially his work in Brazil, where—without finding a single glaciated pebble or polished rock to back him up—he claimed to have found undeniable evidence contradicting evolution; specifically, wide-spread traces of glacial action under the thick tropical canopy throughout the Amazon basin, from which he concluded that a glacial epoch rendered impossible any genetic connection between animals and plants that lived prior to and after it. "Wild nonsense," Darwin called it, telling Gray that Agassiz's "predetermined wish partly explains what he fancies he observed."

Perhaps because he sensed that while he might continue to oppose Darwinism, he no longer could avoid the fact that it seemed to be on the verge of prevailing among biologists—even his son, Alexander, had by and large converted—Agassiz had gone out of his way to mend fences. In the summer of 1864, disturbed and hurt by Gray's public challenges, he had insulted Gray "so foolishly and grossly," as Gray put it, that Gray broke off all personal relations with him. Agassiz apologized two years later, and ever since, the two had shown each other cordial respect. In fact, evolutionary purists like Spencer, Youmans, and Huxley, and "accommodationists" like Gray and Beecher, all welcomed Agassiz's determination to study the world's nether regions afresh in light of Darwin's work, and they wished him unflagging health and success. "Pray give my most sincere respects to your father," Darwin wrote in June to Alexander, a recent member of his ever-widening circle of correspondents. "What a wonderful man he is to think of going through the Strait of Magellan."

The *Hassler* steamed out of Charlestown harbor and into Cape Cod Bay on a gray afternoon on December 4, just before a snowstorm, the first of the season. The hopes Agassiz had formed of this expedition were "as high as those of any young explorer," his wife, Elizabeth, who sailed with him, wrote. For reading, he took along only Darwin's books. A year after despairing that he would never have the chance to finish all that he had started, he looked ahead with gusto to warmer seas. He couldn't wait to get started. "As soon as we reached the Gulf Stream," he reported to Peirce in his next letter, "we began work."

"I AM BACK from Germany more dead than alive," Youmans wrote to his sister, Catherine, from London during the first week of December, "but still a good deal vital." Visiting the Continent—reeling from war, radicalism, and bloodshed—had been "a strange experience" in part due to Spencer, who joined him in Paris ostensibly to help open doors for what

Youmans now called his "international scheme," but whose sensitivity to criticism, Darwin-envy, and dependence on his American friend flashed over during the visit.

Huxley, Darwin's famously combative defender and chief popularizer in England, had challenged Spencer in an article championing a free public school system, which Spencer deplored as useless and destructive. Largely self-taught, Huxley was among England's foremost biologists, having paved the way for *The Descent of Man*—drawing the poison, so to speak—by publishing his own book on human evolution, *Evidence on Man's Place in Nature*, in 1863. Darwinism and radical social theory had become inextricable, yet international events had recently heightened antagonism over the role of government, and Huxley and Spencer, while scientific allies, clashed over how best to improve society. A year earlier, German forces led by Prussia had conquered and humiliated France, where starving Parisians, besieged and bombarded, were reduced to eating dogs, cats, and rats, even the elephants in the zoo. For two months in the spring, socialists and communards ruled the French capital until the uprising was crushed, but not before unleashing the specter of mob rule. A charged political climate in London—the *Times*, in a scathing editorial, attacked the timing of Darwin's release of *Descent* during the Paris Commune as "reckless"—now polarized and inflamed every debate.

Huxley, in addition to writing, teaching, editing, and providing for a household of ten children, was a furious social crusader. He took on too much always, unable to resist new battles. He agreed during the fall to serve with Spencer and Tyndall as English jury for Youmans's project; pledged to write the first book in the series, on bodily motion and consciousness; and took on duties on two royal commissions and the London School Board. In his article on free schools in *The Fortnightly Review*, he called Spencer to task for his views on the proper role of government: that is, as Huxley wrote, "The State is simply a policeman, and its duty is neither more nor less than to prevent robbery and murder and enforce contracts."

Spencer held that societies are organisms and that, like living forms, they evolve. He asserted a gradual evolution from primitive, less organized, to advanced, more organized, societies; and he maintained that as societies become more complex, and individual roles (and property) more varied, government must retreat from vast areas of social life so as to allow each individual to rise by his own exertions. Noting that Spencer compared the role of Parliament to that of the "cerebral masses in a vertebrate animal," Huxley applauded Spencer for the biological analogy, but criticized his conclusion that just as the brain "*averages* the interests of life, physical, intellectual, moral, social," the appropriate sphere of government is to average the interests of various classes in society, not to do anything to improve or alter their relations. Huxley wrote:

> All this appears to be very just. But if the resemblance between the body physiological and body politic are any indication, not only of what the latter is, but of what it ought to be, and what it is tending to become, I cannot but think that the real force of the analogy is totally opposed to the negative view of State function.
>
> Suppose that, in accordance with this view, each muscle were to maintain that the nervous system had no right to interfere with its contraction, except to prevent it from hindering the contraction of another muscle; or each gland, that it had the right to secrete, so long as its secretion interfered with no other; suppose every separate cell left free to follow its own "interest," and *laissez-faire* lord of all, what would become of the body physiological?

In Paris, Spencer bristled for three days while Youmans coped with "my embarrassments here—short time, nobody at home, difficulty of interpretation, torments with cab-drivers, etc." Spencer sought unsuccessfully, in scrambled French, to find a secretary, until one night Youmans finally offered to take dictation. "Spencer couldn't stand it," Youmans told Catherine in a letter, "so he said, 'Huxley has been rampaging around long enough; he must be pulled up.' I wrote twenty pages of manuscript." Polishing the reply upon his return to London, Spencer pushed to have it appear in the next *Fortnightly Review,* explaining his urgency in his autobiography: "[Huxley] put his objection in the form of a question. I could scarcely avoid giving an answer; for otherwise the implication would have been that the question was unanswerable."

While Spencer settled scores, Youmans traveled by train to Cologne, then to Berlin, birthplace and capital of the triumphal new German empire. Increasingly confident that the international series would get off the ground—he had English and French publishers in tow, and a roster of famous authors including ten of the "ablest men in France," as well as Spencer, who succumbed to Youmans's pressure to write a short extra book on sociology—he nonetheless encountered strong opposition at first to the scheme. "Germany is not going to suit me," he cautioned Catherine, who assisted him in business, a well-regarded scientific author in her own right:

> They are too cocky. "We don't want your translations; we can make our own books; the talent is here," is the way the publishers talk. On the other hand, I find that scientific men here have a contempt for "popularization" more intense than anywhere else. They ostentatiously despise it and the countries that tolerate it. It looks like a very bad market for my pigs.

Unable to sleep in the narrow feather beds, Youmans lapsed into self-pity and annoyance, worrying that the country might be a total loss, especially after a side trip to Leipzig, a hundred miles south of Berlin:

> I had a letter to one important man; he is dead. To another, and he is so sick I have been unable to see him. It snows, sleets, rains, and is dark, muddy and detestable in Leipsic. Not a publisher can speak a word of English in Leipsic. I got lost, and could not remember the name of my hotel, and wandered through the mud.

Yet Darwinian theory had enjoyed its greatest initial impact in Germany, which in the past seven years had won three wars, unifying under Prussian control a giant industrial nation overextending its modern borders into parts of Belgium, the Czech Republic, Denmark, France, Lithuania, Poland, and Russia. If the Germans were cocky, they had cause. Darwin himself had recognized early that Germany's nationalism and scientific traditions made its people especially receptive to evolutionary doctrines. "The support which I receive from Germany is my chief ground for hoping that our views will prevail," he wrote. Youmans, buoyed by a letter of introduction from Huxley, managed to meet with many of the country's top scientists, and while they dismissed his publishing ideas, they expressed keen interest in Spencer. As an ideologue employing a competitive view of nature and the evolutionary concept of the struggle for existence as a basis of social theory, Spencer, much more than Darwin, offered great hope and validation for a rising world power.

Back in England, Youmans told Catherine excitedly about the unexpected reversal: "Germany is more ripe for the movement than even England; the best men can be procured. It was Huxley's name which carried the thing there." He added:

Spencer will in time reap his greatest conquest in Germany. The whole nation is pervaded with religious skepticism, and they are without any philosophic guidance. Spencer's subject on the list interested them more than any other, and with the publication of his little book, which I bullied him to write, there will be prompt demand for the Philosophy. When I wrote this to Spencer, the old fellow waked up, went down to King after some circulars, and entered at once upon the finding of a writer.

By the time he sailed for home on December 30, Youmans not only had arranged simultaneous publication of his series in New York, London, Paris, and Leipzig, but also had advanced likely deals in St. Petersburg and Milan. In five years, he expected the series would run to seventy-five or a hundred volumes: "the world's cyclopedia of reading science." Further, he had persuaded Spencer, already overburdened by his monumental system of evolution philosophy, to write an extra book, and that volume was already heavily anticipated despite Spencer's having written not a word. In October, he had told Catherine grimly: "I am bound to this enterprise, and, much as I want to go, I shall be guided absolutely by it. I'm the man to do the work: Nobody else can." Now, spending a fortnight in London tying up loose ends, he was exhausted, but also exuberant.

"My Dear Sister," Youmans reported in his last letter from London:

Last Monday night I met with Spencer and Tyndall at Huxley's at dinner to consider matters. It was precious different from my first dinner there six months ago. They are fairly in harness and trot quite smoothly. . . . It seems to be universally agreed that we have a great thing in prospect and well under way, and which can hardly fail to result in large advantages to many authors and to the public also. I am glad I came now, and glad I stayed it out. . . . Oh, how I will sleep when I get on that ship!

NEW HAVEN, 1872

> au•toch•thon *n* I one of the earliest known
> inhabitants of a place; an aborigine 2 an
> indigenous plant or animal

BEECHER CONSIDERED HIMSELF safe so long as nothing reached the newspapers. He tried to kick Woodhull's threats under the rug and struggled to conceal, if not discipline, his inner nature. One of his congregants had contributed funds in honor of his father, Lyman Beecher, a famously stern Yankee evangelist during the Second Great Awakening, to establish a lectureship on preaching at the divinity school at Yale, the elder Beecher's alma mater—provided Henry taught the first three courses. As a child, he'd cringed and chafed under his father's preaching eternal hellfire for the wicked from his narrow tub pulpit; lacking early promise, he was sent as a youth instead to Amherst. On January 31, he left Brooklyn by launch across the East River—the launches were nicknamed "Beecher Boats" by the press because on Sundays they were packed with Manhattanites streaming to hear his sermons—proceeded uptown to the new Grand Central Depot on Fourth Avenue, and caught a night train to New Haven.

Beecher had no prepared lecture and hadn't decided what to say to the young candidates for the ministry. According to his successor at Plymouth Church and biographer Lyman Abbott, he had a bad night, not feeling well. Went to his hotel, got his dinner, lay down and had a nap. At 2-o-clock he got up and began to shave, without having been able to get any plan of the lecture to be delivered within the hour. Just as he had his face lathered and was beginning to strop his razor, the whole thing came out of the clouds and dawned on him. He dropped his razor, seized his pencil, and dashed off the memoranda for it and afterwards cut himself badly, he said, thinking it out.

Beecher's term for preaching was "pulpit dynamics," and though his Yale lecture was more autobiographical than his sermons, he elected to discuss chiefly what he called "Man Building, the Preacher's Business." In his view, the role of the clergy was ultimately to voice an offer of salvation. In twenty-five years on the broad stage of the Plymouth pulpit, surrounded on three sides by spellbound, well-to-do holders of high-priced pews, he had promoted a gospel of success to equal anything in Spencer. Yale, however, was not Brooklyn, either by temperament or tradition. The conservative Yale Corporation, consisting entirely of Connecticut clergymen, a year earlier had chosen the Reverend Noah Porter, the school's professor of moral philosophy, as president, expecting him to champion the classical curriculum and preserve the ideal of Yale as a Christian college. For the scholars in the audience, especially Porter, men were not built; rather, they were created by God, fell from grace, and either were redeemed through strict adherence to God's moral governance or else staggered by the wayside.

"I have been under the penumbra of doubt," Beecher said, summing up, however unintentionally, his present state. "I look upon the progress of physical science and see the undermining influences that are going on. I see that probably churches as they are now constituted will not stand and that a vast amount of what is called technical theology will have to undergo great mutations. I know there are many minds in the darkness of cloud who ask, Is there a God? or, Is it a pantheistic God? or, Is there a revelation? Can there be an inspiration in this world?

"Young gentlemen," he told them, "true preaching is yet to come."

There is one fact that is not going to be overturned by science; and that is the necessity of human development, and the capability there is in man of being opened up and improved. If there is one thing that can be substantiated more clearly than another, it is that the development indicated by Christianity is right along the line of nature.

Men walk from the fleshly up to the spiritual. If there can be one thing shown to be more true than another, it is that Christianity is walking towards spiritual love as the polar star, the grand centre. If there is one thing in this world more worthy of being worked than another, it is the human soul.

This is the business of the preacher. It is not to grind a church. It is not to turn a wheel. It is not to cuff about the controversies of theology. It is a living work—building work. If you are to be true preachers you are to be man-builders; and in the days yet to come there is to be no labor so worthy of a man's ambition as that of building men worthily, that at last you may present them spotless before the throne of God.

By now Beecher had come to view Christ himself as an instrument of evolution—an all-loving, dynamic force so powerful it could even save a wretched sinner like himself. Man, unlike the lower animals, *bettered* himself, through knowledge. With the Yale lectures Beecher extended his influence to the very center of American religious and social conservatism. Preaching a practical creed—"Beecherism," critics called it—he urged the students to adapt Christianity to their environs: the needs of their flocks, the changing times. "You can manage an average American audience," he advised; "you can make them learn almost anything."

And yet at the peak of his renown, Beecher's double life had begun to subsume him. Woodhull, positioning herself to run for president, seized upon making the international workers' movement her new base of support, and she continued to press him to join her, and threatened to expose him if he didn't. Moving beyond suffrage and free love, she adopted militant positions on wealth and economic equality—leading a demonstration of ten thousand marchers to protest the execution of a leader of the Paris Commune; publishing the first American edition of Karl Marx's *Communist Manifesto* in her *Weekly;* exposing stock manipulation and corruption on Wall Street. Tilton, meanwhile, drinking heavily, also sought help from Beecher. He started telling anyone who would listen that Beecher had seduced Elizabeth, who warned Beecher in an ominous letter about her husband's volatility. Endeavoring, evidently, to blackmail him, Tilton asked Beecher for money to help start a newspaper. Beecher contributed $5,000.

A week after returning to Brooklyn from New Haven, Beecher fell into a pit of despair. Blackness overcame him as he sized up his problems. "To *say* that I have a church on my hands is simple enough," he wrote to a friend,

> —but to have the hundreds and thousands of men pressing me, each one with his keen suspicion, or anxiety or zeal . . . to prevent anyone questioning me; to meet and allay prejudices against T. which had their beginnings years before this; to keep serene as if I were not alarmed or disturbed; to be cheerful at home and among friends when I was suffering the torments of the damned; to pass sleepless nights often, and yet to come up fresh and full for Sunday.
>
> Nothing could possibly be so bad as the horror of the great darkness in which I spend much of my time. I look upon death as sweeter than any friend I have in the world. Life would be pleasant if I could see that re-built which is shattered. But to live on the sharp and ragged edge of anxiety, remorse, fear, despair, and yet to put on all the appearance of serenity and happiness, cannot be endured much longer.

"My dear Peirce," Agassiz reported on January 16, from a station off the Brazilian coast,

> I should have written you from Barbados, but the day before we left the island was favorable for dredging, and our success in that line was so unexpectedly great, that I could not get away from the specimens, and made the most of them for study while I had the chance. We made only four hauls, in between seventy-five and one hundred and twenty fathoms [roughly 450 to 720 feet]. But what hauls! Enough to occupy half a dozen competent zoologists for a whole year, if the specimens could be kept fresh for that length of time.

Agassiz reasoned that deep water conditions approximated "as nearly as anything can in the present order of things upon earth" the heavy atmospheric pressure under which ancient forms of sea life emerged. Though the *Hassler*'s iron, canvas, and leather dredges raked up hundreds of creatures resembling fossil forms from earlier ages, he declared there was nothing in his hauls to show that the living organisms were lineal descendants of long-extinct ancestors—the central claim of evolution. Confidently, he told Peirce that the opposite was true: that the lack of any clear hereditary link proved his conclusion. Such was his standing that the Smithsonian Institution published the finding without the least substantiation.

At Rio de Janeiro, the party remained ashore for a month while the *Hassler* underwent repairs. Coal, as at each refueling stop since St. Thomas, was loaded into the holds by Negro women bearing heavy baskets on their heads—slaves. Agassiz and his assistants packed in alcohol his sixteenth cask of specimens to be sent back to the museum at Harvard, while in American newspapers, a "South American correspondent" reported that during the layover the ship's photographer had conquered the difficulties of taking pictures of live animals in the hot, dank atmosphere of tropical harbors, on a moving ship. Some of the photographed specimens, the *New York Herald* wrote, would fulfill the predictions Agassiz had made to Peirce in his "remarkable letter" on the eve of the voyage.

Agassiz's aura of good luck seemed to have returned. Headlines trumpeted his every exploit, especially in the enterprising *Herald,* which three years earlier had paid Henry Morton Stanley, a journalist and explorer, to travel to the African interior to locate the Scottish missionary Dr. David Livingstone, who had lost contact with the outside world in 1865 and whom Stanley found hungry, ill, and alone on the shores of Lake Tanganyika in October.

THE GREAT DRIFT PROBLEM
Professor Agassiz on his way to Patagonia
From Rio to Monte Video
Quarterdeck Lectures on Northern and Southern Drift
The Professor Quarantined—Goes Ashore—Is Arrested with Rocks in His Pockets

When needed repairs forced the *Hassler* to anchor alongside the windswept bluffs and desolate wilderness of Argentine Patagonia, Agassiz trudged up and down the coastline, securing large boulders crowded with perfectly preserved sea urchin skeletons and immense oyster shells the size of dinner plates. According to Elizabeth Agassiz, who, as during the Amazon expedition, would write a series of colorful articles about the trip for *The Atlantic Monthly,* the few days passed there "were among the pleasantest of the voyage" for her husband. Deep sea work aside, it was geology and natural history that would bring Agassiz face-to-face with the evolutionary argument, as Darwin himself first discovered not far from here a generation and a half earlier. Noticing some broken bones and shells embedded in the low-lying silty banks, Darwin chanced on the incomplete skeletons of three big extinct mammals—his first find as an amateur paleontologist and a scientific rite of passage that established his mode of research for the rest of the voyage: namely, to stay on land as much as possible. Chronically seasick throughout the nearly five-year expedition, Darwin welcomed the prospect.

Rounding Cape Virgens and entering the Strait of Magellan on March 13, the *Hassler* ran the jagged coastline to the bay at Port Famine, midway between the Atlantic and Pacific oceans. In June 1832, at the onset of winter, the *Beagle* had also anchored there. "The Fuegians twice came and plagued us," Darwin later wrote, referring to the dark-skinned Indian tribes of Tierra del Fuego, the arid, inhospitable southernmost populated region in the world. On its previous voyage, the *Beagle*'s mercurial captain, Robert FitzRoy, had taken three Fuegians hostage after tribesmen stole a launch. He brought them back to England, paid for them to be educated, and, after presenting them to the Queen, had returned them recently along with an English missionary to start a fledgling Christian settlement. Darwin, certain that all humans were from the same stock, had studiously compared the Anglicized Fuegians with the wild tribesmen, and the natives with himself, thus establishing the framework for connecting humans to the natural world that would produce *Descent.* According to his description of the encounter, the *Beagle,* a mile and a half off shore, fired its small cannons, while he watched the Fuegians react through a telescope: "It was most ludicrous to watch through a glass the Indians, as often as the shot struck the water, take up stones, and as a bold defiance, throw them towards the ship."

As the *Hassler* left Port Famine, Agassiz and his wife had their own initial brush with a group of natives, who paddled their bark canoes to within shouting distance of the ship, waving animal skins they hoped to barter for tobacco. Agassiz indicated little interest; Elizabeth recoiled. "One could hardly believe that five human beings could make so much noise," she wrote. "The women were naked to the waist: their babies were lashed to them, leaving them free to paddle lustily with both arms and nurse their children at the same time."

Like Darwin, Agassiz viewed race through a prism of personal experience—racial science as a reflection of self. On his first visit to the United States to lecture in 1846, his Harvard-associated sponsors arranged for him, with Gray as his guide, to visit Philadelphia, where they hoped to impress him with the level of homegrown research. There he met Dr. Samuel Morton, eminent physician and a father of American ethnology, who, employing a personal collection of six hundred human skulls of dubious provenance—Morton couldn't identify where most had come from or how they'd been secured—identified twenty-two different species of man. Poring over the specimens of Morton's "American Golgotha," Agassiz quickly agreed with Morton that differences in cranial capacity and geographic distribution could only be explained by separate acts of creation, but it was the shock and revulsion he experienced upon first encountering black waiters at his hotel that converted him into an avowed polygenist. As he wrote to his mother in a long and impassioned letter:

> As much as I try to feel pity at the sight of this degraded and degenerate race, as much as their fate fills me with compassion in thinking of them as really men, it is impossible for me to repress the feeling that they are not of the same blood as us. Seeing their black faces with their fat lips and their grimacing teeth, the wool on their heads, their bent knees, their elongated hands, their large curved fingernails, and above all the livid color of their palms, I could not turn my eyes from their face in order to tell them to keep their distance, and when they advanced that hideous hand toward my plate to serve me, I wished I could leave in order to eat a piece of bread apart rather than dine with such service. What unhappiness for the white race to have tied its existence so closely to that of the Negroes in certain countries! God protect us from such contact!

In 1854, the same year that Longfellow, Holmes, Agassiz, and others organized their Saturday dinner club at Boston's Parker House to discuss philosophy, slavery, and science, Agassiz contributed an introduction to *Types of Mankind,* a 738-page amalgam of pseudoscience and attacks on monogenism that purported to prove Negro inferiority and provide a scientific basis for legal and moral opposition to race mixing. In it, he argued that true science traced human races back to eight "primordial types." Many devout believers in Adam and Eve were offended, and though his abolitionist friends looked away, the book would go into a dozen printings, enjoying its greatest vogue among defenders of slavery.

Darwin, his antislavery fury and his faith in reason rising in tandem, was appalled. He had known Agassiz to be a careful, imaginative naturalist, but he feared *Types of Mankind* undermined the credibility of natural science generally as it sought to explain human development. If God created each race, as other living species, in its proper and assigned place, why put humans in certain zoological provinces and bypass identical zones in other regions? Why do Negroes thrive in different zones? Addressing the problem seventeen years later in *Descent,* Darwin concluded that the polygenists' inability to agree on the number of races—one London ethnologist placed it as high as sixty-three—itself proved that the races could not be ranked as species. "It shews [*sic*] that they graduated into each other," Darwin wrote, "and that it is hardly possible to discover clear, distinctive characters between them."

From the deck of the *Hassler* as it steamed slowly through the plunging mountain scenery of the strait—mile-wide, four-hundred-foot-high glaciers descending to the depths, barely clad natives squatting around fires on shore—Agassiz saw a world that he was certain had only one possible explanation: the judicious exercise of a divine intelligence. Two days out of Port Famine, a storm erupted with sudden fury, lashing the channel into a froth of white foam, the roar of the wind and water so deafening that, according to Elizabeth, "you could not hear yourself speak." With the holds containing miles of hemp dredging rope rapidly flooding, and creaking spars stressed to the breaking point, the captain turned the careening vessel around, seeking shelter. Two days later, with fresh snow blanketing the peaks, Agassiz and several members of the party debarked to explore the glaciers on the south side of the strait, discovering, as he'd predicted to Peirce, that during the Ice Age the movement of ice in the southern hemisphere could be traced from the south northward—the mirror image of Europe and North America. Again Agassiz saw nothing to corrode his catastrophic view of natural development, a universal ice

time explaining whatever inconsistencies, anomalies, and yawning inter-
ruptions existed in the fossil record.

Ebullient, Agassiz decided to spend a second day exploring the glacier
and its environs, while the *Hassler* put out into the strait again for the purpose of taking more soundings and dredgings. Around lunchtime, another group of Fuegians approached the party on shore. Each member of
the party had been issued a Remington rifle for the excursion, and several
of the men held them ready. "I had wished to have a near view of the Fuegians," Elizabeth recalled,

> but I confess that, when my desire was gratified, my first feeling was
> one of utter repulsion and disgust.
>
> I have seen many Indians, both in North and South America, the
> wild Sioux of the West, and various tribes of the Amazon, but I have
> never seen any as coarse and repulsive as these: they had not even the
> physical strength and manliness of the savage to atone for brutality
> of expression. Almost naked, with swollen bodies, thin limbs, and
> stooping forms, with a childish yet cunning leer on their faces, they
> crouched over our fire, spreading their hands towards its genial
> warmth, all shouting at once, "Tabac, tabac," and "Galleta"—biscuit.

When the *Hassler* returned and fired its recall gun, their party hastened
back to the ship, with their "guests" following in two canoes. "Still shouting and shrieking without pause and in every key," Elizabeth wrote, the
natives kept up their pleas for tobacco and biscuits until "we threw them
down both, and they grabbed for them like wild animals." Indeed, long
after the steamer started its engines and pulled away from its anchorage,
two youths and a couple of women clung to the side of the vessel, "dragging the boat below, trying to climb up, stretching their hands to us, praying shrieking, screaming for more tobacco," she wrote.

Agassiz's own impression went unrecorded—he omitted to mention it
in his subsequent report to Peirce—although Elizabeth later claimed he
"regretted" that he had no further opportunities to observe the Fuegians
and compare them to the Indians he had seen elsewhere. Unlike Darwin,
once Agassiz had concluded that the lesser races had nothing more than
a structural relation to Caucasians—much as cattle or monkeys from different continents—there was little left to explicate beyond what he called,

in *Types of Mankind,* "the close connection there is between the geographical distribution of animals and the natural boundaries of the different races of man." Agassiz's science—the science of polygenism, such as it was—exalted classification, not explanation.

"So we parted," Elizabeth wrote, summing up in *The Atlantic Monthly,* which fifteen years earlier had been established by Emerson, Holmes, Longfellow, and several other Boston men of high breeding during a dinner at the Parker House as an attempt to project and promote a distinctly American voice in intellectual affairs, and now served as something of a house organ for the country's educated classes.

> I looked after them as they paddled away, wondering anew at the strange problem of a people who learn nothing, even from their own wants, necessities and sufferings. They wander naked and homeless in snow and mist and rain as they have done for ages, asking of the land only a strip of beach and a handful of fire, of the ocean shellfish enough to save them from starvation.

ONCE SPENCER AGREED TO write *The Study of Sociology,* he took pains to minimize its interference with his other projects, even considering a collaboration until he realized "neither anyone else's version of my thoughts nor anyone else's expression of them would satisfy me." Ever alert to an opportunity, he decided to arrange to have the book serialized and published simultaneously in England and the United States, and he encouraged Youmans to find a fitting journal. Because American monthlies customarily appeared midmonth, while in England they were published a fortnight later, his British publisher, *The Contemporary Review,* wanted protection from undue competition in America. Spencer suggested that Youmans approach a newspaper, urging him to contact Horace Greeley of the *New York Tribune,* America's most famous editor and a defining voice in midcentury affairs. "Under such an arrangement," Spencer advised, "the difficulty as to date would almost disappear."

Youmans doubted the idea. "The newspaper dies in 12 hours," he replied on March 8. "And besides, it is a presidential campaign year, and the papers are already going mad with politics." Greeley, a founder of the Republican Party, reformer, and failed politician, had his own urgent stake in the upcoming election. After twelve years of war and Reconstruction and four years of the administration of Ulysses S. Grant, he was deeply disenchanted with the direction of both the nation and the party, which during the postwar industrial boom together became gripped by money, big business, and a new German-style "blood and iron" ethos of centralized power coupled with imperial ambition. A month earlier, several hundred invited guests including Mark Twain, who'd worked for Greeley as a Washington correspondent, and Greeley's old friend P. T. Barnum celebrated his sixty-first birthday at a lavish private reception, a proto-campaign event organized by a group of prominent New Yorkers who believed Greeley could be nominated and elected as a Liberal Republican, an insurgent party rapidly spreading nationwide in an effort to halt Grant's reelection.

Despite his misgivings, Youmans agreed to approach Greeley about publishing Spencer's articles. "He is as ignorant as a bushman and as prejudiced as a papist," Youmans told Spencer in his next letter, "so that conversation on the subject is hardly possible." Most Republicans, in spite of recognizing the immense tragedy of the war, stressed its successful results—reunification under a militant central government; the emergence of a powerful national entity linked coast to coast by rail, telegraph, and commerce; emancipation, if not equality and safety, for Negroes. But Greeley worried that the country remained torn at its core, and his views on relations between social classes were staunchly anti-Darwinian. A pious, teetotaling moderate once strongly influenced by the French radical Charles Fourier, Greeley promoted a version of social utopianism that he termed "association," in which the goals of eradicating poverty and liberating the human spirit could be accomplished through the shared romantic impulse toward universal brotherhood.

When Youmans told him that the articles in question would be sociological, Greeley lectured him: "As for sociology, Fourier proclaimed more, thirty years ago, than this generation can appreciate." Then Youmans mentioned Spencer, and Greeley said he was "dead and forever opposed to that whole laissez-faire school, and if the articles contained any of that, he didn't want him." By the end of the interview, Greeley told him, noncommittally, "When your articles come, let us see them."

If Greeley, like Agassiz, was grasping for a last chance to assert himself over a surging nation violently recasting itself in every sphere of life,

Youmans in his way was just as ambitious, and he conceived of his mission in terms no less grand. Now that he had launched his international scheme, he believed the timely appearance of Spencer's work was vital to America's advance in the coming industrial age. Spencer's view that human competition was in harmony not only with nature but also with the general welfare and progress of society, and his call for minimal state interference with society and business on scientific grounds—incipient "social Darwinism"—struck across all political and moral discourse, Youmans thought. Unfettered capitalism was Nature's law. Party politics aside, he could hardly allow Spencer's chapters to be published in the *Tribune* even if Greeley wanted them, since he would then have to have them reproduced as pamphlets and distribute them, while in the meantime pirated versions from the *Contemporary* would surely appear, as two other publishers had already threatened.

"But if the *Tribune* prints the papers, what then?" he asked Spencer in his letter. "I shall be uneasy until I know what you are going to do about those articles—whether we are to have them early or not."

As ever, Youmans would not rest. Since the embarrassment with *Appleton's Journal*, he had entertained the idea of publishing his own monthly magazine along the lines of the international series: one in which the world's scientific masters would write for general readers about the most advanced work in their fields. Spencer had heartily encouraged the idea. Yet with publication of the April *Contemporary* now set, and still no arrangement, Youmans grew anxious. Rarely if ever having felt more urgent, he considered wiring Spencer to plead for a reply.

Youmans made up his mind instantly upon receiving the proofs of Spencer's first chapter. "I decided on our course two minutes after getting it," he wrote Spencer on April 3. "I determined to have a monthly at once, and in time to open with this article." In less than three weeks, Youmans conceived and launched *The Popular Science Monthly*. With help from his brother and sister in selecting, writing, and translating articles, he assembled a first issue of 128 pages and lined up D. Appleton & Co. to publish and distribute it. "The first part of it is now printing; the last pages will be closed up to-morrow, and we will have it out in five days more," he told Spencer. The lead article was Spencer's "The Study of Sociology: I. Our Need of It," followed by pieces on a recent solar eclipse, science and immortality, labor, disinfectants, the natural history of man, the causes of dyspepsia, and women and political power. The second number, already in production, would include Spencer's second chapter ("Is There a Social Science?"), an article by Tyndall on the action of dark radiations, a piece on Darwinism and divinity, and a provocative reprint from the *London Journal of Psychological Medicine:* "On the Artificial Production of Stupidity in School."

Youmans was euphoric. In the less than six months since his miserable voyage to England, he had pressured Spencer to write him a book that Youmans believed would make Spencer *the* popular philosopher of the Victorian age ("Being under great obligation to him for all that he had done on my behalf in America," Spencer later wrote, "I could not utter that decided 'No' which I should have uttered to anyone else") and was delivering it in installments to a pent-up public hungering for answers to the pressures, anxieties, and questions of the industrial era. He printed five thousand of the first two issues, then went back to press for another two thousand of each to meet the high demand. "We shall have a large sale on the first two numbers at any rate," he told Spencer, adding:

> Nothing happens as expected, but often the unexpected is best. I am utterly glad that things have taken the course they have. I have long wanted a medium of speech that I can control and now I shall have it. It will consolidate plans and facilitate work. . . . I have not got my amanuensis yet, but soon shall.

MISSOURI JUNIOR SENATOR CARL SCHURZ, the main architect of the Liberal Republican cause, had arrived in Washington in 1869 a committed party man loyal to Grant, but now he and the White House were at war, and his plan to mount a third-party challenge did not include nominating Horace Greeley. Schurz, an immigrant, was himself barred from running, yet Grant was wildly unpopular, especially among intellectuals. The most reform-minded and politically ambidextrous figure in the capital, Schurz at first favored trying to salvage the GOP from within but now led a "small phalanx" in Congress determined to deny Grant reelection. Believing that Grant's stubborn dedication to dubious causes and the lightly principled men who served under him, while advantageous in wartime, represented a fatal political weakness—"a genius for suicide," he called it—Schurz brimmed with full and equal confidence in his talents and his prospects. "Although I cannot become President," he predicted to his brother-in-law, several weeks before the movement's convention in Cincinnati in early May, "nevertheless, between ourselves, I will have to make the next one and can do it, too."

Gangly, stern, and black-bearded, wearing a pince-nez, dark coat, vest, and bow tie, Schurz was a caricaturist's dream—a Teutonic antipatronage moralist and presumptive kingmaker disgusted with American politics. He "was a philosopher; but he seized every opportunity to apply his philosophy in action," Harvard president Charles Eliot, an admirer, wrote. A student revolutionary in Bonn, Schurz was jailed at age nineteen, escaped through a storm drain, fled to Switzerland, then famously returned a year later to Berlin to liberate a beloved professor from the fortress of Spandau prison. He emigrated to America in 1852 to champion democracy. After learning English and practicing law, he campaigned avidly for Lincoln among German Americans, and Lincoln appointed him ambassador to Spain, a job he resigned in order to serve as a major general during the war. At a snowbound winter camp near Chattanooga, he would recall, he huddled long nights in his tent reading Spencer's *Social Statics* by the flicker of a tallow candle. "It became perfectly clear in my mind that, if the people of the South had well studied and thoroughly digested that book, there would never have been any war for the preservation of slavery." Schurz, like Spencer, considered emancipation the central logic of democracy. He thought state interference in social relations to be nearly all bad. And so fighting a war to defend government-sanctioned inequality was antievolutionary: a moral dead end.

While Spencer was most influential among scientists, scholars, and capitalists, Schurz enthusiastically adapted Spencer's arguments from the Law of Equal Freedom—"Every man is free to do that which he wills, provided he infringes not the equal freedom of any other man"—to the business of governing. In the Senate, he clashed with Grant over a range of issues, climaxing with the president's determination to annex the Dominican Republic, which Grant called Santo Domingo. Grant wanted the island nation not just for its rich resources and markets but also as a redoubt against British and French adventurism in the Caribbean, as well as an inroad for further "necessary" expansion in the region and an outlet for freedmen driven out of the South. Like every other president since

James Monroe, he asserted that the United States had the right and responsibility to overspread and defend the American continent—Manifest Destiny. With the nation reunified, the Indians all but extinguished, and the country sprawling along rail lines coast to coast, Grant was anticipating the future. Making the acquisition of Santo Domingo his top foreign policy goal, he dispatched his personal secretary to the island to negotiate a treaty.

Schurz denounced the scheme as an imperialist land grab, anathema to party and national principles. A member of the Committee on Foreign Relations, he revealed in public hearings that Grant's aide and a friend stood to make a fortune through annexation and had secretly pledged to keep Santo Domingo's corrupt ruler in power with military support. He accused the administration of trying to buy his vote with patronage jobs. Along with committee chairman Charles Sumner, Schurz maneuvered to thwart the treaty, presenting Grant with the most embarrassing challenge of his presidency. "The superstition that Grant is *the* necessary man is rapidly giving way," Schurz boasted to an ally. "The spell is broken, and we have only to push through the breach." By early 1871, near the time that Gray learned that Laura Bridgman's doctor was in Santo Domingo assessing whether the natives could be assimilated as Americans, Schurz assailed Grant's mission of tropical expansion explicitly on Spencerian grounds: that is, the presumed unadaptability of the darker races to life in a democracy.

"Suppose we annex the Dominican Republic," he declared in a congressional speech;

> will there be an end to our acquisitions? Having San Domingo, Cuba
> and Porto Rico, you will not rest until you possess also the other
> West Indies Islands; and what then? . . . The grave question arises: is
> the incorporation of that part of the globe and the people inhabiting
> it quite compatible with the integrity, safety, perpetuity, and
> progressive development of our institutions which we value so highly?

Like Spencer, Schurz was a monogenist, but he feared that living in tropical climates and conditions caused native groups to deteriorate morally and intellectually, making them unsuitable for democratic government. Santo Domingo's long history of political unrest and disorder seemed proof enough of the folly of making the island a ward. A racial purist in spite of his libertarian social views, Schurz believed that any lands annexed by the United States would eventually have to be considered for statehood, and that "tropical people, people of Latin race mixed with Indian and African blood" would inevitably degrade the republic.

Schurz broke with Grant as soon as the annexation treaty was rejected two to one despite large GOP majorities in Congress. Swiftly pushing through the breach, he rose within a year to lead disaffected Republicans who no longer saw any vital connection between the party of Lincoln and "the Administration with its train of officers and officemongers," as he wrote. Grant, humiliated, was beside himself. "Sumner and Schurz," he complained to a friend, "have acted worse than any two men."

Now, at the opening session of the Cincinnati convention, two thousand delegates, including those backing Greeley and several other candidates, noisily elected Schurz their permanent chairman. The next day, at the peak of his triumph, Schurz mounted the podium to the strains of "Hail to the Chief." A giant sounding board enabled the throng in the galleries to hear him better. "This is moving day!" he boomed, bringing the delegates to their feet.

But Schurz in his maneuvers proved to be too philosophical by half. He favored nominating Charles Francis Adams, a Massachusetts lawyer, politician, writer, and diplomat, the son of John Quincy Adams and grandson of John Adams—"a first rate man, a distinguished man, a man versed in affairs, and who has filled places of trust and difficulty with ability and fidelity." Schurz believed that society needed to be run by the best men, men of ability and good birth more than wealth and selfish ambition, and he hoped to instill the principle among party members by remaining above factional politics. Yet by letting himself be acclaimed chairman over a fractious body, he squandered his effectiveness. Stuck wielding his gavel at the podium—at the same desk upon which John Adams signed the Declaration of Independence, imported presumably for the occasion of his grandson's historic candidacy—Schurz could do little to influence the activities in the back rooms and on the floor, where, after six ballots, Greeley emerged as the party's candidate. Adhering to his policy of not intervening, Schurz became a bystander at what ought to have been his own coronation, his earlier optimism crushed by the superior deal making of Greeley's supporters.

Schurz, stunned, was flummoxed. The defeat, amplified in the press, was a debacle for him, and he was ridiculed in establishment Republican newspapers like *The New York Times* and the *Chicago Tribune,* and especially by *Harper's Weekly* political cartoonist Thomas Nast, who depicted him as a spidery, played out piano player. He complained to his parents that the whole movement had been "stripped of its higher moral character and dragged down to the level of an ordinary political operation." Further, while Schurz and most of his followers supported free trade, Greeley was a staunch protectionist. "I would do anything," Schurz moaned, "to escape from the necessity of supporting Greeley against Grant." He had inspired and assembled a powerful social force, then been stripped of it by the same coalition of spoilsmen, job seekers, and power brokers it was designed to oppose. And he and they both understood that he had no choice but to support them.

"The result of the Cincinnati Convention has been a severe blow for me," Schurz wrote to his parents. "When somebody with so much effort and under such difficult circumstances has succeeded in building up a great enterprise, then all of a sudden sees it collapse, it is a very hard trial of patience."

For several weeks after the convention, a period of "painful anxiety," Schurz stayed silent in hopes that another candidate would emerge. None did. In late July, after the Democrats, with no better option, also put Greeley on their ticket, Schurz started making speeches in his home state and among German Americans on Greeley's behalf. He often neglected to mention Greeley until the end, extolling instead the party platform—local self-rule, civil service reform, a return to hard money, closing the "bloody chasm" with the South; everything but free trade—while stepping up his attacks on Grant over Santo Domingo. An immigrant par excellence in a nation of immigrants, Schurz was nothing if not adaptable. Where once he had been a leading abolitionist and ardent spokesman for individual liberty and free trade, and though he had been usurped and believed he'd been used, he now joined those who wanted to end Reconstruction and impose steep tariffs.

On Saturday nights when he was in the city, thirty-five-year-old Andrew Carnegie often left the plush suite at the Windsor Hotel on Fifth

Avenue that he shared with his mother and strolled downtown to the Murray Hill townhouse of Anne Lynch Botta, whom Greeley called "the best woman that God ever made." A central figure in the city's progressive social, literary, and artistic scenes, the magnetic and generous Mrs. Botta, wife of a handsome Italian scholar at New York University, was much admired for her sculptures, paintings, and poetry, but more so for the large, cosmopolitan circle she attracted to her parlors. Edgar Allan Poe was a friendless author of gothic tales when she invited him to read early drafts of "The Raven" to gatherings frequented by, among many others, Greeley, Beecher, Margaret Fuller, and Emerson, who dubbed her salon the "house of the expanding doors." When Paris was under German siege, she donated a collection of autographs, photographs, and original sketches by her celebrated friends that fetched five thousand dollars for the suffering women and children.

Carnegie had begun visiting her soirées the year before and soon captured Mrs. Botta's attention. A blond, bearded, self-made phenom just over five feet tall with an impish moonface, bristling energy, furious drive, and rolling Scottish brogue, he had arrived on Wall Street six years earlier and accelerated efforts to build a business empire, it seemed, in all directions at once ever since.

He had been born near Edinburgh, arriving in America in 1848, and started out in industry as an impoverished, unschooled thirteen-year-old bobbin boy working twelve-hour shifts in a cotton factory in Pittsburgh. Within two years, as a messenger in a telegraph office, he had displayed an uncommon gift for memorizing street names and the names and faces of customers, gaining promotion to telegrapher. While still in his teens he became personal assistant to Thomas Scott, superintendent of the Pennsylvania Railroad's western division, then succeeded Scott in that position five years later. After paying a substitute $850 to take his place in the Union Army, he transformed himself into a dazzlingly successful company manager, investor, bond salesman, and international financier while still in his twenties.

Carnegie held dozens of cross-linked interests in railroads, telegraphy, bridge building, iron mills, mines, sleeping cars, real estate, and oil—the core businesses of the frenetically expanding, corrupt, and wholly unregulated new economy. He was now entering his prime, having recently co-engineered the takeover of the Union Pacific Railroad by the Pennsylvania, an audacious coup that earned him a seat on the Union Pacific board two years after the line's Irish laborers met up in Utah with Chinese laborers from the Central Pacific to connect the first coast-to-coast railroad. The *Railroad Gazette* predicted that the Pennsylvania would "control all the transcontinental traffic for many years to come."

Fresh off this "triumphant success," as he called it, Carnegie, whose intellectual, cultural, and social aspirations equaled, if not exceeded, his drive to win in business, plunged into the city's elite discourse over ideas, books, art, and useful opinion. He joined the Nineteenth Century Club, a monthly discussion group on the religious, sociological, and philosophical topics of the day founded by industrialist and speculator Courtlandt Palmer, whose investments in the early technology of lever-action repeating rifles led to the evolution of the Winchester—the "gun that won the West." Preaching positivism, the broad movement of thought that rejected abstract deities in favor of natural phenomena and the "religion of humanity," the club introduced him to the early work of Spencer, which he discovered closely reinforced his own view of human progress. It was Palmer who brought him into the charmed circle of Mrs. Botta, herself sufficiently struck by his outspokenness the first time Carnegie visited to invite him back frequently. "One of her chief characteristics," he recalled,

> was that of recognizing unknown men and women and giving them
> opportunities to benefit, not only from her own stores of wisdom,
> but from the remarkable class she drew around her . . . the literary,
> musical, professional and artistic celebrities—the leading ministers,
> physicians, painters, musicians, and actors, or especially the coming
> man or coming woman in these branches. Millionaires and
> fashionables are poor substitutes for the real lions of a cultivated
> society. Madame Botta's lions could all roar, more or less; they were
> not compelled to chatter, or be dumb.

Driven to compensate for a lack of formal schooling and to avenge the humiliations suffered by his beloved if ferociously possessive mother, Margaret, a genteel woman who held her family together after her husband died a penniless immigrant in America, Carnegie much more than other rising industrial titans reveled in finding himself in such cultured company. Three years earlier, once he realized he'd earned enough to retire, he had laid out his life's ambitions in a memorandum to himself written on hotel stationery, in which he vowed to resign all his business interests by now in favor of a life of study and philanthropy. "Settle in Oxford & get a thorough education making the acquaintance of literary men—this will take three years active work—pay especial attention to speaking in public," he wrote.

> Settle then in London & purchase a controlling interest in some newspaper or live review . . . taking a part in public matters especially those connected with education & improvement of the poorer classes. Man must have an idol—The amassing of wealth is one of the worst species of idolatry. No idol more debasing than the worship of money. Whatever I engage in I must push inordinately therefore I should be careful to choose that life that will be the most elevating in character. To continue much longer overwhelmed by business cares and with most of my thoughts wholly upon the way to make more money in the shortest time must degrade me beyond hope of permanent recovery.

Yet the more his businesses overlapped—heightening potential double-dealing and conflicts of interest—the harder it was for him to let go, and the more greed tempted him. American industry and Wall Street were in the heat of a government-sponsored binge. Washington, swept up by expansionism, wanted coast-to-coast rail service more than investors did, and so the government assumed the risks: chartering new lines, giving away territory (and, as a sweetener, mineral rights), subsidizing construction, guaranteeing loans, and not inadvertently inviting countless scoundrels, stock manipulators, fraudulent accountants, and other hucksters to capitalize on the boon. The men who controlled the Union Pacific before Carnegie and his partners took over, for instance, believed the real money was to be made in building the system, not operating it, and so they created a construction company with the fanciful name of Credit Mobilier of America to overcharge the Union Pacific tens of millions of dollars for building the railroad, all of which went into their own pockets. Union Pacific's financial situation became so perilous that a board member finally approached the Pennsylvania group to rescue the firm.

Carnegie had no part in the fleecing, but he wasn't above taking a quick profit when Union Pacific's stock began to rise after the bailout. He and his partners, using a number of different brokerages to disguise the sell-off, unloaded all but four hundred shares of their stake in the railroad. At Mrs. Botta's and elsewhere, he enjoyed referring to "our Union Pacific," but his sudden, precocious elevation to the upper echelon of the railroad industry turned out to be short-lived and instructive. By March, the other Union Pacific shareholders, getting wind of the scheme, angrily confronted him and two of his three partners. "At the first opportunity we were ignominiously but deservedly expelled from the Union Pacific Board," he later wrote. "It was a bitter dose for a young man to swallow."

Carnegie, in keeping with the positivism of the Nineteenth Century Club, viewed every setback as an opportunity, every disappointment an advantage, every "bitter dose" an edge. He believed, with Spencer, that social organisms including industries and economies evolved from less coherent to more coherent forms, and that American business was in the process of ordering itself through consolidation and the emergence of dominant companies. He agreed that people and societies grow and improve by weeding out the weak and reinforcing the fittest through the "never-ceasing discipline of experience." He held extreme doubts about Christianity and all religion. Now, reading Spencer and Darwin, he recalled in his memoirs, when he reached

> the pages which explain how man has absorbed such mental foods as were favorable to him, retaining what was salutary, rejecting what was deleterious, I remember that light came as in a flood and all was clear. Not only had I got rid of theology and the supernatural, but I had found the truth of evolution. "All is well since all grows better" became my motto, my true source of comfort. Man was not created with an instinct for his own degradation, but from the lower he had risen to the higher forms. Nor is there any conceivable end to his march to perfection. His face is turned to the light; he stands in the sun and looks upward.

Carnegie didn't brood long about his ouster. Centrally positioned now to market the U.S. boom to British investors who found him more companionable and trustworthy than his native-born competitors, he sailed from New York in April to sell bonds in London. Having passed the age he set for retirement busier than ever, he made a point as always to tour British iron and steel mills, including the Sheffield plant of the pioneering metallurgist and inventor Henry Bessemer, who sixteen years earlier had developed a process for producing steel cannons during the Crimean War.

If the helter-skelter laying of tens of thousands of miles of track across the American continent revealed a weakness even more fatal than rampant fraud and corruption, it was the rails themselves. The idea of steel replacing iron had gnawed at Carnegie, among others, for nearly a decade, but steel rails remained too brittle for the main lines where trains traveled at high speed. On certain curves, iron rails needed replacement every six weeks. Breakdowns were costly, time-consuming, and dangerous, spawning yet another new business—civil litigation—and preventing the industry from moving ahead. Railroads had changed America irreversibly—even farmers were buying watches now to keep to the schedule that rail travel imposed on daily life, and twenty-four-year-old Thomas Edison had just invented an improved stock ticker to keep up with Wall Street's mania for trading railroad stocks and bonds—but Carnegie believed the railroad's ultimate effect on the nation's growth depended on the development of stronger and more malleable metals.

Carnegie's ironworks, like several of his competitors', had experimented with Bessemer's process for years but without producing large-enough amounts of steel at a low-enough cost to make a profit in rails. Pittsburgh was growing rapidly as an iron manufacturing center, but the steel business was arising elsewhere. To keep competitive, several of his Pittsburgh partners were assembling a company to build a steel plant. They had surveyed all the existing Bessemer works in America—principally Troy, New York, Philadelphia, and Jonestown, sixty miles east, home of the most advanced and successful plant in the country—and had begun searching for a suitable site. Now, standing before Bessemer's converter, Carnegie "got the flash," as he liked to describe his moments of greatest insight. Bessemer's yields, technology, and product quality had risen to the point where steel was ready to compete with iron in manufacturing. Like natural species competing for survival, one would prevail, the other recede, perhaps go extinct.

Carnegie as a rule profited variously from a single venture. Building the Eads Bridge across the Mississippi at St. Louis, for instance, he procured the contract for his bridge building company, Keystone; sold the construction bonds; rolled the material at his Union Iron Mills; and received a bonus for early completion. By the time he sailed for New York, he had resolved to go into steel with the Pittsburgh group. The time was ripe. After a quick rest, he returned to Pittsburgh to line up subscriptions and begin promoting the idea to customers. "I had not failed to notice the growth of the Bessemer process," he wrote. "If this proved successful I knew that iron was destined to give place to steel: that the Iron Age would pass away and the Steel Age take its place."

On May 11, the *New York Herald* promoted the latest dispatch from the *Hassler* voyage, datelined Valparaiso, Chile:

THE WONDER HUNTERS
Progress of the Agassiz Geological, Archeological, Paleontological, Sounding, Dredging and Impaling Expedition

Horrors of the Graveyards of Santiago
Scientific Scrapings from the Ocean Bed, Botanic Grubbings from the Land, and Savant Chippings from Old Stones

On board, Agassiz remained upbeat, but weary. If there had been real news to report, he'd have written to Peirce, but no letters passed between them for months. Often ill and depleted from working and lecturing and from the boat's incessant rocking, he had begun now to face one bitter disappointment after another, increasing the pressure on the entire party and especially his three intimate companions—the renowned oceanographer and marine biologist in charge of dredging, Louis F. de Pourtales; retired Harvard president Rev. Thomas Hill, whom Agassiz enlisted to conduct the deep-sea soundings; and Elizabeth, his wife.

After the *Hassler* came out of the strait, Agassiz was "very anxious" to pass inside the Isle of Chiloe, where the coastal range cleaved the island into two completely different environments—to "verify some statements of Darwin's," Pourtales reported to Peirce in mid-April. Captain Philip Johnson agreed, but the next morning he abruptly ordered the ship to sea, leaving Agassiz and Elizabeth fuming. Johnson had determined not to run the risk of using outdated charts in treacherous waters, but "Mrs. Agassiz expressed herself rather strongly on the subject," Pourtales warned, "and may have written home in the same spirit (she says the Professor would never have undertaken the voyage had he known how few opportunities for investigations would be afforded him)." Assuming that Agassiz and his wife had already complained to Peirce about the decision, he added, "I have thought you would like to hear all sides."

Pourtales's own underwater researches met with repeated failures, meaning that none of Agassiz's overheated claims for the voyage would have a chance to be proved or disproved—a repeat of the embarrassing Brazil expedition, with what one biographer called its "incredible alleged discovery" of an equatorial ice age. Since the moderate early successes off the Atlantic coast, the hemp lines had rotted, pulling apart on each attempt to dredge in deep water. On April 25, with the seabed yielding no support for his theories, Agassiz decided to split up the party. Accompanied by naturalists, guides, servants, and pack animals, he led an overland expedition to Valparaiso while the *Hassler* made a series of stations during which Pourtales finally had to quit dredging altogether. When he and Agassiz reunited, Pourtales chose to return to Washington with assorted specimens, to publish his scant findings. His departure, Agassiz told Peirce months later, "was a great loss for us all, since notwithstanding his silent nature, he is a powerful standby."

Hill, a Unitarian minister, mathematician, and amateur botanist whom Agassiz brought along chiefly as an intellectual companion and friend, was frustrated similarly in his experiments. After sailing north from Valparaiso, the *Hassler* was unexpectedly forced yet again to lay up on land for three weeks during repairs, and Hill now took the unusual step of complaining publicly about the vessel. "The expedition," he wrote in a letter to the Boston *Advertiser,* published near the end of the voyage,

> has through the inferior manner in which the ship was furnished, turned out quite different from what we intended or expected. We left Boston 29 weeks ago, and of that time the vessel has been lying still and undergoing essential repairs on herself or her engines [for] ten weeks. . . . Six weeks lost in ports have compelled us to hurry while at sea, so that we have not been able to take deep soundings, the temperature in deep water, deep dredgings, chemical analysis of water

from a depth, nor measures of the penetration in light and active force . . . owing to the failures of the builders of the ship to live up to their contracts.

Elizabeth retreated, bored and disappointed, to the stateroom off the captain's cabin that she and Agassiz shared in the stern, reading *Jane Eyre* aloud to Captain Johnson's wife, practicing her German, and writing anxiously to relatives and friends that her husband was troubled that the expedition would fail and "that he would not have any benefit from it for himself or science either." "The voyage was so long when we looked forward," she confessed, "and then all the doubts as to the results!"

Agassiz rested for a few days in Santiago, declining a public reception and dinner in his honor because he felt too ill to attend. Among the correspondence waiting for him was a letter announcing his election as a foreign member of the Institute of France—a crowning honor that elevated his standing internationally even as it reminded him that his contributions were all in the past, and of the bittersweet irony of being celebrated (as Longfellow now was all through Europe, and Beecher at Yale and across America) while engulfed in private suffering. "The distinction pleased me the more because so unexpected," he soon wrote the emperor of Brazil. "Unhappily it is usually a brevet of infirmity, or at least of old age, and in my case it is to a house in ruins that the diploma is addressed. I regret it the more because I have never felt more disposed for work, and yet never so fatigued by it."

By the time the flamboyant headlines appeared back home in May, Agassiz and Elizabeth wanted nothing but to finish the journey and return to Cambridge. He all but quit attempting to work. He had sailed in the mistaken hope that he would recover his health, vitality, position, yet neither he nor the *Hassler* was up to the challenge of confronting Darwinism head-on with evidence—in science, all that finally mattered. "A physical fact," Agassiz liked to tell his students, "is as sacred as a moral principle." Though the expedition would collect thirty thousand specimens for the Harvard museum, placing its collections in marine biology on a par with those of Germany, France, Russia, and especially England, all of which were also scouring deep seabeds around the world for natural treasures, Agassiz had not added measurably to what he already knew.

In June, the *Hassler* approached Charles Island in the Galápagos group, the bleak, black, isolated archipelago 650 miles west of the mainland that Darwin made famous as a laboratory of evolution—"what we might imagine the cultivated parts of the Infernal regions to be," Darwin wrote of his own first sighting. Here was Agassiz's best opportunity to challenge Darwin on the central question of how living forms arise. *The Origin of Species*, Agassiz believed, failed to make a convincing case for evolution since it did not document the origin of a single species. Nothing in the expanding fossil record or the study of biology showed natural selection in action, nor the preservation of one race over another in the struggle for survival. Where, it was fair to ask, were the facts? If, as Agassiz believed, the Galápagos were themselves formed too recently to provide a vast enough time period for the evolution of new species to occur, it presented a powerful rebuke to Darwinism, which had emerged largely as Darwin took note of varying species during and after his five weeks spent collecting there in 1835.

Agassiz "enjoyed extremely his cruise among these islands," Elizabeth wrote, though it remains uncertain whether he left the boat, or what he was able to observe. "Our visits to all these islands were the merest *reconnaissances*," she recalled in the *Atlantic*, "giving time for nothing more than a superficial survey of their geology and zoology." The party visited five islands in a week and then sailed on to Panama, yet Agassiz suggested strongly to Peirce that he had seen enough. The age of the islands, he wrote, "does not . . . go back to earlier geological periods. They belong to our times." Thus the original inhabitants were either created there, or, as Darwin suggested, came from someplace else, either by crossing a former land bridge or being carried by sea or air, then spread from island to island, changing over time into new species. The problem with Darwin's explanation for the islands' diverse biology, he told Peirce, was the presumed mechanism of evolution itself:

> If descended from some other type, belonging to some neighboring
> land, then it does not require such unspeakably long periods for the
> transformation of species, as the modern advocates of transmutation
> claim. . . . If they are autochthons, from what germs did they start into
> existence? I think the careful observer, in view of these facts, will have

to acknowledge that our science is not yet ripe for a fair discussion of the origin of organized beings.

Agassiz, who once described himself to Darwin as "an uncompromising opponent of your views," conceded privately now that Darwin's idea might well be true. Too many other naturalists, including his son, Alexander, had decided Darwin was correct for Agassiz to dismiss them. While anchored off Panama, he also wrote a long, confidential letter to his friend the German naturalist Karl Gegenbauer, explaining, "That is why I am on this voyage"—to help collect evidence to show commonality between species he had previously considered distinct and separately created. But Agassiz, unlike Darwin, had ceased practicing true inductive science long ago. Years after his own expedition, Darwin sought to confirm his theory of seaborne distribution by inviting correspondents around the world to send him seedpods, which he dunked in saltwater for long periods, then germinated in his greenhouse. Measuring the length of time they remained potent against oceanographic calculations, he proved the possibility—if not probability—of his theory. Agassiz by comparison could only play devil's advocate, poking holes in Darwin's case. "I do not argue with the fiery enthusiasm I would have exhibited years ago," he told Gegenbauer:

> But I now examine questions step by step, and I must admit that up to now I have not made any great progress in my conversion to the growing doctrine of evolution.
> P.S. Don't you find a meaning in nature? . . . Is not this world full of the most wonderful combinations;—just think of man himself. . . . From where comes intelligence and how come that we ourselves can stand in a connection with this world which we can understand?

Agassiz's notion of design and purpose in the universe never wavered, and so he kept on collecting, relentlessly, even as the *Hassler* sat in dry dock in Panama for ten days so barnacles could be scraped from her hull, prompting him to dispatch seiners into the bay and the isthmus; even after she sailed for Acapulco, the Gulf of California, and on to San Diego, where he secured the service of Chinese fishermen for their entire catches; even after the ship passed through the Golden Gate on August

24 and anchored off the Third Street wharf. Again declining any public reception because of his frail condition, he spoke briefly to an overflow crowd at the California Academy of Sciences, then spent a month resting up for the difficult train trip back to Boston. The expedition officially ended in San Francisco, but collecting went on in the Bay Area and even a few inland stations were made en route home.

Back in Cambridge, Agassiz wrote at once to Peirce, not about cosmic creation but about more mundane matters. "I am sure the materials we have on hand are better adapted to advance science in the direction in which progress is most needed than the collections of any other similar institutions," he said. "And yet I have before me difficulties which are appalling, for unless I can take care of all this, the whole may crumble to pieces." The collections coming in from the *Hassler* so overwhelmed the museum's capacity that Agassiz now began to pressure Harvard and other sources more insistently than ever for money, assistants, and equipment. What he needed from Peirce was immediate help in arranging continuing federal support to preserve his bounty:

> Will you see Mr. Boutwell, when you are in Washington, and ask him to grant leave of taking 5000 gallons of Alcohol out of the bonded warehouses, free of duty, and in installments of a few hundred gallons at the time, as we have no place in the museum to store the whole. . . . In so doing you would enable me to gain a year in the progress of our institution & when I am so nearly turning the tables in our favor in the relative position of scientific collections in Europe & the U.S. our Government may well be asked to do something for us.

Ever scheming to extend his, Harvard's, and the nation's scientific enterprise—which he still, despite the expedition's notable failures, equated—Agassiz concluded with a postscript:

> Our next step must be to prepare such a course of instruction, that European students, capable of appreciating the difference, may prefer to come to us to finish their scientific education, than to remain at home. I see no difficulty accomplishing this even next year. We must begin enticing the master teachers to our shores, & those who are under a cloud for liberal political views will gladly come & the

students will follow & all will be surprised what we have already of native vigor and growth.

For five days in October the Plymouth Church celebrated "the Silver Wedding"—the twenty-fifth anniversary of its founding and Henry Ward Beecher's arrival as pastor—beginning with a parade past his house on Columbia Heights. Surrounded by friends and onlookers and, in the background, his wife, Eunice, he stood on his stoop at the top of the bluff above the great pulsing harbor while bands and banners and thousands of Sunday school students saluted him, the joyful throng on the sidewalk waving handkerchiefs and cheering wildly, children showering his feet with bouquets. "Mr. Beecher bowed and smiled, and smiled and bowed; he acknowledged his gratitude in every possible manner," according to the official church report. He "looked happier than he had ever been known to look before." Tears streaked his cheeks.

The strains on him had merely intensified during the election season, in which he was far more fatally involved than even the trustees, attuned to each new rumor about his relations with the Tiltons and each fresh newspaper report of Woodhull's scandalous and collapsing presidential crusade, could fathom. After being nominated by the new Equal Rights Party in New York in May and taking as her running mate the freed slave and great abolitionist orator Frederick Douglass, Woodhull had spiraled into disgrace and poverty. Vanderbilt, furious about her communistic leanings and attacks on Wall Street, abandoned her, and she was forced to close her weekly. By July, she and her family had lost their home and were being turned away at hotel after hotel until, desperate, she again appealed to Beecher, who refused to see her. "See to it that she is to understand that I can do nothing!" he told an intermediary. "I shall not, at any and all haz-ards, take a single step in that direction, and if it brings trouble—it must come." Tilton, meanwhile, rebounded from his association with her by managing the campaign of Horace Greeley, who after winning the Lib-eral Republican nomination was also selected by the Democrats, whom Greeley had long vilified but who welcomed his call to "reach across the bloody chasm" and end Reconstruction in the South.

Beecher campaigned ardently for Grant, whose administration was shaken in early September by the news that prominent officials including the vice president, the Speaker of the House, and several Republican congressmen had taken bribe money from Credit Mobilier in the late sixties. Less than a week later, Woodhull spoke in Boston to the American Association of Spiritualists, her one loyal constituency, and poured out what a delegate called "a torrent of flame"—the whole history of the Beecher-Tilton scandal. Every local paper but one—the Boston *Journal* mentioned that Woodhull had slandered a prominent clergyman, but named no names—avoided the story for fear of impropriety and committing libel.

Beecher believed he might yet escape an onslaught in the press. Despite all Woodhull's fervent revelations, which she claimed were divinely inspired, no paper dared take up her crusade. During the silver jubilee he spoke revealingly from the pulpit about the differences between his own preaching and that of the stern, God-fearing New England theology out of which Plymouth Church, a Congregational community formed by Brooklyn's rising industrial elite, had evolved and was still evolving. "That theology," he said,

> had put the emphasis on conscience and that which represents law.
> It has presented the conscience in intimate connection with fear,
> and conscience and fear have been largely developed as the prime
> constituents of religion. But partly from my own personal experience,
> a change of emphasis has been made in my preaching, and I have put
> the emphasis on Divine Love. I have made conscience and fear
> secondary.

"My sun is going down," Beecher confessed, before becoming so overwhelmed that he literally grew speechless by the end of the final encomium—stirring testimony from fellow minister Rev. Richard Storrs. "At its conclusion, Mr. Beecher, with tears, and trembling head to foot, arose, and placing his hand on Dr. Storrs' shoulder, warmly kissed him upon the cheek," according to the church report. "The congregation sat for a moment breathless and enraptured with this simple and beautiful action. Then there broke from them such a round of applause as never before was heard in an ecclesiastical edifice. There was not a dry eye in the house."

"I want to say something"—Beecher shuddered, choked with emotion—"but I am unable to."

WITH ELECTION DAY looming, Woodhull decided that the glorification of Beecher—and its cost to her and to a nation forever uncomfortable with the truth about its own carnality and that of its leaders—had gone far enough. Nearly a year after first approaching him in private to discuss "the most terrific scandal which has ever astounded and convulsed any community," she scraped together the money to revive *Woodhull & Claflin's Weekly*, in which she now published all that she knew about the case. Hoping to reverse her fortunes, she printed—and sold, over a three-day period—150,000 copies. "I will make it hotter on earth for Henry Ward Beecher," she swore, "than Hell is below."

Woodhull's exposé, entitled "The Beecher-Tilton Scandal Case," started on page one and filled most of the paper. A mock interview with herself, it detailed not only Beecher's long-term intimacy with Elizabeth Tilton and the machinations within Plymouth Church to conceal it, but also Woodhull's attempts to exhort him to come forward and admit the truth. It was not Beecher's powerful "amative impulses" that she condemned, she wrote, but his failure to defend them publicly—"to be overawed by public opinion, to profess to believe otherwise than he does believe, to help, persistently to maintain, for these many years the social slavery under which he was chafing, and against which he was secretly revolting both in thought and practice; and that he has in a word, consented, and still consents to be a hypocrite."

Far from denouncing Beecher's sexual nature, Woodhull exalted it. "The immense physical potency of Mr. Beecher," she continued,

> and the indomitable urgency of his great nature for the intimacy and embraces of the cultured women about him, instead of being a bad thing as the world thinks, or thinks it thinks, or professes to think it thinks, is one of the noblest and grandest endowments of this truly representative man. Plymouth Church has lived and fed, and the healthy vigor of public opinion for the last quarter of a century has been augmented and strengthened from the physical amativeness of the Rev. Henry Ward Beecher.
>
> I have been charged with attempts at blackmailing, but I tell you sir, there is not enough money in these two cities to purchase my silence in this matter. I believe that it is my duty and my mission to

carry the torch to light up and destroy the heap of rottenness which, in the name of religion, marital sanctity and social purity, now passes as the social system. I know that there are other churches just as false, other pastors just as recreant to their professed ideas of morality. . . . I am glad that just this one case comes to me to be exposed. This is a great congregation. He is a most eminent man. When a beacon is fired on the mountain, the little hills are lighted up.

Whether Beecher's conscience and fear remained secondary now that the contradictions of his moral life had burst into open view, the crisis was, as Woodhull intended, "a bomb-shell into the ranks of the moralist social camp." Within twenty-four hours, copies of her ten-cent tabloid were reselling for as much as $40. Woodhull was campaigning in Chicago when the *Weekly* went on sale on October 28. By the time she returned to New York, Beecher had met in the library of his home with the U.S. district attorney, a parishioner and political ally, who alerted the commissioner in charge of obscenity and "impure literature" for the New York Young Men's Christian Association, Anthony Comstock, who in turn brought action in federal court. Largely at Comstock's urging, Washington a year earlier had made it illegal to send obscene material through the mail, to combat an explosion since the war of mail-order pornography. On November 2, four days after the reissued *Weekly* hit newsstands, federal marshals arrested Woodhull and Claflin and confiscated three thousand copies, which besides the Beecher exposé featured a short article about a Wall Street banker who allegedly raped two thirteen-year-old girls, and threatened similar disclosures about five hundred prominent men in American society.

The next day—Sunday—Beecher strode to the pulpit of Plymouth Church and issued his first public response to the case, a solemn reading of Luke, chapter 12, in which Jesus, mobbed by adoring followers trampling each other to get near him, warns of the perils of a double life. Hypocrisy cannot succeed, Jesus tells his disciples, because everything is revealed before God. Even the secrets of people's hearts will be uncovered, so it is no use being pious and sanctimonious. Admonishing against self-righteousness, Christ cautions against becoming like a rival Jewish sect that preaches stringent interpretation and observation of scripture.

"Jesus began to say unto his disciples first of all, 'Beware ye of the leaven of the Pharisees, which is hypocrisy,' " Beecher told the immense congregation of some three thousand. "For there is nothing covered that shall not be revealed; neither hid that shall not be known. Therefore, whatsoever you have spoken in darkness shall be heard in the light; and that which you have spoken in the ear in closets shall be proclaimed upon the housetops."

Either Beecher was confessing obliquely to his sins, or he was inviting his followers to wait for the truth to release them all. Either way, he was appealing to his flock to exercise new notions of conscience and morality far more fluid and adaptable than the old laws of the Bible—notions that derived much more from Darwin and Spencer than from the fear of an all-seeing, omnipotent God. Darwin himself, known to be decent to a fault, explained in *Descent* the evolutionary logic of a natural mechanism that makes people behave ethically and fills them with self-reproach when they don't:

> Ultimately a highly complex sentiment, having its first origin in the social instincts, largely guided by the approbation of our fellow-men, ruled by reason, self-interest, and in later times by deep religious feelings, confirmed by instruction and habit, all combined, constitute our moral sense or conscience.

How "moral" Beecher was remained doubtful, but not his ironclad grasp of the Victorian frame of mind, for which hypocrisy served as a safety valve against the constant robust pressure to behave faultlessly. Victorians were at severe pains to seem forever courteous, honorable, and altruistic, and to maintain a sterling reputation; to appear always to be better than they were. Beecher may not have said so directly, but he seemed to be winking at his audience that hypocrisy might in fact *develop* from morality, and that the more moral we become, the more it becomes necessary to distance words from deeds. God in his perfect plan might count the hairs on every head, as Jesus went on in Luke's gospel to tell his disciples, and even know when each will fall out. But that didn't mean moral men couldn't, and shouldn't, conduct secret lives.

On Tuesday, while Woodhull and her sister remained in a four-by-eight-foot cell in the Ludlow Street jail awaiting bond, Grant overwhelmingly won reelection, crushing Greeley despite the mounting corruption scandals within his administration. ("That, two thousand years after Alexander the Great and Julius Caesar, a man like Grant should be called—and should actually and truly be—the highest product of the most advanced evolution, made evolution ludicrous," the historian and journalist Henry Adams sniffed. "The progress of evolution from President Washington to President Grant, was alone evidence enough to upset Darwin.") Still, after twelve years of war and Reconstruction, Americans were disillusioned and worn, and in favoring Grant they elected force over benevolence, militant nationalism over reconciliation and brotherhood. During the campaign, Greeley was mercilessly lampooned as a bumbling appeaser, giving comfort to Southern terrorists like the Ku Klux Klan. He was stripped of editorial control of the *Tribune* and was broke. Days after the election his wife died. In a one-line letter marked "Private Forever," he wrote Schurz to thank him grimly for his support: "I wish I could say with what agony of emotion I subscribe myself Gratefully yours. . . . " Describing himself as the "worst beaten man who ever ran for high office," Greeley suffered a complete physical and mental breakdown and went into a coma, dying at the end of November.

Beecher was asked to speak at his funeral, to an audience that included Grant, his vice president, three senators, the governor, the former governor, the mayor, and scores of lesser dignitaries. Despite the unwavering support of his congregation, by now the scandal haunted his every step. As he ascended the pulpit at the Church of the Divine Paternity on Fifth Avenue, he saw, sitting side by side in a front pew, Elizabeth Tilton and his sister Isabella, Woodhull's worshipful confidante, to whom he confessed afterward "he felt he was going just as Greeley did." Seized by anxiety, heart and head pounding, a beloved and adored man-builder at last facing the wreckage of his own all-too-common faulty design, Beecher was barely able to make himself heard amid the throng.

CHAPTER THREE

NEW YORK, 1873

> *What is the chief end of man?—to get rich. In what*
> *way?—dishonestly if we can; honestly if we must.*
>
> —MARK TWAIN

URING THE FIRST TWO WEEKS of January, Carnegie and his partners took up an option on a hundred-acre riverfront field twelve
miles south of Pittsburgh and, with $700,000 in capital, organized the
firm of Carnegie, McCandless & Co. to build a giant steelworks on the
property. Flush from his bond sales in London, Carnegie personally committed $250,000 to the venture—about twice as much as the total outlay
for a typical Bessemer plant in the United States and, equally to the
point, twice the individual interests of the eight other subscribers, ensuring him a controlling stake from the start. Searching for a name for the
plant, he proposed Edgar Thomson, first president of the freshly dominant Pennsylvania Railroad, whom he hoped to make his largest customer but who remained skeptical of the prospects for native steel. Like
his former boss and promoter Tom Scott, Thomson had mentored him,
was his partner in multiple ventures including the Union Pacific buyout,
and possessed a sterling, almost magical name among the younger generation of entrepreneurs in the thrall of the expanding railroads, despite his
also having been dropped from the Union Pacific board. Thomson let his
name be used only after Carnegie assured him that he would have no lia-

bility for the venture. Carnegie, eager less for capital than for goodwill, savored Thomson's benediction more than his money.

Carnegie strove unstintingly to assemble the industry's most evolved plant and workforce. Bessemer's process for mass-producing steel from molten pig iron involves removing impurities from the iron by injecting oxygen. Air is blown through the molten iron, which is contained in an egg-shaped, clay-lined steel container called a converter. The challenge to business comes in scaling up operations. Carnegie commissioned Alexander L. Holley, a brilliant and prolific railroad engineer and inventor who planned eleven of the nation's first thirteen Bessemer plants, to design his works. All but two of Holley's previous plants had been originally built to make iron, not steel, and he had ingeniously fitted the converters and other equipment into existing layouts; now he had free rein, arranging the buildings organically, as a colleague noted:

> The buildings were made to fit the transportation. [Holley] began at
> the beginning with them, taking a clean piece of paper, drawing on it
> first the railroad tracks, and then placing the buildings and the contents
> of each building with prime regard to the facile handling of material;
> so that the whole became a body, shaped by its bones and muscles,
> rather than a box, into which bones and muscles had to be packed.

America was as much a living laboratory, a crucible, for the evolution of a superior organized labor force as were the Galápagos in the generation of new living forms—a place where the autochthons now faced near extinction and successive arrivals competed furiously for supremacy—and Carnegie hired as general superintendent Captain William Jones, lately of the Cambria Iron Works in Johnstown, who had made a science of selecting men for the brutal, dangerous conditions for making steel. "We must be careful what class of men we collect," Jones wrote:

> My experience has shown that Germans and Irish, Swedes and
> what I denominate "Buckwheats"—young American country boys,
> judiciously mixed, make the most effective and tractable force you can
> find. Scotsmen do very well, are honest and faithful. Welsh can be
> used in limited numbers. But mark me, Englishmen have been the
> worst class of men I have had anything to do with.

By mid-April, when the ground was officially broken at Edgar Thomson, work on the wharf was completed. At Cambria, Captain Jones had lost out for superintendent to a man named Daniel Jones, one of his subordinates whom the mill owner subsequently pressured to cut wages, leading now to widespread disaffection among workers and managers alike. When Carnegie heard in New York about the labor troubles in Johnstown a few days after the groundbreaking, he rushed back to Pittsburgh to offer jobs to all Cambria's department heads. And so even before excavating began, he was able to recruit superintendents for the rail mill, the converting works, transportation, and machinery, as well as his head furnace builder and chief clerk: in all, two hundred men who had gone through the costly apprenticeship of Bessemer steelmaking at the expense of a rival firm. Later, during a tour of the plant for Cambria's general manager, Daniel Morrell, Carnegie asked: "Well, what do you think now of our set-up at E.T.?"

"I can see," Morrell grimaced, "I promoted the wrong Jones."

BECAUSE HARVARD REQUIRED four people to replace him—one to oversee the herbarium and a newly planned botanical garden in Boston's Jamaica Plain, another to keep up with the drudgery of curating plant specimens, and two to teach his classes—Asa Gray freed himself from academic life gradually, in stages. In late 1872, a Boston banker and amateur horticulturalist who had made a killing in railroads, Horatio Hollis Hunnewell, arranged an annual pension of $1,000 provided that Gray return his "undivided attention" to his masterwork, *Flora of North America,* thus unexpectedly ensuring continuous financial support for his research after thirty years of vain pursuit. At age sixty and in relative good health, Gray found himself at last in a position to reap the benefits of being recognized as Agassiz's successor as the nation's foremost naturalist. Emerson invited him into the Saturday Club, Congress nominated him to replace Agassiz on the Board of Regents of the Smithsonian Institution, and the Royal Society of London elected him a foreign member. He grew a "venerable white beard," like Darwin's.

In late February, Gray sent Darwin a "squib" commenting on one of Agassiz's post-*Hassler* assertions and asked him to submit it to *Nature,* the scientific journal that Huxley, Tyndall, and other Darwinians had launched three years earlier to promote liberal science. Unable to "fire off my cracker" in the United States lest the recent cordiality at Harvard be shattered, he insisted that Darwin submit the article unsigned. Darwin, astonished and amused by Agassiz's renewed attacks on evolutionary doctrine and happy to repay Gray a favor, did so, and the piece appeared in March under the title "Survival of the Fittest."

As Gray noted with an arched eyebrow, that doctrine, now widely accepted by scientists if not yet by the lay public, "must be strangely understood in some quarters." He cited in particular a meeting of the Massachusetts State Board of Agriculture, which Agassiz had joined chiefly to enlist farmers, animal breeders, and local politicians to support the museum, and where he had said,

> Hasty generalizing of observation is Darwin all over. . . . Do we find that only the strong beget families? Observe plants at the foot of the White Mountains, where are large trees, and so up to the summit, where they are mere shrubs. The weak may and do survive as well as the strong. Ignorance lies at the base of the discussion.

"Probably no one naturalist, however eminent, can be expected to know everything, or even all simple things," Gray commented. "Can it be possible that Prof. Agassiz supposes (as his argument seems to require) that the dwarf trees in question grow and survive near the top of the mountain, *notwithstanding* they are not the fittest, rather than *because* they are the fittest, for the conditions?. . . . Surely the argument brought out against the doctrine [of natural selection] is a good illustration in its favor, only an extremely simple and elementary one."

"We never could quite comprehend why," Gray wrote, Agassiz should "give himself so heartily and persistently" to the work of demolishing evolutionary science, considering how vital his own work was to its development. After all, it was Agassiz who first proposed that the succession of species in time corresponds with biological rank, a hierarchy somehow paralleled in the embryonic development of individuals among the most advanced species. "In view of his continued but unsuccessful efforts to drive the incoming doctrine out of the land," Gray mused, "we could imagine him addressing his own important discoveries in the words used by Balak to Balaam:—'What hast thou done to me? I took thee to curse mine enemies, and behold, thou hast blessed them.'"

IN THE TWO YEARS since *The Descent of Man*, Darwin had cemented his position at the center of the natural sciences, enjoying—and paying the price for—phenomenal success. *Descent* was the first of his books to earn a healthy profit, going into French, Russian, German, Dutch, and Italian immediately, despite the continuing political upheavals on the Continent, and Swedish, Polish, and Danish soon afterward. Though it was controversial, scientists—Agassiz and very few others notwithstanding—registered far less outcry to his explicitly linking man to apes than a dozen years earlier when he had ducked the issue in *Origin*. While quarreling over the implications for society, most reviewers praised his thoughtfulness, integrity, and candor. "What possible difference can it make to me whether I am sprung from an ape or an angel?" wrote the author of "Darwinism and Divinity," which first appeared in the Tory literary journal *Fraser's Magazine* and Youmans reprinted in *The Popular Science Monthly*. Darwin, grateful to be spared personal attack, noted he was altogether "much impressed by the general assent with which my views have been received . . . everybody is talking about it without being shocked." When *The Expression of the Emotions in Man and Animals* was published in November 1872, there was scarcely anyone left to be affronted, and the book sold more briskly than his previous ones. Even Agassiz, who saw the whole question of human feeling as colliding inevitably with metaphysics, applauded: "I can only rejoice that the discussion has taken this turn," he wrote, "much as I dissent from the treatment of the subject."

With the triumph of his ideas came the season of his great fame, "Darwinism" eclipsing all other forms of evolutionism, including those of Spencer, Huxley, and Alfred Russel Wallace, whose independent discovery of natural selection during a bout of malarial fever in the South Seas first forced Darwin to publish his theory, and with whom he was happy to share credit even though Wallace rejected the continuum of monkey to man. Caricaturists couldn't resist melding Darwin's visage—bald, high-domed forehead, frontal brow, long white beard—into a curious primate stare, as Darwin was satirized widely in newspapers and magazines as an ape. Such recognition pained him, but he realized its value in propelling evolution beyond the realm of learned discussion to the world of common belief. His correspondence grew to about fifteen hundred letters annually, most of it with legions of followers who became his staunchest defenders, and who increasingly made pilgrimages to Downe, hoping to glimpse him in the flesh. "Pope Darwin," Huxley called him, not without mischief.

Darwin's wife, Emma, persuaded him to spend the month of January each year in London, which he enjoyed despite himself, and where he now became distressed to find Huxley reeling from a combination of crushing work obligations and financial worries and verging on a nervous breakdown. Like Darwin and Spencer, Huxley suffered chronic anxiety about his health coupled with bouts of shattered nerves, but unlike them he endured the added stress of supporting a large family on the penurious salary of a professor, author, and lecture grubber—a fact he never quite got over resenting despite rising to the first rank of British science. He had recently had costly improvements done to his house, altering the water runoff, and a neighbor was suing him for damage to his basement. His doctor, Sir Andrew Clark, a Scottish physician and pathologist with whom Huxley had gone to medical school and who now also treated George Eliot and numerous other distinguished sick Victorians for dyspepsia and hypochondria (the two chief idiopathic ailments of the time), had ordered him "to take the most absurd care of my eating and drinking—or I lapse from Grace," he said.

In March, the Huxleys visited the Darwins in Downe. Huxley looked worse than he had in London, thin and haggard, his wife confessing his "profound melancholy" and feeling of "everything having gone wrong in the world" to Darwin's daughter. Dr. Clark had ordered her husband abroad for three months, she confided, adding, "somehow it must be managed, tho' . . . money is not too plentiful." Evolutionarily speaking, money, like sex, is a means of survival, and thus a measure of fitness, and Huxley's crisis not surprisingly spiraled into scorching self-reproach. Darwin—too incapacitated, reclusive, and protective of his cloistered writer's existence to engage in Huxley's brand of direct combat with bishops and other antievolutionists, but not too much to ignore the pummeling heaped upon his major publicist and proxy—was eager to repay his debt for Huxley's long and enthusiastic service. Passing the plate—soliciting fellow Darwinians and X-Clubbers including Spencer, Tyndall, and Darwin's brother Erasmus, whose £100 donation prompted Darwin to raise his own subscription to £300—he arranged within two weeks to present Huxley with £2,100, about two years' salary.

How to present the gift, given Huxley's pride and anger at the fact that in England one had to be an independent gentleman like Darwin to make a vocation of science, required the utmost delicacy. "I tremble about his answer," Darwin told Tyndall on April 18, several days before writing Huxley to inform him that eighteen friends had gathered the fund as a tribute, to "enable him to take a holiday."

Huxley thrashed and paced all night, unable to sleep. "What," he wondered, "have I done to make my friends care so tenderly?" The thought that those he most respected felt he couldn't manage for himself—the bedrock of proud English manhood—plunged him further into blackness. Still, by morning he put Darwin's worst apprehensions to rest, even as he revealed his torment that, despite everything, he'd failed to measure up. "I accept the splendid gift," Huxley wrote, adding,

> for the first time in my life I have been fairly beaten. I mean morally beaten. Through all sorts of troubles & difficulties poverty illness, bedevilments of all sorts have I steered these thirty years, and never lost heart or failed to buffet the waves as stoutly as they have buffeted me. . . . I have for months been without energy & without hope & haunted by the constant presence of hypochondriacal apprehensions which my reason told me were absurd but which I cd not get rid of— for I was breaking down; sliding into the meanest of difficulties, the would be climber of heights mired in a mere bog.

Spencer urged Huxley to get away at once. Nearing completion of his *Study of Sociology,* to be published in the fall, Spencer himself around this time was "compelled to restrict the hindrance to work caused by correspondence," he would recall. He took the extraordinary step of penning a circular that he had lithographed—a form letter—to deter those who might ask something of him. "Mr. Herbert Spencer regrets that he must take measures for diminishing the amount of his correspondence," he wrote:

> Being prevented by his state of health from writing more than a short time daily, he progresses but slowly with the work he has undertaken, and his progress is made slower by absorption of his time in answering those who write to him. Letters inviting him to join committees, to attend Meetings, or otherwise to further some public

object; letters requesting interviews and autographs; letters asking opinions and explanations—these together with acknowledgements of presentation copies of books, entail hindrances which, though trivial individually, are collectively serious, at least, to one whose hours of work are so narrowly limited. . . . After long hesitation, he has decided to cut himself off from every engagement that is likely to occupy attention, however slight, and to decline all correspondence not involved by his immediate work.

Darwin, though he did have a rubber stamp made of his signature and used it frequently, depended vitally upon contact with other minds. He could hardly cut himself off from those who wanted something from him even if he wished to. His life and work were conducted through letters, and each morning at 9:30 he came to the drawing room to retrieve the mail, "rejoicing if the post was a light one and being sometimes much worried if it was not," his son recalled. Most days he wrote four or five expansive letters, starting after lunch and ending at around three, treating correspondents with elaborate patience, answering their questions and, if he saw something to gain, posing his own. Once, when it got too much for him, he complained to Huxley, "I should like a society formed where every one might receive unpleasant letters and never answer them." He threatened to hire a secretary, but nothing came of it.

In August, shortly after Huxley returned from several weeks traipsing in the Alps with Joseph Hooker, Darwin suffered what Emma called a "fit." For twelve hours he lost his memory and couldn't move. Huxley, contacted in London, urged her to call Dr. Clark, who visited the next morning and examined Darwin free of charge. "There is a great deal of work in him yet," Clark declared, placing his chronically dyspeptic patient on a severely restricted diet, probably of small portions, and prescribing strychnine and quinine, bitter alkaloids recognized to improve the tone of the intestines and increase the flow of gastric juices. Darwin spent the next several days in bed with "ugly head symptoms," complaining as always when he was sick about his family's hereditary frailty. "We are a poor lot," he wrote a friend. In mid-September, with Clark's treatment apparently working, he confessed his profound relief to Hooker, recounting the experience as "very bad, with much loss of memory and severe shocks passing through my brain."

"Thank God," Darwin moaned, deep though he was in the most godless period of his life. "I would far sooner die than lose my mind."

CARNEGIE AND HIS MOTHER RETREATED from the stultifying heat and fetid air of Manhattan to spend the summer rejuvenating at the Victorian Gothic cottage he bought at Cresson Springs, a fashionable enclave in the Allegheny Mountains fifty miles east of Pittsburgh. A wide veranda girdled two thirds of the house, which was perched on the town's highest hill and was as near to a home as he had. With his steelworks well advanced, and the towering blast furnace he and his partners operated in Pittsburgh expanding apace to meet the booming demand for pig iron, he continued to diversify his interests even as he yoked them more tightly under his own hand. After trading a life of speculation on Wall Street for the singular discipline of steel making, he spouted a new aphorism: "Concentrate: Put all your eggs in one basket—and watch that basket!" The subject of Carnegie's optimism, focus, and capital—his eggs—was presumed to be the Bessemer process, but the real basket was the man himself.

"All was going well when one morning in our summer cottage . . . a telegram came announcing the failure of Jay Cooke & Co.," he recalled later. New York and Philadelphia banks had capitalized the Union effort during the war and were fueling the epic westward industrial drive, granting Wall Street extraordinary control over the money supply in a political economy reluctant to outlaw even bald conflicts of interest and moral absurdities like insider trading. Jay Cooke, who had been the largest broker of government bonds during the war, enjoyed an honest reputation but had mortgaged heavily to invest in railroads, and the failure of his Northern Pacific Railroad caused his financial house to collapse. With hundreds of thousands of panicked depositors, the failure cascaded instantly through the financial markets. "Almost every hour brought news of some fresh disaster," Carnegie wrote. "House after house failed." Within forty-eight hours, as lenders tried in vain to call in loans from overextended railroads, another fifty-seven banks closed their doors, the stock market crashed, and credit vanished; for the first time ever, the New York Stock Exchange suspended trading, for ten days.

Iron mills and steelworks that had expanded alongside the booming railroads halted production and idled their workers as Carnegie scrambled to protect his holdings. "I then entered upon the most anxious period of my business life," he wrote. "I was at first the most excited and anxious of the partners. I could scarcely control myself." The Davenport and St. Paul Railroad, for which he had sold bonds, failed, drawing a lawsuit against the road, himself as director, and the construction company he had created to build it. Construction halted at the Edgar Thomson works for several weeks while Carnegie trimmed his exposure. When the Texas and Pacific Railroad tottered, and his old friend and mentor Tom Scott turned to him to cover a $300,000 loan, Carnegie didn't hesitate to refuse him, allowing the Texas and Pacific to go under and crushing both the health and reputations of Scott and Thomson, both trustees, who together had given him his start in business. He later wrote:

> It was one of the most trying moments of my life. Yet I was not tempted for a moment to entertain the idea of involving myself. The question of what was my duty prevented that. All my capital was in manufacturing and every dollar of it was required. I was the capitalist (then a modest one, indeed) of our concern. All depended upon me.

After recoiling from the initial shocks, and the remorse of abandoning those who had most helped his career, Carnegie suffered little unease as he surveyed the new economic environment. Having his own capital not being bloated by watered stock—gave him a strong advantage as he realized that the panic would favor certain businesses and punish others. Even though the Edgar Thomson works was a muddy, temporarily idled construction pit, and spreading railroad bankruptcies meant a crashing market for steel rails, he set out to emerge from it better positioned for the future than his competitors. He thought panics, as his biographer Joseph Frazier Wall wrote, "were temporary and even necessary cyclical phenomena, in which the economy, as a man with a fever, burned out of its system that which was dross. Upon its recovery the economy would be stronger and more fit than ever."

"Up to this time I had the reputation in business of being a bold, fearless and perhaps a reckless young man," Carnegie explained later. His career was "thought by the elderly ones of Pittsburgh to have been rather more brilliant than substantial." But the panic—and his financial independence—transformed him, especially in the eyes of the surviving investment bankers, who now sought feverishly to assure themselves that those with whom they did business were solvent, and unencumbered by obligations like those that had done in Cooke and were taking down Scott and Thomson. On the morning after the Texas and Pacific collapse, the president of the Exchange Bank of Pittsburgh, with which Carnegie conducted considerable business, told a meeting of his board that it was "simply impossible" that Carnegie wasn't involved with Scott and Thomson, and suggested that the bank should refuse to discount any more of his firm's promissory notes. Carnegie took the first train to Pittsburgh to "announce there to all concerned that, although I was a shareholder in the Texas enterprise, my interest was paid for." He told the coterie of money men:

> My name was not upon one dollar of their paper or any other
> outstanding paper. I stood clear and clean without a financial
> obligation or property which I did not own and which was not fully
> paid for. My only obligations were those connected with our business:
> and I was prepared to pledge for it every dollar I owned, and to
> endorse every obligation that the firm had outstanding.

If more money was needed to complete the Edgar Thomson works once construction resumed, Carnegie found hope and solace in the fact that he was not already mortgaged to hundreds of investors who bought stock on margin and expected to be rewarded with dividends. And if credit was unavailable in America, he knew he could turn to the banking houses of London. By December, as winter descended on New York and the country plunged into its worst economic depression up to that time, Carnegie, his optimism and bravado restored, wrote with his customary confidence to one of them, J. S. Morgan and Co.: "We are steadily outgrowing the foolish panic here. It is mostly a fright—& the spring will see things prosperous again—but we must drive slower."

All was well since all grew better. Carnegie, as ever, faced the light. "The man who has money during a panic," as he would soon tell Congress, "is the wise and valuable citizen."

WHILE THE DOORS STAYED SHUT at the Exchange, Wall Street at first remained nervous, pent-up, even as the city reeled. Ambitious restaurant keepers uptown furnished stock and news indicators to attract lunch customers. Special police guards were strongly in demand to protect messengers ferrying gold and valuable securities between banking houses. Telegraph companies tripled their volume. The cause of the panic was clear, and seemingly limited. "The banks have been departing from their legitimate line of business," the *Times* editorialized.

> There has been a railroad mania. . . . Last year, over 6,000 miles of new railroads were built, not 500 of which were really needed, or can be turned to any profitable use. The foreign markets have been glutted with these schemes. Many gross swindles of one kind or another have been foisted upon these markets during the last two or three years. At last, confidence has been broken down.

On Monday, September 29, the day before trading resumed, Grant issued a letter urging the banks to give discounts to merchants and announcing improved interest on government bonds, fueling optimism among traders that the economy remained sound and only needed the market to show a decided advance to resume its gallop.

As the time for the start of business approached the next day, brokers burst onto the trading floor, "crowding over each other in the wildest possible confusion," the *Times* reported. The doorways were jammed with masses of onlookers "howling and screeching in the most violent manner" to get in. After the president of the Exchange announced several new trading rules, anxiety spiked: "For several minutes the uproar was uninterrupted. . . . Then the brokers remembered that they had stocks to sell and buy," the paper said. "Brokers rushed toward each other with clenched fists, and uttered loud cries." Then came the quotations, with prices opening about where expected, then dropping abruptly. Sullenness and shock set in. "Many people, who thought that the market would go up like a rocket, before the Exchange opened, now became correspondingly depressed, and began to pipe out dismal croakings about the future," the *Times* noted. By Thursday, Wall Street was "intensely gloomy."

Amid this glum confusion, more than four hundred Protestant religious leaders from throughout Christendom converged on lower Manhattan, uniting for the first time in six years and the first time ever in the United States. All week they arrived—Established Churchmen, Presbyterians, Baptists, Episcopalians, Methodists, Lutherans, Reformers, Wesleyans, Congregationalists, and Free Churchmen—for the sixth general conference of the Evangelical Alliance, an international conclave devoted for forty years to unifying their rival sects. With Protestantism facing the rise of skeptical rationalism, atheism, and communism on one side and Roman Catholicism on the other, ministers and parishioners around the world feared dissolution if their faith continued to splinter. Longing for unity, they gathered at the anxious, bellowing center of American business civilization to shore up what the *Times* called, in an editorial, "a broken and disordered front." Devout in its business Republicanism and Christian ecumenicalism, the newspaper scolded: "The sectarianism of the Protestant Church has been its scandal and its shame."

At Steinway Hall on Friday morning, the Reverend Charles Hodge delivered the opening prayer. At seventy-six, a passionately orthodox Presbyterian divine, Hodge ranked as perhaps America's most eminent theologian, having trained nearly three thousand ministers in fifty years of teaching the inerrancy of scripture at the Princeton Theological Seminary, serving as founding editor and chief contributor of the influential *Biblical Repertory and Princeton Review,* and producing several widely used ecclesiastical texts. Wearing a dress coat and snowy cravat, he leaned on a gold-headed ebony cane. A cirrus of white curls wafted from his temples; round wire-rimmed spectacles magnified his limpid blue eyes and framed the flushed countenance of an aged cherub, inheritances of Scotch-Irish nobility about which his son, who would follow in his footsteps, marveled: "Who ever saw a face more radiant, more serene, more suggestive?"

"Come, Holy Spirit, come!" Hodge intoned, his voice low. Halfway back from the podium, members of the packed audience leaned forward, straining to hear. "We have assembled here from almost all parts of the world. We have come to confess Thee before men; to avow our faith that God is, and that He is the Creator, Preserver and Governor of the World. . . . O Thou blessed Spirit of the living God, without whom the universe were dead, Thou art the source of all life, of all holiness, of all power."

Hodge delivered the keynote address the next day at the session on

Christian union. "Christ pervades his people and makes them one," he said. The son of an impoverished widow—his father had died when he was seven months old—Hodge hewed unswervingly to the doctrine of the unity of mankind. He'd spent his career weighing the facts and truths of the physical world in light of the revelations of the Bible, accepting ultimately the teachings of astronomy and geology while disdaining equally the polygenism of the anthropologists and the evolutionary dogma of Darwin, Spencer, Wallace, and Huxley. Though his wife was a great-granddaughter of Benjamin Franklin and a member of the country's "First Family of Science"—her cousin Alexander Bache was coleader with Agassiz of the Lazzaroni and head of the Coast Survey before Peirce—Hodge had stood vehemently against the racial pluralists, though like many other antislavery men of God he excused Agassiz himself, who he believed had only lent his name to the "niggerologists" out of respect for the anthropologist Samuel Morton; "like a jewel to be worn as on a stage and for a night."

On Monday morning, at the session on "Christianity and Its Antagonisms," Hodge attended a lecture by Princeton College president James McCosh on "Religious Aspects of the Doctrine of Development." Since Youmans reported to Spencer two and a half years earlier that McCosh had urged two dozen Brooklyn clergymen "not to worry" about Darwin's explanation that man descended from apes, the two clerics had maintained an uneasy alliance. McCosh, a lowland Scot who had written major treatises on philosophy and science as a professor of logic and metaphysics in Ireland, was already known as an important religious thinker receptive to the logic of evolution when he first toured America in 1866 on behalf of the Evangelical Alliance. At his Princeton inauguration two years later, Hodge, as senior member of the board of trustees, warned McCosh in his welcoming address: "We desire that the spirit of true religion should be dominant at this college . . . unsanctified learning is a curse. Nothing is more evident that knowledge uncontrolled by religion becomes Satanic." McCosh was equally dogmatic about the supreme role of evangelical Protestantism at Princeton, which more than Harvard and Yale had suffered a sharp slump during the war as it lost students from the South, but he also sought to transform the school, opposing its inbred parochialism by bringing in younger, European-trained faculty and revising curricula.

McCosh used the term "development" in place of "evolution," but as an amateur scientist he believed that life proceeded from a single event, followed by a clear biological progression, with each higher form emerging from lower ones. God anticipated nature's forms according to divine foresight, he explained, although His mechanism was not separate creation but rather a system in which species developed one from another. Detailing the events of Genesis, he said that when on the sixth day of creation there appeared "a nobler creature made after the image of God," it mattered not whether man was created out of an ape or an angel, only that his body, mind, and spirit were divinely inspired and wrought. "This was the special work of Elohim," McCosh said, "the one God with a plural nature who, on finishing the Creation, leaves the living creatures to develop by the powers with which he has endowed them."

During the discussion session that followed, a clergyman from London, George Weldon, praised McCosh for his "able and eloquent" paper and conceded that the "unsolved question of creation ought to make men modest." The problem, he urged, was not development, but natural selection. "We have to decide in the present day," Weldon said, "whether we are to accept the theory of the amiable, but I think mistaken, Professor Darwin of England. In other words, whether we ought to believe that man, as he is, came from clots of animated jelly, or whether he was the work of the Almighty Being, who said, when he brought him forth, that he was very good." Weldon was rebuffed by his countryman, the Reverend J. C. Brown of Berwick-on-Tweed, an amateur botanist who said that in twenty years of studying plants he had found "nothing incompatible" with Darwin's theory. "The hypothesis relates solely to the mode of creation, not the fact," Brown said, "and from the effect of it on my own mind, I anticipate that the confirmation or the general adoption of the hypothesis of development will ultimately exercise a beneficial influence on religion."

Hodge, rising amid what the *Times* called "an immense concourse of people" in St. Paul's Church, propped himself on his cane and offered an impromptu, if long-thought-out, response. "I don't stand here to make any speech at all," he said.

I rise only to ask Dr. Brown one question. I want him to tell us what development is. That he has not done.

The great question which divides theists from atheists—Christians from unbelievers—is this: Is development an intellectual process guided by God, or is it a blind process of unintelligible, unconscious force, which knows no end and adopts no means? In other words, is God the author of all we see, the creator of all the beauty and grandeur of this world, or is unintelligible force, gravity, electricity and such like? This is a vital question, sir. We cannot stand here and hear men talk about development without telling us what development is.

My idea of Darwinism is that it teaches that all the forms of vegetable and animal life, including man and all the organs of the human body, are the result of unintelligent, undesignating forces; and that the human eye was formed by mere unconscious action. Now, according to my idea, that is a denial of what the Bible teaches, and of what the conscience of any human being teaches; for it is impossible for any such organ as the eye to be formed by blind forces. It excludes God; it excludes intelligence from every thing. Am I right?

Hodge had decried polygenism because it conflicted with the scriptural revelation of the unity of man, and also because he suspected that some of America's early anthropologists were using it solely to erode biblical authority. Now, though he and Darwin agreed that humanity shared a common descent, and though he didn't believe that Darwin personally was an atheist, he concluded that Darwinism, followed to its logical end, held no place for a God who not only created the conditions for life and the laws that it followed but also expressed through His creations the very essence of what it meant. If man was created in the image of God as revealed in the Old Testament, how could the human eye, more subtle and intricate than the most complex machines, develop by trial and error from the primitive light-collecting organs of ancient fish? Skipping the remaining sessions on "Christian Life," "Romanism and Protestantism," "Christianity and Civil Government," and "Christian Missions," Hodge returned to Princeton the next day and began at once to expand in writing his questions to Brown.

BEECHER ADDRESSED THE CONFERENCE later that afternoon with a long, emotional oration entitled "The Mission of the Pulpit." The scandal had died down. After her arrest nearly a year earlier, Woodhull had languished for a month in jail before being released, then was rearrested, tried, and acquitted on the obscenity charge, fell gravely ill, and now, in the wake of the panic, was living hand to mouth, shunned by feminists and labor leaders alike. Meanwhile, Beecher had publicly denied the rumors and stories about him as "grossly untrue" while falling into an inner abyss so great that he began hallucinating. He told his doctor that every night around four A.M. he was awakened by voices "on the very borders of Heaven": "I seem to have a double existence, as if another self was beside me in the bed." The doctor prescribed hashish, and the hallucinations waned.

Expounding now on the purpose of ministry in the great hall of the Young Men's Christian Association, at Fourth Avenue and East Twenty-third Street, Beecher expanded on the "man-building" theme of his Yale lectures. "I say the first power needed in every pulpit," he declared,

> is that so signally made known in the first pulpit—the intense sense
> of the need of men, of their limitations, of their ignorance, of their
> want, of their weakness. Call it by what terms you please in your
> systematic theology; call it depravity, total depravity, sinfulness,
> disobedience, ignorance; call it unskilled and undisciplined. . . .
> Men say that the pulpit has run its career, and that it is a little time
> before it will come to an end. Not so long as men continue to be weak
> and sinful and tearful and expectant, without any help near; not so
> long as the world lieth in wickedness; not so long as there is an
> asylum over and above that one that we see by our physical senses; not
> until men are transformed and the earth empty; not until then will
> the work of the Christian ministry cease.

Back in Brooklyn, in his own pulpit, his problems multiplied. A day earlier, at the close of summer vacation, an overzealous member of Plymouth Church formally charged Theodore Tilton with "having circulated and promoted scandals derogatory to the Christian integrity of Mr. Beecher, and injurious to the reputation of the church." Thus Beecher faced an uninvited controversy on his home front just as, the day after his talk, members of the Alliance boarded two dozen carriages outside Association Hall, rode to the Fulton ferry, and steamed across the harbor for a day of sightseeing and entertainment in Brooklyn that culminated in a dinner packed with local dignitaries at the Academy of Music. Following a performance by the Plymouth choir of "Come, Thou Almighty King," Beecher rose to introduce one of the visiting ministers, and offered a brief appeal akin to Hodge's for sectarian reconciliation. "It is well, I think, that the Christian Alliance, which signifies union and seeks it, has had a session upon these shores," he said; "for in this land, as much as anywhere else, it has pleased Divine Providence to develop a spirit of philosophy and of Christian Union."

Whatever the spectacular newspaper reports nationally about the allegations against him, the sizzling hometown gossip, or his ongoing private turmoil, Beecher more than any other religious leader continued to speak for the nation. After the conference concluded on October 12, the foreign delegates and a number of invited guests, some 250 in all, traveled to Princeton and Philadelphia. The Pennsylvania Railroad put at their disposal a special train consisting mostly of palace cars, and when they arrived in Princeton, the elm-shaded route from the depot to the Second Presbyterian Church was lined on both sides by students chanting the traditional "rocket cheer" ("Hooray, Hooray, Hooray! Tiger siss-boom-ah, Princeton!") started by the Seventh Regiment of New York City as it passed through town just days after the start of the Civil War. After Hodge issued the convocation, Beecher was the only American invited to address the audience. Later in the day, in Philadelphia, he issued the formal welcome in the name of the United States at a ceremony in Independence Hall.

On the evening of Friday, October 31—All Saints' Eve—the official body of Plymouth Church, after the usual prayer meeting, recommended that Tilton's name be "dropped from the roll of membership." Tilton hadn't attended church in four years, ever since Elizabeth confessed to him about Beecher's sexual advances, and Beecher saw no value in drumming him out officially, other than to antagonize him. The examining committee persisted. Beecher, as ever, tried to avert a confrontation. When Tilton, rising in his own defense, turned toward him and said, "If I have slandered him I am ready to answer for it to the man whom I have slandered," Beecher replied: "He asks if I have any charge to make against him. I have none. Whatever differences have been between us have been amicably adjusted and, so far as I am concerned, buried. I have no charges. This whole matter has not been with my consent. This whole matter has been against my judgment."

But if Beecher spoke for the country, he could not speak for his parishioners, who saw Tilton's complaints against him as insulting, irreligious, even blasphemous. After some further remarks, members voted 210 to 13 to drop Tilton's name from the roll.

"YOU MUST LEARN to look on fossil forms as the antiquarian looks upon his coins," Agassiz told his Harvard students in his opening lecture in October. "The remains of animals and plants have the spirit of their time impressed upon them, as strongly as the spirit of the age is impressed upon its architecture, its literature, its coinage. I want you to become so familiar with these forms, that you can read off at a glance their characters and associations."

In private, Agassiz knew he was facing the end of his career. After the failures of the *Hassler* voyage, and his ongoing refusal to yield to the intellectual currents of the time, he worried he was doomed to end up on the wrong side of history. And so as classes resumed at the museum, he also undertook a series of articles for *The Atlantic Monthly*, starting with "Evolution and Permanence of Type," in which he sought to reckon ultimately with Darwinism. The series—"Agassiz's last word," Elizabeth called it—was to be a comprehensive appraisal of evolution. Yet by presenting it to lay readers, not scientists, Agassiz guaranteed that it would be disregarded by those most fit to evaluate it. "He is a sort of demagogue," Gray had told Darwin thirteen years earlier when Agassiz denounced *Origin* after reading only a part of it, "and always talks to the rabble." *Atlantic* readers, though educated, lacked the credentials to decide what theories would be of use to future researchers—in the end, the ultimate measure of their worth.

Agassiz now lauded Darwin for placing the subject of evolution "on a different basis from that of all his predecessors," by bringing to the discussion "a vast amount of well-arranged information, a convincing cogency of argument, and a captivating charm of presentation." He conceded that it was "improbable that so many able students of nature should agree in their interpretation of facts, unless that interpretation were the true one."

"It cannot be too soon understood that science is one," he wrote,

and that whether we investigate language, philosophy, theology, history or physics, we are dealing with the same problem, culminating in the knowledge of ourselves. Speech is known only in connection with the organs of man, thought in connection with his brain, religion as the expression of his aspirations, history as the record of his deeds, and physical sciences as the laws under which he lives. Philosophers and theologians have yet to learn that a physical fact is as sacred as a moral principle. Our own nature demands from us this double allegiance.

To Agassiz, the conundrum was that while the Darwinians had furnished a uniquely impressive array of "startling and exciting" information supporting the transmutation of species, they had not produced a single shred of evidence showing one species morphing into another. Meticulous observation of the kind he taught his students was to be used to dissect and dispute fanciful explanations; not, he said, to build them up, since one could not logically erect a theory out of facts unless all facts were known—an impossibility. Darwinians claimed that species evolved from low, primitive, "prophetic" types into higher, more complex ones, but Agassiz himself had documented ancient species of both plants and animals that were unchanged in the modern world, and some even possessing more developed structures than their living correlates. Willfully, it seems, he confused a "higher" organism with one that was more intricate rather than one that was better suited to survive.

"The world has arisen in some way or other," Agassiz concluded. "How it originated is the great question, and Darwin's theory, like all other attempts to explain the origin of life, is thus far merely conjectural. I believe he has not even made the best conjecture possible in the present state of our knowledge."

Agassiz dispatched the article to the magazine's Boston office with extreme urgency. He was simultaneously trying to obtain for his museum the country's two greatest collections of mammal fossils, arranging a permanent exhibit of a giant whale sent by an admirer in Newfoundland, preparing to apply to the federal government for "a million acres of land more or less" to support the museum's programs, and planning how natural history and science generally could play a leading part in the 1876 centennial exposition. All his initiatives were aimed at securing the institution a wider role in the affairs of Harvard and the nation after his death, and he saw the *Atlantic* series as a kind of mission statement, a testament. In November, he wrote to editor William Dean Howells, attesting to what he deemed its crucial importance:

> I have already had this MS copied three times and I would remodel it
> again did I not fear to delay you by retaining it. I send it therefore as
> it is, with the express condition that I shall receive *three* proofs as soon
> as it is set in types. . . . I have too much at stake in this Article to be
> willing to allow it to appear without the severest criticism and
> keeping it for many days before me in its revised form.

Agassiz appeared vigorous, though not hale, but he never let up, and his spiraling concern about his place in history aggrieved and exhausted him. Those around him, Elizabeth especially, noted that every mental effort was followed by great physical fatigue, and she worried more and more about the strain on his system. On December 2, he attended a meeting of the Massachusetts Board of Agriculture in Fitchburg, lecturing on "The Structural Growth of Domesticated Animals." "Those who accompanied him, and knew the mental and physical depression which had hung about him for weeks, could not see him take his place on the platform without anxiety," she wrote. "And yet, when he turned to the blackboard, and, with a single sweep of the chalk, drew the faultless outline of an egg, it seemed impossible that anything could be amiss with the hand or the brain." Agassiz, unlike Gray, loved to teach; during the past July and August, at a rustic new institute for schoolteachers he'd hastily founded on an island in Buzzards Bay, he had lectured twice a day. A mesmerizing showman at the chalkboard, he inhaled adoration and drew power from performing.

Agassiz dined the next day with friends. Two days later, Elizabeth's birthday, he entertained relatives at home, feasted, drank wine, and despite his physician's orders, smoked a cigar. He awoke the next morning feeling, he said, "strangely asleep." After arriving at the museum, he returned home almost at once, collapsed into bed, and never left. For a week he periodically regained consciousness but, his throat paralyzed, he was unable to speak or eat. His doctor prescribed food injections. Suffering no pain throughout this last illness, he died on the evening of December 14 at age sixty-six.

For months the country mourned him heartily; impassioned appreciations poured in. "Three tiny words grew lurid as I read / And reeled commingling: *Agassiz is dead!*" the poet James Russell Lowell wrote famously in a poetic tribute that filled eleven pages of the *Atlantic*. Harvard canceled all business on the day of his funeral, which was attended by Vice President Henry Wilson, senators, governors, mayors, and hundreds of teachers, present and former students, and admirers. Black borders edged Boston newspaper accounts of his burial in Mount Auburn Cemetery. "Seldom, if ever, has the death of a man of science been so deeply felt," declared *The Nation*, which added reverently:

> Never was there a more theistic philosopher. His iterated argument
> against doctrines of evolution, reduced to simplest terms, is this:
> 1. There is order and system in organic nature, such as indicates
> thought. 2. The evolution of species of plants and animals, one
> from another, by natural causation, is tantamount to a denial of this.
> 3. Therefore doctrines of evolution are untrue. If the second term be
> conceded, most people will agree with him.

Agassiz's death left those who agreed with him most on evolution—conservative evangelical Christians like Hodge—bereft. They lost their ablest scientific defender just as they were beginning to discuss formally how to confront a rising set of challenges to their faith from positivists, communists, atheists, evolutionists, feminists, and skeptics—the diverse forces united, however loosely and unsystematically, around Darwin. Without Agassiz as a guiding spirit, many felt vulnerable, exposed, agonizing publicly as they anguished privately over who, if anyone, would emerge to fill his place. His *Atlantic* article—the first and, it turned out, last of his aborted series, published a month after his death—like the *Hassler* voyage, provided no new hard science to rally around, coupled with a renewed insistence upon intelligent design in nature notably unsupported by facts. Yet almost a year after his death, the author of an unsigned article in the Boston *Journal* headlined "Can Christianity Withstand the Assault of Science?" would still mourn his loss:

> It is becoming daily more apparent that the science of this generation
> is largely a Godless and faithless science. Hardly one of the men now
> living who are most prominent in scientific speculation and research is

imbued with the reverent spirit of Christianity, while very many have it for their avowed object to pull down the foundations of the old faith, without troubling themselves overmuch about the construction of a new one. One great secret of the love that was felt for Agassiz, even among people who were unable to follow him in his investigations, was that he stood as a champion of religious truth. From the bewildering speculations and belittling conclusions offered by Darwin and Huxley and Spencer and Tyndall, we were wont to turn confidently to Agassiz and say: Here we have a man equal in learning to any of these, as keen and patient an investigator as any, as acute and thorough a researcher as any, and yet behold his simple faith; his unfaltering fidelity of religious truth, his sustained reverence of spirit. But Agassiz is gone, and who is there to bend the bow of this Ulysses?

NEW HAVEN, 1874

> spe•cie n 1 a commodity metal, historically gold
> or silver, backing money or currency 2 coin, as
> distinct from paper money; from the Latin
> expression *in specie,* meaning "in the actual form"
> 3 an incorrect singular form of species

A S THE DEPRESSION TOOK HOLD, especially across the factory precincts of New England, whole communities tumbled into poverty. Days into the panic, the Delaine woolen mill in Olneyville, Rhode Island, west of Providence, shut down, promising seventeen hundred workers to restart in two weeks. Two weeks later the Riverside worsted mill next door closed. Both remained shuttered for months. Storekeepers at first extended credit, but when neither mill reopened, they reduced supplies. "Large numbers of persons are now suffering for the necessities of life," *The Providence Journal* reported in early January—they stood long hours on soup lines run by Overseers of the Poor, a private relief agency that provided food, fuel, medicines, and sometimes money to "deserving" paupers and vagrants. The more desperate took to the roads, tramping in the bitter cold. In New York, by midwinter, police station basements filled nightly with an estimated thirty thousand "revolvers"—men, women, and children—so called because they were permitted to stay only a night or two.

Business speculators and stock traders clamored for easy money. In Washington, Grant initially allowed the reissue of government notes not backed by bullion in an effort to inflate the economy, then backtracked in his annual message to Congress after alarmed bankers and religious conservatives warned of the perils of inflation and urged a return to the monetary rectitude and moral soundness of the prewar period—before the treasury, as a last resort, started printing "greenbacks" during Lincoln's first year in office to pay for the Civil War. Suggesting the panic might prove "a blessing in disguise," Grant said, "My own judgment is that however much individuals may suffer, one long step has been taken toward specie payments."

Thirty-three-year-old William Graham Sumner, a virtuous and unsmiling Episcopal minister who a year earlier had been "called" to Yale to fill the new faculty chair in political economy after serving for two dispiriting years as rector of a church in New Jersey, thought paper money that was not instantly convertible on demand into gold and silver to be not only worthless, but also an augury of social and moral collapse.

The only son of a self-educated British-born mechanic who both practiced and preached hard work, abstinence, and self-denial, Sumner had attended Yale during the war. As a student, he came to view capital as the basis of civilization, attacking paper money and high taxes in compositions that, he later recalled, laid the foundation for his exit from the pulpit to what he called "an academical career" and from religion to his true calling: the scientific study of society. After the family of a wealthy classmate bought Sumner's way out of the draft by hiring a substitute, then supported him through several years of studying ancient history and languages in England and Germany, he went into the ministry, like Beecher, because it offered a prophetic office for teaching. But he soon grew disaffected with sermonizing and parish duties, unable to discuss from the pulpit, or battle over principle, the issues of currency and tariffs which he considered paramount, threatening the nation at its core. Coming to New Haven from Morristown had meant taking a salary cut from $5,000 to $3,000, but as his wife, Jeannie, noted, a college town "seems to be the only place where poverty is respectable."

Sumner's religiosity about money swelled from an unforgiving Calvinism, which taught that a man made his own worth. It was discovering Spencer that provided him the framework for impressing that ethic upon the mores and actions of society. Sumner would recall that by the time he left preaching in 1872 he had read the *Popular Science* essays that would become *The Study of Sociology*, which immediately gave me the lead I wanted to bring into shape the crude notions that had been floating in my head for five or six years, especially since the Oxford days. [Spencer's] conception of society, of social forces, and of the science of society . . . was just the one I had been groping after, but had not been able to reduce for myself. It solved the old difficulty about the relation of social science to history, rescued social science from the dominion of the cranks, and offered a definite and magnificent field of work, from which we might hope at last to derive definite results for the solution of social problems.

A few weeks after the panic, Sumner became the first Yale professor ever to seek and win political office, as a Republican ward alderman. He hastily published four or five short sketches on monetary history in the banking journal *Financier.* After Grant's annual address to lawmakers in December, which only served to confuse Congress and the public, who couldn't tell what he wanted, sixty inflation bills were introduced in the House. Sumner, under strain both at the college and at City Hall, rushed to turn his articles into a book, *A History of American Currency,* published just as "hard" and "soft" money forces descended on Washington for a showdown in April. Inflationists, led by the railroads, the iron industry, westerners, farmers, and unions, believed that the treasury should float more money to stimulate speculation and growth. The specie men— merchants, bankers, textile manufacturers, reformers, and the religious press, which saw the panic as God's punishment for the corruption of the paper system—warned gravely of social and moral catastrophe.

In Sumner's new evolutionary view of history, capital is energy stored up for the future in the struggle for self-preservation, and thus the most important task for society is to promote capital accumulation, which is only "rendered possible by consistent renunciation of the present," he once wrote. Savings were the wage of discipline, patience, and virtue. Millionaires were a product of natural selection; "the bloom of a competitive civilization," as Richard Hofstadter wrote. Capitalism ratified nature's and God's plan, and helter-skelter changes in government policy only eroded progress. Now, in his book, Sumner derided the issuance of greenbacks as a grievous wartime mistake. "The question whether it is necessary to issue legal tender notes is a question not of law, but of political economy, and political economy declares that it never can be necessary," he wrote.

The proposition involves an absurdity. Whatever strength a nation has is weakened by issuing legal tender notes. One might as well say that it is necessary to open the veins of a weak man who has a heavy physical task to perform. All history shows that paper money with a forced circulation is not a temporary resource. It cannot be taken up and laid down as we choose. It is a mischief easily done but most difficult to cure.

Sumner—bald, heavy-lidded, with piercing greenish eyes that a follower remembered as being like "the end of an ominous rifle barrel sticking out of a firing slot," and a bristle-brush mustache overarching a resolute mouth and aggressive chin—testified before the House as it deliberated over what became known, disapprovingly if accurately, as the Inflation Bill. "The sum of all iniquity," hard-money men called it. Most lawmakers and newspapermen believed Grant supported the legislation, which would increase the nation's money supply by $100 million. The president, who had failed bitterly at every venture he tried until he led the North to victory as head of the Union Army, had campaigned as a workingman; he knew poverty and sympathized with those the bill was meant to help. Yet when it reached his desk, he vetoed it, arguing much in the same terms as Sumner that any short-term benefit would be far outweighed by the long-term threat to the national economy from ensuing inflation.

Grant's veto cemented the position of the Republican Party as the party of capital, tilting it toward the forces favoring a return to specie. At the same time, it infused Sumner with a potent sense of intimate association with public affairs, launching the "magnificent field of work" he foresaw for himself, Yale, and the rapidly expanding legion of young scholars who intended to make sciences of politics, economics, history, and morality by divining the laws that governed them. Here was a new type of professor: "hard-headed, aggressive, with a large fund of information about government and finance, as much interested in the concrete problems of the day as in books and theories, and not above joining hands with his fellows in the actual work of [government] management and political combat," his biographer Harris Starr noted. Though reviewers skewered *A History of American Currency* as sloppy, rushed, unfocused, and unorganized, even as they lauded its timeliness, it sold briskly and

was considered influential, positioning Sumner to exploit his new visibil-
ity in national political and academic circles.

Within weeks, he enthusiastically reviewed Spencer's latest project,
Descriptive Sociology. Starting in 1867, Spencer at his own expense had
employed a succession of research assistants to help him assemble the
first systematic analysis in the history of social science. "I had arranged,"
he recalled, "to have collected for me, and put in fitly classified groups and
tables, facts of all kinds, presented by numerous races, which illustrate social evolution under its various aspects." The first volume dealt with the
uncivilized races, the second with extinct and degraded civilized races. A
marvel of modern scholarship, the folio volumes detailing the environ-
mental and internal forces governing human relations up and down the
scale of time and across the globe nonetheless plunged Spencer, yet again,
into worrying over money and complaining to his American friend. "No.
2 of the *Des. Soc.* is out," he wrote Youmans in March,

> and I have ordered a copy to be sent to you. It will be a very valuable
> installment for all people sufficiently rational to appreciate it; of
> which, however, there are unfortunately but a few. The third volume
> of Forster's *Life of Dickens* sold ten thousand copies in ten days. The
> first part of *Descriptive Sociology* has been asked for by the public to
> the extent of not quite 200 copies in eight months.

Youmans employed Spencer's glum report, as always, to solicit further
financial support, bringing an offer from a St. Louis actuary to raise
£1,000 or more for Spencer to use as he saw fit. Sumner's review signaled,
meanwhile, that Spencer's call for an emerging academic discipline of social science would be taken up, as Beecherism had been, within the
neogothic citadel of American social and religious conservatism: Yale.
That Sumner was a member of the secret campus society Skull and Bones
promised expanded influence among men of power, on Wall Street and in
government. Praising both volumes mightily, he argued that Spencer's
work was the new type of sociology the country needed. "It presents history as a social evolution in which no fact is contemptible," Sumner
wrote, "because the social outcome of a nation's life is a resultant of a vast
number of forces, each of which must be estimated for what it was in its
day, not for what it would be now."

CHARLES HODGE'S STUDY HAD one door opening toward the seminary for students, and another into the hall of his house, and when his eight children were young he removed the second door's latches and put springs on it so that even the smallest toddler could wander in. He was a voluminous writer: during the past two years, Scribner's had released his three-volume, 2,260-page magnum opus, *Systematic Theology*. By mid-January, just weeks after Agassiz's testament appeared in the *Atlantic*, he was able to read a "paper on Darwinism" to his colleagues. Within three months he issued a book, *What Is Darwinism?* expanding his comments at the Alliance meeting in New York into a full-blown polemic. Hodge considered the ambiguities that enabled Christian leaders like McCosh and Beecher to adopt evolutionary doctrine "a great evil." Though "visibly ripening for another life," as his son observed, he set the terms starkly: "It is obviously useless to discuss any theory until we are agreed as to what that theory is. The question, therefore, What is Darwinism? must take precedence of all discussion of its merits."

What Darwinism was was not at all clear, even to most avowed Darwinists; even to Darwin himself. Not merely the notion of evolution through survival of the fittest, the term was coming to represent an explosion in thinking that eclipsed and absorbed—at least in name—the work of Spencer, Huxley, Gray, Wallace, and many others who accepted the overall truth of gradual development as a principle of biological descent, but disagreed sharply among themselves on other essential questions, and on the deeper implications for society, and for God. Fourteen years earlier, during the run-up to the war, Hodge wrote an article "What Is Christianity?" asserting that it was both "a doctrine" and "a life." He believed that all prior scientific revolutions that had threatened Christian philosophy and scripture left Christian life whole and unscathed. He worried that that was not the case now.

To Hodge, what gave Darwinism its "peculiar character and importance" was its rejection of teleology—the proposition that the universe has design and purpose—an essential argument for the existence of God reaching back to Aristotle. Darwin's "blind and designless nature" banished out of the universe an all-provident intelligence that creates life to conform to an idea, a final cause. To ask Darwin "to give up his denial of final causes is like asking the Romanists to give up the Pope," Hodge wrote. "That principle is the life and soul of his system." No middle ground existed. By personifying the laws of the universe and supplanting a supernatural architect with a natural one, Darwinians submitted everything to brute force and chance.

"This is the vital point," Hodge wrote, mounting his central argument near the end of his treatise:

> The denial of final causes is the formative idea of Darwin's theory, and therefore no teleologist can be a Darwinian. . . . We have thus arrived at the answer to our question. What is Darwinism? It is atheism.

Distinguishing belief from believer, and perhaps not wanting to roil further the unsettled climate among evangelicals, Hodge took care to clarify: "This does not mean that Mr. Darwin himself and all who adopt his views are atheists; but it means that his theory is atheistic, and that the exclusion of design from nature is . . . tantamount to atheism." He completed the book, prayerfully, personally, with a recitation from scripture—the dying words of the apostle Paul:

> The time of my departure is at hand. I have fought the good fight, I have finished my course, I have kept the faith; henceforth there is laid up for me a crown of righteousness, which the Lord, the righteous judge, shall give me at that day; and not to me only, but unto all them that love his appearing.

GRAY, EXTRICATED AT LAST from his numbing routine at Harvard, welcomed—relished—Hodge's challenge. He had long argued, most notably to Darwin, the opposing position: that Darwin in fact had reinjected teleology into natural history, rescuing it from godless materialism. Gray found natural selection itself a majestic, if not infallible, mode of design. It explained the utilitarian purpose of biological mechanisms that scientists had previously found unintelligible. Take a burr, he suggested. Classical botanists, examining form and structure without regard to function, defined a burr variously as a seed, a fruit, a part of a fruit, the outermost whorl of a flower, or something else. But one saw clearly in light of

Darwin, and final causes, that it was an exquisite adaptation that enabled a plant to disseminate seeds far and wide by hitching rides on cattle and other animals. What a living form did in the struggle for survival determined its structure. Purpose implied intelligence. Hodge, Gray believed, had mistaken the essential point.

Writing anonymously in *The Nation,* Gray rebutted *What Is Darwinism?* with the same analytic zeal with which he had once attacked Agassiz, and which more recently he had reserved for Huxley and the other radical evolutionists who believed that natural selection negated the design argument. After trumping Agassiz's metaphysical biology, he'd encountered the fiercest resistance to his Christian evolutionism not from churchmen, many of whom agreed with him, but from other scientists. The problem now was Darwin himself. Six years earlier, Darwin had taken the uncharacteristic step not only of denying the design argument in one of his own books, *Variation of Plants and Animals Under Domestication,* but also of directing his criticism specifically at Gray. "However much we may wish it," he wrote, "we can hardly follow professor Asa Gray in his belief."

On March 3, Gray wrote to a friend: "I dare say I am much more orthodox than Mr. Darwin; also that he is as far from being an atheist as I am." Yet despite his confidence, Gray knew little about Darwin's spent religious beliefs, which Darwin carefully concealed. No one did. And so in answering Hodge in *The Nation,* a liberal Republican soapbox, Gray was reduced to attributing the theological difficulties presented by Darwinism to the misguided interpretation of unnamed others. He wrote, with barely disguised frustration:

> The taint of atheism which, in Dr. Hodge's view, leavens the whole lump is not inherent in the original grain of Darwinism—in the principles posited—but has somehow been introduced in the subsequent treatment. Possibly, when found, it may be eliminated.

Gray maintained instead that the skepticism of modern science was misplaced. "Having nearly despaired of converting scientists to the possibility of evolution and theism dwelling together," his biographer A. Hunter Dupree wrote, "he now tried to convince a theologian of the same thing." Gray borrowed for his conclusion excerpts from a paper delivered three years earlier to London clergy on the problems confronting the church from the rise of modern theories. Did doing away with the theory of Creation do away with that of final causes? "Not in the least," the speaker had declared; "We know of old that God was so wise that he could make all things; but behold he is so much wiser than even that, that he can make all things make themselves."

Gray sent Darwin a copy of the review in mid-June, jauntily soft-pedaling, as always, their disagreement over final causation. "You will see what uphill work I have of making a theist of you, 'of good and re-spectable standing,' " he wrote. Darwin, likewise skirting a confrontation, responded a week later. "I read with interest your semi-theological review, & have got the book, but I think your review will satisfy me. The more I reflect on this subject, the more perplexed I grow."

EVER SINCE HIS "FIT" the previous August, Darwin had been spending more and more time ambling around a short loop through a nearby acre of fields and woods that in January he finally was able to buy from a neighbor, though for considerably more than he thought he ought to pay. Routinely, he piled a mound of flints at the turn, then with each pass knocked one away with his walking stick so as to complete a set number of laps without having to interrupt his cogitation with keeping count. The path was where he plumbed his deepest thoughts.

The design question was dead, he believed. Now that the law of nat-ural selection had been discovered, there seemed to be no more intelli-gence behind the variability of living things than "in the course which the wind blows," he soon would write. But man was a moral animal, and nearly every culture throughout history worshipped an all-powerful spirit. False religions spread across the world "like wild-fire." Even up to the point of publishing *Origin*, Darwin had tried to invent evidence to convince himself of the existence of a divine being and the truth of Christian revelation. In 1862, he told the London *Illustrated News:* "I feel most deeply that this whole question of creation is too profound for human intellect. A dog might as well speculate on the mind of Newton! Let each man hope and believe what he can." But the effort to keep faith finally became useless. Disbelief "crept over me at a very slow rate, but was at last complete" about the time he turned forty.

Out of respect for Emma's orthodoxy—and coupled with his determination not to let the debate over evolution devolve into personal attacks on him—Darwin kept his lapsed faith largely to himself. But on his daily walks he reflected much on the central questions raised by the failure of the old design argument: "How can the generally beneficent arrangement of the world be accounted for?" If not God, what? And what about evil? In the end, was the world as a whole, ruled as it was by blind forces and laws, and filled with suffering, "a good one or a bad one?"

Darwin, trellising his thoughts, judged there to be more happiness in the world than misery, though he knew he couldn't prove it. Assuming he was right, that is what might be expected from the law of natural selection, since "if all the individuals of any species were habitually to suffer to an extreme degree they would neglect to propagate their kind." Much suffering was to be expected in the battle for life. Given the prevalence of happiness, though, he theorized that all sentient beings have developed in such a manner that pleasurable sensations—"eating, drinking, the propagation of the species, &c"—serve as "habitual guides." In other words, survival rewarded overall goodness. Joy and pleasure enhanced survivability; pain and suffering did not. All else was elaboration.

In January, Darwin and Emma attended a séance. A rage for spiritualism, and scientific answers about life beyond death, had sprouted in the United States and now gripped Britain. To his dismay, some of Darwin's closest friends and relatives, including Wallace, had been swept up in it, even as other skeptical X-Clubbers, Huxley in the lead, found time to attend spirit-rapping sessions and expose fraudulent mediums. (Huxley had gone so far as to teach himself to crack the bones of his feet inside his boots to replicate the alleged tapping of the dead.) More than commercialized entertainment, spiritualism had become a religious force, and Darwin's own views, like those of other leaders, were vigorously sought. He said robustly he believed "none of it"—echoing Lincoln's classic remark: "Well, for those who like that sort of thing, I should think it is about the sort of thing they would like." But Emma's brother Hensleigh Wedgwood had become obsessed with the spirit world, and Darwin and Huxley now succumbed to Hensleigh's invitations.

Darwin's son George and his brother Erasmus arranged the session. They hired a medium whom they secured hand and foot, spent an hour beforehand inspecting under chairs and carpets in the drawing room of

Erasmus's London home, and attracted a guest list that also included Darwin's half-cousin Francis Galton, a fellow scientist so gripped by Darwin's observations concerning the breeding of domestic animals that he devoted the rest of his career to devising novel ways to measure the hereditary nature of human traits, especially intelligence. Also attending were the crusading positivist George Lewes, making jokes, and his wife,* Mary Ann Evans—the novelist George Eliot—although she and Lewes "left in disgust," she told her diary, after the medium insisted on complete darkness. So did Darwin, who nonetheless detailed the scene afterward in a letter to a friend:

> We had grand fun, one afternoon, for George hired a medium, who made the chairs, a flute, a bell, and candlestick, and fiery points jump about in my brother's dining room. . . . I found it so hot and tiring that I went away before all these astounding miracles, or jugglery, took place. How the man possibly could do what was done passes my understanding. . . . The Lord have mercy on us all, if we have to believe in such rubbish.

SPENCER'S HABITUAL PIQUE about the slow sales of *Descriptive Sociology* aside, he now also enjoyed a reputation as a giant—if not more famous than Darwin, more influential among the rising class of intellectuals, businessmen, and liberal preachers. Legions of readers of his serialized *Study of Sociology* made the book a success as soon as it appeared, earning Spencer his first substantial royalties as it became one of the three top-selling titles in the International Scientific Series and stoked widespread interest in his other work. George Eliot would read it three times. "Strange to say," Spencer wrote Youmans, "I am getting quite popular with women." Spencer's social philosophy sparked more attention than his evolutionary doctrine, but it was Spencer, more than Darwin, who addressed what the struggle for survival meant for human society. Darwin, above all a naturalist, expressed his relief at ceding him that role, nodding

---

* Although Evans and Lewes lived together from 1854 until his death in 1878, they were never married. Evans called Lewes her "husband" and I have referred to her here and elsewhere as his wife in recognition of that bond.

his appreciation in a letter after reading Spencer's argument against the Great Man Theory of human history in *The Contemporary Review:*

> I never believed in the reigning influence of great men on the world's progress; but if asked why I did not believe, I should have been sorely perplexed to have given a good answer. Every one with eyes to see and ears to hear . . . ought to bow their knee to you, and I for one do.

Long-suffering, Spencer savored the attention and acclaim, even as he thought it insufficient and overdue. As English gentlemen, he, Darwin, Huxley, Wallace, and the other evolutionary pioneers exhibited a rare public willingness to share credit and submit to having their ideas lumped together. At the same time, he relied on Youmans to promote the view in America that it was he, not the others, who had promulgated the key insights, and at a time when it was far more dangerous to do so. Spencer had paved the way, borne the brunt. He dared not express his resentments, but others could. Though acknowledgments of his genius by Darwin and other eminent thinkers offered vindication, they were weak consolation for the public's failure to understand that much if not most of what people called Darwinism was his.

On June 5, Youmans addressed the New York–Manhattan Liberal Club, a less dogmatic offshoot of the positivist Nineteenth Century Club of which Carnegie was an acolyte. Held in club chambers in Plimpton Hall, at Stuyvesant and Ninth streets, the assembly offered a chance to clarify Spencer's true position as *the* philosopher of the age to an audience already versed in his and Darwin's views. Youmans's health had declined commensurate with the demands of his and Spencer's success, with both the international series and *The Popular Science Monthly,* which, as he boasted, had "met an urgent public need" and was "the most valuable magazine now before the American public." ("It comes to me like the air that they send down to the people in a diving bell," Oliver Wendell Holmes had written in a recent review.) His ravaged eyes verged on giving out entirely, so strained and painful that Spencer had beseeched him ten months earlier to cease lecturing and "adhere rigorously to this course of abstinence."

Youmans took the rostrum and launched a spirited defense of Spencer and the doctrine of evolution. He lectured excitedly for three hours without pausing. "Twenty years ago that doctrine was almost universally scouted as a groundless and absurd speculation," he began;

now it is admitted as an established principle by many of the ablest men of science. . . . It is, moreover, beginning to exert a powerful influence on the investigation and mode of considering many subjects, while those who avow their belief in it are no longer pointed to as graceless reprobates or incorrigible fools.

With this general reversal of judgment regarding the doctrine . . . there is naturally an increasing interest in the question of its origin and authorship; and also, as we might expect, a good deal of misapprehension about it.

The name of Herbert Spencer has long been associated in the public mind with the idea of evolution. And while that idea was passing through what may be called its stage of execration, there was no hesitancy in according to him all the infamy of its parentage: but when the infamy is to be changed to honour, by a kind of perverse consistency of injustice there turns out to be a good deal less alacrity in making the revised award.

Youmans blamed the general misunderstanding—and perhaps much professional resentment—on what one critic called Spencer's "weakness of omniscience." Intellectual fashion pitted old-line generalists against a new generation of specialists, who largely due to Darwin and Spencer were narrowing their inquiries even as they expanded the reach of skepticism and reason into new academic fields. Holmes, for instance, lauded Spencer's "periscopic" mind: "No specialist is safe," he wrote in a review of *The Study of Sociology*. Others were somewhat less generous. Youmans noted that Holmes's fellow elder, Emerson, politely if backhandedly praised Spencer in a newspaper interview on his opinions of great men as a "stock writer, who writes equally well on all subjects."

"These are not the circumspect and instructive utterances which we should look for from men of authority whose opinions are sought and valued by the public," Youmans argued.

They are gross and inexcusable misrepresentations, and exemplify a style of criticism that is now so freely indulged in that it requires to be met, in the common interest of justice and truth.

By their estimates of Mr. Spencer, the gentlemen quoted have raised the question of his position as a thinker, and the character and claims of his intellectual work. . . . My object will be . . . to trace his mental history, and the quality and extent of his labors as disclosed by an analysis and review of his published writing.

If any philosopher—save Plato in Aristotle, or Jesus in Matthew— ever had a more committed student and proselytizer, Spencer could scarcely hope to do better than Youmans, who went on to explicate in minute detail the history of evolutionary ideas throughout the century and Spencer's primacy among those propounding them. Earlier thinkers, he said, had recognized that the present system of things resulted from gradual change and that there had been progressive development of living forms, but no one before Spencer had proposed how it was done. Starting from the point of view that nature was guided by a system of laws, and assuming that the existing order must grow out of a preexisting one, it was Spencer's unique contribution to consider "all the contents of nature" in the same way.

> It was therefore apparent that life, mind, man, science, art, language, morality, society, government, and institutions, are things that have undergone a gradual and continuous unfolding, and can be explained in no other way but by a theory of growth and derivation.
>
> It is not claimed that Mr. Spencer was the first to adopt this mode of inquiry in relation to special subjects, but that he was the first to grasp it as a general method, the first to see that it must give us a new view of human nature, a new science of mind, a new theory of society—all as parts of one coherent body of thought.
>
> In a word, I maintain Spencer's position as a thinker to be this: taking a view of Nature that was not only generally discredited, but was virtually foreclosed to research, he has done more than any other man to make it the starting point of a new era of knowledge.

Others might well have quarreled with this assessment, especially with Youmans's claim that evolution was "virtually foreclosed to research," since at the time that Spencer experienced his flash of cosmic insight and began deducing from it the varied parts of his system, Darwin was buried in the twenty-five laborious years of observation, experimentation, and endless correspondence that resulted in *The Origin of Species*. Indeed, despite the seeming admiration and gratitude in his letter, Darwin thought Spencer's generalizing from incomplete information and his self-absorption—Spencer read narrowly, and spoke proudly of it—disqualified him from the greatness and crucial role in the history of ideas that Youmans advocated for him. Within a year Darwin would write, in a memoir:

> Herbert Spencer's conversation seemed to me very interesting, but I did not like him particularly, and did not feel that I could easily become intimate with him. I think that he was extremely egotistical. After reading any of his books, I generally feel enthusiastic for his transcendent talents, and have often wondered whether in the distant future he would rank with such great men as Descartes, Leibnitz, etc. . . . Nevertheless, I am not conscious of profiting in my own work by Spencer's writings. His deductive manner of treating every subject is wholly opposed to my frame of mind. His conclusions never convince me: and over and over I have said to myself, after reading one of his discussions,—"Here would be a fine subject for half-a-dozen years' work."

Youmans saved for last the most sensitive and crucial misapprehension: "a word or two regarding Mr. Darwin's relation to the question" of evolution; likewise, Spencer's role in—and view of—"Darwinism": "While this illustrious naturalist has contributed immensely towards the extension and establishment of a theory of organic development, he has made no attempt to elucidate the general law of evolution. His works do not treat this broad problem; and nothing has tended more to the popular confusion of the subject than the notion that 'Darwinism' and Evolution are the same thing."

Darwin and Spencer had been drawn so tightly together by their insights that the public identified them more and more as one, even though they disagreed on the central question of teleology. They embraced similar conclusions as to the social function of natural selection—which now, in the wake of the panic, were coming suddenly into vogue as "social Darwinism," but which, in their extreme conservative, laissez-faire, antigovernment formulation would more accurately be labeled "Spencerism." As Darwin postulated in *Descent:*

> With savages, the weak in body and mind are soon eliminated; and those that survive commonly exhibit a vigorous state of health. We

civilized men, on the other hand, do our utmost to check the process of elimination; we build asylums for the imbecile, the maimed and the sick; we institute poor laws; and our medical men exert their utmost skill to save the life of everyone to the last moment. There is reason to believe that vaccination has preserved thousands, who from a weak constitution would formerly have succumbed to small pox. Thus the weak members of civilized societies propagate their kind. No one who has attended the breeding of domestic animals will doubt that this must be highly injurious to the race of man.

As Youmans spelled out again and again throughout his lecture, the two thinkers were promoting distinctly different enterprises: Darwin's chiefly scientific, Spencer's social and philosophical. And claiming, as ever, to have little use for each other. The day after the lecture, Youmans mailed Spencer a copy of his remarks, and within two weeks Spencer replied, "Of course I cannot but rejoice at the complete success of your address and exposition. . . . You have put in immense claims for me, and doubtless greatly astonished your audience."

In a second letter in mid-July, written as Spencer busily prepared for a fishing trip in Scotland, and as Youmans's oculist advised him to stop reading and writing lest he ruin his eyes for good, Spencer followed up with a list of additional talking points to help Youmans further set the record straight. He encouraged him to establish a chronology which would show that from 1842 onward he developed the idea of evolution in his own mind and that he had enunciated the universal law of evolution in 1857—two years before *Origin*. "You have clearly enough stated at the end this independent origin of the doctrine," Spencer told his friend; "but what strikes me is that this fact would be much more clearly seized if in the narration you briefly indicated the stage it had reached before Darwin published." He added, taking elaborate care not to seem presumptuous or invite grievance: "But I leave this hint for you to act on or not, as you think well."

WITH FRIENDS LIKE HIS, Beecher needed no enemies. In March, a Congregationalist assembly was called to examine the affairs of Plymouth Church. The Reverend Leonard Bacon of New Haven, an old evangelical ally of Beecher's father and perhaps the most influential Congregational minister of his day, presided. Beecher, seeking as ever to defuse tensions with Theodore Tilton, declared that no one, by joining a church, renounced the right to withdraw from it; the board, he claimed, should have let Tilton resign rather than expel him. His opponents disagreed. Distressed by the stalemate, and by the rancor and suspicion festering behind closed doors, Bacon decided to take matters into his own hands. In a speech to Yale divinity students in April, he compared Tilton to a "knave" and a "dog," criticized the Plymouth elders, and urged a full public airing of his charges. The *Tribune* reported his comments: "There are many not only in Brooklyn, but elsewhere, who felt that the church had not fairly met the question, and by evading the issue had thrown away the opportunity of vindicating its pastor," Bacon said. "Mr. Beecher would have done better to have let vengeance come on the head of his slanderers."

Beecher could only stand by helplessly as his last hope for keeping the scandal out of the public eye vanished. Within days Tilton threw down the gauntlet, in a long reply to Bacon that appeared in all the major New York papers. He claimed that Beecher had committed an unnamed crime against his family and invited Bacon to ask Beecher "to inform you, on his word of honor, whether I have been a slanderer—whether I have spoken against him falsely . . . and whether he has not acknowledged to me, in large and ample terms, that *my* course towards *him* in this sorrowful business has been marked by the magnanimity which you apparently intimate has characterized *his* towards *me*." Lashing back after years of public silence, of humiliation and scorn, his rebuttal forced Beecher to appoint a six-man investigating committee to examine the intimate history of the relations between the two of them, and with Elizabeth. "There is only one thing that I was born for," Tilton would soon tell the panel, "and that is war."

War it was. On July 11, the same day Beecher announced the formation of the Plymouth Church Investigating Committee, Elizabeth Tilton awoke her husband to tell him she was leaving him. "I rose quietly," she recalled, "and having dressed, roused him only to say: 'Theodore, I will never take another step by your side. The end has indeed come!'" Ten days later Tilton counterattacked by denouncing her and Beecher as adulterers and charging Beecher with "criminal seduction." More than a mere love triangle gone sour, or a *Scarlet Letter*–like tale of clerical philandering and retribution, the affair now heaved into public view as an apocalyptic struggle among three prominent Christians—the accused, the accuser, and the alleged victim—that exposed an upheaval in bourgeois morality and marriage, much as Woodhull had forecast it would almost three years earlier.

Bitter statements and counterstatements, documents and counterdocuments, saturated newspapers across the country. After picking up *The Brooklyn Argus* from a newsboy and reading Tilton's charges, Beecher composed an emphatic denial in which he conceded that Elizabeth, who had grown up in the church and helped him edit his novel *Norwood,* had over a period of years confided in him about her deepest feelings and relied more and more upon his judgment, but only because Tilton had strayed into "religious and social views" that she "deemed vitally false and dangerous"—in particular, denying divine revelation and preaching free love. She denied, likewise, any sexual intimacy with Beecher, declaring provocatively, however, that she "had been treated by my husband as a non-entity from the beginning, a plaything, to be used or let alone at will," and "With Mr. Beecher I had a sort of consciousness of being more: he appreciated me as Theodore did not; I felt that he respected me; I think Theodore never saw in me what Mr. Beecher did."

Tilton, countering, released two hundred and one love letters that she had sent to him and that he deftly expurgated to illustrate their mutual tenderness and affection, allowing the missives to be printed as a special supplement to the *Chicago Tribune.* The biggest story since the Lincoln assassination, the scandal received more coverage than the impeachment of Andrew Johnson, which Tilton had also helped engineer. Papers resumed the wartime practice of issuing second editions, and crowds, bloated by the ranks of the newly unemployed, surged around the massive bulletin boards outside their offices to read the latest news. Mothers complained that children got up before breakfast, watched out for the newspaper deliverers, grabbed the papers, and imbibed the scandal before their parents could intercept them.

That Beecher chose the six committee members from among his closest friends and church allies rendered the proceedings suspect from the start. And so all parties—including him—campaigned to try to win over the public's support: "Trial by Newspaper," *Nation* editor E. L. Godkin called it. Testimony, documents, and statements were leaked to favored publications almost as soon as they were submitted. Circulations spiked, even as Godkin and a few other commentators wrung their hands. "A committee nominated by him, and composed of his own personal friends and members of his congregation, although it might satisfy the church over which he presides, was sure not to satisfy his opponents or the public," he wrote.

> No one will now care what its finding is, or whether it comes to any conclusion or not. The trial is transferred to a different forum. This forum consists of the newspapers and their readers, and a more unsatisfactory one, in some respects, there could hardly be, but it is the one before which a man in Mr. Beecher's position must plead, sooner or later, to any charge brought against him. From this neither civil nor ecclesiastical courts can save him. When the community exalts a man as it has exalted Mr. Beecher, it insists on deciding in the last resort whether its confidence has been misplaced.

Whether or not the committee could get to the truth, or inspire the public's trust if it did, Beecher battled on as if its conclusions would vindicate him. Now that the cover-up had officially ended—indeed, as in any scandal, now that his step-by-step history of concealment became as much a source of interest as what he sought to conceal—his private and public selves collided, inverting so that the multitudes who knew, honored, and admired him before for his public positions and pronouncements eagerly whispered about his inmost feelings and most private behavior, his secrets. His hair grew noticeably grayer.

Beecher appeared before the panel on August 13, vowing to explain all. "Gentlemen of the committee," he said, reading from a prepared statement,

> It is time for the sake of decency and of public morals, that this matter should be brought to an end. It is an open pool of corruption exhaling deadly vapors. For six weeks the nation has risen up and down upon scandal. Not a great war nor a revolution could more have filled the newspapers than this question of domestic trouble. . . . Whoever is buried with it, it is time that this abomination be buried below all touch or power of resurrection.

On cross-examination, much was made of several letters Beecher had written in the first week of February 1872, around the time he returned to Brooklyn from delivering his first Yale lecture, when he confessed to his and Tilton's mutual friend Frank Moulton about living "on the sharp and ragged edge of anxiety, remorse, fear, despair." Six weeks earlier, Elizabeth, bedridden after a miscarriage, had signed a written confession about her affair with Beecher under pressure from Theodore, then, the same night, had retracted it in writing at Beecher's urging. Both letters were to be given to Moulton for safekeeping. A day later, Moulton convinced Beecher that Tilton might be placated by a written apology, and Beecher dictated a contrite letter: "I ask through you Theodore Tilton's forgiveness," it began, "and I humble myself before him as I do before my God." According to Tilton, Beecher then confessed to Moulton and his wife that he had had sex with Elizabeth, but "that it had been through love, not through lust." Within the month Beecher gave Moulton $5,000 to start up a newspaper with Tilton as editor.

Beecher assured the committee that there had been no attempt at blackmail, and he was questioned repeatedly about his state of mind during that period. "I have had stormy days," he said, "more from this than probably all other causes in my life. Yet, taking the four years together, I have had more religious peace and more profound insight into the wants and sufferings of men since I have become acquainted with trouble and despair. I have had an experience in the higher regions of Christian life that is worth all the sorrow and suffering I have had to go through to get it."

John Winslow, a lawyer and district attorney for Kings County, brought the questioning around to Beecher's ultimate subject—love, and its unspoken corollary, sexual morality. As the success of Beecher's liberalism and "religion of gush," Woodhull's spectacular rise and fall, the Comstock Laws, and the popularity of the doctrine of evolution all testified, the country was convulsed with clashing notions of what love meant—between women and men, but also between men and men and women and women. Anyone who put love and feeling on a par with duty and restraint or held the view that intimate friendships with married people of the opposite sex were fitting, as Beecher and Tilton both did, was liable to attack for advancing "free love," an ill-defined term that could mean either promiscuity or abolition of marriage laws. As Woodhull now resurfaced to announce that she and Tilton had been lovers, Tilton and Beecher each made a major part of his defense that the other, according to historian Richard Wightman Fox, "had slipped over the moral precipice into debauchery."

Facing Beecher, Winslow now importuned: "An anonymous letter to the committee, from a free lover, says that you have a reservation in your philosophy which would enable you to say, I had no wrong conduct or relations with Mrs. Tilton, having in your own mind a belief that what you are charged with doing is right. What are your ideas on the subject?"

"I am not versed in the philosophy and casuistry of free love," Beecher replied. "I stand on the New England doctrine, in which I was brought up, that it is best for a man to have one wife, and that he stay by her, and that he do not meddle with his neighbors' wives. I abhor every manifestation of the free love doctrine that I have seen in theory, and I abhor every advocate of the free love doctrine that I have known."

"Did you ever know anybody who took hold of it seriously who was not ruined by it?"

"No, sir; provided they were susceptible to ruin. I have had women write to me that if I did not send them $10 they were ruined, and I wrote in reply that they were ruined before."

After several more questions, the banker and broker S. V. White, who was church treasurer and a leader of its Sunday school, came to the crux of the dispute:

"Did you admit at any time to Mr. Moulton or Mr. Tilton, or to any other person, that you had ever had any relations with Mrs. Elizabeth R. Tilton, or ever commit any act to or with her, or said any word to her, which would be unfit for a Christian man to hold, do or say with the wife of his friend, or for a father to hold, do or say with his daughter, or a brother with his sister—did you ever admit this in any form or in any words?"

"Never," Beecher said.

"Did you ever, in fact, hold any such relations, do any such act, or utter any such word?"

"Never."

Two weeks after examining Beecher, the committee issued its report. Plymouth Church was filled to overflowing with parishioners and onlookers as the final resolution was declared, asserting there was "nothing whatever in the evidence that should impair the perfect confidence of the world in the Christian character and integrity of Henry Ward Beecher." Moulton, vilified in the proceedings and in the press as Tilton's negotiator in a vengeful blackmail scheme, had to be escorted by police from the church lest righteous congregation members, shaking their canes and shoving to get near him and shouting "Rush him!" and "Kill him!" conduct their own brand of punishment. Beecher, absolved, sobbed with relief.

But he was not—could not be—let go. Within days Tilton sued him for $100,000 in damages suffered as a result of Beecher's seduction of his wife, to which Beecher responded by going before a grand jury with a representative of the investigating committee to seek indictments against Tilton and Moulton for malicious libel. As *The Nation*'s Godkin had warned, it was the country now, and not just his congregation, that needed to know whom to believe. After the spectacle of "Scandal Summer," the questions surrounding Beecher loomed larger than ever. The country expected answers. As the *New York Tribune* observed in an editorial:

If Mr. Beecher is innocent these men are guilty. If he is acquitted they are condemned. There is no middle ground.

The community is directly interested in the issue now joined. If these men tell the truth, then Mr. Beecher should not be allowed to pollute the Christian religion by his ministrations. If they lie, it would be a general disgrace to permit them to escape punishment after having for so many months filled the public mind with such poisonous defilement. Mr. Beecher might forgive, if he chose, the crime against himself. But he has no right to forgive the crime against the public involved in that unwholesome familiarity with the vilest forms of domestic misery which Moulton and Tilton have propagated throughout the length and breadth of the land. Ten thousand immoral and obscene novels could not have done the harm which this case has done, in teaching the science of wrong to thousands of quick witted and curious boys and girls.

It is the fate of Mr. Beecher and nothing else which is to be decided by the result of this trial. . . . The public now waits to hear a court of justice say merely what kind of man Mr. Beecher is.

LIKE SUMNER, Harvard Spencerian-without-portfolio John Fiske was an institutional bellwether, his—and the school's—own progress providing compelling evidence of the success of his evolutionary mission. As an intense, rebellious eighteen-year-old undergraduate in 1860, Fiske had read all the scientific literature he could lay his hands on, and although Harvard was known to offer a more liberal intellectual atmosphere than Yale, he nearly earned a full year's suspension for reading the positivist Auguste Comte during chapel. "My soul," Fiske would recall of his youthful Faustian hunger for knowledge, "was on fire." Fiske's minister back home, urged by his grandmother to investigate his religious backsliding, met with him and concluded that he was "an atheist, an infidel, a blasphemer, a hypocrite, an immoral person, and finally . . . a Unitarian."

The product of a conventionally religious New England family, Fiske found himself after graduation faced, like Sumner, with need of employment. He turned unenthusiastically to the law, entering Harvard Law School in 1863 and finishing enough of the course in nine months to pass the Boston bar examination. With a growing family and few clients, he decided in 1866 to quit his practice and concentrate instead on a literary career, despite financial prospects no more promising. In one of his first articles, "University Reform," published in *The Atlantic Monthly*, he took up the cause of academic liberty, describing Harvard as "a place where boys are made to recite from textbooks . . . the principle is coercion. Hold your subject fast with one hand and pour knowledge into him with the other. The professors are taskmasters and police officers, and the President is Chief of the College police."

When Agassiz's friend and fellow *Hassler* voyager Rev. Thomas Hill resigned as Harvard's president in 1868, a few members of the Board of Overseers felt strongly it was time to break the nearly two-and-a-half-century-old tradition of electing a clergyman. Godkin invited Fiske to write an article on the situation for *The Nation*, which Fiske hoped would pave the way for a liberal reformer who, not incidentally, might install him on the faculty. "What we do not want," he wrote, "is a mere business man, a fossil man, an ultra-radical man, or a clergyman. What we do want is a man of thorough scholarship, not a specialist . . . but a man of general culture . . . endowed with sound judgment, shrewd mother-wit, practical good sense."

sense, Fiske believed it could be explained by the nearly two decades it took humans to develop fully into adults. Such prolonged enfeeblement of the young required what now would be called "high parental invest-ment," necessitating strong family and clan ties and structures that led, over generations, to the emergence of social and sexual morality.

Fiske's other article, published in *The Popular Science Monthly*, assailed Agassiz's forthcoming "last testament"—a preemptive rejection of the claim that a "sort of scientific pope" had emerged in America to dispel the advance of evolutionary thought. Appearing two months before Agassiz's death, the article signaled Fiske's emergence as an important defender of the new scientific faith. In England he conferred, frequently at length, with Darwin, Spencer, Huxley, Lewes, Tyndall, and others, impressing them with his determination to extend their theories into metaphyics— an area which, as a group, and in the interest of unity, most assiduously avoided. After returning home in February, he began organizing their discussions into a book that, with Huxley's assistance and over Spencer's objections, he titled *Outlines of Cosmic Philosophy*.

Despite his irreligion, Fiske never stopped believing in a deity. Now, amid the chaos of a growing household and the pressures of his work at the library, he set out to show that the concept of evolution, far from spi-raling inevitably into sin and godlessness as Hodge and others argued, ac-tually was the strongest evidence ever put forth for the imperative of good behavior and the existence of an infinite unknowable power. Fiske had long rejected an anthropomorphic conception of God, a knowable per-sonal deity with human characteristics who created the universe and took a hand in events. As he later would recall, his own early idea of God was a "tall, slender man, of aquiline features, wearing spectacles, with a pen in his hand and another behind his ear" standing behind a ledger-bound desk in a roofless office "just over the zenith" from which He could view the whole world. "That all my words and acts were thus written down, to confront me at the day of judgment, seemed naturally a matter of grave concern," he noted.

But under Cosmic Philosophy, where everything is constantly being transformed in conformity with immutable law, he now wrote: "There ex-ists a Power, to which no limit in time or space is conceivable, of which all phenomena, as presented in consciousness, are manifestations, but which we can only know through these manifestations." God, in other words, was not in doubt, but vastly beyond the comprehension of "one petty race of creatures . . . in one tiny quarter of the universe." Nor was science at odds with faith, but indeed its greatest supporter, since science concerned itself ultimately with how those manifestations worked, and worked together. In social terms, order and unity ruled. Fiske thus foresaw "the continuous weakening of selfishness and the strengthening of sympathy," leading to "the gradual supplanting of egotism by altruism."

It was Fiske's conclusion, his biographer John Spencer Clark wrote, that "the Christian religion was steadily undergoing a purification through scientific criticism whereby it would ultimately be stripped of its anthropomorphic and much of its ecclesiastical accretions, and brought down to the simple yet comprehensive formula of its Founder: 'Thou shalt love the Lord thy God with all thy heart, and with all thy soul, and with all thy mind: and thou shalt love thy neighbour as thyself.' "

Fiske's discovery of a more rational form of religious faith brought him, like Carnegie, a new serenity and optimism: all was well because all grew better. His soul still blazed, but ecstatically. He recognized that his Cosmic Philosophy was consonant with America's Christian value system in a way that not even Spencer, who also believed in an unknowable deity but doubted Fiske's excursion into metaphysics, could match. Released simultaneously in the United States and Britain in October, the book generated considerable attention, quickly becoming influential. The New York *Daily Graphic* published a full-page cartoon that depicted him standing, back arched, fist to the sky, holding a kite to the wind, and bore the caption, "Professor John Fiske flies the evolution kite in America." An apelike Darwin holds the tail; an orangutan crouches nearby, reading Spencer's *First Principles*. Fiske enjoyed it so much he framed it and put it on his library wall.

From zealous acolyte to national spokesman, Fiske had launched himself into a position of exceptional prominence. In mid-December, he received back-to-back congratulatory letters from Darwin and Spencer. "My Dear Sir:—" Darwin wrote on December 8,

> You must allow me to thank you for the very great interest with which
> I have at last slowly read the whole of your work. I have long wished
> to know something about the views of the many great men whose
> doctrines you give. With the exception of special points, I did not

even understand H. Spencer's general doctrine, for his style is too hard for me. I never in my life read so lucid an expositor (and therefore thinker) as you are.

Darwin thanked Fiske for referring to his works, especially *The Descent of Man,* which "must have appeared laughably weak to you." Three days later, Spencer responded equally in character:

As yet, I have myself read but parts of the first volume. I am so continually hindered by multitudinous distractions and my small reading power proves so inadequate for getting up the matter bearing on my immediate work, that I have an increasing difficulty in getting any knowledge of the books I receive; even when they concern me very nearly, critically or otherwise.

What I have read, however, which has been chiefly in the new parts, has pleased me greatly. . . .

The progress of things is amazingly rapid. The public mind is everywhere being ploughed up by all kinds of disturbing forces and prepared for the reception of rational ideas. Indeed, the process of sowing needs to be pushed on actively, lest a crop of weeds takes possession of the soil left vacant after the rooting up of superstitions.

Neither founder of the evolutionary cause, however, committed himself to the religious implications of Fiske's argument: Darwin because he had already forsaken the existence of a God; Spencer, it seemed, because he hadn't.

CHAPTER FIVE

BROOKLYN, 1875

Young gentlemen, true preaching is yet to come.
—HENRY WARD BEECHER

BEECHER'S CIVIL TRIAL for adultery began in City Court Chamber II during a blustery January cold snap that froze the East River. The massive Gothic stone bridge tower near the Brooklyn shore was rising to completion, seven years into the project, and on several days, with the ferries idled, many of the eleven lawyers couldn't get over from New York, and court was canceled. Since the facts of the case were already known to schoolchildren across America, each side had no choice but to make the issue the moral character of the other. Facts were superfluous. It was Beecher's word against Tilton's and Moulton's.

Facing the bench, Beecher reposed at a long table beside Eunice, his son, and his six lawyers. He "appeared in perfect health and spirits," the *Times* said. "There was not the slightest indication of what he himself would term 'soul weariness' about him, and he occupied his time attentively reading a copy of yesterday's *Times,* to which at intervals he called the attention of his counsel"—former U.S. attorney general William Evarts. It was Evarts who had successfully defended Andrew Johnson against impeachment charges. Boston bred with bloodlines tracing back on both sides to the *Mayflower,* educated at Yale College and Harvard

Law School, he recently had won the nation's case before an international tribunal in Switzerland that ruled unanimously against England for claims arising out of the Civil War, when British shipyards violated England's neutrality by supplying naval cruisers disguised as merchant ships to the South. Evarts's adroit arguments set an important precedent for solving major international disputes and laid the foundation for dramatically improved relations between the United States and Britain. Beecher was far from alone in believing he had at his side the country's ablest legal advocate.

As the trial got under way and the prosecution called its star witnesses—Tilton, Moulton, and Moulton's wife, Emma—Beecher appeared to enjoy the proceedings. He sniffed a nosegay of wild violets, while in the packed gallery men spat tobacco juice and cigar smoke choked the air. He displayed a confidence in the outcome that very few accused men could hope to exhibit. Given what the country knew of his prior state of anguish from the now famous "ragged edge" letter, and his abject plea for Tilton's forgiveness from his "letter of contrition," his demeanor suggested a calm faith that his connection to God was secure. As the *Herald* observed, he "presents for the investigation of scientific men, a psychological problem which they must despair of solving." Eunice, too, bore up without evident strain: attending every day throughout the six-month trial, observed close-up by sixty reporters, her chiseled face never once flickered with emotion, except now and then a hint of a smile.

It was Moulton, as keeper of the letters, who launched the first blow. During two days of cross-examination, one of Beecher's lawyers challenged him to repeat his libelous charges before the church investigating committee: "Didn't you say that Mr. Beecher was a damned perjurer and a libertine?"

"I don't know whether I said he was a damned perjurer and a libertine," Moulton replied. "I may have said he was a perjurer and a libertine—as he is."

And yet the more Tilton and Beecher and their proxies accused each other of lying and depravity, the more necessary it became for each to exalt the piety and purity of Elizabeth, who aroused breathless fascination, especially among the reporters. From the time she first appeared, a petite, shy woman wearing a black silk dress, dark velvet cloak, veil, and black velvet hat plumed with an ostrich feather, the mystery of who she was infatuated the nation. What woman could provoke such a conflict? While news of the trial resounded across the country—in a saloon near the new Fulton ferryhouse, the owner banned men from talking about it after a Beecher man threw a beer bottle in the face of a Tilton man; elsewhere, there were reports of obsessed readers being driven into insane asylums—Elizabeth sat wordlessly in the courtroom, fewer than a dozen feet from Tilton and Beecher.

Evarts badgered Tilton for several days of cross-examination in February. Tilton acknowledged that when he and Beecher first became friendly in the late fifties and during the war, "Mr. Beecher was my man of all men . . . I loved him, Sir, next to my father." As the population knew, they had kissed back then at least once—Beecher recalled it was on the lips, Tilton on the forehead—and Evarts understood that the more each portrayed himself as having loved and trusted the other, the better the opportunity to act the righteous victim. Indeed, Tilton's story was that he loved both Elizabeth and Beecher so much that it made perfect sense for him to encourage their friendship, especially knowing her deep, almost spectral religious faith and spotless decency.

What were Elizabeth's views on "feminine chastity," Evarts asked her husband.

"I think my wife loves everything good and hates everything bad," Tilton testified. "I believe today she is a good woman—"

"Well," Evarts interjected, trapping Tilton in his own logic, "we do not differ from you." If Elizabeth was innocent, so, presumably, was Beecher.

"I was going to say," Tilton pleaded, "that I have never blamed her for the blame which belongs, not to her but to her betrayer." Two days later, he elaborated:

> I think she is a pure woman. I hold, with Mr. Beecher, that she is
> guiltless. . . . I think she sinned her sin as one in a trance; I don't think
> she was a free agent. I think she would have done his bidding if, like
> the heathen priest in the Hindoo-land, he had bade her fling her
> child into the Ganges or cast herself under the juggernaut. That was
> my excuse for Elizabeth.

When Emma Moulton took the stand as a witness for the prosecution, she testified with a directness that startled the court. "Both Mrs. Tilton and Mr. Beecher," she said, "admitted in language not to be mistaken that a continued sexual intimacy had existed between them." She detailed Beecher's tearful confession and frank talk of suicide. Beecher's lawyers endeavored to use her candor against her. "Gentlemen," one of them told the jury, "you have seen for yourselves that Mrs. Moulton is naturally a lady. She could no more have made that coarse and vulgar speech to her pastor, at that time than she could have cut off her hand." That is: she was too respectable to do what she claimed and thus must be lying. As Beecher's biographer Debby Applegate observes: "The defense team's great weapon was the inane paradox of the sexual double standard: Anyone base enough to speak of such sordid sexual matters was, de facto, too immoral to trust."

By now, the evidence "pinched Monsignor Beecher very hard," diarist George Templeton Strong wrote after her testimony. "He is probably ruined by his utterly fatuous confidences and confessions." Even if found not guilty, Beecher hereafter would have to account for why, if he had nothing to hide or apologize for, he had gone to such ridiculous lengths to conceal and atone for so much. And for how his placing God's love above conscience and fear might help to explain his predicament. "But then he evidently fails to see," Godkin wrote in *The Nation*, "what most other thinking people see, that the calamity which has overtaken him, and bids fair to cloud his declining years, is the not unnatural result of his philosophy of life."

THE DEFENSE BEGAN its presentation on February 24, introducing a dozen witnesses to discredit and disparage Tilton and Moulton before calling Beecher himself on April 1.

The balconies that day were jammed; thousands more massed outside, trying to get in. Beecher, nosegay in place, strode to the stand and created a murmur by refusing to swear on a Bible, asking instead to "swear in the New England custom . . . by the uplifted hand . . . in the presence of the ever-living God." Under friendly questioning, he recalled events and conversations in extraordinary detail, acting them out, mimicking voices. To frequent applause, sobbing occasionally, he denied any impropriety, explaining once again that he was no more intimate with Elizabeth than with his own family, or for that matter, Theodore Tilton. But on cross-examination, he stumbled. By turns vague, evasive, and forgetful, he fed the impression that something had gone on with Elizabeth that he was struggling to conceal.

Tilton's lawyer, Judge William Fullerton, asked him about two carriage rides the pair had taken together in early 1870. Had there been others? "I think before these that I had taken some rides, but I have no recollection of them definitely," Beecher said. Might they have taken place in a closed carriage? "I have no recollection, Sir, of it." So Fullerton went until it appeared that, at the very least, Beecher was reluctant to talk about their buggy rides. Then Fullerton turned to the subject of their much-noted physical affection. Part of Beecher's defense was that intimacies of more than one kind were fitting among close friends, and he'd brought gales of laughter when he recounted on direct examination a meeting in 1871 when he and the Tiltons reconciled briefly even after Tilton had already charged him with seducing his wife: "When we arose, I kissed him, and he kissed me, and I kissed his wife and she kissed me, and I believe they kissed each other." Now, Fullerton invited him to clarify:

Were you in the habit of kissing her?

I was when I had been absent any considerable time.

And how frequently did that occur?

Very much; I kissed her as I would any of my own family.

I beg your pardon. I don't want you to tell me you kissed her as you did anybody else. I want to know if you kissed her.

I did kiss her.

Were you in the habit of kissing her when you went to her house in the absence of her husband?

Sometimes I did, and sometimes I did not.

Well, what prevented you on the occasions when you did not?

It may be that the children were there then; it might be that she did not seem in the—to greet me in that way.

Well, what do you mean by that, that you didn't kiss her when the children were present?

I sometimes did, and sometimes did not.

Did you kiss her in the presence of the servants?

Not that I ever recollect.

Was it not true that you did not kiss her in the presence of the children or the servants, but did kiss her when she was not in their presence?

No, Sir, it is not true in any—as I understand your question.

I don't know how you understand the question; it is about as plain as I can make it. Did you not purposely omit to kiss her in the presence of the children and the servants?

No, Sir, I did not; in the presence of the children, certainly not.

Having cast the impression that Beecher was reluctant to discuss his involvement with a woman he admitted kissing except, it seemed, when her children and servants were around, Fullerton finally grilled him on what came to be known as the "clandestine letters." In January 1872, just as he was preparing to leave for New Haven to deliver the first Yale lecture—when, after cutting himself with his razor, he'd preached to divinity students on "man-building"—he wrote to Elizabeth about his upcoming trip, adding: "My wife takes the boat for Havana and Florida on Thursday." In a second letter, also written while Eunice was vacationing, he invited Elizabeth to send him "a letter of true inwardness . . . it would be safe, for I am now at home here with my sister; and it is permitted to you."

"Why did you say it would be safe for her to do it?" Fullerton asked. "Your wife was away, was she not?"

"She was."

Fullerton neatly established that Beecher desired secret, soul-baring communication with Elizabeth Tilton, which did not prove adultery, but which looked suspicious when Beecher lamely tried to explain that the only reason he mentioned Eunice's travels was his desire to let Elizabeth know what was going on in his life. After more than two months of appearing immune to, even dismissive of, the charge against him, he suddenly looked—and acted—like a guilty man.

FOLLOWING BEECHER'S TESTIMONY, Evarts and the defense team faced two remaining obstacles: how to answer the court's—and especially the public's—interest in hearing from the last two major players in the drama, Victoria Woodhull and Elizabeth Tilton. However discredited themselves, either one could still be lethal to Beecher's tottering credibility. Anticipation spiked when Woodhull, her face heavily veiled, appeared in court in late April. Eunice rose and left the courtroom, though Woodhull was only asked to submit some letters and did not testify. Then, on May 1, the defense rested, and it appeared that Elizabeth would not be heard from either.

Two days later, on the seventy-seventh day of the trial, Elizabeth abruptly stood up and addressed the judge—rising "like an apparition," the *Herald* reported. "Your Honour," she said, "I have a communication which I hope Your Honour will read aloud." When Judge Joseph Neilson refused, several newspapers took up her cause, editorializing that she had been silenced by the court, and Elizabeth promptly and inevitably released her statement to the press. In fact, Elizabeth had changed her story so many times that neither side dared expose her to questioning, but her letter astutely placed the onus on the court to clear her name.

"I have been so sensible of the power of my enemies," she wrote, "that my soul cries out before you and the gentlemen of the jury that they beware how, by a divided verdict, they consign to my children a false and irrevocable stain upon their mother." In effect, Elizabeth argued, anything less than full exoneration for Beecher condemned her and her innocent son and daughter as well. Though the statement was reported to be her own, most reporters saw it as a shrewd effort by Evarts to divert what historian Richard Fox calls "the tepid victory of a hung jury—no finding of guilt, but no ringing declaration of innocence either."

Closing arguments stretched on for twenty-five days. The jury was conducted to a small room on the top floor of the courthouse on June 24. A heat wave engulfed the Northeast, but the fanlight over the door was shut so that their deliberations would not be overheard. One juror passed out from heat exhaustion, and Neilson provided mattresses for sleep. After eight days and fifty-two ballots they gave up. When the jurors, ill and depleted, filed into the courtroom, only Eunice among the two married couples was in court, sitting in her accustomed seat, waiting. The clerk asked if they had a verdict.

"No, we have not, I regret to say," the foreman said. "We cannot. We ask to be discharged."

Deadlocked 9 to 3 in Beecher's favor, the jury effectively delivered a decision that he and Evarts claimed vindicated him, but which could not erase the stain of the scandal, or put an end to his troubles. "It can hardly be said," Godkin wrote, "that this is a victory for anybody, but it is something very like a defeat for Mr. Beecher." To his relief, he found himself redeemed in Brooklyn, where the next night Plymouth Church overflowed with well-wishers who heard him appeal for their forgiveness and the trustees hiked his salary for the year to $100,000 so he could pay his legal bills. But the country, which had seen his private life and his marriage turned inside out, harbored more questions than ever about what type of man Beecher was. Having survived one ordeal, he confronted another: rebuilding a shattered reputation throughout a stern Christian nation reacting against a threatening liberalization in its social views—a point made most compellingly in the religious press. As the New York *Evangelist* asked:

Is Mr. Beecher free from all blame?

The best, the only plea made for him by his friends or by himself confesses a degree of folly which is amazing. It is impossible to hold him innocent without confessing him capable of absurdly foolish behavior. Probably he himself would speak more severely than this. Will he profit by his dear-bought experience? Will he choose better associates or wiser counselors? Will he cease from that unbridled extravagance of speech, which has so nearly made him a ruinous witness against himself: which so often moves his crowds of admiring hearers and readers to derision of men as faithful as himself, or wiser; which sometimes makes his truest and best friends doubt whether he holds fast fundamental truth: and which shows less sympathy with the stern conscientiousness of his heroic ancestry than with the self indulgent and self applauding liberality of that "long-haired, gushing, kissing crowd," who first courted him and then tried to tear him in pieces?

Beecher fled the city as soon as he could pull himself away, retreating to his farm in Peekskill, where, surrounded on his porch by family and friends, he told a local crowd, "I have no new course to take. I am too old to change my position. I shall go on trusting men. I have pursued that doctrine all my life and only once in forty years have I made a mistake. I shall love men; I shall not stop to think of their faults before I love them." He went to Twin Mountain House, New Hampshire, to minister to his summer parish. Whatever he may have learned from his ordeal, he now exerted the last powers that belonged to him, contacting the district attorney to drop the case against Moulton and Tilton, purging the Plymouth congregation of any who opposed him, and having ten thousand copies of Evarts's speeches in his defense sent to every library, college, and important church in the country. By the time he returned to Brooklyn in September, most Americans had concluded that Beecher, if no adulterer, was at least guilty of behavior "entirely unworthy of his name, position and sacred calling," as the *Times* wrote. The great majority of churchgoers believed he would go to hell, though he himself had long stopped fearing damnation. "I will *not*," he would soon declare, announcing his final break from the Calvinist legacy of punishment exalted by his father, "worship cruelty."

CARNEGIE ANTICIPATED that launching the Edgar Thomson works would position him to dominate a risky, fractious industry in which he had yet to land his first customer. Capitalizing on the depression— cutting wages, renegotiating contracts, ratcheting demands on suppliers: "reef sailing," he called it—the firm had trimmed its building expenses by nearly a quarter, and as the plant neared completion his managers now assured him that it would be able to manufacture steel rails at a lower cost than his competitors. In mid-June, the country's established steelmakers met in Philadelphia "for the purpose of considering questions connected with the trade." These "Fathers-in-Israel," as Carnegie called them, disdained him as an upstart, but they had heard much about Holley's state-of-the-art design and Jones's recruiting coup, and they invited the company's part-time general manager, William Shinn, to sit in. At the gathering, the industrialists formed the Bessemer Steel Association, a loose trade alliance for exchanging information and promoting common interests such as favorable tariffs.

Carnegie wanted much more from them. From the time of his entry into the iron industry nearly two decades earlier, he had discovered that while he and his fellow producers all exalted free competition, nothing in truth could be worse for business. Out in the wild, competition for survival rewarded the ablest, most self-sufficient individuals and species, but markets operated best when they remained stable, favoring a cooperative spirit. To keep prices from falling so low as to eliminate profits, mid-century capitalists established "pools"—more or less formal pacts to set prices, quotas, and geographical territories, and to share orders. To gain a foothold in steel, and thus ensure E.T. a future, Carnegie suggested in the weeks following the meeting that the group establish a rail pool. The indignant steel men, their relationships with their customers and one another squarely in place, rejected the overture.

No one in the steel business was strong enough to try to end harmful competition, as John D. Rockefeller had begun doing in the oil business, simply by eliminating his competitors. Rockefeller reputedly trumpeted that process in starkly Darwinian, and also religious, terms, writing: "The growth of a large business is merely a survival of the fittest, the working out of a law of nature and a law of God." Carnegie bought a few shares in each of his competitors' companies in order to see their annual stockholder's reports—a scrutiny he had no fear of facing himself, since his own company was a closed association with no paper on the open market. He studied their costs and pressed Shinn to develop an accounting system that let him know to within a hundredth of a cent what it cost to produce each rail. He later recalled that he mustered his first order for what his biographer Peter Krass called "a mere morsel of two thousand tons of rails" from the Pennsylvania Railroad by exploiting not only longtime connections but the steel aristocracy's ripening disdain for his venture. He wrote:

> Our competitors in steel were at first disposed to ignore us. Knowing the difficulty they had in starting their own steel works, they could not believe that we would be ready to deliver rails for another year, and declined to recognize us as competitors. The price of steel rails when we began was about seventy dollars per ton. We sent our agent through the country with instructions to take orders at the best prices he could obtain: and before our competitors knew it, we had obtained a large number—quite sufficient to justify us in making a start.

The first "blow" at E.T. commenced in mid-August, and the first steel rail rolled off the line on September 1. Dignitaries arriving by special train from Pittsburgh followed Carnegie on a personal tour through the block-long buildings, beneath towering chimneys belching smoke. They recoiled in trepidation as workmen blew a blast of air through the rumbling converter and produced a violent, blinding shower of pure white sparks the size of quarters. "The liquid pig metal contains a percentage of manganese silicone and carbon," a company history later explained. "If we could conceive of these elements as endowed with human emotion we might say that every particle is in love with some atom of oxygen. The converting vessel is the meeting place of the lovers and the scene of their marriage. With noisy celebration the union of the little globules of air and the tiny atoms takes place, and emerging from the lip of the converter in sparkling radiance the happy pairs soar away to spend their short lives together." Carnegie, still single and living with his mother, exulted at the fireworks.

The steelworks, which cost less than $800,000 to build, earned $11,000 in profit in its first month, and $18,000 in October. Carnegie received a note from Shinn showing that rails sold at an average of $66.32 per ton, at a profit of $9.86 per ton: "pretty good for second month," Shinn wrote. But Carnegie had not received a reorder from the Pennsylvania, which like all roads granted contracts through established relationships and favoritism, and he worried about the months ahead. He now suggested that the railroad's board of directors invite sealed bids for winning rail orders, certain that he could beat his rivals on price. The board, like his fellow suppliers, rejected his plea for relief. Carnegie anxiously told Shinn to see if two of his partners with connections on the Pennsylvania board could find out where the firm stood, hoping to avert even a temporary shutdown. "Urge them to go down," he wrote. "We are in grave danger—the importance of starting right is so obvious I need say nothing to impress you—now is the time to get the E.T. just right on its feet—Please telegraph me what is decided upon."

Carnegie resolved to shore up E.T.'s competitive position. If he could not, like Rockefeller, crush his competitors, he would force them to reckon with him by squeezing them hard on costs. By the third week of November, he instructed Shinn to prepare for a price war:

Of course we are in for a year of low prices. I have seen this from the day of our failure to combine, but if we meet it rightly the track will be clearer after the war is over—One year without dividend on Cambria, Penna. Steel, Joliet and North Chicago will make some amicable arrangement possible.

Nine days later, he issued his marching orders:

Two courses are open to a new concern like ours—1st stand timidly
back, afraid to "break the market" following others and coming out
without orders to keep our works going—that is where we are going
to land if we keep on.

2nd To make up our minds to offer certain large consumers lots at
figures that will command orders—For my part I would run the
works full next year even if we made but two dollars per ton.

Carnegie commanded the battle from New York. Though he had focused everything on steel, his preferred habitat remained the brokerages
on Broad Street, the Windsor Hotel, the Nineteenth Century Club, Delmonico's, and Mrs. Botta's parlors. Boosted by "the new venture in steel
having started off so promisingly," he began to think of taking a holiday,
he later recalled. Carnegie understood that he alone among his competitors was in a position to sacrifice profits in order to undercut the others,
and it simplified his mission: to reduce costs. In December, he told Shinn:
"Please call all our people together & advise me how low you are willing
to go. You know my views—fill the works at a small margin of profit—get
our rails on the leading lines next year. The year after, take my word for it,
you will make profit enough."

As YALE'S FIRST PROFESSOR of political and social science, "Will" Sumner enjoyed wide latitude in defining both an emerging area of academic
interest and how it ought to be taught and discussed within the college's
dreary, quasireligious, overheated lecture rooms. He was hired to teach
political economy—the equivalent of modern economics—but, riled by
Spencer and his own public aspirations, Sumner pressed his students
from the start to embrace higher interests. He spoke in an "iron voice,"
one would remember: cold, authoritative, towering with rectitude.

"The duty of the economist," he said in his introductory lecture,

is not simply how to avoid waste of what has been won but to learn
the laws by which there may be no falling short of the utmost that
might be attained; and the duty of the social scientist is to teach that

moral and social deterioration follows inevitably upon economical mistakes.

My aim will be to give to those who visit this university faith in science, in thought, in training as applies to politics. I desire to use the opportunity given me to furnish the country with citizens of sterling worth, and to give to the professions men whose public influence will tell in the cause of liberty, industry and honesty.

Republics learn only by experience, but the bitter experience will not be wanting. The men of this generation are not doing their duty by the men of the next. They are putting off hard duties and are shirking responsibilities and are relaxing the political virtue of the country. In one way or another the results will inevitably come. When they come, I am of the opinion that the American people will find that it does not pay to be ruled by small men. They will look out in their need for men who know what ought to be done and how to do it.

Sumner saw his escape from the pulpit in Morristown as a means to try to reconcile Christianity and science, which he thought could be achieved best at the lectern, where impressionable young men were molded. The laws of production, distribution, and scarcity discovered earlier in the century by Adam Smith and the other masterminds of nineteenth-century economics were pure, inviolate, even divine, he told his students—"fixed in the order of the universe . . . God's laws." Yet this very universality led Sumner during this time to study biology, and after rereading Spencer and reading all of Darwin, Huxley, and the other reigning natural scientists, he visited paleontologist O. C. Marsh and viewed his parade of fossil horses, which converted him almost at once— he would recall the process as nearly effortless—to the doctrine of evolution. "I never consciously gave up a religious belief," he would write. "It was as if I put my beliefs into a drawer, and when I opened it there was nothing there at all."

Exchanging faiths, Sumner preached no less hard, nor was he less moralistic. Though too severe and impersonal for active ministry, at Yale he signaled something new and exciting. Fastidious as he was stern—he always looked as if he had just stepped from the "bahth," as he called it, and he pared his fingernails to precise angles—he dazzled appreciative young students who dozed through President Noah Porter's classical curriculum of ancient Greek, Bible studies, and natural theology with his modern, hard-bitten brand of economic and political discipline— Darwinian evolution applied to society, politics, and behavior. As a later student would remember, he reproached dissenters with both barrels— stern, conservative Christian principles fused to the harsh imperatives of survival:

Professor, don't you believe in any government aid to industries?

No, it's root, hog, or die.

Yes, but hasn't the hog got a right to root?

There are no rights. The world owes nobody a living.

You believe then, Professor, in only one system, the contract competitive system?

That's the only sound economic system. All others are fallacies.

Well, suppose some professor of political economy came along and took your job away from you. Wouldn't you be sore?

Any other professor is welcome to try. If he gets my job, it is my fault. My job is to teach the subject so well that no one can take the job away from me.

"He broke upon us," a man in the class of 1874 reported, "like a cold spring in the desert."

Sumner offered unalloyed, scientific, *masculine* reproof to the yawning sentimentality of the age: Beecherism, women's rights, spiritualism, communism—all the belief systems that softened and modified and that he held, even beyond Spencer, weakened the natural competition that produced better men, societies, and nations. Throughout the fall, he lectured on the nascent study of sociology, several years before the subject was introduced to undergraduates at other schools. Like Harvard and Princeton, Yale had begun its headlong transformation into a university, adding graduate studies to reflect the explosion in knowledge and confront the emergence of more secular institutions like MIT and Cornell and the booming, diversified, state-funded schools arising under the widely popular postwar land grant system. But undergraduates generally were still thought too inexperienced and malleable to be exposed to social

True to Fiske's manifesto, the board chose Charles Eliot, a reform-minded chemist exiled to the Massachusetts Institute of Technology six years earlier after Agassiz and the Lazzaroni blocked his appointment as a professor and dean of sciences. Wasting no time, Eliot arranged immediately for seven lecture series on philosophy for the upcoming year, including two on recent thought: he invited Emerson to address "The Natural History of the Intellect" and Fiske to discuss "The Positive Philosophy." Here was Fiske's revenge. Less than a decade after the college charged him with "undermining the faith" of his fellow students with his too-ardent defense of his views, he delighted in his new position as lecturer, which Eliot went on to renew for the 1870–71 term.

Much in the way that Youmans sought to affirm Spencer's evolutionary bona fides before the Liberal Club in New York, Fiske used his Harvard lectures—under the tutelage of Spencer—to delineate Spencer's positivism from that of Comte, the French philosopher who first proposed to launch a naturalistic science of society and who coined the word "sociology." Both Harvard series were published in the New York *World*, garnering Fiske, at age twenty-nine, instant national popularity as an authority on evolution. He was invited to lecture in Milwaukee, then Boston, and he began to consider writing a book that would flesh out the spiritual implications of Spencer's doctrine—the one realm Spencer had yet to pursue. But Fiske's hopes for a professorship encountered vehement faculty opposition, and in the fall of 1872 he began work as Harvard's assistant librarian. Eliot appointed him expecting that a few years' loyal service to the university would help establish his collegiality. While no one thought Fiske anything but grossly overqualified, the job was no sinecure; his duties involved supervising new collections and the cataloging of tens of thousands of books and pamphlets.

A woman from Boston was so impressed with one of Fiske's lectures that she gave him a check for $1,000 so he could travel to England to consult Spencer and others on his project, and the following August, after securing a leave of absence, he set sail. Just before he left, Fiske "planted his flag" in the evolution debate, completing two articles that he believed would propel him to the front rank of interpreters. In one he set forth for the first time his argument for social and moral evolution based on man's prolonged infancy. While Darwin and others continued to struggle with how *Homo sapiens,* apparently alone among beasts, had developed a moral doctrines that in their implications might be antichurch. With no text-book available, Sumner lectured largely from his own limited scholarship, mostly regarding the effect of import taxes.

Meanwhile, he pressed to apply his beliefs, promoting his moral and economic principles at public gatherings, serving as a delegate at the Republican congressional convention, and addressing the Chamber of Commerce on the urgency of resuming specie payments. In his introductory lecture, Sumner told his students: "I dislike to hear politicians sneered at and the career of politics tossed aside as if it were the career of a swindler, for I hold politics—or, if we must abandon the degraded word, statesmanship—to be the grandest calling open to men." In practice, he encountered vigorous resistance. Many in New Haven were out of work. In December, as Christmas approached, the question came before the Board of Aldermen whether to allocate any money from the budget to provide employment for the jobless and needy. A prominent Democrat, Thomas McGrail, demanded that some portion of the $14,000 for the grading of streets and $18,000 for "ordinary labor" be used to assist "the poor laboring man."

Sumner opposed the project, calling it unjust since it would result in benefiting a selected few at the expense of the rest. When McGrail responded that if the money went to laborers, the town would have no one to provide for but poor widows, Sumner decided to have "a little fun" with him, according to his biographer Harris Starr. Sumner asked if the appropriation could be used to employ seamstresses; McGrail said no. "Why not?" Sumner asked. He loudly questioned the propriety of making a distinction as to classes to be provided with work in hard times.

New Haven, however, was not Yale. Sumner lost the vote, the laborers got city jobs, and McGrail strengthened his popularity.

YOUMANS, TOO, DISCOVERED how hard Darwin had made it to rest social policy on evolution. Pouring out editorials and reviews in *The Popular Science Monthly,* he promoted what historian Robert Bannister calls "the staples of Gilded Age liberalism: free trade, hard money and good government." But other publications, even those generally sympathetic to evolutionary theory, rejected the unsparing claims of those like Sumner who interpreted the universal laws of nature to endorse not just the view that man inevitably heightens himself, but that the biological struggle for survival requires him to be ruthlessly selfish in doing so, and that any attempt to improve society violates the natural order. Spencer had made the point publicly before Darwin that the biological world was competitive and favored the best-adapted individuals, but natural selection was widely understood to clash with the enlightened presumption that society progresses also through sympathy and fellow feeling, and that it can be induced to leap ahead by the spread of new ideas and social action.

Youmans seldom employed the phrases "struggle for existence" or "survival of the fittest," and he attacked any intimation that he and Spencer were Darwinists. In March, *The Popular Science Monthly* published a portion of Spencer's forthcoming *Principles of Sociology,* his long-delayed book on social science. In the excerpt, Spencer explored the origins of superstitions, theorizing that primitive man—"with no one to answer his questions, and no ideas of physical causation"—necessarily concluded that all phenomena were exactly as he experienced them through his senses. Uncivilized races, unlike their more educated descendants, accepted as "fact" even what was demonstrably false, he wrote.

The magazine also reprinted an article on "Social Evolution" from *The Contemporary Review* by Irish political economist John Elliott Cairnes, who challenged Spencer's habit of legitimating niggardly social policies on the basis of natural imperatives. A fifty-three-year-old invalid suffering on his deathbed, Cairnes wrote: "Never before has the conception of a social science been put forth with equal distinctness and clearness; and never has its claim to take rank as a recognized branch of scientific investigation been placed upon surer grounds, or asserted with more just emphasis." The problem, according to Cairnes, derived from Spencer's analogy of society as a "social organism." The main goal of a biological organism is to survive as a whole, and it is the purpose of its parts—cells, organs, systems—to serve the general good. But in society the opposite is true; the overall scheme is meant to foster the existence and happiness of the individuals who compose it. "This being so," Cairnes wrote, "what can be more preposterous" than applying modes of organization from the animal and plant kingdoms to regulate social life?

Cairnes recalled Spencer's spat with Huxley four years earlier, when Spencer, traveling in France with Youmans, had decided that Huxley needed to be "pulled up" and insisted on dictating a rebuttal. "If the analogy of the body politic with the body physiological counts for any thing," Huxley had then pointed out, "it seems to me to be in favor of a much larger amount of governmental interference than exists at present, or than I, for one, at all desire to see." Now with his own magazine, Youmans took it on himself to administer the correction. In an accompanying editorial, he attributed Cairnes's obtuseness to "his prejudices as a politician, or an Englishman, or some other perversity."

"Professor Cairnes goes back to an old essay on the 'Social Organism,' in which Mr. Spencer nearly twenty years ago, pointed out some analogies between the structures and actions of the body politic and those of individual organisms, and says that Spencer's Doctrine of Evolution is based upon this analog," Youmans wrote.

> We cannot conceive a grosser misapprehension than this. Mr. Spencer maintains that the Law of Evolution is universal because the evidence of it is found in each of the great divisions of natural phenomena.
>
> In the social sphere the principle rests upon observed effects, and is an induction from the facts belonging to that sphere, just as strictly as the law of organic evolution is derived from the facts in the biological sphere.

Darwin's shadow loomed over all Youmans's efforts to present Spencer to America as the true progenitor of the new epoch in evolutionary thinking, and he used *The Popular Science Monthly* to conduct a running campaign against Spencer's critics. In another editorial the same month, he upbraided *The Nation,* which shared most of his political views, for ignoring Spencer's intellectual paternity in a recent account on the history of evolution. This time Youmans drew on Huxley's authority as Darwin's fiercest advocate. Huxley had said in a Royal Society lecture in which he avowed his own belief in evolution, "the only complete and systematic statement of the doctrine, with which I am acquainted, is that contained in Mr. Herbert Spencer's 'System of Philosophy'—a work which should be studied by all who desire to know wither scientific thought is tending."

"But the *Nation* thinks differently," Youmans wrote. "It not only does not commend Mr. Spencer's works to readers seeking information on the 'Theory of Evolution,' but such readers are tacitly warned against them."

In mid-July, Youmans returned to England to tend to the International

Scientific Series, accompanied by his sister, Catherine, and a nephew. Spencer, who had urged him to take some time off to relax, left them "in possession" a week after their arrival, going north to rest, fish, and attend a meeting of the British Association for the Advancement of Science between dictating the final sections of *The Principles of Sociology*, polishing a reissued version of *The Study of Sociology*, and starting a new project— an autobiography. Usually when traveling by train Spencer showed up with whatever manuscript he was working on tied to his waist by meters of thick string pouring from under his coat. According to his biographer Mark Francis, "He would arrive at the station with a small entourage consisting of his amanuensis or secretary, a woman companion to read to him and to wave him off when the train left, and a couple of porters carrying the luggage." He would have his temperature taken by the secretary, and, so long as it wasn't too high, board a reserved first-class compartment where a hammock had been strung up for his journey.

Hauling around London in summer, meanwhile, wore Youmans out, and after returning to America late in the fall, he sent Spencer "a discouraging account of himself." On December 18, Spencer, alarmed, reprimanded him, responding pointedly with "a trait of my nature—a somewhat too candid expression of my opinions." He took the occasion to lecture Youmans at length on the risks of disregarding his health. "Turning to your letter," he told him,

> let me say first that I have regretted greatly to have an account of your state that is so unsatisfactory, alike by what it says and what it implies. To think that you should have come over here mainly to recruit, and now that you should apparently be no better than when you left; and all because you would go on working and worrying instead of resting! Your inattention to be careful now amounts to nothing. . . . That you will cut short your life or incapacitate yourself, is an inference one cannot avoid drawing; seeing that in your case, as in a host of other cases, experience seems not to have the slightest effect. It is a kind of work-drunkenness; and you seem to be able to no more resist the temptation than the dipsomaniac resists alcohol. . . . What is the use of all this propagation of knowledge, if it is to end in such results?

CHAPTER SIX

WASHINGTON, 1876

> *Our generation has to open the second century of our*
> *national life, as the Fathers opened the first. Theirs*
> *was the work of independence, ours is the work of*
> *reformation.*
>
> —CARL SCHURZ

BESET BY POLITICAL SCANDALS, the deepening depression, and the violent unraveling of Reconstruction amid torrents of racist intimidation and murder in the South, Grant entered his final year in the White House at a low ebb. After gaining passage of the Resumption Act of 1875, which called for returning to full specie payments within four years and which subordinated the party of Lincoln from then on to the interests of Eastern business, he grasped at the hope of running for a third term, but faced near certain rejection by the party, again split by a liberal insurgency.

Schurz remained influential among liberals despite having lost reelection, and he again aimed to "make" the next president. The more Grant's regime collapsed from within, the more Schurz's reluctant support for Greeley, instead of a humiliation, appeared prescient and courageous, even to steadfast Republicans. Facing renewed financial concerns after years of separation from his family—during his Senate term, his wife, Margarethe, and three children lived in Germany, only recently resettling in America—he maintained a furious schedule of writing, traveling, and lecturing.

Schurz attacked Grant on all flanks. A year earlier in Ohio, Democrats had nominated a greenbacker for governor, and Schurz had campaigned exhaustively for the Republican candidate, a specie man and retired reformer named Rutherford B. Hayes, whose victory catapulted him into contention for the White House. Meanwhile, Democrats had won back the House of Representatives, and to salvage his administration Grant was forced to appoint an aggressive and ambitious new treasury secretary, Benjamin Bristow, to purge it of corruption. Since April, Bristow's investigators had exposed a powerful ring of payoffs by whiskey distillers that now reached to Grant's inner circle, and Grant's son Fred told the *New York Herald* that the indictments stemmed from a conspiracy between Bristow's solicitor and Schurz. Angling to stave off another third-party fiasco, Schurz and other liberals began planning an independent conference "to devise means to prevent the campaign of the Centennial Year from becoming a mere scramble of the politicians for the spoils," he would write.

In early February, Grant received a rebuke from a troubling new quarter. Blanche Bruce, a Mississippi Republican and the Senate's only Negro, took the floor in executive session and accused the president of deserting freed blacks. Bruce said that the party could no longer be trusted and that southern Negroes would be "forced to make peace with the Democrats and form a political alliance with honest and trustworthy white men of the South," according to historian Dee Brown. "Shake not your bloody shirt at me!" Bruce exploded, attacking as hypocritical and dishonest Washington's retreat in rebuilding and reforming the region under federal authority.

Eleven years into Reconstruction, the postwar struggle over power, wealth, and race in the vanquished, economically ruined states of the former Confederacy had produced extraordinary constitutional rights guaranteeing equality but also a potent opposition movement promoting "Redemption"—a return to white supremacy and home rule. While Grant's reelection at first seemed to affirm Washington's commitment to Reconstruction, Redeemers, aided by terrorists, had rapidly reversed the tide, capturing state governments in Arkansas, Alabama, and Texas. The previous summer a band of white men in Clinton, Mississippi, had fired into a crowd at a Republican barbecue—two women and four children were among the dead—then rampaged through town killing blacks.

When similar reports soon poured in from around the state, the governor requested federal troops to restore order. From his summer home on the New Jersey shore, Grant rejected the plea. "The whole public are tired out with these annual autumnal outbreaks in the South," he wrote, "[and] are ready now to condemn any interference on the part of the government." In November, Mississippi Democrats captured the state in a landslide in which counties with large black majorities recorded Republican votes as low as zero.

The successes of Redemption meant that Reconstruction—"the last battle of the Civil War," as historian Nicholas Lemann calls it—could only be won through sustained judicial and military intervention. But neither Grant, who had conquered the South in battle before, nor the Republicans, who had come to power promoting free labor and equality, nor Schurz, who denounced federal efforts to uphold the radical Republican government in Louisiana, had the will to struggle on. Bruce's outburst most disconcerted Republican leaders, who feared losing the White House in the fall unless they could regain some southern districts lost in the midterm election.

Grant's troubles mounted week by week. Every one of his cabinet departments was now under investigation by Bristow or Congress. In late February, the papers reported that Secretary of War William Belknap was alleged to have accepted bribes in return for arranging lucrative trading post assignments. (As rumors flared that a broken Belknap had killed himself, reporters, confusing his name with Beecher's, conflated the two scandals, rushing to Brooklyn only to discover the minister still alive.) Movement activists urged Schurz to accelerate his calls for an independent conference, and he appeared to be on the verge of wiping away the last of the political damage from four years earlier.

While Schurz traveled extensively to rally support, Margarethe, expecting their fourth child, suffered a difficult pregnancy, unable for months to climb stairs or go out. Schurz was lecturing in upstate New York when he got word that his father was fatally ill and, after racing to Illinois to see him, he quickly returned to Manhattan to care for Margarethe during her confinement. On March 5, his second son was born; ten days later, Margarethe died of complications from the delivery. Schurz, proudly steely and optimistic, a dutiful and loving if distant family man, crumpled. "The loss of the wife of one's youth is unlike any other bereavement," he mourned to a friend. "It is the loss of the best part of one's life."

Grant, too, sank more and more into depression, leaving the White House often to walk alone through the city, ignoring passersby. He skipped appointments, letting languish in his anteroom men he disliked, including the showy Indian fighter George Armstrong Custer, who'd been called to Washington by Democrats to testify against the war secretary, had implicated Grant's brother in the scandal, and was now eager to return to the Dakotas where war loomed against the tribes of the northern plains. Grant lashed back at his pursuers, who, he complained to a friend, were even investigating his conduct of the Civil War. On March 28, he suffered severe head pains, diagnosed as "neuralgia of the brain" brought on by extreme physical exhaustion; after improving slightly, three days later he relapsed. As stories spread that he had had a mild apoplectic stroke, his friends and family feared for his life. The few callers to see him in his office reported that he was pale and listless, but well enough to smoke a cigar. His doctor, he told them, was giving him quinine for a tonic.

IN PHILADELPHIA, the United States formally celebrated a century of restless progress. On May 10, amid thunderous cheers lasting more than a minute, Grant took the podium in front of the main hall of the Centennial Exhibition—scores of massive new iron-and-glass buildings sprawled across hundreds of acres of muddy bottomland along the Schuylkill River. (Carnegie, a member of the construction committee, had persuaded the committee to change its original plans for wooden structures and to give the iron orders and building contract to his companies.) Grant donned his eyeglasses, removed a wad of foolscap from a side pocket, and opened the proceedings. He spoke so low that few could hear him. "One hundred years ago our country was new and but partially settled," he recited dully.

> Our necessities have compelled us to chiefly extend our means and time in felling forests, subduing prairies, building dwellings, factories, ships, docks, warehouses, roads, canals, machinery. Most of our schools, churches, libraries and asylums have been established within

a hundred years. Burdened by these great primal works of necessity, which could not be delayed, we yet have done what this exhibition will show in the direction of rivaling older and more advanced nations in law, medicine, and theology; in science, literature, philosophy and the fine arts. Whilst proud of what we have done, we regret we have not done more.

Escorted by four thousand federal troops and an honor guard wearing white sashes and black-plumed helmets, he led a cortege of dignitaries to Machinery Hall. Inside stood thirteen acres of idle industrial machines— for spinning wool, combing cotton, printing newspapers, making shoes, lithographing wallpaper, pumping water, sewing cloth, sawing logs, shaping wood, and scores of other laborious tasks—all dwarfed by a towering Corliss steam engine rising more than forty feet above the floor in the main transept. Thousands of feet of underground shafts, belts, wheels, and pulleys connected the machines to the engine, its giant steam boilers placed outside the hall to quell the roar. Looking wan and exhausted, Grant climbed the stairs to a metal platform, joined by Emperor Dom Pedro of Brazil, the second monarch to visit the country after the king of Hawaii. Together they turned a pair of control levers that, with a gush of steam, moved two tremendous walking beams and a geared flywheel. The machines clattered suddenly to life. The throng erupted.

Here was the nation's glorious technical might put wholly to peaceful use—innovation yoked to utility. Despite the rafts of moral, political, and economic uncertainty testing the new society as never before, Grant's burden of "great primal works of necessity" had achieved this much. "It is in these things of iron and steel that the national genius most freely speaks," *Atlantic Monthly* editor William Dean Howells marveled; "by and by the inspired marbles, the breathing canvases, the great literature; for the present America is voluble in the strong metals and their infinite uses." Machinery Hall became by far the most widely attended attraction among the fair's ten million visitors—one in four Americans. Among the technologies on exhibit was a new device that allowed people to speak at a distance, connected by a wire.

The other great theme was westward expansion, the all but concluded continental conquest. Grant, who believed that the Indians were human but inferior and required Christianity to civilize them, had personally supported establishing an encampment of 300 aborigines from 53 tribes to populate the Smithsonian's ethnography exhibit. The Department of the Interior, which controlled Indian affairs, balked at the plan, even though the Smithsonian's naturalist promised that "only the cleanest and finest looking Indians" would be displayed, those who could speak English and—testifying to their domesticity—could bring with them a child, dog, and pony. Life-size mannequins were used instead, the mock encampment imparting a frisson that dominated the other attractions at the two-acre United States building, which showcased the nation's natural bounty. One mannequin wore a belt full of dangling scalps, another a grizzly-bear-claw necklace. "The red man, as he appears in effigy and in photographs in this collection," the *Atlantic's* Howells observed, "is a hideous demon, whose malign traits can hardly inspire any emotions softer than abhorrence." The solution to the Indian problem is "extinction," Howells wrote.

Despite his prostration, Grant returned to Washington still aspiring to win a third term, and he found galling the desertions and betrayals of party leaders. A few days later in New York, liberals led by Schurz met in anticipation of the upcoming party convention. Schurz told representatives from eighteen states, including veterans of the Greeley campaign E. L. Godkin, Sumner, and others, that the liberals had no appetite for starting a third party, but that they needed to back a candidate who stood for reform above all else. "Every true American," Schurz declared in a heavy German accent, "must have the courage of his duty." When Charles Francis Adams—Schurz's favorite for the Liberal Republican nomination four years earlier—spoke in favor of Bristow, however, Schurz equivocated, saying he was unsure whether he could support either party and would remain for now on the fence "because the mud was too deep on both sides to drop into it."

GRANT WITHHELD CUSTER'S ORDERS to join the fight against the Sioux up to the last minute, relenting only after Custer realized the price for disloyalty and pleaded with him in a letter from Chicago: "I appeal to you as a soldier to spare me the humiliation of seeing my regiment march to meet the enemy and I not share its dangers." Two summers earlier, Custer had led twelve hundred troops illegally into the Black Hills in Sioux territory and discovered gold, which, in the frenzy to rebuild specie reserves in the wake of the panic, incited a gold rush and extreme pressure on Grant. In November, Grant decided against sending troops to try to restrain frantic prospectors from entering the area, just as he had refused to send soldiers to enforce federal authority in Mississippi. "He knew that in a racial battle," his biographer William McFeely wrote, "white Americans would support their white brethren, across regional lines." Sioux warriors were arming in response, though Grant and Custer both trusted that the Indians would disperse, as always, when confronted with a cavalry and superior weapons.

In Cincinnati for their nominating convention, the Republicans stood deadlocked. Schurz and the liberals lined up behind Bristow, while the front-runner, Maine senator James Blaine, known by his admirers as "the Plumed Knight," rebutted accusations that he had profited illegally from the sale of worthless railroad bonds. Then dispatches from Washington delivered the news that Blaine, an anti-Grant moderate, had collapsed from apoplexy while mounting the steps of his church, and for days, while his opponents sowed uncertainty and confusion, even his own loyalists didn't know whether he was alive or dead. So effectively did Bristow's men cast doubts upon Blaine's fitness—it was widely rumored that he was paralyzed—that administration supporters attempted to revive the third-term movement for Grant, whose most frequently mentioned running mate was the obscure but reputedly moral governor Rutherford B. Hayes, a favorite son who monitored the proceedings from his office in Columbus.

At midweek, Blaine recovered consciousness and was said to be moving about, and it appeared that swelling sympathy for his recovery might overwhelm the doubts about his character and that he might win the nomination. Hayes, a fifty-four-year-old former major general severely wounded at Antietam whose safe liberalism, party loyalty, and military record made him a popular second choice throughout the hall, voiced strong opposition. "The indications point to the nomination of Blaine on the first or some early ballot," he wrote to his campaign manager. "I feel that his nomination would be fatal to the cause. . . . I have the greatest aversion to being a candidate on the ticket with a man whose record as an upright public man is to be in question—to be defended from the beginning to the end . . . withdraw my name, if it is proposed, in connection with the Vice-Presidency."

The deadlock snapped on June 16. With supporters making last-minute deals, it came down to Blaine and Hayes on the seventh ballot, and Hayes won the nomination by five votes. Angry that the party so quickly left him behind, Grant could see that his enemy, Schurz, was right: the campaign would be a repudiation of him and "Grantism." "Governor Hayes is a good selection and will make a strong candidate," Grant told a newspaperman. Other GOP voices rejoiced. THE REPUBLICAN PARTY HAS ALMOST MIRACULOUSLY ESCAPED POLITICAL DESTRUCTION, exulted the headline in the *Chicago Tribune*. Democrats' gains in the South and Congress notwithstanding, the party entered the fall elections discredited, but whole and intact.

In the Montana Territory, Grant's "peace policy" neared its ultimate refutation in the war against the Sioux. He and the other reformers who had rejected the previous military approach in favor of placing Indians on reservations administered by Protestant church groups now witnessed in helplessness and dismay the fiercest fighting in a decade as gold miners and other business interests poured into the area. A week after the conventioneers boarded their trains for home, Custer, his famous long blond curls shorn for battle, led his regiment over the last divide between the Rosebud and Little Bighorn rivers. A Union Army general at age twenty-three, his style of boldly assaulting enemy positions verged at times on the reckless. He wore buckskins instead of a uniform and appeared to be a civilian.

Custer's orders were to lead one of three columns dispatched to force the large army of the warrior Sitting Bull back to the reservations, but he ignored instructions to wait, attacking instead a nearby group of about forty fighters. He divided his forces, hoping to surround the Indian encampment, then found himself outnumbered three to one. "As the Indians closed in, Custer ordered his men to shoot their horses and stack their carcasses to form a wall," according to one account, "but they provided little protection against bullets. In less than an hour, Custer and his men were killed in the worst American military disaster ever." After the battle, the Indians stripped and mutilated all the uniformed bodies, believing mutilation would force their souls to walk the earth for all eternity. Custer inexplicably was discovered shot through the brain and heart but without being scalped or mutilated.

It took more than a week for news of the defeat to reach the nation, just as the centennial celebration reached its zenith on Independence

Day. Grant, exhausted, remained in Washington rather than travel to Philadelphia, site of the official ceremony, where feminists led by Susan B. Anthony and Elizabeth Cady Stanton interrupted the orations by reading the Women's Declaration of Independence. Customarily, out-of-town visitors expected to shake the president's hand, and by early summer the hordes attending the Centennial Exhibition and taking a side trip to Washington were so voluminous that he was greeting between five hundred and six hundred visitors per day—"Centennial Pilgrims," he called them. On the great question of American society—race—he was inundated by renewed calls for all-out extermination of the Indians, and a reversion to, if not slavery, the violently segregated social and property relations of the Old South. On July 8, a murderous attack on blacks in Homburg, South Carolina, prompted the state's Republican governor to request federal troops. Though well aware that he was likely to repeat the previous year's result in Mississippi, Grant told him to try to punish all the offenders "without aid from the Federal Government." In the fall, he would send guards to protect polling places and voters from terrorist attacks, but it was too late: Redeemers handily recaptured the state.

"A GERMAN EDITOR HAVING WRITTEN to me for an account of the development of my mind and character with some sketch of my autobiography," Darwin wrote on an afternoon in late May,

> I have thought that the attempt would amuse me, and might possibly interest my children or their children. I know that it would have interested me greatly to have read even so short and dull a sketch of the mind of my grandfather written by himself, and what he thought and did and how he worked. I have attempted to write the following account of myself, as if I were a dead man in another world looking back at my own life. Nor have I found this difficult, for life is nearly over with me. I have taken no pains about my style of writing.

As with his eight-year obsession with barnacles, which produced two books while he strenuously delayed writing *Origin,* or his current immersion in observing the mechanisms of flesh-eating plants, Darwin set out to probe his own emergence as an original thinker in light of natural selection. He worked on the project for nearly an hour most afternoons through the summer, sifting from the facts of his family life, health struggles, and journey from amateur naturalist to leading man of science a narrative of epic ambition coupled with Victorian scruples—the need to leave a good impression. Learning from life who he was, Darwin found himself, though an invalid, exceptionally well suited in the struggle not only to survive but to prevail.

"I can say in my own favour," he wrote, "that I was as a boy humane, but I owed this entirely to the instruction and example of my sisters. I doubt indeed that humanity is a natural or innate quality." Darwin's mother died when he was eight, and his father, a towering, corpulent physician much admired in his district and by his gangly, underperforming son, was a giant presence in the household. By the time Darwin left school, which he disdained in favor of collecting beetles and shooting birds, to study medicine at the University of Edinburgh, he now wrote, "I believe that I was considered by all my masters and by my Father a very ordinary boy, rather below the common standard in intellect. To my deep mortification my Father once said to me, 'You care for nothing but shooting, dogs and rat-catching, and you will be a disgrace to yourself and all your family.' "

Taunted by low expectations—and discovering at about this time "from various small circumstances that my Father would leave me property enough to subsist on with some comfort"—Darwin resolved to go his own way. An orthodox Christian, drenched in the mores of the church and of his class, he trained for the clergy, then took off to see the world aboard the *Beagle*, believing in moral strictness and austere self-governance. He was kind to a fault in acknowledging help from others, but readily dismissed their influence on him. Having read by then his grandfather Erasmus Darwin's *Zoonomia*, in which the elder Darwin speculated four decades earlier "that the strongest and most active animal should propagate the species, which should thence become improved," he now wrote that he read the treatise "without [its] producing any effect on me." Darwin, like Spencer, was happy to share intellectual credit so long as it was clear that the big ideas were all his.

Darwin was already established as a rising naturalist and author—and suffering from undiagnosed vomiting, heart palpitations, itching, and flatulence—when, nearing thirty, he reached a turning point. In June or

July 1837, living in London, he opened his first pocket-size red notebook on "transmutation of species"—an idea so heterodox that he mentioned it to no one. He understood by now that species transformed, but not how. Meanwhile, he grappled rigorously with whether to get married, writing himself a memorandum the following summer weighing the pros and cons. "Eheu!!" he shuddered in the con column. "I should never know French,—or see the Continent—or go to America, or go up in a balloon, or take a solitary trip in Wales—poor slave—you will be worse than a negro." "My God," he wrote at the end of the pro column, "it is intolerable to think of spending ones [*sic*] whole life, like a neuter bee, working, working, & nothing after all. No, no—won't do."

Two months later, Darwin "got the flash." For "amusement," he read the economist Thomas Malthus's famous essay on population, which observed that in humans, mechanisms such as war, disease, and famine check the growth rate, which otherwise would outstrip food supplies. "Being well prepared," he now recalled in his autobiography, "to appreciate the struggle for existence which everywhere goes on from long-continued observation of the habits of plants and animals, it at once struck me that under these circumstances favourable variations would tend to be preserved, and unfavourable ones to be destroyed. The result of this would be the formation of new species. Here, then, I at last got a theory by which to work." Within two months, Darwin proposed to Emma Wedgwood, his first cousin, a plain and caring woman of deep faith who, a year older, possessed an independent fortune of her own and was more than a decade into her childbearing prime.

During these two years, Darwin "was led to think much about religion," he recalled. Though he was "very unwilling" to give up his faith, he gradually dismissed Christianity as a divine revelation, finding it "more and more difficult, with free scope given to my imagination, to invent evidence which would suffice to convince me." Fearing even now that he would upset Emma, Darwin insisted that his memoir was not to be published, but he confessed in it that he had "never since doubted even for a single second that my conclusion was correct."

"I can hardly see how anyone ought to wish Christianity to be true," Darwin wrote, barely masking his bitterness, "for if so the plain language of the text seems to show that the men who do not believe, and this would include my Father, Brother and almost all my best friends, will be everlastingly punished.

"And that," he wrote, "is a damnable doctrine."

"The old argument of design in nature . . . ," he continued,

> which formerly seemed to me so conclusive, fails, now that the law of natural selection has been discovered. We can no longer argue that, for instance, the beautiful image of a bivalve shell has been made by an intelligent being, like the hinge of a door by man. There seems to be no more design in the variability of organic beings and the action of natural selection, than in the course which the wind blows. Everything in nature is the result of fixed laws.

"Nor must we overlook," Darwin added, commenting on the evolution of religious faith itself, "the probability of the constant inculcation of a belief in God on the minds of children producing so strong and perhaps an inherited effect on their brains not yet fully developed, that it would be as difficult for them to throw off their belief in God, as for a monkey to throw off its instinctive fear and hatred of a snake."

Darwin had long been anxious about his own genealogical fitness, between his physical ailments and his marriage that yielded ten children, six of whom survived to adulthood, but, until July, no grandchildren. But in all his decisions he had put to use highly effective patterns of behavior for advancing his purposes; for instance, his pained gratitude toward his correspondents versus his dismissal of his grandfather. "Darwin lavished credit on scores of minor league researchers, while diminishing the few predecessors who might have been even remote contenders for his crown," wrote his psychological interpreter Robert Wright; "he thus incurred the debt of many young, rising scientists, while risking the offense mainly of the old and the dead." Even his poor health became an asset and a goad, keeping him at home, on a rigidly enforced schedule, surrounded by a loving family, "saved . . . from the distractions of society and amusement." "My life goes on like Clockwork," he'd written thirty years earlier to Captain FitzRoy, "and I am fixed on the spot where I shall end it."

Darwin completed his sketch by the first week of August, writing mostly in the early afternoons, then spending "the remains of the day lying on the grass under the lime trees, lazily drifting in and out of his memories," according to his biographer Janet Browne. And yet if he had developed through his life and work a balance that favored intellectual and social success, he also regretted what he had sacrificed: not just moral certitude but the "higher aesthetic tastes." Up to the age of thirty, he had relished poetry and music. "But now," he wrote near the end, "for many years I cannot endure to read a line of poetry: I have tried lately to read Shakespeare, and found it so intolerably dull that it nauseated me. I have also almost lost any taste for pictures or music. . . . I retain some taste for fine scenery, but it does not cause me the exquisite delight which it formerly did.

"On the other hand," he continued,

> novels that are works of imagination, though not of a very high order, have been for years a wonderful relief and pleasure to me, and I often bless all novelists. A surprising number have been read aloud to me, and I like all if moderately good, and if they do not end unhappily— against which a law ought to be passed.
>
> My mind seems to have become a kind of machine for grinding general laws out of large collections of facts, but why this should have caused the atrophy of that part of the brain alone, on which the higher tastes depend, I cannot conceive.

Troubled perhaps as much by this lapse in evolutionary logic as by the loss of his youthful pleasures, Darwin lamented, "The loss of these tastes is a loss of happiness, and may possibly be injurious to the intellect, and more probably to the moral character, by enfeebling the emotional part of our nature."

BUILT FOR SPEED, the White Star *Germanic* sailed from Queenstown, in County Cork, on July 27. In February, the liner had made headlines with a record-breaking eastbound crossing of the Atlantic—seven days, fifteen hours, and seventeen minutes at an average speed of 15.79 knots—and was expected to take the westbound record soon. Two huge funnels belched black smoke from the furnaces and fog whistles blasted through the night as the ship plowed through the waves; it also was fitted with four towering masts and carried spars and sails—for emergencies.

Huxley, at age fifty-one and traveling with his wife, Nettie, had long entertained visiting "Yankeeland," as he called the United States in letters to friends. But his chronic financial straits, hectic public life in Britain, and black moods, as well as the young ages of their children, had delayed the trip up to now. He looked forward to seven weeks of conferring and sightseeing with Youmans, Marsh, Fiske, the publishing Appletons, and others, replenishing his funds by lecturing, and reuniting with an older sister, living in Alabama, whom he hadn't seen in thirty years. But the real prize was the nation itself. "I will take for lecture days September 18th, 20th, 22nd, and be off on the 23rd," he told Youmans on the eve of the trip, "leaving the whole population of New York on the quay in tears at my departure."

Standing on deck as the *Germanic* steamed up the harbor to New York—in seven days, nineteen hours, still several hours off the westward record—Huxley surveyed the grand panorama; hundreds of ships, schooners, ferryboats, and barges "shoved like a child's toys against a confused jumble of buildings," as Gore Vidal has written. He asked an acquaintance about the two most conspicuous towers, the Tribune and Western Union Telegraph buildings. "Ah," Huxley told him, "this is interesting; that is America. In the Old World, the first things you see as you approach a great city are the steeples; here you see, first, centres of intelligence." He stared at the tugboats chugging up and down and across the bay. "If I were not a man I think I should like to be a tug," he commented.

A few reporters scrambled aboard to interview Huxley before Youmans, joined by William Appleton and his son, met the couple and whisked them to the publisher's estate in Riverdale, a half-hour's sail from lower Manhattan. It was the hottest summer on record, and Nettie wrote to her sister-in-law asking if they could meet in Nashville instead, to avoid the discomfort of train travel to Montgomery in late August. Scientists, educators, and Christian conservatives all regarded Huxley's visit keenly, but few ordinary Americans knew his name, and he expected traveling over long distances to be arduous enough. He was pleased and surprised during a brief sightseeing excursion to New York City when, after he announced he was planning to visit scientists in New England, the New York and New Haven Railroad promptly offered to put a private parlor car at his disposal—"a new idea of the possibilities of railway traveling," he called it.

While his wife went with friends to Saratoga, Huxley plunged into the most anticipated week of his stay: several long days examining paleontologist O. C. Marsh's skeletons at Yale's new Peabody Museum, with a side trip to see fossilized dinosaur footprints along the sandstone banks of the Connecticut River north of Springfield, Massachusetts. At about the same time that Darwin had published *Descent* and Agassiz was renewing his attack on evolution as bereft of facts, Huxley had undertaken with a Russian collaborator to assemble the fossil lineage of a single modern mammal, concentrating on the horse. It had become one of his most popular lectures—the making of the age's "exquisite running engine"—as he illustrated how from ancient five-toed, fox-sized ancestors, through larger three-toed intermediary species, and finally up through asslike dew-clawed creatures, the modern European equine arose. Where there were gaps in the fossil record, or he had trouble explaining the streamlining or toe rejection, Huxley deferred the question.

Marsh was an imposing, great-bearded figure, swaggering and ambitious. He had unearthed the fossil remains of hundreds of long-vanished species during four frantic summers collecting out west with students. He believed his own findings told a richer, fuller story. "My own explorations led me to conclusions quite different from his," he later wrote, "and my specimens seemed to prove to me conclusively that the horse originated in the New World, not the old, and that its genealogy had to be worked out here. With some hesitation, I laid the whole matter frankly before Huxley, and he spent nearly two days going over my specimens with me and testing each point that I made."

Marsh knew that Huxley planned to discuss the evolution of the horse during his three lectures in New York near the end of his trip, and he meant to be central to that discussion. He was locked in a celebrated scientific battle with another paleontologist, Edward Drinker Cope of Philadelphia, that the press called "the Great Bone War" or "the Great Bone Rush"—two equally apt analogies describing the rapacious rivalry over the prehistoric spoils and relics vanishing, like the Indian and the buffalo, before the onslaught of westward expansion. Marsh had been a Yale senior when *Origin* was published, and though he was only six years younger than Huxley, he revered Huxley's intellect and status as "Darwin's bulldog." In his "relentless, methodical, acquisitive way," as historian Mark Jaffe notes, Marsh had pieced together a sixty-million-year history documenting thirty different species of quadrupeds in three families that "was not just a tale of the evolution of anatomy but of the transformation of the earth itself."

According to Marsh's theory, the early ancestors of the modern horse were built low to the ground and walked on several outspread toes, to accommodate travel on the soft, moist floor of primeval forests. As grass species flourished, diets shifted from foliage to grasses, leading to the development of larger and more durable teeth. Meantime, as the prairies emerged, the horse's predecessors required longer legs to outrun predators. Gradually some toes lifted from the ground so that the weight of the body was shifted onto just one of them—the third. "It was not simply a story of specialization as Huxley thought," Jaffe wrote, "but rather one of the complex interrelationship between environment and species, and also a tale of trial and error."

Darwinians had learned, in large part from engaging with Agassiz, not to rely too heavily on fossil records, which were well recognized as hosting too many dead ends, anomalies, and missing links. And Huxley resisted departing from his own popular theory. He pored over box after box of Marsh's bones, assiduously, challenging him again and again, calling for a hoof from this ancient species or a molar from that one. With each challenge, Marsh beckoned an assistant to fetch another crate. "I believe you are a magician," Huxley finally blurted. "Whatever I want you just conjure up." Huxley declared the collection "the most wonderful thing I ever saw," telling Marsh: "The more I think of it, the more clear it is that your great work is the settlement of the pedigree of the horse."

"He then informed me," Marsh recalled, "that all this was new to him, and that my facts demonstrated the evolution of the horse beyond question, and that for the first time indicated the direct line of descent of an existing animal."

Possessing for the first time physical proof of evolution, Huxley lit out for the rest of his trip with a heightened urgency. No other Victorian scientist proselytized more for science itself, nor was any more connected to the view that evolution disproved the argument from design. Huxley claimed to be agnostic, a term he coined, on the question of God; that is, it simply was impossible to know. Though he was politic enough not to lecture a Christian nation in the throes of a depression, a political tempest, a moral and intellectual revolution, and an evangelical revival on matters of faith, Marsh's bones convinced him that the moment was ripe here for a bold public leap in favor of facts, reason, and education. The foremost expositor of godless evolution, Huxley prepared to rebut Hodge's challenge: *What Is Darwinism?* It is America.

Rejoined by Nettie, Huxley left New Haven on August 15 for Newport, where he spent three days with Alexander Agassiz, an authority on
starfish who, having made a fortune developing a copper mine in Michigan, donated $1 million to sustain his father's beloved museum at Har-
vard. Huxley was not much given to luxury, but his fervent reception by
men of wealth and power—the governor of Connecticut traveled to see
him, telling reporters afterward that he was "affable" and surprisingly of
"the commercial or mercantile type"—proved as pleasant as it was unexpected. "We may be rich yet," he told Nettie.

In Cambridge, Huxley visited Gray. No two members of Darwin's
inner circle stood further apart on the religious implications of species
transmutation, but Youmans, hoping to capitalize on Gray's fame and
credibility among orthodox Christians, had invited him to assemble his
essays and reviews on evolution into a book, *Darwiniana*, which Appleton planned to publish to coincide with Huxley's New York lectures. Gray
had prepared for it a final chapter on teleology in which he suggested a
new analogy for reconciling blind chance and providence—reversing, not
inadvertently, the one Darwin posed in his autobiography: "Natural selection is not the wind which propels the vessel, but the rudder which, by
friction, now on this side and now on that, shapes the course . . . variation
answers to the wind . . . the *Divine* it is which holds together all Nature."

Gray and Huxley were cordial, but while Gray "tried hard" to entertain
him, as Gray's biographer A. Hunter Dupree wrote, it was Fiske who
"managed to monopolize [Huxley's] time while he was in and near
Boston."

Huxley, beginning to feel as if the country was "killing me with kindness," fled the city as soon as he could, he and Nettie taking their private
rail car to Athol, in the north central part of the state. From there Fiske
took them by carriage to the big rambling summer home of his brother-
in-law, overlooking the placid eighteenth-century green in the village of
Petersham, where it was cool enough at night for a fire. For two days they
wandered the countryside, and after supper, with other guests including
Hawthorne's daughter and Emerson's widow, they played charades. Fiske
had never seen Huxley—whose massive head, piercing gray eyes, thick
gray whiskers, compressed lips, and air of perpetual gravity seldom gave
away his drollness—more playful. Before departing for a meeting of the
American Association for the Advancement of Science in Buffalo, Hux-

ley left in the guestbook a signed sketch of two apes—one dangling from a tree limb entwined by a snake and handing a piece of fruit to the other on the ground. He titled it:

THE TRUE HISTORY OF ADAM AND EVE
(*from specimens in New Haven; Marsh's collection*)

SPEAKING WITHOUT PREPARED REMARKS, Huxley told the assembled scientists at the Tifft House hotel in Buffalo: "I am not by nature a man of many words, and have thought the highest eloquence was in condensing what one has to say." Marsh had preceded him to the city, eager to announce Huxley's benediction upon his theory of horse ancestry, but Huxley preferred to wait until his lectures in New York to make a thorough presentation, and he confined his comments on evolution to a flat statement that the theory had now been proven as fact. Spencer's X-Club nickname was Xhaustive; Huxley's was Xalted. He would not be goaded into haste.

"I have heard a great deal from your own writers about the degeneracy of the present American stock from the primitive English type," Huxley quipped, acknowledging the national longing to know what sophisticated Europeans thought of American society. "The late Nathaniel Hawthorne used an expression which rather rubbed us; he spoke of the distinction between English and American women, and he told us English women were rather too teethy. Now that was his expression, not mine."

Huxley gracefully turned his hosts' insecurities back on themselves. He referred to an oft-heard hypothesis that differences in their two races—English and American—derived from climatic conditions causing a reversion to aboriginal behavior, but said he had only noticed such regression in the form of extreme hospitality, a well-recognized savage trait. "I have visited your wigwams—and they are pretty good wigwams too," he said, to laughter. "You entertain us with your best, and not only give us your best, but are not quite happy unless we take the spoons and plates away with us."

Huxley cited another striking difference: in England, men of wealth amassed estates and founded families; in America, they founded colleges. As for the notion that Americans had to visit Europe to discover antiquities, he noted, he had found much older and more compelling objects here: Marsh's fossil collection. "There does not exist in Europe anything approaching it," he told the audience,

> as regards extent, and the geological time it covers, and the light it throws on the wonderful problem of evolution . . . which has occupied so much attention since Darwin's great work on species.
>
> Before the gathering of such materials as those to which I have referred, evolution was more a matter of speculation and argument, though we who adhered to the doctrine had good grounds for our belief.
>
> Now, things have changed, and it has become a matter of fact and history. The history of evolution as a matter of fact is now distinctly traceable. We know it has happened, and what remains is the subordinate question of how it has happened.

Setting the stage for the rest of his tour—and to get some rest before the grueling thirty-hour train ride through Cincinnati to Nashville, the only hinterland city where he would deliver a public address—Huxley joined a scientific party including Youmans and Marsh for a week at Niagara Falls, where he led an expedition to the gorge under the falls and prepared his upcoming lectures. The Right Reverend A. Cleveland Coxe, Episcopal bishop of Buffalo, denounced him as a "gratuitous assailant of revelation" and "an intellectual suicide." But otherwise Huxley's remarks sparked little protest even in the religious press, which was preoccupied with the imminent arrival of the urban revivalist Dwight Lyman Moody and his chorister Ira David Sankey, who since February had produced riots and mass faintings in city after city promoting "instant salvation" by rejecting science and reason in favor of "something so much better"— spiritual but unemotional Christian conversion. A Chicago shoe merchant turned soul saver, Moody shunned the tent-show staples of writhing, shaking, and going into convulsions. "We don't want your money," he beseeched adoring crowds, "we want your souls."

IN NASHVILLE, instead of pressing his case for evolution directly, Huxley apologized "for being a sort of fanatic in this matter" and begged forgiveness "if I ride my hobbyhorse before you." He urged improved elementary education and scientific literacy, so that people might decide for themselves the validity of new discoveries. "It is quite useless for persons who have not been so trained, to attempt to pick out of books what is said of these matters—they will only cut their fingers by using tools which they are not competent to handle."

This was Huxley's driving theme—the man- and society-building usages of scientific truth. Five weeks' travel in America convinced him of nothing so much as the need for advanced practical ideas for promoting intelligence and keeping society informed, to accompany the country's astonishing wealth and breakneck growth. He and Nettie traveled overnight to Baltimore, where he had been invited to deliver the inaugural address at Johns Hopkins, the nation's new temple of organized science, and where he reunited with Marsh. Railroad moguls had organized the new institution to stem the flow of advanced students to Europe, and they welcomed Huxley's imprimatur. "Boom money," as his biographer Adrian Desmond noted, "was bouncing Baltimore into the vanguard of American higher education . . . Hopkins professors were to be paid to research, and, with the largest bequest in U.S. history, paid well. The trustees saw friend Huxley as their man."

Huxley learned that the New York papers wanted advance copies of his address, which was not on the subject of evolution but on university education. Eager to promote his evolution lectures, he accommodated the press by dictating the Baltimore lecture beforehand to one of the reporters to take down in shorthand. When the printed copy was returned to him, however, too late, on flimsy paper, he already was seated alongside the governor, the mayor, the Japanese minister, federal officials, and other dignitaries on the Hopkins stage, facing a crowd of more than two thousand, and unable to read a word of it. Huxley strained to recall his exact words so as not to deviate from the printed versions, delivering an oddly stilted and flat oration until, at the three-quarter mark, he recovered full force. "I cannot say that I am in the slightest degree impressed by your bigness, or your material resources, as such," he said, continuing,

Size is not grandeur, and territory does not make a nation.
The great issue, about which hangs a true sublimity, and the terror of overhanging fate, is what are you going to do with all these things?

What is to be the end to which these are to be the means? You are making a novel experiment in politics on the greatest scale which the world has yet seen. Forty millions at your first centenary, it is reasonably to be expected that, at the second, these states will be occupied by two hundred millions of English-speaking people, spread over an area as large as that of Europe, and with climates and interests as diverse as those of Spain and Scandinavia, England and Russia.

You and your descendants will have to ascertain whether this great mass will hold together under the forms of a republic, and the despotic reality of universal suffrage; whether state's rights will hold out against centralization, without separation; whether centralization will get the better, without actual or disguised monarchy; whether shifting corruption is better than permanent bureaucracy; and as population thickens in your great cities, and the pressure of want is felt, the gaunt spectre of pauperism will stalk among you, and communism and socialism will claim to be heard.

Truly America has a great future before her; great in toil, in care, and in responsibility; great in true glory if she be guided in wisdom and righteousness; great in shame if she fail. I cannot understand why other nations should envy you, or be blind to the fact that it is for the highest interest of mankind that you should succeed; but the one condition of success, your sole safeguard, is the moral worth and intellectual clearness of the individual citizen. Education cannot give these, but it may cherish them and bring them to the front of whatever station of society they are to be found; and the universities ought to be, and may be, the fortresses of the higher life of the nation.

Widely reproduced, then quickly sermonized upon from pulpits across America, the speech catapulted Huxley to instant, widespread fame. *"The great issue . . . is what are you going to do with all these things?"* On the verge of the first genuinely contested national election in sixteen years, the country was about to learn. The Democrats, having nominated the reform New York governor Samuel Tilden at their convention in St. Louis, launched their fall campaign with a promise to curb the excesses, concentration of power, and immorality of the postwar era. Huxley's question seemed to presage a historic choice.

The next day he and Nettie boarded a private rail car for four hours of sightseeing in Washington, where the unfinished Capitol rotunda hovered, wooden scaffolding half exposed, like a huge hatching egg over the sweltering, deserted city. Though they were scheduled to stop next in Philadelphia to tour the exposition, Huxley made no comment about it in either of the two small daybooks he carried, leaving the question of whether he thought it could explain anything he hadn't already seen.

THEY ARRIVED IN NEW YORK, at the Westminster Hotel, on September 15. Nettie felt "tired and stupefied" by the constant "sightseeing & traveling," but Youmans promptly arrived, and Marsh, and the crush of people who wanted to see Huxley became so great that she had to guard their sitting room for five hours, barring all entry, so he could finish writing his lectures. Youmans wrote to Spencer: "His tour has been a laborious ovation rather than a restful vacation, for which he can blame nobody but himself. If he had been less good-natured he would have been more free."

The *Times,* which reported daily on what prominent guests were staying at which hotels, commented in an article on his arrival: "That Prof. Huxley will be heartily welcomed on Monday evening there can be no doubt," adding, "The religious mind of our people is becoming gradually convinced that Darwinism is in no way opposed to theism." The paper echoed the point the next day with a highly favorable two-column review of Gray's *Darwiniana* that began: "When the Darwinian hypothesis was first put forth many of the 'weaker brethren' felt there was not only an assault on revelation but upon religion itself. They dreaded that if the theory should ever be made probable or prove true the famed 'argument from design' would be weakened or overthrown."

As Youmans anticipated, Gray's religiosity gave wide cover to Huxley's agnosticism and reputation for "parson skinning," and the audiences that attended the packed lectures at Chickering Hall, at Fifth Avenue and Eighteenth Street, were "of New York's best society," according to the *Tribune.* English workingmen who comprised Huxley's legions back home readily enjoyed the subtleties of his sardonic glances, but even learned and sophisticated New Yorkers were accustomed to the broad rhetoric and theatrical gyrations of lyceum speakers, and Huxley the first night was thought to have underperformed. By referring to Milton's *Paradise Lost*, with its epic descriptions of the Creation, instead of the biblical version, he sidestepped offending religious conservatives directly.

Two nights later, Huxley traced in detail the known evidence favoring an evolutionary succession from dinosaurs to birds. Behind him were pictures, blown up under Marsh's supervision, of sensational extinct species unearthed across America—a large swimming bird with teeth dug up in western Kansas that Marsh described as "essentially a carnivorous swimming ostrich," a chicken-sized dinosaur that walked on its hind legs, shared anatomical features with birds of the same era, and made birdlike tracks that he had seen fossilized in New England sandstone on his side trip up the Connecticut with Marsh. Unlike the case with Marsh's horses, the evidence here was tantalizing but incomplete, and Huxley declined to overstate it. There was no indication, for instance, whether the latter creature had feathers, "but, if it did, it would be hard indeed to say whether it should be called a reptilian bird or an avian reptile."

"I do not think, ladies and gentlemen, that I need insist on the value of evidence of this kind," Huxley said. "You will observe that, though it does not prove that birds have originated from reptiles by the gradual modification of the ordinary reptile into a dinosauran form, and so into a bird, it does show that the process may possibly have taken place; and it does show that there existed in former times creatures which filled up one of the largest gaps existing in animated nature, and that was exactly the kind of evidence which I stated to you at starting we are bound to meet within the rocks, if the hypothesis of evolution be correct."

On Friday night, Huxley delivered his final address—on the evolution of the horse. "You are all aware," he told his audience, "that when this country was discovered by Europeans, there were found no traces of horses in any part of the American continent. . . . Nevertheless, as soon as geology began to be pursued in this country, it was found that remains of horses, like horses existing at the present day, are found in abundance in the last superficial deposits."

Digging deeper, Huxley said, American paleontologists had found new and curious animals. Here he praised Marsh—and America. "I have had the advantage of glancing over his collections at New Haven, and I can undertake to say that so far as my knowledge extends, there is nothing in any way comparable to them in extent, and the care with which the remains have been got together or their scientific importance." Drawing patriotic applause, he then walked his audience through the evolution of the horse, and predicted confidently at the end that as older geological strata were explored, a specimen of an earlier ancestor would turn up.

"This is what I mean, ladies and gentlemen, by demonstrative evidence of evolution," Huxley concluded, speaking as much on behalf of science as of Darwinism.

> An inductive hypothesis is said to be demonstrated when the facts are shown to be in accordance with it. If this is not scientific proof, there can be no inductive conclusions which can be said to be scientifically proved, and the Doctrine of Evolution at the present time rests upon as secure a foundation as the Copernican theory of the motion of the heavenly bodies.

Not all were convinced. Though the audience cheered him, the *Times,* so welcoming a week earlier, charged in a harsh editorial that Huxley had presented no new ideas, and no real proof. "Mr. HUXLEY himself stands on the baseless fabric of a fancy or a dream in his 'Evolution,' " the paper told readers:

> The absence of all link between man and the simian in fossil remains, the high character of the skulls of the oldest human relics, the difficulty of obtaining the survival of a hairless creature under natural selection, the obstinate difficulty now in crossing even related varieties, and the fact that no authentic instance is afforded among animals of a new species arising from hybrids, all are objections which have not been fairly met, and which it cannot be said that the English Professor has fully answered.

Amid champagne toasts afterward at the Westminster, Youmans, as always, sought to capitalize on the moment by proposing to assemble the lectures as soon as possible into book form with Marsh's illustrations. By 8:30 the next morning, the *Tribune* issued a ten-cent commemorative containing all of Huxley's speeches. Huxley received $4,800 for the three lectures, and seemed greatly pleased, if exhausted, as Youmans, Appleton, and Marsh saw him off two hours later aboard the liner *Celtic,* which for twelve days tossed about on stormy seas. Huxley, rebellious about overcoats, strode the frigid decks until he caught a cold and for three days lay in his bunk wrapped in linseed-and-mustard poultices. On returning to England, faced right away with more lecturing, he wrote hurriedly to Marsh, "I am thinking of discoursing on the birds with teeth. Have you anything new to tell on that subject? I have explicit faith in the inexhaustibility of the contents of those boxes."

Huxley's faith was promptly rewarded. By the end of November, Marsh told him that he had indeed discovered the "five-toed dawn horse" that Huxley had predicted in his last lecture—not out west, but in an unopened crate. "I had him 'corralled' in the basement of our museum when you were there," Marsh told him, "but he was so covered with Eocene mud that I did not know him from [his successor] Orohippus. I promise you his grandfather in time for your next Horse Lecture if you will give me proper notice."

DESPITE HIS GRIEF, Schurz cultivated a major role in the race for president, crafting with Hayes his acceptance speech and becoming a close political adviser and popular stump surrogate. "Unless I am very much mistaken the Cincinnati convention has nominated our man without knowing it," he explained to Adams. As he had predicted, both parties pledged wholesale reform, to purify the nation after eight years of Republican corruption. In part because all those who held patronage jobs were expected to give two percent of their salaries to the party that had appointed them, Schurz championed civil service reform, and Hayes, despite GOP concerns that such a move would deplete party coffers, came out strongly in favor. So did Tilden, who had prosecuted machine politicians in New York and sent legendary wire-puller Boss William Tweed to jail. So narrowly did the party platforms vary that other liberals bolted for the Democrats, including Sumner, who told his students he preferred Tilden's brand of "hard money, free trade, and local self-government" to Hayes's presumed mediocrity.

Hayes doubted he could win, telling Schurz in late October, "I shall find many things to console me if defeated." Fraud and violence, especially in the South, were expected, and gubernatorial elections a month earlier had yielded Democratic victories in Indiana and West Virginia, auguring losses there, too. With the odds great that the party would surrender the White House for the first time since before Lincoln, the campaign was bitter, tightening right to the end. On the morning after the election, with ballots still being counted, and incomplete and contested voting results converging on Washington by overnight telegram, "Centennial Sam" Tilden was all but unanimously declared the victor.

It was an editor at the *Times* who first noted late on election night that, although Tilden led by more than 250,000 votes and appeared to have enough electors to win, if Hayes could claim victory in South Carolina, Louisiana, and Florida—states where the Republicans still controlled the balloting machinery—Republicans would have a one-vote victory in the Electoral College. He roused party functionaries to wire local leaders to hold their states for Hayes, who two days later revised his outlook, telling reporters: "I think we have undoubtedly been elected. That's the way it looks to me now."

The country, thrust into uncertainty and crisis, reeled. Business halted. Rumors of local and national uprisings, of militias marshaling, swirled. Grant took a train to Philadelphia to close the Centennial Exhibition with a nine-word speech, reassuring many who believed he wouldn't leave Washington if the threats were serious, but not before ordering more troops to Louisiana to ensure a fair count of votes. In spite of severe pressure from within the party, he strove to remain neutral, fearing that any Republican victory in the South that looked as if it had been compelled by federal enforcement would be "stigmatized as a fraud." He would soon quietly order three companies of artillery and troop reinforcements to Washington, as he and Congress groped toward an orderly resolution.

Schurz received word of the apparent reversal in St. Louis, where he had moved his four children into a hotel and was searching for a house. Quite sure at first that the cause was lost, he now quickly reconsidered, writing immediately to Hayes to suggest that reputable observers be sent to Louisiana to monitor the vote gathering. Hayes asked if Schurz himself could go—as Sumner would soon do for the Democrats—but he declined. After installing his children in a furnished apartment with his newly widowed mother, Schurz turned to counseling Hayes on how to win the White House without "any suspicion of unfair dealing," proposing a constitutional amendment to settle the dispute. No doubt aware that Hayes had started considering names for his cabinet, he understood that those who helped him gain office would be positioned to benefit.

By law, electors in each of the thirty-eight states cast their ballots on

December 6. But South Carolina, Louisiana, Florida, and Oregon—where the Democratic governor ruled a Republican elector ineligible because he was a federal employee—forwarded two separate election certificates to Washington. Hayes was freshly encouraged, telling Schurz, who remained skeptical, "I have no doubt that we are justly and legally entitled to the presidency." By now, conjectures were ripe regarding secret negotiations to end the standoff. Although Grant believed privately that Tilden had won, Hayes's men began discussing with Southern Democrats what they needed in order to concede defeat, and the southerners were naming a steep price: home rule, economic improvements, a new transcontinental rail system, and a cabinet post or two. Meantime, Vermont senator George Edmonds proposed turning the dispute over to the Supreme Court. Schurz, fearing Hayes's deteriorating legitimacy if the improperly certified votes were counted, urged Hayes to embrace the plan.

"We must look the undeniable fact in the face, that the Republican party is today very much morally weaker than it was on the day of the election," he counseled Hayes, "and it will grow weaker still in the same measure as it countenances arbitrary acts of power."

This time Hayes rejected Schurz's advice, leaving his letters unanswered. Tilden, fearing widespread instability if the crisis continued, called for calm, while Grant issued a declaration that "any demonstration or warlike concentration of men threatening the peace of the city or endangering the security of public property or treasure of the government would be summarily dealt with"—and vowed, if necessary, to declare martial law in Washington. He was scheduled to leave office on March 5, but a former Confederate general announced he'd been offered command of an armed force of Democratic volunteers to ensure Tilden's inauguration, and the New York papers were carrying reports about a group of Eastern Democrats forming a paramilitary unit to block Hayes from taking office. "Sixteen years after the secession crisis," historian Eric Foner observed, "Americans entered another winter of political confusion, constitutional uncertainty and talk of civil war."

NOT UNTIL LATE JANUARY did Congress enact a compromise and form an electoral commission of fifteen members, representing equally the

Democratic-controlled House, the Republican-led Senate, and the Supreme Court. Already, Hayes had begun soliciting views about his inaugural address and his cabinet, and Schurz had suggested keeping the probing Bristow at Treasury and making Beecher's defense lawyer William Evarts—whom the Republicans had now selected as their lead counsel in the electoral dispute—secretary of state. Schurz coveted the diplomatic post himself, and despite his outspokenness and unsolicited advice, Hayes liked him and valued his support. Still, Schurz understood the need for indirection, allowing friendly journalists to float his qualifications. He urged Hayes to accept the commission bill, cautioning that if Republicans defeated it, "the sentiment of the country will be so overwhelmingly against you that, if the House sets up Tilden as counter-president, as it then will certainly do, it will be no mere puppet show."

Hayes and Tilden both initially opposed the commission, Hayes believing it unconstitutional, Tilden accepting it with weary reluctance only as a last resort. "What is left but war?" he asked. Then, amid suspicions of a deal, the lone high court justice who was an independent was named to the Senate by his state legislature, delivering the Republicans an 8–7 majority on the panel. Outraged Democrats urged Tilden to declare himself elected while the military transferred more troops to the Capitol area and drilled them daily. Congressmen began carrying sidearms. Someone fired into Hayes's dining room in Columbus while his family ate supper, although no one was hit.

All Schurz's fears of illegitimate government re-arose, as did his ambitions to complete his political comeback, penetrate Hayes's inner circle, and become the first foreign-born cabinet secretary since the start of the century. So many leaders of both parties were negotiating separately on so many fronts that it was unclear who held the power to make and enforce real agreements, even as a string of one-vote victories on the commission ratcheted the inertia for a Republican victory. It seemed as if, in a warlike spasm, society was purging itself of the last of the postwar political order, which had sprung ultimately from the exigencies of ensuring the participation of freed slaves in Southern political life.

On the evening of February 26 a group of Southern Democrats secretly met with Hayes's men in Evarts's room at the black-owned Wormley Hotel in Washington, on the corner of Fifteenth and H streets near the White House. The frantic final week of Grant's term had begun, and no successor had yet been named. The last four national elections had all turned on the use, or threat, of military force; American politics seemed permanently "Mexicanized." At a House Democratic caucus a week earlier, a majority of members preemptively adopted a resolution to be inserted into a military spending bill that forbade using troops in the South without House approval. Thus the upshot of the Wormley Conference was to ratify what had already been done: granting Redemption, and the end of Reconstruction, in the two remaining states in the South where Republicans still held control, Louisiana and South Carolina. In exchange, the southerners promised to defeat their party's filibuster over accepting the last of the electoral votes that would give Hayes a 185–184 victory, see to Hayes's peaceful inauguration, safeguard the rights of Negroes, and forswear bloody reprisals. "In effect," the historian C. Vann Woodward wrote, "the Southerners were abandoning the cause of Tilden for control over two states, and the Republicans were abandoning the cause of the Negro in exchange for the peaceful possession of the Presidency."

As news of the "bargain," as it was called, traveled, Hayes and his family boarded a private rail car for Washington. Civil order prevailed—barely. The country had averted war, but at a moral price. "These are the days of humiliation, shame and mourning for every patriotic American," editor Charles A. Dana of the New York *Sun*, a staunch Democrat and Tilden man, wrote. "A man whom the people rejected at the polls has been declared president of the United States through processes of fraud. A cheat is to sit in the seat of George Washington." America's original sin—the race question—was put silently away, along with the last of the Republican commitment to solve it. Godkin rued, "The negro will disappear from the field of national politics. Henceforth the nation, as a nation, will have nothing more to do with him."

By naming Evarts secretary of state and Schurz secretary of the interior—he also appointed a former Confederate officer to a cabinet post—Hayes "passed the Republican party to its worst enemies," a friend of Grant's moaned. Schurz arrived in the capital the morning before the inauguration, and he became an immediate member of Hayes's inner circle, the stern, black-bearded general in charge of the nation's Indians, patents, lands, and pensions—the largest, most complex portfolio of any department. He faced special venom from party loyalists who derided him as "a godless German philosopher, as mercenary as he was fickle," his biographer Hans Trefousse wrote. Within three weeks, he wrote to his children that his relations with the administration couldn't be better.

Sumner, on the other hand, faced a swift and instructive reckoning as a political turncoat. Though he had twice been elected alderman as a Republican, the party now refused to support him. Although the Democrats nominated him for a third term, he lost the next election. Maintaining a keen interest in state affairs, Sumner abandoned his political career in favor of lecturing, writing, teaching, and bringing Spencer and evolution to Yale. He "had not known the rules of the game," he later wrote, "and did not want to learn them."

BALTIMORE, 1877

*The power of money has become supreme over
everything. It has secured for the class who control
it all the special privileges and special legislation
which it needs to secure its complete and absolute
domination. . . . This Power must be kept in check.
It must be broken or it will utterly crush the people.*

—New York *Sun*

ON BOARD THE SLEEPER en route to Richmond, Beecher's new lecture manager, Major J. B. Pond, received a telegram that read as follows: "No use coming. Beecher will not be allowed to speak in Richmond. No tickets sold." Despite Plymouth Church's generosity, Beecher's ordeal had left him in debt, and he had turned to the lyceum circuit for salvation, as well as to find the funds to complete the grand riverfront mansion he was building in Peekskill. The restless, depressed country, a seventh of its people out of work, reeling from a succession crisis, awaited the chance to see and hear him in the flesh. Beecher had been guaranteed as much as $1,000 a lecture.

Pond put the telegram in his pocket and told Beecher nothing about it. After completing their January southern swing, he had scheduled forty lectures in seven weeks beginning in Oswego, New York, on February 5, and boycott threats only boosted the public's curiosity. When they arrived in Richmond and the warning was repeated, the local agent abandoned the lecture. Pond rented the theater and issued bills and dodgers announcing that Beecher would appear, and on the night he spoke the theater was filled—with men only; women were barred. According to

Beecher's biographer Lyman Abbott, Pond was informed "the gallery is full of eggs."

Hoots preceded Beecher as he rose to speak. He launched a good-humored jest at the state legislature, many members of which were in the crowd. Within minutes, he had the audience laughing. Afterward, at an informal reception at his hotel, he was urged to stay and lecture a second night so women could come to hear him.

What Beecher would have to say once he won over the public was more in doubt than his ability to command attention. He did not so much lecture as preach, and his old ethical discourses on equality and the rights of women were eclipsed by events both national and personal. As in Richmond, where his most eloquent passage consisted of a tribute to the Commonwealth of Virginia—"mother of presidents"—he was confined mostly to patriotic assertions and flattering the locals.

At his Cleveland lecture, curiosity seekers offered up to $10 for standing room. In Chicago, he preached at Rev. Dwight Moody's church, the largest in the city, and ten thousand to twenty thousand people were turned away. In Madison, Wisconsin, the legislature invited him to open a session of the House with prayer, and in St. Louis he was asked to preach in the oldest church in the city, where police couldn't contain the throng trying to get in. "No event," a local pastor wrote, "not excepting even the National Democratic Convention, has awakened the general interest that was manifested in his coming." "In the balmiest days of my life," Beecher told one friend, "I never had such audiences." To another he said, "The old scandal is hardly thought of; one hears no allusion to it, and the papers do not touch it."

It wasn't quite true. In Iowa, a snarling crowd rushed his private rail car as it stopped outside Decatur. Pond grabbed a poker from the fireplace and sliced it across the face and arm of the first man through the door. Beecher lectured that night "as if nothing had happened," his biographer Debby Applegate wrote. And yet while he returned from the tour with more than $40,000, the question remained whether he was being primarily vilified or celebrated, and if so, exactly why. *The American Socialist*, which was associated with the country's most radical utopian experiment in Oneida, New York, observed that Beecher's "glorious triumph" reflected a new morality. "What is the meaning of this almost national ovation?" it asked:

Is it not a sign of enlarged liberality in the public mind toward "true inwardness" in love matters? Is it hardly possible that any body believes in Beecher's entire innocence of heart-trespass? Are not the people condoning the encroachments of religious love on matrimonial territory? Is there not a squint toward church familism?—which is one promising form of Socialism.

Since the Oneida Community's notion of "church familism" included "complex marriage," wherein every man and every woman was wed to every other, and "male continence"—a form of birth control in which teenage boys were trained by postmenopausal women not to ejaculate during and after intercourse—its members and supporters stood to gain from the perception that the nation's embrace of Beecher reflected a growing enthusiasm for free love, and that his trial exposed both Beecher's hypocrisy and the public's. Others more orthodox would have none of it. As Dana's *Sun* sneered, excoriating not only Beecher but the churchgoing, apparently forgiving public that fawned on him and flocked to see him:

Still, there is a morbid curiosity existing within the minds of many people in regard to monstrosities of every description: and the same impulse that would lead a man of low tastes to pay to see the bearded woman, or a two-headed calf, or to get a good sight of a convicted murderer, would also induce him to pay 25 or 50 cents to look upon Mr. Beecher and hear him crack his jokes upon religion and other matters.

CARNEGIE BY NOW set the terms at Edgar Thomson Steel, and he moved hard to press his advantage. He consolidated his control within the company by buying out two of his overextended partners: one who had bought into outside suppliers without telling the others, putting the firm legally at risk; the other who was sick of Carnegie and Shinn's relentless accounting regime and refusal to pay dividends now that the works was strongly profitable. A zero-defects man, Carnegie conveyed a heartless, if sunny, obsession with costs. When a manager wired "We broke all records for making steel this week," he replied, "Congratulations! Why not do it every week?" When an agent landed a big contract: "Good boy! Next!" "The gravest danger to Carnegie's impressive start in the steel business—the final component in the template for success, as it were—was Carnegie himself," Peter Krass writes.

With his competitors all under the same grueling pressure—new Chicago steelworks were arising quickly, cutting off western markets—the Bessemer steel men decided finally to attempt a rail pool and reluctantly invited Carnegie to join them at a meeting in Philadelphia. He prepared for it by combing through their annual reports, determining the salaries of the men who would be attending the meeting and estimating the cost to each of producing rails. At the table, he learned their proposed arrangement: Cambria 19 percent, Pennsylvania Steel 15 percent, and so on. E.T. was allotted the smallest share: 9 percent.

Carnegie stood up, raised himself to his full height, and banged on the table. He revealed that he was a stockholder in each of their companies, then went on to state the salaries and personal expenses of each of the industry elders, exposing them to embarrassment while playing them off each other. "Moreover," Carnegie announced, "Mr. Holley, the engineer who built the Edgar Thomson works, has informed me that it is the most complete and perfect in the world and will turn out steel rails at cost far lower than its competition.

"So, gentlemen," he bluffed, "you must be interested to know that I can roll steel rails at $9 a ton. If Edgar Thomson Co. isn't given as high a percentage of this pool as the highest, I shall withdraw from it and undersell you all in the market—and make good money doing it."

No pool emerged. Carnegie realized that some alliance in pricing was inevitable and began at once to pursue a partnership with Cambria. "I know there is more profit for each of us in harmonious working than in fierce competition for every order that comes on the market," he wrote to its president, "and I am disposed to try any plan you think likely to make." By autumn, his relationship with Cambria prospering, he turned next to Bethlehem Steel, in Pittsburgh, touring its operations and afterward writing a flattering note to its president. "I might say that everything I saw," he concluded, "tended to convince me that on the Darwinian principal of the survival of the fittest, you have no reason to fear the future."

SPENT AND DEPLETED after four brutal years, the railroads—America itself, it seemed—verged on a general failure. On July 11, the board of directors of the Baltimore and Ohio, noting that the continuing "depression in the general business interests in the country" was hurting earnings, voted a 10 percent pay cut throughout the line—the second reduction since January. Brakemen, who risked dismemberment and death earning $1.75 for a twelve-hour day and who had to pay their own return fares after their jobs took them hundreds of miles from home, went on strike. Conductors earning $2.78 per day and firemen making $1.90 joined them. In Martinsburg, West Virginia, workers walked off the job, uncoupled the engines, ran them into the roundhouse, and pledged to stop all traffic until the cut was reversed. When a supportive crowd gathered, the company asked the governor for military protection. Days later, a militiaman shot and killed a striker.

With six hundred freight trains clogging the Martinsburg yards, the governor applied to President Hayes for federal troops. The U.S. Army numbered twenty-five thousand soldiers, down from a high of about one million during the war, and most of them were deployed against the Indians. Hayes as governor had used state guardsmen to restore order after labor troubles, and he now ordered two small detachments to Martinsburg. Once the trains resumed running, strikers in Baltimore assembled at the Camden yards, three miles from the city, and halted them there, and the Maryland governor ordered out that state's militia.

Baltimore erupted. Across the teeming city, thousands of poor families lived in cellars and drank contaminated water. Liquid sewage ran through the streets, and each summer children got sick in alarming numbers: 139 babies died during the first week of July alone. After an angry mob of more than two thousand men, women, and children surrounded the armory, 150 militiamen marched on the crowd, killing nine people and wounding many more. Again, Hayes replied with a presidential proclamation and ordered in five hundred soldiers. During the next several days, as the strike spread from state to state, shutting down transit, crippling commerce, and threatening civil order, he also sent troops to Pittsburgh and Chicago.

"The sixth and seventh days of the revolution," *Harper's Weekly* reported, "were the darkest and bloodiest of all." Local authorities in Pittsburgh tried to arrest strikers at the Union Depot and were met by a shower of stones and a revolver shot fired into the ranks. For the next three minutes, guardsmen shot into the crowd, killing sixteen and wounding many more. Then, as news of the slaughter spread through the city, the streets filled with rolling-mill hands and other workers who broke into a gunworks and captured two hundred rifles and additional small arms. By nightfall, twenty thousand people squared off at the large roundhouse at Twenty-eighth and Liberty streets against eight hundred soldiers with Gatling guns and two other large battery pieces. Over the next two days, amid running street battles, seventy-nine buildings were burned to the ground, twenty-four people were killed (including four soldiers), and a nascent general strike developed as mill workers, car workers, miners, and laborers all walked out. Carnegie's steelworks was briefly affected. The entire national guard of nine thousand men was called out. In Chicago and St. Louis, workingmen's parties with large followings among immigrants sponsored militant protests and called for nationalizing the railroads.

In Europe, Karl Marx wrote optimistically to Friedrich Engels that the summer's Great Railroad Strike was "the first uprising against the oligarchy of capital which had developed since the civil war" and predicted that, though he was sure it would be defeated, it "could very well be the point of origin for the creation of a serious worker's party in the United States." Hayes's decision, meanwhile, to send federal troops to restore order crossed a new threshold: less than a year after Grant had refused to deploy government forces to protect lands deeded to the Indians by treaty or enforce the political participation of blacks or ensure fair elections, his successor for the first time in U.S. history used them to suppress strikes.

Like many religious leaders, Beecher, back in Brooklyn, denounced the violence flaring coast to coast. He sermonized at great length on the elementary principles of political economy, which he believed required that in a free market no man ought to be guaranteed work if another man can do the same job and is willing to do it for less. "The necessities of the great railroad companies demanded that there should be a reduction of wages," Beecher declared. "There must be a continual shrinkage until things come back to the gold standard, and wages, as well as greenbacks, provisions and property, must share in it."

"It was true that a dollar a day was not enough to support a man and five children, if a man would insist on smoking and drinking beer,"

Beecher went on. "Was not a dollar a day enough to buy bread? Water costs nothing." There was uneasy laughter in the pews. "Man cannot live by bread, it is true; but the man who cannot live on bread and water is not fit to live," he said. "When a man is educated away from the power of self-denial, he is falsely educated. A family may live on good bread and water in the morning, water and bread at midday, and good bread and water at night." Here the laughs grew continuous.

"Thousands would be very glad of a dollar a day, and it added to the sin of the men on strike for them to turn round and say to those men, 'You can do so, but you shall not.' " There may be cases of special hardship, Beecher said, but the great laws of political economy could no more be denied than the laws of God. And so in the end the men on strike would be defeated, trade would resume, and prosperity would be restored.

Beecher exalted workingmen; it was the unions and communists that he despised. Flush from his triumphal return to the national stage, he withstood the predictable scorn of the strikers and their sympathizers, who thought his widely reprinted "bread and water" sermon sanctimonious and hypocritical—profoundly unchristian. More lacerating were the barbs of established opinion. "Suicidal and the part of a lunatic," the New York *World* called the sermon. By the next Sunday, July 29, thirty plainclothesmen mingled with the packed congregation at Plymouth Church as Beecher sought to explain himself amid threats and condemnation. His call to let nature take its course in eliminating the unfit through the merciless discipline of the depression had become Beecher's next great theme, which he hoped would put the Tilton scandal finally to rest. Once again he consoled his followers that the present economic order, brutal as it was, was God's will and His way. The poor, he said, must "reap the misfortunes of inferiority."

"Is the great working class oppressed?" Beecher asked. "Yes, undoubtedly it is. . . . God had intended the great to be great and the little to be little. . . . The trade union, originated under the European situation, destroys liberty. . . . I do not say that a dollar a day is enough to support a working man. But it is enough to support a man."

IN EARLY APRIL, Marsh got a letter from Arthur Lakes, an Oxford-educated Episcopalian minister, schoolmaster, and part-time geologist, about a find Lakes had made while rambling around the sandstone hog-backs in the little town of Morrison, Colorado, fifteen miles west of Denver: "I discovered in company with a friend, Mr. Beckwith of Connecticut, some enormous bones apparently a vertebra & a humorus bone of some gigantic saurian in the upper Jurassic or lower Cretaceous." Fossil bones of large extinct reptiles had been found in England and Western Europe for more than fifty years, and fragmentary dinosaur remains had been unearthed in Montana. But Marsh's fossilized horses and birds with teeth, addressing more directly the central question of evolution, had produced far more excitement, consuming his attention. He at first neglected Lakes's note, which included two sketches of the bones and geologic cross sections of the hills, as well as a follow-up letter about another bone Lakes had discovered; a femur fourteen inches across at its base, which Lakes calculated had belonged to an animal "not less than sixty to seventy feet" long.

Lakes shipped some of the bones to Marsh—more than a ton by mid-May—in the hope that Marsh would contract with him to continue digging. Still with no answer, he also sent some vertebrae to Marsh's arch-foe, Edward Drinker Cope, who pressed Lakes to send along the skull and teeth that went with them and who promised "pecuniary aid in continuing the work." When Marsh heard of the correspondence between Lakes and Cope, he decided that the Morrison region warranted interest after all, sending Lakes a check for $100 and wiring his chief collector, Benjamin Mudge, to proceed there at once from another excavation in Kansas—although not before Lakes had crated two skulls and some teeth and shipped them to Cope in Philadelphia. On June 29, Mudge arrived on horseback, promptly hired Lakes and two assistants for the summer, and instructed Lakes to telegraph Cope to ask for his fossils back. Marsh took no chances, hurriedly dispatching his most trusted aide to Philadelphia. "Please say to Prof. that the fossil [sic] are now the property of Yale College," he instructed.

Marsh beat Cope to become the first scientist to describe a new and gigantic extinct land beast to rival in size the great sea creatures, announcing in the July 1 issue of the *American Journal of Science* the discovery of what he called *Titanosaurus montanus,* estimated to be fifty feet in length. By July 14, Mudge and Lakes had shipped another 2,500 pounds of bones to New Haven, and in early August they extracted the remains of a dinosaur even larger than *Titanosaurus*—Marsh named it *Apatosaurus,* "deceptive lizard." With Cope hastily announcing new species just as spectacular from a fossil field a hundred miles to the south near Canon City—he claimed one animal perched on its hind legs could reach 130 feet in the air, grazing from the treetops—the rush was on throughout the territory for new beds to quarry.

In late July, Marsh received another unsolicited offer from two would-be collectors—"Harlow" and "Edwards"—announcing the discovery of some large fossil bones in the Wyoming Territory. The note was cagey and misleading, written by a pair of railroad men who thought they might make a lot of money and who, wary of exposing the exact location of their find, used fake names and rode more than fifty miles to hand the letter to the station agent in person. (Marsh, stealthy and suspicious, routinely instructed his own assistants to communicate in code in order to throw off Cope and his operatives.) The letter writers referred to a shoulder blade measuring four feet eight inches and a vertebra measuring two and a half feet around, pledged to send a few fossils at their own expense, and concluded: "We would be pleased to hear from you, as you are well-known as an enthusiastic geologist, and a man of means, both of which we are desirous of finding—more especially the latter." Suspecting more dinosaur bones, this time Marsh responded promptly, urging the men to ship the materials to New Haven.

While awaiting shipment, Marsh traveled to Nashville, the most anticipated speaker at the yearly meeting of the American Association for the Advancement of Science, which he served as vice president. There were perhaps three thousand trained scientists in America, but few who were truly distinguished, and Marsh's elevation to the fraternity of Huxley and Darwin conferred on him a new standing which he now aimed to exploit. He lectured for an hour on "Vertebrate Life in America," dismissing in the process the last gasp of resistance among native scientists toward Darwinism. "[I] am sure I need offer here no argument for evolution," he said, "since to doubt evolution to-day is to doubt science, and science is only another name for truth." He went on to conclude:

> In this long history of ancient life, I have said nothing of what Life itself is. And for the best of reasons, because I know nothing. Here at

present our ignorance is dense, and yet we need not despair. Light, Heat, Electricity, and Magnetism, Chemical Affinity, and Motion, are now considered different forms of the same force; and the opinion is rapidly gaining ground that Life, or vital force, is only another phase of the same power. Possibly the great mystery of life may thus be solved, but whether it be or not, a true faith in Science knows no limit to its search for Truth.

The first crates of dinosaur bones from Como Bluff, a prominent ridge along the Union Pacific line near Cheyenne, arrived at the basement of the Peabody Museum by mid-October. Marsh immediately identified a leg bone and a piece of a shoulder blade as coming from a large creature similar to the Morrison fossils. The railroad men told him in a letter that they had unearthed another fifteen hundred pounds of bones of every description and "discovered the bed of two more animals which we judge to be of the same kind." Marsh wasted no time in answering: "Bones came today," he wired them. "Send rest with all small pieces." But it was their next letter that drew Marsh unreservedly into the fray. "We are keeping our shipment of fossils to you as secret as possible," the two men wrote, "as there are plenty of men looking for such things and if they could trace us they could find discoveries which we have already made and which we do not desire to have known."

Disturbed by the warning that Cope's men might soon invade the area, Marsh dispatched to Como Bluff another collector from his Kansas operation, who after two days reported: "Canon City and Morrison are simply nowhere in comparison with this locality both as regards perfection, accessibility, and quantity. . . . [The bones are] magnificently preserved and scattered for six or seven miles. The shales are clean and exposed and it will be the grandest place imaginable to hunt for small specimens." Fearing that "Harlow" and "Edwards" might be lured away by other parties, and with winter descending, Marsh at once handwrote a contract pledging them to

work for Prof. Marsh for one year from date collecting and shipping vertebrate fossils in the region around Como, Wyoming and vicinity, to take all reasonable precautions to keep all other collectors not authorized by Prof. Marsh out of the region and to use their best efforts in every way to promote Prof. Marsh's interests for the sum of ninety dollars per month each.

Marsh, unlike Carnegie, viewed competition as zero-sum, win or lose. Science and America were conjoining in the West to produce, and unearth, untold abundance, and those who controlled the territory controlled the future. Dinosaurs promised perhaps little in the way of understanding the vital force that Marsh called life, but their monumentality made them a kind of living version of the great Corliss engine: an iconic public sensation.

While winter set in hard over Wyoming, a glittering celebration was held in New York for the opening of the Museum of Natural History. The building, founded by a special act of the state legislature, formed one twelfth of the proposed structure, which was to frame a quadrangle in the West Seventies, directly on Central Park. Guests mingled amid a stuffed camel from Armenia, a moose from Nova Scotia, an elk from the Rocky Mountains. The main hall on the second floor was occupied with stuffed birds from France and the South American collections of the German prince Maximilian. Hayes delivered the formal address. Marsh received admiring applause as he was introduced to speak on behalf of American science.

"The opening of this museum," he began, "is an important event in the annals of natural science. In all that pertains to ancient life, the Western Continent has countless treasures that are unknown in other lands. This museum will fail of its highest good unless the workrooms in the upper stories are made the most important elements of the whole. . . . If the museum founded to-day does not take an important part in this great work it will not do justice to its founders or to its opportunities."

SINCE THE PUBLICATION of the first volume of *The Principles of Sociology* the previous June, Spencer had conceived of a new approach for distributing the second volume. All his previous work had been serialized for subscribers, but with his international sales growing and the success of *The Study of Sociology*, he now began "entertaining the thought of preliminary publication in chapters," he told Youmans in May. Spencer was about to examine the role of government and the evolution of various forms of social control, beginning with the influence of ceremonial institutions. "The subjects will be popular and novel, as well as instructive, and will bear detachment in the shape of magazine-articles, under the titles of 'Mutilations,' 'Presents,' 'Obeisances,' 'Salutations,' 'Titles,' 'Badges,' 'Dresses,' etc.," he wrote. "I shall probably propose them to Morley for the *Fortnightly*, and they would probably suit you also." As he prepared the series of articles over the next six months, arrangements were made for simultaneous publication in France, Germany, Italy, Hungary, and Russia.

During the summer, Spencer busied himself with "entertainments," seeking respite from the rank air of London as well as a fuller social life. Well-off and profitable at last, thanks to Youmans and *The Study of Sociology*, he resolved to enjoy the privileges of success. Picnics and "water parties" given by his friends in the country had been very pleasant, and he decided: "Why should not I give a picnic?" He selected a hilltop in the Surrey countryside and invited more than a dozen friends. "The experiment was a success," he wrote in his autobiography, "but it created considerable surprise. One of the ladies, I remember, could not refrain from expressing her astonishment—'A philosopher, and giving a picnic!' She exhibited afresh what I have before remarked on: she identified philosophy with disregard of pain and contempt for pleasures.

"Picnics," Spencer continued, discussing the subject at length,

generally drag a little towards the close; and to avoid the dragging I adopted the device of changing the scene. The carriages were ordered to fetch us between 5 and 6, and in them we drove to the Oatlands-Park Hotel. After an hour or so spent by some in playing a game of one kind or another, and by some in rambling about the grounds, we went indoors for a "high tea." The animation was thus kept up to the last. A like routine was followed on subsequent occasions, which occurred annually until my bad health compelled desistance.

He visited the Leweses, who had just bought a country house. Often he'd urged them to stop reading to each other at night and get a billiard table instead: "They were deaf to my arguments," he wrote. Now, he was delighted to see they'd taken up lawn tennis, recalling: "It is a great mistake for adults, and especially for adults who work their brains much, to give up sports and games. The maxim on which I have acted, and the maxim which I have often commended to my friends is—Be a boy as long as you can."

Rheumatism prompted him to stop on his way north in Buxton, a spa town in Derbyshire, and from there he went to Whitby to visit the Huxleys, who were about to spend the fall there. He traveled on by excursion steamer, train, and carriage to Ardtornish, a rolling enclave of estates on a peninsula on the west coast of Scotland where he intended to fish, stalk deer, and shoot grouse. "Have I, or have I not, named the fact that yachting had become one of the recreations at Ardtornish?" he recalled in his memoir, detailing the trip. A friend, Valentine Smith, invited him for a cruise on a private 450-ton steam yacht on which eight passengers were attended by a crew of twenty-one. Returning to port, the vessel went aground. As the passengers scrambled into lifeboats, it heeled over and began to sink. "Spite of all protests," Spencer wrote, "Mr. Smith, with the daring characteristic of the family, insisted on going on board again to get the ship's papers and other valuables; and presently returned, bringing, among other things, a quantity of wraps for the ladies."

In early September, Spencer prepared to return to London, writing to Youmans from Ardtornish: "The last week has been doing me great good." In the city for the fall to meet with authors and foreign publishers and to review manuscripts, Youmans reported to his brother William a month later: "Mr. Spencer, I think, looks extremely well, but he cannot keep steadily at his work." As ever, Spencer complained of being too racked by insomnia and illness to go on much further, and he confessed that he was thinking of accelerating his next project, the evolution of ethics. The urgency of the times, the pressure presented by others like Darwin, Huxley, and Fiske weighing in, and his own fear of giving out completely before stating his views on the "moral sense" now impelled him to jump ahead.

"It is probable that slight circumstances derange him more now than formerly," Youmans continued in his letter:

> He talks of the possibility of his not being able to get through with
> his enterprise, and promises to outline some important features of
> his Principles of Morality at odd times, so that this most important
> portion of his work shall not be left blank in case of a breakdown. He
> is going very thoroughly through *The Study of Sociology*, revising it
> with a view to style, proposing to make it his most perfect work

in this respect. It is funny that a volume that I bullied him into preparing should be chosen for this honour. It is interesting to look over the volume to see what thorough work he is making with it; every page is blackened with erasures and slashings.

Youmans found autumn in London unusually dry and bracing, until the damp cold set in in midmonth and he, too, succumbed. His right wrist began to ache as he wrote, and within a day the pain kept him from sleeping. He told his sister: "Sunday morning I was pretty badly off and was thoroughly scared. It was so much like the old attack of inflammatory rheumatism at Saratoga that I began to contemplate another siege. I could dress myself only with great difficulty, doing everything with my left hand. My right wrist was much swollen, and it pained me acutely to touch it. Spencer was in a great fume. Lord, how he did give it to me at breakfast!"

For years there had existed between them a dynamic whereby Youmans cosseted Spencer while Spencer admonished Youmans for doing too much and neglecting his own needs. As Spencer now took charge of Youmans's care, he "forbade" him to go out, and "after preaching till he was tired about my imprudence, etc. . . . went out to a druggist's and had some liniment made, brought it in, and called 'Jeames,' the waiter, who came," Youmans told Catherine:

Then he told me to take off my coat, which with "Jeames's" help I did, and it nearly killed me. Then the servant was ordered to rub my arm with the liniment. The brute went at it and nearly killed me. It was horribly excruciating, but he kept at it, rubbing around the sore place, and finally I took it up myself, and by very gentle friction at first I was able, after a time, to increase the friction, and in an hour the acute pain was all gone.

"It is raining like great guns, and I am again forbidden to go out," Youmans continued. "It is just as well. This sitting in the house and doing nothing is a great thing, and I think it is doing me much good. Spencer went to Busk's, and put his dressing gown on me over my coat before he left, and covered my pate with his smoking cap, and so I snoozed by the fire."

Once recovered, Youmans ventured out at Spencer's insistence to see the Leweses, just back from the country. He visited Huxley, whose *American Addresses* had come out in the spring and was selling briskly, and who had completed the first book in Britain to make the case for evolution based on fossils. "So far as animals are concerned I am quite satisfied that Evolution is a historical fact," Huxley now said. "What causes brought it about is another matter." As it had not during Youmans's visit six years earlier, the "Darwin Party" had conquered British intellectual life, and Huxley's concession to God's unknowability seemed an invitation to the religiously disaffected. As Youmans returned to New York, Spencer decided to give himself a gift: a set of his own books, permanently bound.

"Why should I not treat myself to copies in handsome bindings?" I asked. So I went to the binders to consult and order. Various samples of leather were shown to me. Some I objected to as unfit in colour—too gay, perhaps, or too somber; while this was too dark, and that too light. At length the manager, seeing the kind of thing I wanted, put his mouth to the speaking tube and called—"Mr. Jones, send me some light divinity calf." The sample brought down proved to be just the thing I wanted.

CHAPTER EIGHT

BROOKLYN, 1878

> *Worship is ever the dark side of the shield, of which*
> *knowledge is the bright side.*
>
> —JOHN FISKE

ON A DAY IN MID-APRIL, Elizabeth Tilton, her hair having gone white during the past year, visited her lawyer. She handed him a personal letter and urged him to make it public as soon as possible. After two years of living in semireclusion with her mother and opening a school that quickly failed, she and Theodore were reported to be reconciling—he had inquired about summer lodgings upstate for her and the children; a desk clerk had tipped the newspapers. Tilton, like Beecher, was away lecturing. Her attorney had the letter set in type and distributed to papers across the country, which printed it the next day under page one headlines: MRS. TILTON PLEADS GUILTY, the *Times* stated.

A few weeks since, after long months of mental anguish, I told, as you know, a few friends, whom I had bitterly deceived, that the charge brought by my husband, of adultery between myself and the Rev. Henry Ward Beecher, was true, and that the lie I had lived so well for the last four years had become intolerable to me. That statement I now solemnly reaffirm, and leave the truth with God to whom also I commit myself, my children, and all who must suffer. I know full well the explanations that will be sought by many for this acknowledgment; a desire to return to my husband, insanity, malice, everything save the true and only one—my quickened conscience, and the sense of what is due to the cause of truth and justice.

The papers agreed that, unlike her offer to testify in court, the card appeared to be genuine; that is, whatever her state of mind or her motives, she seemed to have come forward on her own. They also agreed, given her previous history of confessing and then retracting her confession, she wasn't to be believed. "This weak and erring woman has so hopelessly forsworn herself as to forfeit all claim to attention or credence," the *Times* editorialized. Those who trusted in Beecher's innocence celebrated his vindication—they concluded since the case against him was based on malicious lies, this final direct accusation must exonerate him hands down. But the paper warned against such reasoning: "As for Mr. Beecher, he remains the impure and perjured man which any rational construction of his own letters proved him to be.

"There is but one thing more to be done to demonstrate beyond the possibility of doubt that Mr. Beecher is a perfectly innocent man," the *Times* commented, lampooning the tortuous logic of the majority of the Plymouth congregation, who still vigorously supported him. "Let him rise up in his pulpit next Sunday and remark that a quickening of his conscience compels him to confess that the charges of adultery and perjury heretofore made against him are completely true." As reporters hounded Elizabeth—she confirmed that the letter was real, but refused to give further details—parishioners denounced her and moved for her to be excommunicated.

Upstate in Elmira, where Beecher was set that night to lecture, Major Pond issued a fresh denial. "I believe Mr. Beecher is convinced that Mrs. Tilton is now under the absolute control of her husband, that she loves him, and that this letter of confession is the price she pays for reconciliation," Pond told reporters, "and you will see that they will be living together before three months roll around." Beecher himself told them he knew no more than they did and wouldn't comment, but three days later the *Times* quoted him as telling an interviewer from the *Rochester Express:* "Poor woman! She is the strangest combination I ever knew. You see her one time and you would think her a saint on earth; at another time she is a weak, irresponsible being and anything but a saint." He went on, at her expense, to say that "the confession reminded him of a story of a negro waiter who was asked by a guest if it was the second bell for breakfast that had rung. 'No Sah, it's not de second bell, it's de second ringin' ob de fust bell.'"

Now that he had won back a prominent place in the national discourse—now that he had survived—Beecher was in full throat. As the story soon died out and Elizabeth was banished from Plymouth Church, he again took to the summertime lyceum circuit, publicly no worse for the fact that his alleged victim had come forward and confessed, heaping shame on herself and her children. "They had to survive in a culture that cared a great deal whether one's mother was an adulteress," as Richard Wightman Fox notes. Whatever Elizabeth had hoped to accomplish by confessing, it didn't divert Beecher from his prospering new business of preaching about society and the science of it, and she and her husband remained apart.

In Minneapolis in early August, Beecher lectured on "The Reign of the Common People," showcasing the new Spencer-like perspective that only seemed to have grown in the year since his "bread alone" sermon. For the first time in his career, he brought Eunice along, and Pond had booked an extended tour of the Far West. The journey was a grim one for her. In Grinnell, Iowa, she complained to acquaintances in detail about his extravagances, leading him to tell their daughter that "this morbid craving for sympathy over fictitious woes seems like the appetite of the inebriate." By the time they reached Minnesota, he'd declared to Eunice that his married life had been a failure.

On stage, Beecher spoke about the varied influences of life upon intelligence, beginning with the effects of work. "New labor," he said, "especially manufacturing industries and commercial industries, are most powerful educators; they stir up the brain; they make it nimble; they make it various; they make it fruitful; and drive men forward in the way of life." In America, he said, numerous conditions combine to both broaden and deepen this operation. Climate, for one: "We breathe more in one breath here than they do on the other side in three. I mean more oxygen," he said. Beecher told the crowd of having met shipmasters who drank heavily in Liverpool but couldn't bear to drink in New York because they became overstimulated by the combination of alcohol and the atmosphere.

"Did you ever take notice throughout the whole North how lean the faces of men are, how sharp the features of men are, how keen and radiant the eyes of men are?" he asked. "Did you ever walk the streets and see how busy men look? Even lazy men look active, if you take their features for it." A chorus of laughs shot up.

If that intensity was not enough, Beecher said, there was our volatile democracy. "When a prairie is on fire everything must feel the light or the heat of it, and so our people are continually ruling through the stimulus of political excitement." Likewise the industrial element: "We all believe in moral wealth and all believe in educational wealth; but nevertheless there is nothing that tends in society to measure quality as much as wealth does today."

"And to a certain extent it is right," he added, "for although wealth, and especially selfish and sordid wealth, is not an honor to a man, yet that man that has begun in industry and preserved himself in it for ten or twenty years, and finally by generalship has erected a fortune, that man deserves laurels as much as he who has been on the battlefield, and it is a credit to a man to have amassed property by legitimate and lawful means. It means thought; it means self-denial; it means morality in the long run."

Finally, there was religion: after all the stimulation of life, men are transformed again in the crucible of a fiery and active church. "They are put on the anvil again, and beaten with other hammers, and developed into new forms of excitement."

As Beecher groped toward his own renewal, he seemed to have decided that the country itself was a kind of great forge where better minds were formed.

In our own land, upon this continent, the tendency towards cerebral development which has been going on slowly and augmenting through the generations, in respect to its impulses and highest stimulation, has resulted in a positive development of brain. I believe there is more brain matter in man than there used to be. I think they have bigger thinking power than they used to have. I think it is better disciplined, and more exercised, but, being developed, it is more fruitful and versatile—certainly more than it was in any previous period since the race began on the earth.

Back in Brooklyn for the fall, Beecher attended to the ongoing work on his upstate retreat; an amateur botanist, he would in time surround the house with three hundred varieties of trees. In Fort Greene Park, overlooking downtown, three thousand men and boys assembled on a night in September to listen to the California populist leader Dennis Kearney, an Irish immigrant best known for his nativist and racist political views toward Chinese immigrants. Kearney was invited by the Eighth Ward Greenback-Labor Club, and after alluding to "the muck vomited forth by that lousy, slimy hypocrite who runs the *New York Herald*"—James Gordon Bennett, Jr., a flamboyant yachtsman who flaunted his opulent rail cars and lavish mansions—he directed what the *Times* called "some awkward thrusts at Beecher."

"I will read a chapter of the Bible to see how it will sit upon the stomachs of the fat, lazy tricksters who listen to Henry Bread-and-Water Beecher," he said. "It is the fifth chapter of St. James. In those days all the saints were tramps. If Henry Bread-and-Water Beecher had been compelled to live upon bread and water there would be no scandal to relate." Kearney recited the chapter, in which the rich are condemned without pity and without the possibility of conversion, then said, "I have read enough to prove that God almighty is with the workingmen of the United States."

"MY DEAR YOUMANS," Spencer wrote from London on July 22,

> I have seen a good deal of Prof. Marsh while he has been over here, and had the opportunity of showing him some civility by asking him to join a picnic at Weybridge for some dozen or more friends (as I did also last year). He seemed to enjoy it much, and is, as I gather, enjoying his stay here greatly. He is evidently doing very careful work in the preparation of his monographs on these fossil types and promises to do good service for us.

Marsh also visited Darwin at Downe, but he cut short his trip and the glow of being celebrated by the chieftains of evolution to tend to a sudden unexpected opportunity back home. Being a bachelor and independently wealthy—Yale paid him no salary, and he was financing his burgeoning dinosaur war as well as the museum with money from his inheritance—freed him from the necessity of adjusting himself to others. Still he had a knack for winning elections, and in March he had been chosen vice president of the National Academy of Sciences, the distinguished but near-moribund commission engineered during the war by Louis Agassiz and the Lazzaroni. Then the academy's president died, making Marsh acting president just as Schurz and other reformers in Washington decided to enlist the organization in a pivotal new battle.

On June 30, Congress acted to require the academy to advise the government on how to map—essentially, how to develop—the new territories of the West. As soon as he heard what was happening, Marsh arranged to sail home. He sent letters to key scientists and initiated a committee to study the issue, which consisted mainly of how to merge the several redundant and competitive government geographical surveys that since the war had made the effort one of the most fractious and politicized in American science. Both Marsh and Cope had been deeply involved in those rivalries, and the current political battle represented the best hope for each to extend his ambitions, which far exceeded scouring prehistoric boneyards for new species. With science yielding dramatic new power in society, both foresaw a bonanza as the relationship between government and research evolved from the "My darling Ben" coziness of Agassiz and Peirce.

Schurz had set the political struggle in motion, in conjunction with the chief of the smallest survey, John Wesley Powell. Powell had become famous after leading a descent of the Colorado River in 1869, despite army surgeons having amputated his shattered right arm above the elbow after the Battle of Shiloh, leaving him in ceaseless pain. He was largely self-taught. While the other military and civilian explorations dwelled on the bounteous topography of the region, he had devised a revolutionary view of how it ought to be settled, which in March he had sent to Schurz under the title *Report on the Land of the Arid Regions of the United States.* It began:

> The Physical Conditions which exist in the arid lands, and which
> inexorably control the operations of men, are such that the industries
> of the West are necessarily unlike those of the East, and their
> institutions must be adapted to their industrial wants. It is thus that a

new phase of Aryan civilization is being developed in the western half of America.

Powell believed that it was too dry west of the 100th meridian—the geographical zone referenced on most maps as the Great American Desert—to sustain a growing population unless the government stepped in and regulated development. He proposed classifying all remaining public lands according to their likely uses. He urged imposing a twenty-fold increase in the size of homesteads, a move that would slow migration and settlement, enable settlers with limited capital to compete with large cattle companies, and purposely antagonize timber and mining interests that seized lands through dummy homestead entries. He recommended village cooperatives, large-scale government irrigation projects, and declaring some lands off-limits to all exploitation.

Marsh returned to New Haven in August and immediately selected a committee to explore the problem and make recommendations to the academy. It consisted entirely of like-minded civilians—a group with strong associations to Harvard, Yale, and Columbia, and that included MIT founder William B. Rogers and Alexander Agassiz. Marsh's temporary billet at the helm of elite science was fortuitous, but his own position on Powell's document was fervently held. Four years earlier, on his last expedition, during the same tense weeks that Custer invaded the Black Hills and found nuggets of gold, he had met Oglala Sioux chief Red Cloud, who came to trust him and showed him evidence of corruption in the Indian bureau. Marsh delivered it to Grant, ultimately forcing out the interior secretary. Marsh cared less about corruption than about creating a favorable environment for exploration and a profitable relationship between government and scientists. His purposes dovetailing neatly with Schurz's mandate to clean up the notoriously corrupt land and Indian bureaus, he now made himself a crucial ally in helping Schurz promote Powell's plan.

Within a month, Marsh circulated a draft report based on Powell's recommendations. In early October, he wrote Schurz outlining the committee's progress, and Schurz passed the report to Powell, who was busy proselytizing to newspaper after newspaper and visiting Congress, where western politicians denounced him as a dangerous radical bent on impeding the "big barbecue"—unfettered and wholesale exploitation. The committee's report, citing the "paramount importance of the public lands," endorsed Powell's plan to merge all the existing surveys, military and civilian, under civilian control, and transfer them from the Treasury Department to Interior along with the General Land Office. Reflecting Marsh's particular concerns, the report also proposed that all fossil and rock collections made by the surveys be deposited in the national museum.

Marsh delivered the two-thousand-word report to a special meeting of the academy at Columbia on November 6, and it was adopted by a vote of 31 to 1, with only Cope opposed. Three days later, Marsh traveled to Washington "and in less than two days got the approval of Secretary Schurz, Secretary Sherman, General Sherman, the President (so far as he had the plan before him), and Supt. Patterson of the Coast Survey," he wrote to Rogers at MIT. He submitted the plan to Congress when the session opened in December, sparking the first major battle over government-funded science. The opponents of the Powell program characterized it as "an effort of 'new-fledged collegiates' and 'scientific lobbyists' to shut off development of the West," as historian Henry Nash Smith wrote. "For them, the unpardonable sin was criticism of Western resources and doubt concerning the endless splendid future of the 'Great West.'" Marsh thrust back by enlisting, among many others, the presidents of Yale and Harvard to lobby congressmen. Schurz, meanwhile, steered the resulting bill to organize the United States Geological Survey to the powerful Appropriations Committee, where he had allies and influence. When it passed three months later, Schurz handpicked the first director.

H.R. 6140—essentially Powell's *Arid Regions* channeled through Marsh's report—elevated the National Academy of Sciences from a kind of reference panel to an initiator of reform. Although he would yield the role of acting president in the next election (only to return later for two terms), Marsh now became, like Sumner, a political force. Less than six years after Agassiz's death, he emerged as a top evolutionary scientist with perhaps more influence among scientists and in Washington than Agassiz had wielded at his height, yet unlike Agassiz, his identification with the leading edge of research—and his priority in his field—seemed secure. Darwin, Spencer, and Huxley celebrated him. Out west, Como Bluff disgorged one new dinosaur species after the next, despite the fact that Marsh had neglected to pay the railroad men for several months and they verged on quitting. As soon as Schurz's nominee was approved, Marsh wrote to Powell: "Now that the battle is won we can go back to pure Science again. I therefore invite you and Mr. Gilbert to attend the coming meeting of the national academy . . . and hope you both will have some papers to present."

TWO WEEKS AFTER BEECHER LECTURED in Minneapolis on the enhanced American brain, Sumner addressed a House committee selected to investigate the causes of the depression, now in its fifth year of long-term, widespread, involuntary joblessness and misery, grinding on with no end in sight. After the election, Hayes had traveled to New York with Schurz and Evarts to convince the city's Chamber of Commerce that the government was determined to get the country moving again. Evarts told the group, of which he was a long-standing member, that with the agony of Reconstruction "ended, and forever," the suppurating gash of the Civil War was finally closed, positioning the nation for unified economic growth. Resumption of specie payments was scheduled to begin in January. The *Times,* meanwhile, advised readers to buy dogs to ward off beggars and vagrants.

Since his conversion to evolution, Sumner took an increasingly pitiless view of humanity, and of government involvement in the economy. He believed natural law dictated social inequality and no reform could abrogate that fact. "If we do not believe in survival of the fittest," he liked to say, "we have only one possible alternative, and that is survival of the unfittest." The "iron spur" of suffering was necessitated by the progress of the race, and the state had no place as mediator in that struggle. "Nature's remedies against vice are terrible," he wrote. "She removes her victims without pity. A drunkard in the gutter is just where he ought to be, according to the fitness and tendency of things." Now addressing lawmakers, Sumner counseled a severe hands-off approach, especially regarding any kind of assistance to those in need or who lost jobs to industrial progress.

"What is the effect," he was asked, "of machinery on those laborers whom for the time being it turns out of employment?"

"Of course, a loss of income and a loss of comfort," Sumner told the legislators. "There are plenty of people in the United States to-day whose fathers were displaced from their labor in some of the old countries by the introduction of machinery, and who suffered very great poverty, and who were forced to emigrate to this country by the pressure of necessity, poverty and famine. When they came to this country they entered on a new soil and a new system of industry, and their children today may look back on the temporary distress through which their parents went as a great family blessing."

"But the fathers had to suffer from it?"

"They had to suffer from it."

"Is there any way to help it?"

"Not at all," Sumner cautioned. "There is no way on earth to help it. The only way is to meet it bravely, go ahead, make the best of circumstances: and if you cannot go on in the way you are going, try another way, and still another, until you work yourself out as an individual."

Massachusetts Republican William Rice, a former insolvency judge, invited Sumner to elaborate: "Then the pressure of necessity is one of the prime elements in the progress and civilization of mankind?"

"Yes; we have been forced to progress, and that is the reason we have made it," Sumner explained.

"Do you think that there is any remedy that might be applied by legislation or otherwise to relieve labor from the consequences of this speculative era?"

"Legislation might do a great deal of mischief, but nothing else."

Sumner volunteered near the end of his testimony a lesson in the value of forced idleness. The problem of an oversupply of workers, he said by way of analogy, must inevitably correct itself. He continued:

Of course, I have not any remedy to offer for such a state of things as this. . . . I do not know of anything that the government can do that is at all specific to assist labor—to assist non-capitalists. . . . The general things that a government can do to assist the non-capitalist in the accumulation of capital (for that is what he wants) are two things. The first thing is to give him the greatest possible measure of liberty in the directing of his own energies for his own development, and the second is to give him the greatest possible security in the possession and use of the products of his own industry.

I do not see anything more than that that a government can do in the premises.

Committee chairman Hendrick Wright of Pennsylvania referred to earlier testimony by workingmen who raised the point that when in the natural operation of society there are fewer jobs, certain people who are just as deserving as others find it impossible to work. "They say that society owes them a living; that, if they cannot get work in private hands, the public should intervene for the time being and provide some place where their labor could be employed, and where they can get a livelihood. . . . Can that be done?" Wright asked.

"Sir," Sumner concluded, "the moment that government provided work for one, it would have to provide work for all, and there would be no end whatever possible. Society does not owe any man a living. In all cases that I have ever known of young men who claimed that society owed them a living, it has turned out that society paid them—in the State prison. I do not see any other result. . . . The fact that a man is here is no demand upon other people that they shall keep him alive and sustain him. He has got to fight the battle with nature as every other man has; and if he fights it with the same energy and enterprise and skill and industry as any other man, I cannot imagine his failing—that is, misfortune apart."

SPENCER BEGAN THE YEAR with a bad cold that kept him indoors, feverish, heart galloping, for eleven days—"the most miserable eleven days I remember," he told Youmans, who from his silence Spencer feared was also seriously unwell. "More and more each winter there is forced upon me the experience that five months of bad weather—cold, wet, gloomy, relaxing, by turns—is trying to my system, and that I profit greatly by getting away to some sunnier and drier region," he wrote:

But the difficulty of meeting the mental requirements is insuperable.
I cannot take my friends with me; and in the absence of the ability to
pass the time in reading to any extent, I get dreadfully bored; so that
when I go away for a week, and have profited by the better sleeping
and other physical advantages, I always rejoice greatly when the last

days come, enabling me to return to town from my wearisome banishment.

Spencer managed to travel with his friend Edward Lott for a week in May to Paris for the International Exhibition. "Reluctant to sacrifice wholly the working power which each day gave me," he later recalled, he corrected manuscripts while sitting in the garden of the Trocadero Palace, as laborers scrambled nearby to ready a site for the completed head of the Statue of Liberty. They visited the Salon show, which opened while they were there, but left before, on a night in June, a switch was thrown and electric lightbulbs invented by Thomas Edison, who also had a phonograph on display, illuminated the Avenue de l'Opéra. Throngs of fairgoers flocked to a human zoo called a "negro village" populated with four hundred "indigenous people."

The latter part of June was beastly in London, and Spencer took his shorthand secretary to Kensington Gardens, hired two chairs in the shade, and dictated rough drafts of sundry chapters on ethics throughout the mornings, stopping usually after half an hour to walk awhile. He had leaped ahead to the utmost question—morality—because he believed that "the gap left by the disappearance of the code of supernatural ethics" in light of the recent gains in evolutionary theory had to be filled by a "code of natural ethics," and he urgently pieced together, from scraps of memoranda, prescriptions for "a right rule of life, individual and social." He now planned to publish an immense book, *The Data of Ethics*, before returning to his *Sociology*. Toward the end of July, after reporting to Youmans his pleasure in meeting Marsh and having him on his picnic, he traveled to the countryside for three weeks to read, revise, and fish for salmon, though the weather was disappointing. According to his diary for August 17, he hooked and lost four fish in a row.

Spencer's pursuit of leisure took on a new urgency as fall again closed in. "I wish I could make you more fully realize the fact than you generally do that care for health and the relaxation needed to put yourself in better state are really demanded by regard for your work," he lectured Youmans, who Fiske lately had noticed looked haggard and weary, "and that you will in the long run be able to do much more in discharging your obligations if you do not persist in working when ill than if you do persist." He pressed Youmans to take "a good holiday," something Youmans had never considered, much less done, and invited him to come to London, then accompany him for two months to the Mediterranean. "If you could make up your mind to come with me and do a little idling in pleasant places," he wrote, "I am convinced that you would find it in the long run a great economy of time."

Whether chiefly for Youmans's good, or else to fulfill his own desire for a traveling companion to help him avoid another winter like the last one, Spencer refused to let the matter rest. "Pray yield to my pressure," he wrote two weeks later, "and to the pressure I doubt not others also put upon you. . . . My going abroad will very much be determined by your answer. It is quite out of the question for me to go alone." Deciding in favor of the south of France, Spencer argued that the change of scene, forced rest, and salubrious climate could only do Youmans good. Anxious that Youmans might delay so long in making up his mind that the trip might have to be delayed a year, Spencer goaded him by reminding him of his mortality: "You have not so very great a length of time left that you can with wisdom put it off. You should remember that you have not only got to do your *work,* but you have got to *live;* and ever since I have known you you have been thinking only of the work and never of the living."

Youmans finally relented in mid-November, agreeing to book passage on the *Germanic* on December 7, and to spare two months away. He warned Spencer to lower his expectations. "I must, however, say again, that I am in a miserable condition for such an expedition, and will probably give you as much occupation in dragging me around as you will want," he warned. "It will certainly alleviate your monotony, if that is the main thing." Indeed, Youmans was eager to hear Spencer's views on morality, and could scarcely resist the compulsion to prod and question him at length. He thought he could use the opportunity to counter critics, religious and otherwise, who challenged the role of evolution in divining right from wrong—the question that had plagued Darwin in *Descent.* "Nothing," he wrote, "but the desire to be in some way useful to yourself in promoting your work, and at the same time of helping myself in the way proposed, would induce me to encounter another winter passage across the Atlantic."

As he prepared for the trip abroad, Spencer was thrown off his routine by the death, after an agonizing illness, of George Lewes. He broke his own rule not to attend funerals "partly because my absence would have been generally misinterpreted, and partly because it might have given pain to one whose feeling I should have been very reluctant to hurt, though probably she would have understood my motive"—Lewes's wife, George Eliot, who was too distraught herself to leave the house. Once, she had loved Spencer, and his awkward rejection led more or less directly to her twenty-five-year marriage to Lewes as well as to Spencer's encrusted frigidity—he would die, as far as is known, a virgin. "I can but dimly perceive what such a parting must be," he now told her in a note. "But I can conceive it with clearness enough to enable me to say, with more than conventional truth, that I grieve with you."

The *Germanic*, after sitting at anchor in dense fog five miles off the Irish coast, docked on December 16, providing Youmans with barely enough time to turn around before meeting Spencer and venturing on. "I got off at Liverpool at half past one; got through the customhouse at ten minutes of two; got to Lime Street Station at two; got to the train with not a second to spare, and got into London at half past eight, the train being an hour behind time," he wrote to his sister.

> Spencer met me at the door. He is very well, and was ready to start on the instant for the Continent. Everything was ready, tickets taken through, circular notes procured, etc. . . . We shall be off at nine tomorrow morning by Dover and Calais to Paris, where we spend one day, and then take the night train for Marseilles, and that is all I know.

Now that he was in Spencer's protective care, Youmans offered neither protest nor resistance. "We are resting, giving the animal a chance," he wrote to Catherine from Hyères on December 24. "Spencer will let me do nothing but walk and eat. Can't read or write. Have to steal moments to write letters, and hence haven't written much." The rigors of leisure, Youmans discovered, left little time or energy for anything else. Spencer, he told her, "is working like ten horses in quest of what he came for—relaxation! So we walked two hours this afternoon on the piazza, seventeen feet long and ten feet wide, passing each other at every turn. Lord, how the people stared? But Spencer didn't care, and I'm sure I shall never see them again."

A few days later, after the rain stopped and the weather turned pleasant, he issued a fuller report, one in which he bristled with mixed feelings at the forced exercise and constant watchfulness, and chafed at his host's inconsistency: "While not relaxing a jot of his theoretic *laissez faire,* he is still more irritably denunciatory of people doing as they can and may." Spencer, Youmans wrote,

> meddles with me, and interferes with me, and criticizes me, and takes care of me, all for my good, of course, in the most assiduous manner. I am beginning to count on momentary escape from his vigilance to do a little writing and reading.—At this point he came for a walk, "a slight ramble of half an hour." It was very wet and muddy but we rambled through the lanes and alleys, up around the side of the mountain behind us, climbing for an hour, steady pull. Then he struck off into an obscure path that promised more direct descent. We lost the path, and lost our way, and had to plunge down a steep, broken, rocky, muddy side of the great hill full of gorges and deep channels. . . . We got back after two hours' tramp, and I was quite used up.
>
> . . . I promised to write of his Morals, which is to be a great thing, *of course,* though I have not seen it. . . . He is now revising the first four chapters, but will not let me see them till they are all corrected and all together, which it will take two to three weeks to bring about. It will now begin to be seen what "Evolution" is for, and I find the main reason he has jumped over to ethics is that people had got tired of waiting for some result, and the ethical writers—mainly Sidgwick [*sic*] of Cambridge, have said, "After all morality is found to have nothing to do with evolution." *I* can begin to see that it does, and *how* it does.

Youmans cut himself short: "Here comes Spencer, bullying me for writing, and I tell him this is the last letter I will write in the next seven weeks."

"WHAT WAS MOST REMARKABLE about Carnegie's newfound success as a capitalist," his biographer David Nasaw wrote, "was how little it required of him." Carnegie once told a Pennsylvania businessman: "What I do is to get good men, and I never give them orders. My directions seldom go beyond suggestions. Here in the morning I get reports from them. Within an hour I have disposed of everything, sent out all of my suggestions, the day's work is done, and I am ready to go out and enjoy myself." With Jones and Shinn handling operations at E.T., the cost of manufacturing rails had been cut by half, profits were a striking 32 percent return on capital, Carnegie's original $250,000 investment had tripled in value, and he held the last word on every decision. In three years, he had leaped over his rivals to position himself to dominate the Steel Age. Relentless as ever, he now turned to keeping the vows he'd made to himself in his hotel room a decade earlier. He resolved to continue his education, succeed in literature, develop his social influence far beyond Pittsburgh and New York, and seize a leading role in "the education & improvement of the poorer classes."

On October 24, Carnegie and an old Pittsburgh friend, John Vandevort, sailed from San Francisco for China—the first leg of an around-the-world survey of human civilization. "Spencer and Darwin were then high in their zenith," he would recall. "I began to view the various phases of human life from the standpoint of the evolutionist." On board the White Star line's SS *Belgic*, a cargo vessel and passenger tender, were eight hundred Chinese natives returning home, and the steward assigned Carnegie and Vandevort to dine with a missionary, his wife, and "two young lady missionaries in embryo," he wrote in his travel diary. The second Sunday at sea, curious, he attended the missionary's sermon. "He spent the morning attempting to prove to us that the wine Christ made at the marriage feast was not fermented, as if it mattered, or as if such could ever be known! And I was in the mood to preach such a magnificent sermon myself, too, if I had had his place. No; I shall never forgive him—never!"

Carnegie's disgust was as impassioned as that of any religious convert encountering heathenism in the flesh, and it fused into principle. Later, when one of the young women from the table wrote him asking him for $4,000 for a new dormitory for her mission in Foochow, he denied her request, writing back that foreign missions in China were "not only money misspent, but that we do a grievous wrong to the Chinese by trying to force our religion upon them against their wishes." He explained:

> I believe that all religions are adapted to those for whom they are
> provided. The ten great religions are very much alike in their
> fundamental ideas, and I do not wonder at the attacks made upon

foreign missions by the Chinamen. If the Chinamen were to come here protected by warships of their government and try to prove the falsity of our religions, against our earnest protests, I fear they would not meet with better treatment. Besides, I think that to force our religious views on others is not Christ-like. He never used force, but was always gentle and persuading. I commend his example to all your missionary friends in China, who are there simply because our warships or guns protect them.

If, like Darwin, Carnegie did not set out to see the world with the unseating of Christianity explicitly in mind—he had long ago concluded that the whole scheme of Christian salvation and the conception of an angry God was "diabolical" and "libelous"—he could not help, as he traveled, seeing evidence everywhere of Darwin's theory, or of its stark contrast with religious superstition, prejudice, and racial chauvinism. "The Unknown," he wrote, "does not deserve such abuse." Yet unlike Spencer, Sumner, and Beecher, he had been an immigrant, and poor, and had never been subsidized, and he saw less to celebrate in nature's cruel indifference. His optimism was all-embracing. As ruthless, self-serving, and self-aggrandizing as he could be with his rivals, partners, and employees, Carnegie now developed into a humble and respectful traveler, a pilgrim ardently, ecstatically testing a new faith.

In China I read Confucius; in India, Buddha and the sacred books of the Hindoos; among the Parsees, in Bombay, I studied Zoroaster. The result of my journey was to bring a certain mental peace. Where there had been chaos there was now order. My mind was at rest. I had a philosophy at last. The words of Christ "The Kingdom of Heaven is within you," had a new meaning for me. Not in the past or in the future, but now and here is heaven within us. All our duties lie in this world and in the present, and trying to peer into that which lies beyond is as vain as fruitless.

After more than three weeks at sea, the *Belgic* steamed into Yokohama Bay, under a setting sun that bathed fourteen-thousand-foot Fujiyama in light. Carnegie and Vandevort—"Vandy"—took a sampan to the custom-house and reached their hotel. Venturing out, they encountered shoeless cabmen wearing loincloths and hats as big as barrelheads to shield them from sun and rain, and coolies "naked as Adam" pushing a load of iron. Repulsed by the blackened teeth of married women, Carnegie was forced to look away. "How women can be induced to make such frights of themselves I cannot conceive," he wrote, "but Fashion—Fashion does anything."

In Tokyo, the great city of empire, he witnessed the bustling New Japan in the grip of unprecedented upheaval. Since Commodore Matthew Perry and his Black Ships had forced open Japan at gunpoint twenty-five years earlier, feudalism had been overthrown, the imperial line had been restored, and Japan had catapulted itself into the modern age—destined to become one of the world's major industrial and military powers. Carnegie marveled at many of the gains, particularly Japan's arsenal, postal system, vigorous press, and ability to absorb the manners and norms of Western civilization, but he detected in the lurching transformation an easy mutability that made him wary. After visiting a magnificent tomb, he wrote, "It is gorgeous in color, and the extreme delicacy of the gold is surprising." He continued,

> But these tombs totally failed to impress me with any feeling akin to reverence; indeed nothing in Japan seems calculated to do so—the odor of the toyshop pervades everything, even their temples. As for their religious belief, it is hard to tell what it is, or whether they have any. One thing is sure, the educated classes have discarded the faith of the multitude, if they ever really entertained it, and no longer worship the gods of old. . . . It is in Japan as it was in Greece—one religion for the masses, and another, or rather none in the ordinary sense, for the educated few.

Evolutionarily speaking, Japan's explosive emergence from extreme isolation (during the two and a half centuries of the Tokugawa shogunate, which ended barely a decade earlier, the penalty for leaving the country was death) and xenophobia (before Perry's arrival, only China and the Netherlands had trading rights, each with a single island and a single port) had left its people politically undeveloped. Carnegie was appalled while visiting the arsenal, where native-designed warships were under construction, to note the deep, religious submission to official authority. "We had another opportunity of seeing the bowing practice in its fullest development," he wrote:

The various foremen as they approached bowed three times almost to the ground, and in some cases they were first upon their knees and struck the floor three times with their foreheads. We were afterward informed that only a few years ago these would have added to the obeisance by extending the arms to their full length and placing the palms of the hands flat upon the ground; now this is omitted, and I have no doubt, as intelligence spreads, less and less of this deference will be exacted.

Carnegie was surprised and amused to learn that just a few years after the demise of the official *Gazette*, read only by functionaries and containing little of general interest, several hundred newspapers existed, many publishing daily, and that their observations were piquant. "Here is a specimen," he recorded in his diary, which by now had begun to take rough shape as a travel book that he planned to publish privately on his return:

"In America during the Civil War paper currency was issued and made legal tender. At every successive issue the premium rose higher and higher till the currency was not worth more than a third of its face. The Southern states followed in the same path, but they kept on till their issues were found to be good for about one purpose only— to line trunks withal—such fools these Americans be. Happy Japan! Blessed with rulers of preeminent ability, who keep the finances of our land in such creditable form."

Happy, indeed. Cruising on the Inland Sea in late November, Carnegie described

a panorama of busy, crowded life, but life under most beautiful surroundings . . . [a] fairyland. The rivers and seas abound with fish; the hills and valleys under irrigation grow their rice, millet and vegetables. A few dollars per year supply all the clothing needed, and a few dollars buys their light wooden houses. Thus they have everything they need, or consider necessary, and are happy as the day is long, certain of one established fact in nature, to wit, that there is no place like Japan; and no doubt they daily and hourly thank their stars that their lines have fallen in pleasant places, and pity us—slaves to imaginary wants—who deny ourselves the present happiness they consider it wisdom to enjoy, in vain hopes of banqueting to surfeit at some future time, which always comes too late.

American intellectuals lately had discovered in Japan—chiefly the old, endangered Japan of stillness and simplicity—an antidote to the jarring dislocations of modern life, even as they played a leading role in modernizing it. Since the centennial, a great vogue had developed in the United States for "all things Japanese," as historian Christopher Benfey writes— "prints and porcelain, judo and Buddhism, geisha and samurai." A Massachusetts zoologist, Edward Morse, had recently visited the country in search of coastal brachiopods; in little more than a year, he helped found Tokyo University, where he delivered a popular series of lectures on Darwinism, opened the study of archaeology and anthropology in Japan, and was now collecting historic pottery and shipping it back to the Museum of Fine Arts in Boston.

After more than a month traveling in the country, Carnegie tempered his estimation with a measure of scientific skepticism. "Surely no other nation ever abandoned its traditions and embraced so rapidly those of a civilization of an opposite behavior," he wrote.

This is not development under the law of slow Evolution; it seems more like a case of spontaneous generation. Presto, change! and here before our very eyes is presented the strange spectacle of the most curious, backward, feudalistic Eastern nation turning into a Western one of the most advanced type.

That Japan will succeed in her effort to establish a central government, under something like our ideas of freedom and law, and that she has such resources as will enable her to maintain it and educate her people, I am glad to be able to say I believe; but much remains to be done requiring in the race the exercise of solid qualities, the possession of which I find some Europeans disposed to deny them.

CHINA—EIGHT TIMES MORE POPULOUS than America, its government forty times older, originator of the compass, porcelain, gunpowder, and the art of printing, yet without a mile of train track or telegraph wire or macadam—beckoned slumberingly ahead. Carnegie and Vandy reached Shanghai on December 5, finding ample accommodations in the Astor House, in the American settlement. The Chinese government had set aside a riverside enclave for foreigners where broad streets, as well tended "as in an English town," were thoroughly drained and lit by gas, but just beyond it lay what seemed a dense, trackless human wilderness. "There is not a street or road in the region, outside of the reservation, in which a horse can travel," he recorded; "only footpaths, where a wheelbarrow pushed by a man is the only possible vehicle." Communications existed solely by means of rivers and canals.

Carnegie marveled at the oddity of the world's oldest civilization neither possessing, nor apparently having any desire for, modern ways. "China's difficulty," his biographer Wall writes, "had been that she had evolved to a high degree of civilization too early in the history of the human race." When ancient Englishmen were still barbarians huddled in forests, the Chinese were reading and writing. With no incentive to mix with other races, her people grew insular and conservative, wary of change. Carnegie understood little of China's culture, but he recognized its evolutionary predicament.

He learned that the obstacle to building railroads was that "China is one vast cemetery," as he wrote.

> Go where you will, in any direction, the mounds of the dead intrude
> themselves upon you at every step. There are no cemeteries set apart for
> burial purposes; on the contrary, the Chinaman seems to prefer having
> his dead buried on his own land, and as near to him as practicable. In
> this neighborhood, their mode of sepulture is revolting. The coffins are
> not put into a grave at all, but are laid directly on the surface of the
> ground and covered with but a few inches of earth.... The stench from
> the coffins became so offensive last year that the European authorities
> had to enter complaint to the Chinese Mandarin.

Having lately begun to consider whether at age forty-three and still living with his sainted mother he was missing deeply the satisfactions of love and sexual intimacy, he studied Chinese marriage practices, and especially the companionability of its women. "Do not mourn too much over the sad fate of a young Chinaman compelled to marry one whom he has never seen," he wrote:

for indeed there seems little difference between the young ladies of China. Thousands of years of seclusion, of unvarying customs, have at last moulded women into the same form, mentally and physically, and anything like individuality can exist only to a small degree, and in exceptional natures. They are like as peas, and one may as well marry one as another.

Carnegie found the "universal sameness" of China monotonous, but on the scale of races, he held the Chinese to be at the top, because they had succeeded in moving beyond the military mode of society—a lower evolutionary stage, as Spencer explained, than the higher mode of noncoercive civilization toward which all societies ultimately are driven. The more heterogeneous an organism, the more self-regulating and internally balanced, and the less dependent upon force. "China is, as far as I know, the only nation which has advanced beyond the so-called heroic age when the soldier claims precedence," Carnegie observed. "No general, no conqueror, be his victories what they may, can ever in China attain the highest rank. That is held only by successful scholars who have shown the possession of literary talent. . . . These are the Mandarins, and there is no other aristocracy in China."

Whether Carnegie imagined himself reaching a higher position in society as an author or as a steelmaker, his high esteem for the Chinese model remained with him through Canton to Hong Kong, where on Christmas Eve he and Vandy received a single American paper and rejoiced greatly over the "triumph of hard money views" in Congress. The next day, having "been so long out of the region of music," he rose early and went to the English Cathedral to hear the Hallelujah Chorus. Afterward, strolling about the church, he noticed thirty-odd sedan chairs with up to four coolies each "in gorgeous liveries" lying in the shade, a few playing dice, awaiting the closing of prayers. "Really," he wrote, vowing to walk to church from now on unless his mother seriously objected, "three men kept at work so that one may pray seems a shade out of proportion."

By New Year's, Carnegie was aboard a luxurious French-owned liner sailing through Indochina and the island of Singapore before heading west toward Ceylon and India. The tropical heat forced him and Vandy to shed their vests and overcoats, reducing their washing and dressing time to seven minutes. Of East Asia and its two modes of accommodating Western advancement—Japan's servile imitation versus China's cult of intelligence and slow adaptation—he confidently predicted victory for the latter. "Here the 'survival of the fittest' is being fought out under the protection of the British flag," he wrote while at anchor in Singapore,

which insures peace and order wherever it floats. In this struggle, we have no hesitation in backing the Heathen Chinese against the field. Permanent occupation by any Western race is of course out of the question. An Englishman would inevitably cease to be an Englishman in a few, a very few, generations, and it is therefore only a question of time when the Chinese will drive every other race to the wall. No race can possibly stand against them anywhere in the East.

FRENCH RIVIERA, 1879

> *The question is not whether the college shall, or shall*
> *not, teach theology, but what theology it shall teach.*
>
> —Yale president NOAH PORTER

SPENCER AND YOUMANS ARRIVED IN CANNES on January 2—
"a rich, prosperous watering place, a kind of Saratoga on a side hill,"
Youmans wrote to his sister. He understood that Spencer intended to
push him to the limit while continuing to talk in only the most general
terms about his treatment of ethics, which Youmans now believed would
"rank morality with the sciences." Submitting abjectly to his regimen, he
cajoled Spencer for details, dashed off hasty dispatches to his sister and
parents when Spencer wasn't around, and surrendered gloomily whenever
Spencer turned up to administer the next therapy. "The scenery is fine
and clear, and the air mild and very pleasant," he reported to Catherine:

> The place is quiet and both Spencer and myself slept well last night,
> having mosquito nets which were effectual—the first time, Spencer
> says, he ever slept under one. —Back again from another pull. This
> time it has been through the town, but it is all the same. The mistral
> today has dried the mud, and the walking is better but I am utterly
> tired out. It would seem as though this would either kill or cure. I am
> abundantly conscious of the stupidity of all I have been writing, but
> there seems nothing else to say or talk about.

That Spencer believed he was on a lifesaving mission left no doubt; it matched his conviction that only by treating himself in the same manner could he go on with his work. "Spencer," Youmans wrote, "pegs away at his revising an hour or two a day, but is greatly and continuously disgusted at not getting letters, having had but one or two in a week from England." Though the days were warm, the nights were cold, and Spencer, after setting their routine, announced he was satisfied with his choice of destination and the climate. "This is a region of extremes," he told Lott in a postcard, "winter and summer mixed. Now sitting crouching over the fire with great coat and cap on, and piling rugs on the bed at night, and now walking in bright sunshine, seeing butterflies about and peas six feet high in blossom, and being obliged to use mosquito curtains!"

After a week that Spencer described as "pleasant" and Youmans as "enjoyable and profitable," Youmans complained to his sister: "I am undergoing a sharp discipline; and what between a revolutionized diet, cessation of smoking, and triple my former exercise, I *ought* to pick up." Spencer scouted their next stop—Mentone, a picturesque town at the foot of the Maritime Alps on the shore of the Mediterranean—while Youmans took advantage of his absence to write one editorial and a short note to his parents promising to try to "squeeze out" another in time for the March *Popular Science Monthly*. A few days later, they drove the Corniche road fifteen miles east of Nice to Mentone, where they settled for a month. Feeling stronger, Youmans tried to work whenever he could, but after a stretch of grim weather his eyes became "very bad," he wrote on January 27. Confronted by Spencer, his hopes sank to a new nadir:

Since Spencer has commenced working with my eyes and begins
really to find out in how bad a state the left eye is, he is very
vehement against my reading at all, or even writing. He says: "I never
saw a person so subject to changes of aspect: sometimes your face
looks coloured and healthy, and at other times pale, flabby and
haggard: and from what I can see it is reading that makes that change.
It is clear to me that you will have to stop writing and go to
lecturing."

Youmans had hoped for "bright, exhilarating weather," and two days later the skies cleared and it turned brutally hot. In the afternoon, he and

Spencer took a four-hour walk, clambering up a mountain to a tumble-down village of stone houses in the midst of which stood a Catholic church "all gilt and decked out in great style." Too exhausted the next day to go out, Youmans remained in his room, writing a few letters and not reading at all, while Spencer took a side trip to a seaside town with a ru-ined stronghold above it. He climbed for an hour above the ancient fortress to admire the magnificent panorama, then took out a portion of *The Data of Ethics* and worked on it for half an hour. "Remembering what the place had witnessed during the times when it was a refuge for the people of the district, and during other times when it was held by the in-vading Saracens, I was struck by the odd contrast between the purposes to which it was then put, and the purpose to which I was putting it," he later recalled.

Youmans, eyes aside, and Spencer, despite the demands of tending to his friend and scrambling to finish his manuscript, each found in Men-tone and in their side excursions a relief from overwork and solitude. "I am getting up an appetite for exercise, and regret that it is raining today, so that I have to keep indoors," Youmans told his sister in early February. "It is my improvement in this that makes Spencer think that if I would follow his directions in all things implicitly I would be born again. . . . Spencer will not budge from here until the time is up and gets angry if I propose going before. He also insists that I should stop a month in Lon-don and have not less than a three months break." No doubt to the sur-prise of them both, Youmans now found himself "inclined to listen."

Equally reinvigorated, Spencer, whose usual problem toward the end of a vacation was a feeling of "wearisome banishment," marched Youmans through several more side jaunts. "Of course we made expedi-tions," he wrote in his autobiography. "There was a trip to Monaco and Monte Carlo to see the gaming tables, where the faces of the players were less repulsive than I had expected."

By the middle of February, each had accomplished his goals, spurred on by the other. Youmans, revived, conceded that Spencer had been right. Extolling the benefits of leisure, he agreed to spend some extra time in London, although he surreptitiously resumed work as soon as he got to his hotel. "I have been bothered to snatch intervals to get these things done," he confided to his brother, "for Spencer watches me constantly and will listen to nothing. He does not know that I have written anything for the *Monthly*." Spencer, though there had been more fine days than dull or rainy ones, expressed disappointment with the French weather but declared the trip nonetheless a success. His completed book on the evolution of right and wrong and the science of proper behavior in hand, he reported to Lott from his rooms in Bayswater, "the change was beneficial in some respects and enjoyable; and as I did my full stint of work or rather more, and have come back perhaps a little better than I went, I am content."

In Singapore, Carnegie made the acquaintance of a collector who worked for Henry Augustus Ward, a former assistant of Agassiz who had moved to Rochester, New York, and founded a pioneering enterprise that gathered wild specimens from all parts of the world, then mounted them and sold them to colleges and museums. The man had just returned from four months in Borneo, where he had shot forty-two orangutans, and he asked Carnegie a favor. The collector had brought out two very young apes alive and was shipping them to a naturalist in Madras. Would Carnegie, who was sailing west on the English mail steamer *Teheran*, look out for them on board?

"At first every lady we took forward to watch them was compelled to run away laughing and exclaiming, 'Oh, they are so much like babies! It's just horrid to see these nasty, hairy things carry on so!'" he wrote in his travel diary. "Confirmation strong, I suppose, of our kinship." Carnegie tried to tempt the smaller of the two with a banana, but the animal wouldn't take it. "Then I tried the larger one," he reported. "He took it in his paw, peeled it at one end and put it to his lips, then looking up at me with a sad, puzzled expression, dropped his prize, and resting his head on his paw laid slowly down on the straw, telling us all as plainly as could be that he was seasick.

"They are much too human," he wrote.

Even more than Japan and China, it was India—where Grant, on an around-the-world tour of his own, was also traveling—that aroused Carnegie to take in and consider the role of human nature in modern affairs, just as he began to launch himself from steelmaker to man of letters and, ultimately, public benefactor. If Japan evolved too readily and China too early, India developed too slowly, hidebound by an ancient caste system and governed by superstition and idolatry. At the same time, its 250 million people were ruled, in elaborate degree, by England, which was caught up in what Carnegie called the "colonizing craze" and fielded a local army of sixty thousand soldiers. Debarking in Madras on January 28, Carnegie got his first glimpse of the three main castes, devotees of three different gods with their foreheads marked to denote their status, and soon realized both the magnitude of India's evolutionary challenge and the futility of foreign dominance.

Calcutta tested his faith and optimism. Accompanied by the U.S. consul, he and Vandy visited the temple sacred to the dark goddess Kali, from which the teeming city derived its name. Hordes of pilgrims from hundreds of miles around arrived daily, many of them traveling by measuring their bodies on the dusty ground: lying flat, marking their length, rising, and lying down again, begging for food and water all along their route. The four-armed Hindu goddess drew her power from drinking human blood, and each pilgrim brought a goat, buffalo, or kid to sacrifice at the shrine, hundreds a day in a shrieking, bloody spectacle. Carnegie recoiled. "I gave up all hope of improvement in these people," he wrote. He consoled himself that the children brought to witness the rite knew that the goddess was a symbol of power and not power itself, and that "around this fact the forces able to overthrow superstition may be evolved hereafter. The germ is there." Invoking Spencer, who wrote that each religion reflects "as near an approximation to the truth as it was then and there possible for men to receive," he philosophized: "In the progress of the race such dreadful conceptions of God must apparently exist for a time."

Far more promising, Carnegie decided, were the subcontinent's fifty million Mohammedans. "The claims which Mohammed has upon the gratitude of mankind rest upon a solid basis," he wrote after leaving Calcutta by train and arriving in Benares,

for it is he who proclaimed to the East that there is but one God, and announced himself as his prophet only, instead of demanding that he himself should be worshipped; but he performed another great service, for he abolished the abominable system of caste, and thus it comes that the most popular religion in existence hails all its disciples, from the peasant to the Sultan, as one of brotherhood, as Christianity does with hers . . . it is to them we must chiefly look for the regeneration of the native races.

It was the status of the European, however, that most thoroughly impressed him. Pushing through the city's narrow, teeming lanes, their native guide cracked and brandished a whip among the crowd, calling out "Sahib! Sahib!" People glanced behind, then scurried out of the way.

Here was India's great sorrow—fear and poverty galvanized over generations into inherent deference and subservience. And yet resentment seethed, and resistance did erupt. Carnegie's next stop, Lucknow, had twice come under siege as Indian soldiers broke into open rebellion in 1857, following widespread rumors that the cartridges for their new Enfield rifles were greased with a mixture of beef and pork fat. Soldiers then had to bite off the ends of the cartridges to prepare for firing, which would defile both Hindus and Muslims, and they refused. After a mutiny at the Lucknow garrison, a number of European women and children had been massacred. Carnegie discovered no traces of the slaughter, but after wandering Lucknow's crowded bazaars and visiting the tombs of the Englishmen who died putting down the rebellion, he shuddered for the future of any world power that presumed to control a native population, even one as beaten down as India's:

> Who can assure us that these bronzed figures which surround us
> by millions may not again in some mad moment catch the fever of
> revolt. This is the anxious question that I find intruding upon me
> every hour. Truly it is a dangerous game, this, to undertake the
> permanent subjection of a conquered race; and I do not believe that
> after General Grant sees India he will regret that the foolish Santo
> Domingo craze passed away. If America can learn one lesson from
> England, it is the folly of conquest, where conquest involves the
> government of an alien race.

Carnegie ached for feminine contact. "The absence of women, other than coolies, which has struck us everywhere in the East, is if anything even more marked in India, where, so far, we have scarcely seen one woman of high caste," he complained in his journal. After leaving Lucknow in mid-February, he and Vandy took a train to Agra, hoping to drive out and see the Taj Mahal, the world's great monument to married love, by moonlight. Having read the tormented and ecstatic travel writer Bayard Taylor, who warned that the "Taj is like a lovely woman: abuse her as you please, the moment you come into her presence you submit to her fascinations," Carnegie girded himself to be disappointed. He wasn't. After eight hours of solitary meandering among the mausoleum's creamy marble curves, he declared:

> It is as warm and sympathetic as a woman. . . . If I am ever
> sentenced for hard labor for life for some unlawful outburst of wild
> republicanism, I will make one request as I throw myself upon the
> mercy of the court: Let me be transported to India, and allowed to
> perform my daily task in beautifying and preserving the Taj. This
> would be a labor of love, and I should not be unhappy with my idol to
> worship.

En route from Bombay to Delhi in their sleeping car, Carnegie and Vandy passed Grant and his entourage headed to Calcutta—"but there was no chance to get at him to shake hands," he recorded. He had forsworn doing business while he was away, but now business intruded. One of his original partners in the steelworks, E.T. chairman David McCandless, died suddenly, and his general manager, William Shinn, eager to advance, immediately wrote Carnegie applying for the position. His concentration on Spencer, Darwin, and the world jarred, Carnegie grew agitated, responding: "Let me get a little time for breathing please—You travel fast in this direction." With a struggle emerging, he had no choice but to turn his attention back to Pittsburgh and steel, and for the next several weeks, as he and Vandy sailed from India to visit Arabia and Egypt, Sicily, and finally Rome, he resented more and more the intrusion, taking it personally. "I think Mr. Shinn might have spared me his long letter of complaint," he wrote to another partner. "It has of course cut my holiday short and made me uneasy. Surely he couldn't expect me to act on such a matter until my return. What use then in annoying me. I would not have done it to him had he been away."

By the time Carnegie returned to his home at Cresson Springs in midsummer, his dedication to evolutionism and a cooperative spirit among nations, and his growing opposition to religious expansionism and wars of empire, were never firmer—he had "suffered a sea change, into something rich and strange," he wrote. He had observed and compared the world's peoples through their struggles to survive and had come away opposed more than ever to "those parochial prejudices and false claims of superiority that most of his fellow countrymen subscribed to in their attitude towards the people of the exotic East," according to biographer Joseph Frazier Wall.

"No nation has all that is best," Carnegie wrote, concluding his travelogue as he took time in the mornings to engineer Shinn's ouster; "neither is any bereft of some advantages, and no nation, or tribe, or people, is so unhappy that it would be willing to exchange its condition for that of any other.

"Another advantage to be derived from a journey round the world is, I think, that the sense of the brotherhood of man, the unity of the race, is very greatly strengthened thereby," he concluded.

> Wherever we have been, one story met us. Everywhere there is progress, not only material but intellectual as well, and rapid progress, too. . . . We saw no race which had retrograded, if we except Egypt, which is now in a transitional state, and will ultimately prove no exception to the rule. The whole world moves, and moves in the right direction—upward and onward—to things that are better than those that have been and those to come to be better than those of today.

DESPITE HIS SEVEN YEARS of cheerful service, John Fiske, at age thirty-seven, was sadly misplaced as an assistant college librarian. Privately he was bitter, and in February he finally quit. During the previous summer, he had been invited to give a lecture series at the Old South Church in Boston. The historian Francis Parkman, who shared many of his views on society, suggested the early history of America as a fruitful new subject, advising him: "I believe that you could do the work better than anyone else." Having examined and cataloged twenty thousand volumes and pamphlets in Harvard's "America Room," Fiske eagerly agreed.

Since the publication of his *Cosmic Philosophy*, he had been drawn "more and more to sundry problems and speculations connected with the transplantation of European communities to American soil, their development under new conditions, and the effect of all this upon the general progress of civilization." The commodious new house on Berkeley Street and the Petersham retreat had both been provided by his mother and stepfather, a wealthy New York lawyer whom Hayes had appointed minister to Russia and who supported Fiske's work enthusiastically, so his family was secure financially. Now, as he applied the doctrine of evolution to human history, he began to view the emergence of the American people as its crowning creation. Having produced only a few essays in recent years—but urged on by Darwin, Spencer, and Huxley—he let himself imagine a large audience eager for such a theory.

Fiske's course on "America's Place in History" opened on March 10. The basilica was filled for his first lecture, on "The Era of Maritime Discovery." "The voyage of Columbus," he began, "was in many respects the most important event in human history since the birth of Christ." By putting the conquest and settlement of America in the context of earlier European attempts to extend Christianity's reach throughout the world, notably the Crusades, he attempted to show how the westward migration held high moral and religious purpose "with immense significance to the future development of man's social and political institutions," according to his biographer John Spencer Clark, who was in the audience. The response to Fiske's "luminous survey," Clark wrote, removed any doubt as to Fiske's "ability to interest the American people in the subject of their own history." Writing the next day to his mother, Fiske exulted: "The audience was the very cream of Boston, the enthusiasm prodigious, the success complete. Everybody says I went miles ahead of anything I had ever done before."

By the time he lectured a week later on the influence of the Spanish and French explorers and colonists during the sixteenth century, Fiske understood that he had discovered the great theme that would propel him to the position of public acclaim and influence he had envisioned for himself since college and never quite given up expecting. He described the scene the same day, again to his mother, and while Clark noted that Fiske delivered his talk "with an entire absence of egotistic self-consciousness," Fiske's own account brimmed with heated ambition, outsize confidence, and a newly energized lust for platform speaking:

> This was the worst of nasty March days—pelting snow, slush up to
> your knees, dark as Egypt—a day when ordinarily nothing would
> have tempted me to leave the house. But the Old South Church was
> *packed full* of the very best of Boston, in spite of the weather. I felt
> every pulse quickened by this fact, and they say I was so eloquent as

to seem almost like a new man. The applause was great. I felt the sense of having the people drinking in every word and tone with hushed breath and keen relish. Half unconsciously I deepened and intensified my voice and began to lose myself in the theme, with which I was greatly fascinated myself. I had a sort of sense that I was fascinating the people and it was delicious beyond expression. . . . This thing takes the people, you see: they understand and feel it all, as they can't when I lecture about abstract things. The fame of it is going about briskly; and I believe I shall get full houses all over the country. The Centennial has started it, and I have started in at the right time.

Fiske culminated the series with "The Manifest Destiny of the English Race." He rejected the widely favored term "Anglo-Saxon," which described a culture that existed between the fifth and eleventh centuries, instead calling the agglomerated Aryan population in America "English" because "it is a race which has shown a rare capacity for absorbing slightly foreign elements and moulding them into conformity with a political type that was first wrought out through centuries of effort on British soil."

"When the highly civilized community, representing the ripest political ideas of England, was planted in America, removed from the manifold and complicated checks . . . of the Old World, the growth was portentously rapid and steady," Fiske said. Like Carnegie, he rated races on an evolutionary scale according to Spencer's explanation that primitive societies develop a military aspect while more advanced ones transcend militarism through trade, science, and political flexibility. He noted that "the assaults of barbarism"—war with the Indians—"constituted only a petty annoyance as compared with the conflicts of ages which had gone on in Europe. . . . There was no occasion for society to assume a military aspect. Principles of self-government were at once put into operation, and no one thought of calling them into question."

Fiske predicted that the next stage in human history—"the dispersion of this magnificent Aryan political system over the world, and the complete elimination of warfare," as Richard Hofstadter later wrote—depended on the robust expansion of Anglo-American civilization. England was leading the world through Empire; America could support a population of seven hundred million and rise unrivaled to world power if only it would drop its tariff and compete freely and peacefully with the rest of the world, which Fiske said would convince Europe it could no longer afford military competition. Fiske proffered scientific hope for human society to pass from barbarism to true Christianity. "It is enough to point to the general conclusion, that the work which the English race began when it colonized North America is destined to go on until every land on the earth's surface that is not already the seat of an old civilization shall become English in its language, in its political habits and traditions, and to a predominant extent in the blood of its people," he said.

Here—at the juncture of natural selection and business civilization, especially in the United States as it leaped over other nations—stood the manifest destiny of the race. "The day is at hand when four fifths of the human race will trace its pedigree to English forefathers, as four fifths of the white people in the United States trace their pedigree today," he said, adding, "and the world's business will be transacted by English-speaking people to so great an extent, that whatever language any man may have learned in his infancy he will find it necessary sooner or later to learn to express his thoughts in English."

If Carnegie's scientific humanism led him to envision a supreme but humble American race avoiding the doom of empire, Fiske foresaw a glorious hegemony—"the language of Shakespeare may ultimately become the language of mankind," he told his audience. Upper-class Bostonians, following their Puritan forebears, already believed themselves to be beacons of humanity, and many were accustomed to Fiske's marrying evolution to the spread of Christian doctrine. It embraced all their self-beliefs. Yet even Fiske, used to being hailed, was astounded by their fierce enthusiasm. News of the success of his Boston lectures spread rapidly, and he was besieged with speaking invitations. However, the lecture season in America was all but over. Accordingly, he wrote to Huxley and other English allies regarding lecture opportunities in London. Huxley, who in his own lectures on Marsh's fossils was greatly helping to improve America's scientific and philosophic standing in England less than fifteen years after both had receded sharply during the Civil War, cabled back a terse reply: "Come."

FISKE HASTILY PREPARED for a two-month trip. He was so swept up and exhausted by the whirlwind change in fortune that he slept most of the first three or four days aboard ship. Huxley arranged for him to lecture on successive weeks at a theater seating four hundred at University College, London, and on the night of the first lecture in early June, Fiske was "nervous beyond my wont," he told his wife. "I felt sick all Wednesday forenoon, and was unstrung with anxiety. I feared there wouldn't be 50 people." Just as during his second lecture in Boston, it poured: "a gloomier day I never saw." Ten minutes before he was to begin, only two young American girls were in the room. "I was so unhappy," he confessed, "I could hardly keep from tears." Then all at once "came a rattle of hansom cabs and in poured the people! Within five minutes in came two hundred. . . . Then entered Huxley, and the two hundred applauded." Five minutes more and the room was filled.

"My spirits rose to the boiling point," Fiske wrote home. After he finished the lecture to three long rounds of cheers followed by chorus after chorus of "Bravo!," Huxley rushed up to squeeze his hand in congratulation. A week later, eighty to a hundred people stood in the aisles and the applause was "huge." "Huxley," he wrote, "told me he thought I was making a really 'tremendous hit' (those were his words,—'tremendous hit'), and that a great deal would come of it hereafter."

"For my own part, my dear Fiske," Huxley announced, holding Fiske's hand upraised before the crowd, "I will frankly say that I have never before been so enchanted in all my life. Henceforth I shall tell all my friends that there is no subject so interesting as the early history of America."

The sudden toast of London's scientific and intellectual set, Fiske alternated lunches and dinners with Huxley and Spencer, who he noted was "extremely jolly and friendly," having retained the spiritual benefits of his trip to the Riviera. Darwin, who was unwell and under his doctor's orders to limit his exertions, invited him to Downe. "The old man was as lovely as lovely could be," Fiske wrote. The two shared a smoke on the veranda and stayed up late talking. The next morning, Darwin emerged for a session with a portrait artist, dressed in a red academic gown, grandchildren capering at his feet.

Later that same day, Fiske went for a nineteen-mile tramp with Spencer and the publisher Henry Holt, roaming and "now and then lounging under great beeches and oaks, telling stories, making jokes, philosophizing." While he was away, Harvard appointed him to its Board of Overseers.

Again, as in Boston, the emotions of his final lecture overwhelmed him. "Room jammed: every seat full, extra benches full, people crowding up on the platform where I stood, all the aisles packed full of people standing, people perched up on the ledges of the windows, and a crowd at each door extending several yards out into the entry ways!!!" he wrote home. He went on:

When I began to speak about the future of the English race in Africa, I became aware of an immense *silence,* a kind of *breathlessness,* all over the room—although it had been extremely quiet before. After three or four more sentences, I heard some deep breathings, and murmurs, and "hushes." All at once when I came round to the parallel of the English career in America and Africa, there came one stupendous SHOUT, —not a common demonstration but a deafening SHOUT of exultation. Don't you wish you had been there, darling? —It would have been the proudest moment of your life.

At the end of the lecture they fairly *howled* applause. Gentlemen stood up on the benches and waved their hats: ladies stood up on the benches and fluttered their handkerchiefs; and they kept it up until I had to make a pretty little speech. Then they clamoured again. . . . Spencer kept his bright eyes fastened on me all through the lecture and after all was over he said: "Well, my boy, you have *earned* your success: it was the most glorious lecture I ever listened to in my life."

On July 4, Fiske dined with Spencer and Huxley. "An evening of unrivalled glory and bliss," he wrote of the occasion. "I have never learned so much in one evening before. I have since heard back from Huxley and Spencer that the two would look back on this as one of the happiest evenings of their lives." No other American—not even Marsh—had been so embraced by the leaders of evolution, or by the mother country.

By the time Fiske returned to Cambridge in midsummer, he had given the study of modern history, and that of America in particular, instant intellectual currency. Huxley began arranging for him to return the following year for a series at the Royal Institution of London, proposing a syllabus that would trace the genesis of American political ideas back to the early Aryans. Invitations arrived for some thirty lecture engagements in New York, New Jersey, Philadelphia, Washington, Buffalo, and Ohio. Brief as his first lecture campaign had been, Fiske had won elite acclaim

in both nations. On Christmas, he wrote his mother that he'd been selected to write the introduction to one volume in a British series called
"Portraits of the 100 Greatest Men in History." Emerson had written the
introduction to the whole work. "So you see," Fiske told her, "your boy is
in very good company."

"I AM INVITED," Asa Gray told the ministers-in-training at Yale's theological school, "to address you on the relations of science to religion. . . .
But, until your invitation reached me, I had no idea that I should ever be
called upon to put this passing thought into practice." Gray himself
thought the discussion of evolution and God was "now a little thread-
bare." He and Darwin had talked themselves out, and the argument
about supernatural intelligence and design had receded to the pages of the
Princeton Review and a few other conservative religious journals. He was
driving to complete his long-overdue *Flora of North America* and hated to
pull himself away, but he felt himself uniquely qualified to comment—as
a biologist, friend of Darwin, and reconciler between evolution and the
Bible—and so had agreed to deliver two lectures in New Haven.

Marsh attended both, as did Yale's president Noah Porter. Far more
than McCosh at Princeton or Eliot at Harvard, Porter, approaching
eighty, remained staunchly unconverted by the surge in scientific evange-
lism. He defended against the rise in secularism by striving to keep Yale
"distinctly and earnestly Christian" in its influence, discipline, and course
of study. Yet as a professor of moral philosophy and metaphysics he had
used Spencer's *First Principles* and *Principles of Psychology* as textbooks in
his graduate classes, and he recently had spoken on behalf of the convention of Congregational ministers that, after Beecher's trial, investigated
Plymouth Church and affirmed its faith in Beecher's innocence. He'd assured Beecher, whose views on evolution were becoming more public and
pronounced, that the council retained complete confidence in him.

Gray used his first lecture to summarize the major changes in scientific
belief since he had launched his own research. "Half a century ago," he
began, "the commonly received doctrine was, that the earth had been
completely depopulated and repopulated over and over, each time with a
distinct population; and that the species which now, along with man, occupy the present surface of the earth, belong to an ultimate and indepen-

dent creation, having an ideal but no genealogical connection with those that preceded.

"This view," Gray continued, "died a royal death with Agassiz, who maintained it with all his great ability, as long as it was tenable. I am not aware that it now has any scientific upholder."

He proceeded to explain natural selection. "It is a truth," he said, "of the same kind as that which we enunciate in saying that round stones will roll downhill faster than flat ones. There is no doubt that natural selection operates; the open question is, what do its operations amount to?

"Darwinism does not so much explain why we have the actual [life] forms, as it does why we have only these and not all intermediate forms—in short, why we have *species*," Gray explained. "The point I wish to make here is that natural selection—however you expand its meaning—can not be invoked as the cause of that upon which it operates, i.e., variation." Gray had no problem with the idea of natural selection so long as it didn't claim to explain the force behind the changes that nature selected. And he understood that his audience, while perhaps not expecting to be persuaded, yearned to hear how a first-rate scientist who professed to be a devout Christian handled the question of first and final causes. If Darwin had "destroyed the argument from design in nature as a logical basis for religious belief," as Gray's biographer Dupree suggests, it was now left to Gray, all but alone among his peers, to "recast the argument."

Gray pursued the question in his second lecture, "The Relations of Scientific to Religious Belief." "There are perplexities enough to bewilder our souls whenever we look for the causes and reasons of things," he said, "but I am unable to perceive that the idea of the evolution of one species from another, and of all from an initial form of life, adds any new perplexity to theism." Like many conscientious people, Gray could not believe that science and religion were ultimately at war. The key to life through evolution was the fact of variability—that throughout the reproductive realm, there were imperfections and changes that resulted in new and different forms in each generation. But what caused the changes, and what their true purposes were, remained unseen. Within each variation, Gray said, "lies hidden *the mystery of a beginning.*"

Darwinism "is therefore a good hypothesis, so far," he resumed. "But is it a sufficient and complete hypothesis? Does it furnish scientific explanation of (i.e., assign natural causes for) the rise of living forms from low to high, from simple to complex, from protoplasm to simple plant and animal, from fish to flesh, from lower animal to higher animal, from brute to man? I answer, Not at all!"

So long as the *causes* of variation remained mysterious—and taking into account irrefutable evidence that nature followed explainable laws and was basically orderly—Gray could see no alternative explanation *but* design. "It must be reasonably clear to all who have taken pains to understand the matter that the true issue is not between Darwinism and direct Creationism, but between design and fortuity, between any intention or intellectual cause and no intention or no predictable first cause," he said.

Gray had long avoided commenting publicly on man's place in nature, with its "grave ulterior considerations," but he now felt compelled to address the subject, however cautiously. "You are aware," he said, "from my whole line of thought and argument, that I know no natural process for the transformation of a brute mammal into a man. But I am equally at a loss as respects the processes through which any one species, any one variety, gives birth to another." On the creation-evolution spectrum, theologians now distinguished between two views of how matter became existence. In the first view, creation was universal and immediate, the raw materials of the universe arising at once out of nothing. The second involved gradual creation through natural, and supernatural, processes, forged with existing materials: as Charles Hodge put it, "the power of God working in union with second causes." As far as humans were concerned, Gray said he found ample evidence of both, and did not think them exclusive of each other.

"I do not allow myself to believe that immediate creation would make man's origin more divine," he declared. "And I do not approve either the divinity or the science of those who are prompt to invoke the supernatural to cover our ignorance of natural causes, and equally so to discard its aid whenever natural causes are found sufficient."

If Gray could not win over Darwin, perhaps he was likelier to persuade earnest young Christian theists who craved both religion and science. He offered his own attempts to reckon with the problem as an instructive example. A lifetime spent upholding both faiths had only convinced him that "with all life goes duality," he said.

Gray's lectures were not an apology, but neither did he provide the rousing defense of the design argument that Christian Darwinists still hoped would arise. In theological terms, it was "near beer"—as Gray himself seemed to affirm. Near the end of the second lecture, he confessed,

> I accept Christianity on its own evidence, which I am not here to specify or to justify. . . . I take it that religion is based on the idea of a Divine Mind revealing himself to intelligent creatures. We shall perhaps agree that the revelation on which our religion is based is an example of evolution; that it has been developed by degrees and in stages, much of it in connection with second causes and human actions; and that the current of revelation has been mingled with the course of events.

DURING THE FIRST TERM, Sumner introduced a course for Yale upperclassmen in social science—"years before any such attempt was made at any other university in the world," he would recall—and he assigned as his text Spencer's *Study of Sociology*. Troubled by the perils it posed to young minds, a few orthodox faculty men informed Porter, who read it, belatedly. Porter was appalled, especially by the chapter titled "The Theological Bias"—Spencer's term for the religious turn of mind that "brings errors into the estimates men make of societies and institutions." Spencer regarded several other biases—class, political, emotional, educational—as equally troublesome. He argued that patriotism, which he defined as national egotism and identified chiefly with America, also clouded judgment, distorted truth, and warped conceptions of good and bad in social affairs. But his examination of religion struck Porter as a deliberate affront to Christianity.

Spencer classified theological bias as any obstacle to scientific knowledge deriving from a fanatical belief about the relation of man to God. He cited South Seas cannibal tribes who believed they honored their gods by roasting their victims alive before they ate them, and who yet at the same time looked upon other tribes in horror because they had no religion, didn't believe in deities, and didn't engage in human sacrifice. "The ferocious Fijian doubtless thinks that to devour a human victim in the name of one of his cannibal gods is a meritorious act," he observed, "while he thinks that his Samoan neighbor, who makes no sacrifice to these cannibal gods, but is just and kind to his fellows, thereby shows that meanness goes along with his shocking irreligion. Construing the facts this way, the Fijian can form no rational conceptions of Samoan society.

"Speaking generally, then," Spencer wrote, extrapolating, "each system of dogmatic theology, with the sentiments that gather round it, becomes an impediment in the way of Social Science." He introduced as further illustration the sectarian struggle among Christians regarding the Holy Trinity:

> Here we have theologians who believe that our national welfare will be endangered, if there is not in all churches an enforced repetition of the dogmas that Father, Son, and Holy Ghost, are each of them Almighty; that yet there are not three Almighties, but one Almighty; that one of the Almighties suffered on the cross and descended into hell to pacify another of them; and that whoever does not believe this, "without doubt shall perish everlastingly." They say that if the State makes its priests threaten with eternal torments all who question these doctrines, things will go well; but if those priests who, in this threat, perceive the devil-worship of the savage usurping the name of Christianity, are allowed to pass it by in silence, woe to the nation! Evidently the theological bias leading to such a conviction entirely excludes Sociology, considered as a science.

According to Spencer, any special religious bias accompanied by a special set of doctrines "inevitably prejudges many sociological questions." Such prejudice blinds cannibals and Christians alike:

> One who holds a creed as absolutely true, and who by implication holds the multitudinous other creeds to be absolutely false as they differ from his own, cannot entertain the supposition that the value of a creed is relative. That a particular religious system is, in a general sense, a natural part of the particular society in which it is found, is an entirely alien conception; and, indeed, a repugnant one. His system of dogmatic theology he thinks good for all places and all times. He does not doubt that when planted among a horde of savages, it will be duly understood by them, and work on them results such as those he experiences from it. Thus prepossessed, he passes over the

proofs found everywhere, that a people is no more capable of suddenly receiving a higher form of religion than it is capable of suddenly receiving a higher form of government.

On December 6, Porter wrote to Sumner, registering his disapproval with the use of Spencer's text. The assignment, he noted, "has made a great deal of talk and is likely to make still more." Porter criticized Sumner's decision to offer the book to undergraduates, whose ability to "discriminate between the valid and the invalid is much below that of a graduate," and said:

> As I am presumed to authorize the use of every textbook, I must formally object to the use of this. The freedom and unfairness with which it attacks every Theistic Philosophy of society and of history, and the cool and yet sarcastic effrontery with which he assumes that material elements and laws are the only forces and laws which a scientific man can recognize, seem to me to condemn the book as a textbook for a miscellaneous class in an undergraduate course. . . . I feel assured that the use of the book will bring intellectual and moral harm to the students, however you may strive to neutralize or counteract its influence, and that the use of it will inevitably and reasonably work serious havoc to the reputation of the college.

Sumner thought better than to reply in writing and a few days later went to see Porter in his office. Like a gentleman's club, Yale preferred to handle disputes quietly, and Sumner presumed Porter's letter was an invitation to discuss the matter personally, outside the official channels of faculty and trustees. By long-standing protocol, departments decided their own remedies. "If there are defects in our system," the previous president had advised Porter at his inauguration in 1872, "the faculties are, as they ought to be, mainly responsible; if an inefficient or unfaithful officer comes into a chair of instruction, the faculties, who know him best, and not the corporation, are to bear whatever censure is justly due." And Porter, fiercely paternal, had shepherded Sumner's career at Yale since his undergraduate days, when in a letter of introduction abroad he commended Sumner as "a young gentleman of superior powers and mind, a very fine scholar and writer . . . a very excellent and promising man." The two men—alike stern and unyielding—were friends.

Porter laid out his concerns. "The book, he thought, was open to grave objections," Sumner recalled. "It treated sacred subjects in a tone that, however disguised, seemed to him sneering and flippant, and liable to give a wrong bias to the thoughts and opinions of the students using it." He "did not specify any particular passages which he considered as being of an infidel or irreligious tendency, but contented himself with a general objection to its tone of dealing with sacred things." He therefore requested that Sumner discontinue its use, "if possible."

Sumner, regretting the attempt at interference, explained that if the use of the book were prohibited, "I should resign my position, as I did not think I could properly fill the chair of Political and Social Science if I was hedged about and restricted in such a manner." Sumner believed firmly that no other textbook was either as authoritative or as elucidating as Spencer's. While he also disapproved of Spencer's tone and disagreed with him on many fundamentals, he saw no way to teach sociology without it, he told Porter.

Porter vacillated. "I stated my view of the case to President Porter very frankly," Sumner recalled, "and, while he did not at all change his view of the book, he yielded so far as to permit the book to remain on the schedule, and even went so far as to announce it as one of the subjects of study at the commencement of the January term." They agreed it would be used only by the senior class, and for just one term—New Year's to Easter.

If Sumner hadn't won—Porter still believed it was within his jurisdiction to tell professors what books they could use in their classrooms—he believed now he also hadn't lost. He trusted that his interview with Porter had brought the matter to a close, and he expressed satisfaction with both its handling and its outcome. "President Porter throughout acted in the most courteous and kindly spirit," he later told a reporter, "and while he still retains his original opinion of the book, he has not gone so far as to exclude it."

WASHINGTON, 1880

> *There is apparently much truth in the belief that the wonderful progress of the United States, as well as the character of the people, are the results of natural selection: for the more energetic, restless and courageous men from all parts of Europe have emigrated during the last ten or twelve generations to that great country, and have there succeeded best.*
>
> —CHARLES DARWIN, *The Descent of Man*

JOHN FISKE HAD SPECIFIED to the architect who designed his home that he wanted his capacious study to open to a music room at one end. Self-taught on the piano, he could perform from memory certain Beethoven sonatas, Chopin nocturnes, and pieces by Schubert, and he regularly slipped away from his overrun desk to the keyboard, where he played and sang with great feeling and enthusiasm. "Next to his love for his family was his love for music and nothing gave him more happiness," a friend observed. "In speaking of a future life he always associated it with music."

In January, Fiske embarked on his first full lecture campaign in abundant spirits. Uplifted by his whirlwind popularity, he now anticipated his first real financial success. The fame of his lectures in London had reached New York, where large audiences poured into Chickering Hall and he was invited back to speak to women only; but apparently not Philadelphia, where Fiske was "sadly disappointed" with the turnout. When the fact became known that he'd had meager crowds there, a few wealthy citizens "made up a purse" for him.

Official Washington opened its arms for Fiske. With Hayes preparing to fulfill his promise to serve only one term, Republican aspirants for president—a long list that again included Grant and James Blaine and, for a final time, fleetingly, Beecher—were positioning themselves to run for nomination, while Schurz and other reformers scrambled to put forth a suitable candidate at the upcoming convention in Chicago. Schurz, whose sympathy for Fiske's racial views had been apparent since Schurz's opposition to Grant on Santo Domingo, was also under attack in a growing tempest over the rights of Indians. But he took time out to play a leading role in getting together the formal invitation to Fiske, which was signed by Hayes, senior members of his cabinet, the chief justice of the Supreme Court, senators, generals, historians, scientists, and other distinguished residents. Hayes, in signing the document, said he had heard much about Fiske's success in London and asked, if Fiske came to the city, to meet with him.

Fiske arrived in Washington in mid-February to give four lectures in the Congregational Church. "Got here to breakfast, Wednesday morning, and saw Schurz, who is lovely and very jolly and who invited me to his house *sans* dress-suit in the evening," he wrote home. Schurz too cherished a normal home life and revered music, and he had just fallen in love with a woman he would remain intimate with for the rest of his life but never marry. The administration's Southern policy had failed utterly, the South more lost to the Republicans than ever. Finding the possibility of a third term for Grant utterly unacceptable, Schurz was ardently fostering two other candidates.

That night Fiske dined with Schurz and his two grown daughters and "a profoundly meditative old German chap who beamed on us all the evening and vouchsafed three 'Ja's' as his contribution to the conversation," he wrote. He went on:

Carl and I soon got on to music; he made me play. I was in my most *cantabile* mood, *very* happy and ready to play all night. Schurz has a *magnificent* Steinway grand, every tone of which entranced me. I played *my best*. Then Schurz extemporized. He has a wonderful gift for improvising. He played one very delightful nocturne, making it up as he went, but couldn't play it over again. Most such things are trash: but Schurz's playing is not trash. Then he played a sonata of Chopin's with great fire and expression. His *touch* is beyond measure delightful.

Staid till 1:30 am and the girls sat up. Truly we had a magnificent time.

During the evening, Schurz reiterated Hayes's invitation. The president was interested in having what Fiske liked to call a "chin wag" with the celebrated stepson of the Honorable Edwin Stoughton, who along with Evarts had argued Hayes's claims before the electoral commission three years earlier, and who had recently retired from his posting in St. Petersburg after the harsh Russian winter seriously weakened his health. Two days later Fiske visited Hayes at the White House, recalling:

> He received me very warmly and said he felt very proud of my going over to England to speak to John Bull about America, and of my reception there. When I thought it time to go, the President urged me to stay as long as I could; and he treated me with very marked deference. He kept me more than an hour, till all the Cabinet came in for a Cabinet meeting. The President then introduced me to all the members I didn't know, and we had a jolly talk for fifteen minutes before "biz," when I left.

Fiske hoped that the government's embrace would translate into ticket sales, but his audiences in the capital, while distinguished, were small, and financially the Washington lectures were a failure. Following so closely on his experience in Philadelphia, he began to doubt that he would succeed after all as a writer and lecturer on American history—"his historical undertaking," as Clark called it. His apprehension diminished, however, as he returned to New York, fulfilled three overflow engagements, visited his mother, and returned to Cambridge to find a letter from Huxley inviting him to deliver three lectures on "American Political Ideas" at the Royal Institution of London in May. As Hayes had confirmed, the surest route to distinction for an American artist, scientist, or intellectual remained on the other side of the Atlantic. Fiske resolved to use his London series to broaden both his domestic audience and the scope of his subject.

He spent twenty-three days preparing new lectures, the last four in Huxley's library in London. He planned the series to be "one of the most lucid and powerful peace arguments that has ever been made," Clark wrote. Fiske's prediction of historical supremacy for English-speaking peoples had morphed into an argument for the natural easing of man's imperative to make war, even as Europe, especially since the rise of modern Germany, faced a growing anxiety that the great industrial nations inevitably must try to destroy each other. Fiske offered a more benign view of social evolution, and again English audiences flocked to hear him speak.

Upon sailing for Liverpool, he had written to Darwin, telling him about his plans. "I am unable to follow you in detail quite so closely as I used to," Fiske told him,

> for year by year I find myself studying more and more nothing but history. But Huxley told me last year that he thought I could do more for the "Doctrine of Evolution" in history than in any other line. To say that all my studies to-day owe their life to you, would be to utter a superfluous compliment; for now it goes with out saying that the discovery of "Natural Selection" has put the whole future thought of mankind on a new basis. When I see you I shall feel a youthful pleasure in telling you what I would like to do, if I can.

Again earning an invitation to Downe, Fiske, accompanied by his wife, Abby, visited Darwin overnight before leaving for Edinburgh and more lectures. Darwin gave Abby flowers from his garden, which Fiske carefully pressed and kept. Huxley feted them in London, and when they returned from Scotland before traveling on to the countryside and Paris, Spencer invited them for lunch in his rooms. "Spencer is in better health than he has known for years and is one of the jolliest companions I have ever taken a glass of beer with," Fiske reported to his uncle. "I never met a man in my life who for brilliant conversation could be compared with him; and then his voice is so rich and musical you could never get tired of hearing it."

Fiske's marked success in England was widely noticed in the American press, and when he returned home in late July, the demand for his lectures spiked. With a repertoire of nine lectures, which could be delivered singly or in courses of three, four, or six parts, he had adapted his range of topics and the level of his discourse "so as to meet the great variety of local conditions," Clark wrote. Invitations for the following season arrived from cities across the East and Midwest.

Fiske's prominence now appeared guaranteed, although he was disconcerted to discover a new challenge, from Harvard philosopher William James. Earlier in the decade, Fiske had been a member of the circle of James and others in Boston who rebelled against the more mechanistic interpreters of evolution who discarded the role of metaphysics and the human spirit in society. Now, in a lecture to the Harvard Natural History Society reprinted in the *The Atlantic Monthly*, James launched a blistering attack on "Mr. Herbert Spencer and his disciples" that centered on Spencer's attempts to extend the laws of biological evolution to social history. Asking what caused communities to change from generation to generation, James dismissed the explanation of blind development and improvement. "The difference is due to the accumulated influences of individuals, of their examples, their initiations and their decisions," James declared.

Though Fiske hadn't been identified by name, he felt compelled to rebut James in print, penning a reply for the *Atlantic* that turned James's polemic back on James himself by pointing out his own considerable debt to Spencer's writings. James, a pioneering psychologist and pragmatist, responded with a backhanded thank-you: "I have received your spanking, and I shouldn't mind having some more from the same rod. I kiss the rod that chastises me! It is pleasant to find one who so perfectly endorses all I have to say about the facts and laws of sociology; and reading your last pages has made me more than ever regret that you are not teaching history in college."

SUMNER WAS NO DISCIPLE of Spencer. His laissez-faire social creed was premised more upon observable experience than cosmic theory, and he resented Spencer's neglect of the isolated "forgotten man"—the middle-class laborer who toils and sacrifices despite nature's cruel odds. Though his religious beliefs had evaporated, he still on formal occasions wore his ministerial vestments, and he distrusted Spencer's absolute faith in secular truth. Large and forbidding—six feet tall, with a big frame, broad shoulders, and imposing head—Sumner in person was formidable; he swaggered. As he introduced Yale seniors to the study of sociology, using Spencer's book through the winter term, the volume became instantly popular. But it was "Will" Sumner himself, and the lean, unsentimental human world he represented in his lectures, that his students exalted.

Around end of the term, the grumbling over his use of *The Study of Sociology* burst into public view after an unnamed faction, most likely faculty opponents of Sumner's, brought the story to the New York papers. The *Times,* especially, fueled the controversy, running two long articles on consecutive days that began atop page one. The first, on April 4, amplified sharply the stresses underlying Porter's and Sumner's ambiguous arrangement back in December:

YALE AS BATTLE-GROUND
Scientific Research Face to Face with Dogmas of Faith

THE DISCUSSION CAUSED BY PROF. SUMNER'S USE OF SPENCER'S
"STUDY OF SOCIOLOGY"—THE OBJECTIONS OF PRESIDENT PORTER—
THE FACULTY DIVIDED—FEATURES OF THE CONTROVERSY

Referring to Sumner incorrectly as "Wilber"—it identified Spencer the next day as the "White Czar of Agnosticism"—the *Times* catapulted the dispute into the national arena by inflating it into a proxy war. "In its full scope and significance," the paper reported, "it involves the whole issue between science and religion, and its final settlement will decide the attitude of the college toward the modern spirit of inquiry, which proposes to be guided by reason rather than faith." Sumner himself was less certain. He had no desire to stake his career on defending Spencer, and he had agreed, at Porter's urging, to explore alternative readings. As an evolutionary historian, Sumner "hated reformers and their emotionally charged 'causes,' those absurd efforts to remake the world," the historian Burton Bledstein wrote, and he feared losing his rank and respectability if Porter drove him to the wall and he had to resign. Though he had hoped to settle the matter discreetly, now he had no choice but to take a public stand, to address the issues as he saw them—to "stick," as his friends urged him.

Sumner spent a few days at the New York home of William Whitney, his old friend and benefactor who now served as the city's corporation counsel—in effect, the barrier between the city treasury and claims growing out of the ring frauds. As a young lawyer, Whitney had been one of Tilden's famous "boys," who aided in rescuing New York from the Tweed ring and engineered Tilden's presidential bid. Since college, when as classmates he and Sumner divided the prize for English essays and Whitney paid Sumner's way out of the Union Army and then financed his years of study in Europe, Whitney had promoted Sumner's ideas while easing his way socially and financially. They were key allies in the "Young Yale" movement to modernize the institution by severing old ecclesiastical ties and replacing them with economic ones, staking the college's future on its strength in the sciences and connections to business. "Those men who think the classics will recover their ascendancy in education are like bats in sunshine," Sumner would say. "Greek is dead and philosophy is moribund. If we stick to them they will sink us."

Sumner met with a *Times* reporter at Whitney's house at Fifty-seventh Street and Fifth Avenue, one of New York's most splendid. The affair, he stated, had been very much exaggerated. "The controversy, if you choose to call it such, was carried out in the most amicable manner on both sides," he said.

With Mr. Spencer's individual opinions on matters of religion I have nothing to do, but his work on sociology is the only book of the kind in the English language, and coming from as great a philosopher and student as Mr. Spencer, and embodying as it does, the results of years of the most exhaustive and discriminating investigations into a particularly complex subject, it naturally commends itself to those engaged in the study of social science. Indeed, it would be difficult to see how English students could study social science at all, if the works of so high an authority as Spencer were to be debarred them.

The work was a popular one with certain of the younger students and tutors, and I have been at some pains to restrain the hot-heads among them from getting up a public controversy over the affair. As it was, the whole question was settled by President Porter and myself three months ago, without the intervention, to my knowledge, of a single one of the Faculty, and it has not been reopened since. . . . President Porter throughout acted in the most courteous and kindly spirit, and while he still retains his original opinion of the book, he has not gone so far as to exclude it. I sincerely trust that the press will let the matter alone, as its agitation would only call forth useless controversy and be prejudicial to the college's interests.

Provoked, counseled by Whitney, Sumner girded himself as he played for time. The news stories no doubt would bring pressure on Yale's trustees, more than half of them Christian ministers, to become involved. O. C. Marsh, who had taught evolutionary biology at Yale for nearly a decade, and other young progressives offered strong support in any faculty fight, but the struggle had abruptly shifted beyond Yale to Spencer and his book.

While Sumner and Porter alike feared ruinous consequences for themselves and the college, others—Youmans and Spencer above all, and understandably—rejoiced. Spencer's impromptu volume, urged upon him by Youmans during the latter's grim and doubt-ridden European slog nine summers earlier, and which in turn launched *Popular Science* and nearly topped the list in the International Scientific Series—the linchpin, really, in all Youmans's slaving to elevate Spencer's standing among enlightened men of the age—now became a cause célèbre, sparking the first public academic-freedom battle of the new era in higher education. The dominance of God and Christ in the college classroom appeared to be at stake, and Spencer, the "mastermind" of evolution, had ignited, and now loomed over, the battle—eclipsing Darwin at last. In less than a decade, Youmans and Spencer had thrust Spencer's ideas about society and his name from the periphery to the center of American intellectual life and elite opinion, simultaneously storming Yale and, with Fiske's lectures, Harvard.

Youmans joyfully sent Spencer two copies of the *Times*, which Spencer reported back he read with "amusement and satisfaction." "Very probably," Spencer advised, "this local fight will set going a general fight, which will be highly advantageous no doubt." He included a list of suggestions regarding the Yale affair that Youmans, who already had an editorial in type at *Popular Science*, received in time to incorporate into his own comments. In his editorial, Youmans reported that the controversy was spreading. He cited the chancellor of New York University, also a minister, who was said to have declared that "if the works of Herbert Spencer should be introduced into the institution over which he presides, he would resign his position."

Yet despite his attempts to flog the story, Youmans in mid-May told Spencer: "The Yale College flurry is over, so far as exciting public criticism is concerned, but the antagonism is deep, and will quietly deepen still more." Nearing sixty, and ruefully arranging to turn to lecturing as Spencer insisted, he struggled more and more now just to keep at his work, his perennially threatened health undercutting his exertions. A decade ago he'd have risked nearly anything for such publicity, but now Youmans lacked the energy to do much but let the episode run its course. "I am getting sensibly stronger, and feeling better, but I am old, sore, and decrepit in my legs and feet," he reported to Spencer in the same letter. "I walk, however, considerably and increasingly, and hope to gain permanently by it. But I suspect an early old age is upon me, and that I must go tottering through my remnant of days." He added, "I am rejoiced to hear that you are not only holding out well but are advancing, so that you can again take hold. Don't you think you can take your vacation next year on the Rocky Mountains? I want to cross the continent very much but hate to go alone." Spencer, having wintered in Egypt, confessed in reply that he was behind in his work and felt too overburdened to "think of anything in the shape of a long holiday."

During the annual meeting of Yale's governing board in June, Porter issued a formal statement on the matter of Sumner and Spencer. He understood that while unsympathetic to Sumner, the Corporation's members were likely also to feel that he, Porter, hadn't acted vigorously enough to bar the use of a heretical and dangerous text. His wavering hadn't helped him. He now took the position that Sumner's "materialistic agnosticism" and "supercilious contempt" for Christian ideals made *The Study of Sociology* pedagogically inexcusable—"substantially atheistic." Former president Theodore Woolsey held ready, if Porter decided to ask for it, a resolution on the power of the president with respect to textbooks, but the question failed to come up. Apparently attempting to disarm impending criticism, Porter told the trustees that Sumner had given his assurance that he would no longer use the book as a text in his course in sociology, rendering the issue moot. That same month, Porter published a blistering review of the book in the *Princeton Review.*

Sumner, trusting the matter was closed, learned nothing about Porter's ex parte statement to the governors for six months. While preparing in late December to reopen his sociology course, he received a letter from Porter informing him that the use of Spencer's text had come up at the June meeting. Attached was the statement Porter had read to the members. Sumner—rigorously, even relentlessly ethical—erupted with indignation. He believed he had never agreed not to use Spencer's book, only to search for an alternative, and inferred that Porter had represented him as capitulating so as to derail Woolsey's resolution. "I have never yielded the point or authorized any assurances that I would not use the book again," he soon declared, "if I should still find myself so situated that I could not teach sociology without it." In other words, he had not intended his offer to look for another text to imply that he wouldn't use Spencer's if he couldn't find one, and he concluded that Porter was disingenuously using his willingness to compromise to corner him. Considering his position at Yale now untenable, Sumner decided he had no alternative but to resign. Contacting Whitney and others, he reluctantly began to seek out an opening in business or banking.

ON THE NIGHT of June 14, every seat from the stage to the topmost gallery of the Brooklyn Academy of Music was filled with fashionably dressed men and women who had paid fifty cents apiece to attend a mass meeting to ratify the results of the Republican convention in Chicago. Tricolored streamers festooned the proscenium and national flags draped the boxes. Beecher—loose, thinning white hair stringing around his jowls, the cords and hollows of old age visible in his neck—rose to speak, with the throng bursting into round after round of applause. Men threw up their hats; women waved their handkerchiefs. The band struck up "Hail to the Chief."

"Fellow citizens," Beecher boomed.

It gives me great pleasure to-night to appear before you and to advocate the claims of the Republican Party to the administration of the government for the next four years.

I, for one, first, second and last, desired that General Grant should have been nominated. But since he was set aside, should I go to my tent and sulk? Shall I refuse support because I am not gratified in my choice? God forbid! And all the more when the second choice gave to us a man in many respects admirable, a man that for some functions seems to be expressly adapted by the providence of God for the emergencies of our day.

Since the summer of 1863, when he had returned from England after delivering a series of volcanic speeches that were said to have convinced

Britain to cut off arms shipments to the Confederacy, it had not been hard for Beecher to imagine himself so adapted—to be such a man. Lincoln told his cabinet afterward that "if the war was ever fought to a successful issue there would be but one man—Beecher—to raise the flag at Fort Sumter, for without Beecher in England there might have been no flag to raise." Despite the Tilton scandal, his gift for oratory and his party service made him one of the Republicans' most cherished, if not respected, figures. In Chicago, however, with Grant and Blaine deadlocked, and Schurz and the reformers assaulting both of them as tainted and corrupted by graft, exhausted delegates turned to a dark-horse candidate, James Garfield, on the thirty-sixth ballot. After Garfield, a self-made lawyer and wartime major general who had risen to House floor leader, was nominated, Beecher confided ruefully to Pond that he no longer held any idea of becoming president.

At sixty-five, Beecher's vague ambitions as a politician expired, but his star billing at political rallies and the vast applause he elicited were just the stimulus he needed to extend his theological influence, in and beyond Plymouth Church. His congregants were Republicans almost to an individual. He would remain a staunch party man, no matter who the candidate, gaining in return the esteem, favors, and access to power that would help foster and promote his more provocative preaching. But he would no longer defend religious dogma; if he burned bridges, so be it. During the weeks after the Brooklyn Academy of Music rally, Beecher's Sunday sermons began to reveal a stark new unorthodoxy. "It is a gigantic lie," he preached in July,

> . . . that man was created perfect and then fell. . . . The world is
> as God meant it to be. There was no trick. God did not make a bad
> job and then paint it pretty and plaster it up. Such an idea is not
> worthy of Him. In the childhood of thought such ideas might prevail;
> that they continue in the manhood of the world is pitiable and
> confounding. . . . In a sense, God made laws to be broken—that is,
> He knew that nascent and imperfect beings would break them. The
> idea is to be disclaimed and trampled under foot that men must
> do thus and thus, or be destroyed. . . . I don't hold the theory of
> Atonement. . . . I hold that the Divine nature broods over the human
> family everywhere, and tenderly stirs men to rise from a lower to a
> higher state of action.

Beecher made no pretext of being scientific; he exploited evolutionary principles for evangelical aims where it suited him. But now, often in tears, he seemed to purge himself of the last shards of his father's admonishing Calvinism, and of the stain and embarrassment of the scandal. "The truths of the Bible are not to be swallowed whole," he told his parishioners, "but to be sifted." Having won his freedom at last, Beecher decided to preach his own religious and scientific faith, reserving to himself the right to declare the truth as he saw it about God and the human soul, and urging his congregants to follow. "I have never expressed any theology but my own," he announced. "If I am not permitted to hold fellowship with other churches, let it be so. I will not engage in controversy. I have not many years here—I cannot afford to spend them foolishly."

"SCHURZ AND YOUR MOTHER ARE the happiest people you ever saw," Hayes wrote to his son Webb following the convention. In his service to the administration, Schurz had probably worked harder at the real business of government than any cabinet officer in fifty years, and he was the first to apply a scientific spirit not only to the problem of how to survey the bounteous West but to other institutions and policies. He pressed hard for civil service reform—the moral and intellectual improvement of government workers—and by winning several sharp jurisdictional and policy battles with the War Department, he had made himself the man most responsible for the Indians now that major hostilities had all but passed. "The country is to be congratulated as well as yourself," he wired Garfield. In July, after urging the nominee to stress civil service reform in his acceptance letter and being disappointed when Garfield didn't, he embarked on his second lengthy trip to the West to inspect Indian agencies and reservations, a favorite perquisite of the job.

Inheriting Grant's policies, Schurz had taken charge of some 250,000 Indians living on millions of acres at a time when racial views toward them fluctuated, often violently, between vengeance and philanthropy. In his first year, he enforced the removal of a minor tribe of eight hundred farming people, the Poncas, from their reserve in Dakota to the Indian Territory (Oklahoma), but subsequently he pursued a more sociological approach to native affairs. Schurz met with Indians from many tribes, increased his knowledge of their societies, studied their character, and came to regard them as an able race deserving of government aid and relief.

Concluding that rapid settlement, the building of the railroads, and the extermination of the buffalo and other large game augured the end of their subsistence by hunting, he pressed to teach them agriculture, herding, and freight hauling. He cleaned up the bureaus, swept out corrupt agents, and specified that annuities and supplies go directly to heads of families instead of tribal chieftains. The previous summer he'd traveled with Webb Hayes and other friends, partly by private car, partly by horse and wagon, to meet various Indian leaders in their native lands; Chief Crazy Horse of the once warlike Oglala Sioux presented him with a tomahawk and put a war shirt over Schurz's head, declaring: "He Ogalalla."

Now Schurz stopped in Indianapolis on his way west to help open the Garfield campaign, speaking at a rally at the Wigwam. The hall, easily holding three thousand people, was uncomfortably crowded, with hundreds upon hundreds standing.

The vast audience, the *Times* reported, "listened greedily."

"As a member of the present Administration, now on the point of yielding its powers into the hands of a new set of public servants, I may be permitted to appeal to the candid judgment of the American people as to the manner in which the public business has been conducted during these last years," Schurz began.

It has, under trying circumstances, when the public peace was disturbed by riot and violence on the part of a numerous class of citizens, greatly aided the restoration of order and security by a calm and moderate employment of the limited power at its command, without in any case resorting to a doubtful stretch of authority. It has reformed many abuses in the public service, infused a higher sense of duty into its different branches, raised its moral tone, increased its efficiency, punished dishonesty, and kept the service unsullied by the scandals arising from lax notions of official integrity.

Withal, the country is on the whole, in good condition. The people are prosperous again; business is reviving; our industries are active; labor finds ready and remunerative employment; the Government enjoys the confidence of the business community in a rare degree, as our financial management has won the confidence of the whole world.

Schurz's upbeat assessment, by and large true, reflected a new national self-assurance since the conclusion of the Great Railroad Strike and the end of the depression, which a year earlier finally receded everyplace but California. On the thirtieth, Schurz stopped to give a campaign speech in San Francisco before traveling with a military escort and an immense retinue to Yosemite and Yellowstone. The nativist Irishman Dennis Kearney, capitalizing on fierce social and economic discontent throughout the state, had propelled the rise of the Workingmen's Party of California into a force so popular that in 1878 it elected a third of the delegates to a state constitutional convention. Democrats and Republicans were able to stop them from controlling the proceedings only by joining forces, and the uprising had drawn keen interest from Karl Marx, who wrote to an American friend that California "is very important to me because nowhere else has the upheaval shamelessly caused by capitalist concentration taken place with such speed." Schurz in his speech blamed California's continuing hard times on "the disorderly and dangerous elements of society . . . the agitators and their followers . . . who are connected with the Democratic organization."

"I know that you are disturbed by questions more or less foreign to the rest of the country," Schurz said.

> The Chinese problem, and the evils springing from a distasteful immigration, is a problem perplexing to you and the government. . . . The government, under wise control, has solved many perplexing problems—problems as perplexing as this—and it is hoped that they will solve this, too, with honor to themselves and with benefit to all. Let me impress upon you that attempts of a lawless character on the part of any of your people to solve it would be more calculated to injure than relieve it; and I trust—no, I am sure—that this is the conclusion which every good citizen of California has formed for himself.

Schurz possessed a faith in republican government—and in his own righteousness—that at times blinded him to the limitations of both. Earlier in the year, a month before his evening of music making with Fiske, the novelist and poet Helen Hunt Jackson, who Schurz recalled "wished to be to the Indian what Harriet Beecher Stowe was to the slave," sought to enlist his support for the Poncas. She had heard Ponca chief Standing Bear, noble and poignant in his full Indian regalia and feather headdress, lecture through a translator in Boston on the story of his people, which social reformers were using as the basis of a legal appeal on Indian citizenship and rights that they hoped to bring to the Supreme Court. Jackson demanded that Schurz assist the Poncas by bringing suit to recover their original reservation. But Schurz, after investigating and discovering that the Poncas had built new homes and planted crops, quashed the appeal, recommending instead that she use the funds she and others had raised to help the Poncas get individual title to their new farms. The "wise control" of government Schurz extolled in San Francisco presumed the noble intentions and inerrancy of those who asserted it.

After leaving the city, Schurz visited the snowcapped, steel-colored hulks of the High Sierra and then Salt Lake City before traveling on to Yellowstone Park to hunt for elk, moose, and, he hoped, grizzly bears. "His large wagon train furnished excellent meals, which he liked to wash down with champagne," his biographer Hans Trefousse wrote. The tribes he visited along the route seemed content, confirming, Schurz believed more now than ever, that his and Hayes's Indian reforms had been correct.

In Brooklyn, one of the largest and most stirring meetings of the campaign was held in a mammoth tent at Flatbush and Fifth avenues. Beecher both presided and served as featured speaker. The tent's four thousand seats were filled, and a thousand cheering men stood on the fringes while another thousand or more besieged the doors, unable to get in. Organized by the Young Men's Central Garfield Club, the meeting gave Beecher an opportunity to address an audience new to politics, and he spoke little about Garfield ("as pure a minded man as lives upon the Continent of America," he called him) and less about his Democratic opponent, Civil War general Winfield Scott Hancock ("I have nothing to say of General Hancock that is not good. He tried to serve his country"). Instead, he re-summoned the specter of the bloody shirt.

"Down to this hour we find that the Democratic Party, in the greatest conflict known to this age, has never got over the virus that was injected into its veins by slavery," Beecher said. "Now young men, just of age, do you want to vote for the night or the day? For darkness or for liberty?"

"For liberty every time!" a voice shot out.

"That's the voice of the people," Beecher said. "The South and the Democratic Party have for more than thirty years been working for slavery interests, for caste, and now they want the government put into their hands. I suspect them. They were not even cunning. Is the South in a condition to dictate terms to the Nation?"

"No!" came the hearty reply.

"The Southern people in many respects have behaved wonderfully well," Beecher continued,

> but it is the unconscious influence of men and systems that tells the story. While the South ought to have its own local independence recognized, the Southern states are not yet in condition to go beyond that. The army is withdrawn; there is no hindrance. The people are allowed to take care of themselves, but it is wanton almost to the verge of insanity to say that they shall be allowed to take care of us.
>
> They now hold votes in their hand in the Senate and the House, and I would not take them away from them. But they are not yet in a state that fits them to manage the affairs of New England and New York and the great West. My interest in this particular meeting centers in the young men; I cannot understand how a young man born and bred in the North, should go into the Democratic Party.

Beecher then conjured "the anxious careworn face of the martyred Lincoln," beseeching the young men by proxy, "Will ye abandon me?" Deafening cheers erupted as he concluded his address.

And yet if bringing up the Civil War remained, fifteen years after it ended, the Republicans' strongest issue, Democrats countered by attacking Republican corruption and the contested 1876 elections, of which memories were fresher. As the campaign narrowed in the closing weeks, Beecher, Grant, Schurz, and other surrogates for Garfield avoided direct attacks on Hancock, widely respected for his service at Gettysburg, but they claimed he would act as a figurehead for Democratic interests. That the Republican Party had long since become an instrument for men of wealth and power—Grant himself, initially dejected after losing the nomination, was now hastily consorting with railroad owners, trying to become a capitalist—went unsaid.

Beecher presided over the largest meeting of the campaign in Brooklyn on October 30. The speaker was Colonel Robert Ingersoll, the most popular orator of the age. The son of a conservative Protestant minister, Ingersoll was a successful trial lawyer and evangelical agnostic. He ranged across the country, holding spellbound huge audiences that paid to hear his eloquent diatribes against the clergy, the Bible, and the Christian faith, and there were few Americans who didn't recognize him by now as the nation's most outspoken infidel. Beecher, after receiving an ovation lasting several minutes, "paid high tribute" to Ingersoll in his introduction, according to the *Times*. Ingersoll, who committed his speeches to memory, spoke for two hours, delivering a message of confidence in man and optimism for the future. At the conclusion, he proposed three cheers for Beecher, who, anticipating the inevitable public attacks on his moral judgment in standing shoulder to shoulder with Ingersoll, distributed a one-paragraph letter to the papers:

> If it would promote the cause, I would preside at twenty meetings
> with twenty Robert Ingersolls to speak. This is no time to ask
> questions about a man's religious beliefs. If he believes in his country,
> in manhood, in liberty, he has the right to march in the ranks with me
> or any other man. Do whatever you think best about it, and I will be
> obedient.

Beecher's partisanship paid off. Garfield's slight victory in the election—he won by fewer than twenty thousand votes, the narrowest margin in history—kept the White House in Republican hands, while Beecher returned to his ministry better connected politically than he had been during the Hayes interregnum—that is, between the rejection of Grantism and the yet undefined mystery of Garfield, a former team driver on a canal whom Republicans promoted as a hardworking, self-made man but one whose loyalties and positions were still to be revealed. More heterodox in his theology than ever, Beecher resumed his place on the Plymouth pulpit a rebuilt man.

The second Sunday after the election he chose as his text Paul's statement to the Corinthians "For when I am weak, then I am strong." Beecher explained that the whole problem in human life consisted in the struggle between the animal and the spiritual man. The great question, he said, was not how men came into life, or how they went out of life, but how, with reason and morality grafted on animal instincts, one schooled oneself so that reason and the spiritual part prevailed.

There were three states of humanity, he explained. The great multitude of men were in a state of nature, with the lower appetites and passions predominating, but with occasional gleams of spirituality. Another class was notoriously corrupt, scheming, and given to bad conduct. "I have one man in mind now," Beecher said, apparently referring to Tilton, "but I won't mention him." In a smaller multitude, reason and moral sensibility were ascendant, but now and then they faltered. Beecher urged his congregation to strive toward that higher state, by resisting the power of pride, pleasure, and seducing love. What Paul meant in the paradoxical text was, "When I am weak down below I am strong up above," Beecher explained. To strengthen the spiritual life we must weaken the animal life. Always, though, there was the struggle.

With the election peacefully, if ambiguously, concluded, the nation got back to its first order of business—economic and technological progress—with its usual impatience and zeal. Grant, needing something to do to make money, cultivated his friendship with Matias Romero, formerly minister from Mexico to the United States. In June he had written Romero promoting railroad building in his country, assuring him "there is no doubt the work of the railroads will progress rapidly and that Mexico will commence to enjoy a progress admirable and a prosperity extraordinary." Now, on November 11, Romero gave a banquet in honor of Grant at Delmonico's uptown restaurant that was attended by leading men of Wall Street. Grant reassured investors that the shaky and impoverished Mexican government should not deter them, explaining that it was friendly to business, and that while the United States had had nearly a century of peace to develop, Mexico had enjoyed only thirteen years. Two weeks later, just moments before Beecher planned to launch an attack on Calvinism in his sermon, Grant and Romero arrived unannounced at Plymouth Church and took seats in a pew near the altar.

Beecher, in his prayers, asked the divine blessing upon "the strangers within our midst," while all eyes rested on the former president. Beecher said in his sermon: "I won't have any of the medieval doctrines. If God forgives men He does it because of His infinite love and tenderness for His creatures. The moral administration of God is forgiving and forgiving and forgiving, because God is love." After the doxology had been sung, no one rose for ten minutes, the crowd declining to leave so long as Grant sat still. At last, Beecher decided he had to make them go. "I will thank the audience to disperse. A special service may be held if you want to worship a man. The house was built for the worship of God. I will thank you not to block up the aisles any longer. You will go out," he instructed.

"General Grant rose smilingly and started for the door," the *Times* reported the next day. "The policemen on duty succeeded after hard work in making a passage for him through to his carriage, and he finally got away."

DESPITE HIS EFFORTS to reform Indian affairs, Schurz came under mounting attack for his evacuation of the Poncas, and he countered in early December with a vigorous defense. "When I took charge of this department," he wrote in his final annual report,

> the opinion seemed to be generally prevailing that it was best for the Indians to be gathered upon a few large reservations where they could be kept out of contact with the white population, and where their peaceful and orderly conduct might be enforced by a few strong military posts. It was, perhaps, natural that, with limited knowledge of the character and needs of the Indians, and no experience in their management, I should at first accept that opinion.

Though Schurz recognized the removal of the tribe, the subsequent deaths of up to a quarter of its members from malaria, the incarceration of Standing Bear when he tried to return to his native land to bury the bones of his sixteen-year-old son who had died in exile, and numerous other depredations inflicted on the distraught natives as a "grievous wrong," and though he had soon reversed the initial policy himself and pressed Hayes and Congress to redress the abuses, Schurz repeated that the condition of the Poncas in the Indian Territory had recently improved, and that it would be much better if they weren't disturbed by "reports from outside that they would soon be returned to Dakota." High-handed in his liberal humanitarianism, resentful of the criticisms lodged against him, Schurz disliked intensely being blamed for the Poncas' suffering, and his lawyerly, carefully worded response provoked sarcastic editorials even in normally friendly papers such as the *Times*, which noted: "If these banished Indians are enamored of their surroundings in the Elysium of Indian Territory, it is difficult to see why they should be unsettled by vague reports of their being returned to Dakota."

The night after Schurz released his report, the governor of Massachusetts and the city's mayor were among those to address a huge audience at the Tremont Temple in Boston, epicenter of a growing national movement to support the Poncas that now included Holmes, Longfellow, and the antislavery paragon Wendell Phillips, who also delivered an impassioned and eloquent speech. Easterners historically blamed frontier vengeance for the condition of the Indians, but Governor John Long vilified Schurz: "I tell you the infamy of this business is in Washington, not in the West." Former Omaha journalist Thomas Tibbles, who had served as the Poncas' press agent, ushering Standing Bear through his celebrated lecture tour, quoted from the equal protection clause of the Fourteenth Amendment guaranteeing "all persons within the jurisdiction of the United States" the right to legal redress. Why is it, Tibbles asked the crowd, that the government refused to grant to red men rights now accorded "to the negro and the Chinaman"?

Schurz responded indignantly, sending Long a seventeen-page letter in which he reviewed the facts of the case at great length, blamed the Grant administration and Congress for bringing about the Poncas' unlanded status and powerlessness in the courts, and spoke again about the bettering of life for the tribe and the illegal invasion of Indian lands by whites. "But more remains to be said," he noted. "It was reported in several speeches in your meeting that now at last that great wrong to the Poncas has been 'unearthed.' It was fully disclosed and published three years ago, and who did it? Not you, Governor, nor Mr. Tibbles, nor Senator Dawes, nor Mayor Prince. But I did it myself."

Hayes, displeased by a controversy that disturbed him personally and was interfering with his valedictory months in office, intervened the following week. He had relied on Schurz's reporting on the condition and general will of the Poncas to stay where they were, and he had been furious when Schurz, who had stated repeatedly that the Poncas were living in good houses with woodstoves, had been forced to concede to Congress that, three years after their removal from their homeland, all but two families were living in tents because the cabins were too shoddy to inhabit. Hayes stunned a senator by showing up at the man's boardinghouse, slamming his fist on the table, and announcing that he intended to fire Schurz. Collecting himself, he stood by his cabinet secretary in late October when Schurz told him that the Ponca chiefs had written to say they wanted to stay put. Now confronted by the party's abolitionist old guard, Hayes appointed a commission to investigate.

The commissioners visited the Ponca agency in the Indian Territory, meeting with the remaining tribe members, then traveled to Dakota to interview a smaller group who had returned to cultivate land near their reserve. In both places tribe members indicated their desire to remain where they were. Two days after Christmas, a delegation of Ponca chiefs presented Hayes with a declaration offering "to relinquish all their rights and interests" in their former territory. Schurz, worried, kept confidential tabs on the proceedings.

He felt relieved and vindicated when Hayes declared that the evidence demonstrated that the Poncas were "healthy, comfortable and contented" and remarked that "the time has come when the policy should be to place the Indians as rapidly as possible on the same footing with the other permanent inhabitants of our country." In issuing his Indian recommendations in the waning days of his term—industrial education for boys and girls to prepare them for citizenship, land allotments for individual family groups, fair compensation for lands, citizenship—Hayes subtly reproached Schurz's handling of the problem: "I do not undertake to apportion the blame for the injustice done to the Poncas. Whether the Executive or the Congress or the public is chiefly in fault is not now a question of practical importance."

The dispute was not over. Massachusetts senator Henry Dawes, who emerged as Schurz's chief antagonist, attacked Schurz on the floor of Congress, though not by name, for using methods that were "not American in origin" against "weak and defenseless people" and that bore "too striking a resemblance to the modes of an imperial government carried on by espionage and arbitrary power." Schurz retaliated with an open letter to Dawes and had copies placed, since he had no official privilege to speak from the floor, on the desk of every member of the Senate. He complained that he was being attacked because he was German American. The letter disputed and dismissed Dawes's assertions while assuming the high ground: "Senator," Schurz wrote, "let these Indians at last have rest."

As Schurz prepared to leave office, Evarts hosted a reception for him in Washington, while his defenders organized a retirement dinner in Boston, no doubt to inflame his opponents. Dawes's supporters, refusing to sit quiet, put together a counter-reception honoring Dawes on his re-election, and Governor Long drafted a paper signed by state and local officials "to show that the sense of Massachusetts is not on the side of Mr. Schurz—but with you." The Schurz reception at the Hotel Vendome, in the newly filled Back Bay, was followed by a gala dinner attended by 250 of the state's most eminent citizens, who cheered him enthusiastically as he noted that the Poncas, the government, and the public all seemed satisfied. Attempting to seize the last word in the aftermath of his Boston triumph, Schurz published an article on the Indian problem in *The North American Review* justifying his conduct. He seemed to believe to the end that the Indians were now better off than if they had been allowed to return to their homeland, and that he had not made a mistake in enforcing their relocation, even long after he concluded it was wrong.

"Still less would I justify some high-handed proceedings on the part of the government in moving peaceable Indians from place to place without their consent," Schurz wrote, "trying to rectify old blunders by new acts of injustice."

CHAPTER ELEVEN

NEW YORK, 1881

> *Were anyone to call me dishonest or untruthful he*
> *would touch me to the quick. Were he to say that I am*
> *unpatriotic, he would leave me unmoved.*
>
> —HERBERT SPENCER

M Y DEAR SPENCER," Youmans wrote from New York in mid-April,

It was ten weeks ago day before yesterday that I was struck with a
chill, the result of writing in a cold room, and came down with
pneumonia. I was prostrated bodily and mentally from the outset. I
grew better but the stupid nurse washed me with cold water, which
brought on a relapse with pleurisy. . . . The pleuro-pneumonia came
on again in an exaggerated form, and I had a hard time with it. I am
again much better, but the left lung is in a bad way, and, I fear,
threatens long to remain so; but I am free of pain, have a good
appetite, am gaining strength, and begin to walk around the room,
though with a very tottering step. I was terribly reduced, the first
month living chiefly on brandy. . . . Of course in a business way, the
last three months have been a blank.

During his illness, Youmans lost touch both with Spencer and with the
postinaugural fever in Washington, where thousands of office seekers
scrambled from boardinghouse to government office to Congress to the

White House in search of remuneration for their support during the campaign. Despite the acid split between the Stalwarts—the faction of the party's old guard that supported Grant—and those who at first backed Blaine, known derogatorily as Half-breeds, the Republican spoils system remained secure. So did Spencer's grim view of the evolution of politics and political institutions, the subject of his latest work, which, as with his *Data of Ethics*, he was serializing in *Popular Science Monthly*. As Youmans's condition improved over the next month, his brother gave him some of the letters he had missed, including one from Spencer explaining his views on the evolution from the militant type of government to the industrial type.

Classifying societies by evolutionary stages, Spencer characterized militant societies as those based upon coercive rule. "As the soldier's will," he wrote, "is so suspended that he becomes in everything the agent of his officer's will, so is the will of the citizen in all transactions, private and public, overruled by that of the government . . . just as in the individual organism the outer organs are completely subject to the chief nervous center." Industrial social systems, on the other hand, are arranged according to the individual freedoms implied in all acts of commerce, and people cooperate voluntarily rather than because they are compelled by any authority. Spencer feared, however, that the new industrial economy, fueled by a fetish for armaments, wars, and military sentiment, also caused a malignant spread of compulsory regulations, and that the freedom of individuals was actually diminishing, and states becoming more and more coercive.

Youmans, exhausted by a forced jaunt to the country, revived noticeably as he read Spencer's latest installment. "I consider that [to be] the most interesting and the most important part of your series of papers; we cannot get enough of this kind of discussion for our magazine," Youmans told him. "There is no salvation for this continent except in the acquirement of some proximately scientific conception of the nature of Government. We are without the stability that comes from long habit, and without any guidance in the shape of national theory. I am so clear that this is the next subject of supreme public moment that I am glad to devote the *Monthly* largely to its elucidation."

To Spencer, as the old coercive arrangements of societies governed by force and caste relaxed and gave way, new institutions arose to take their place, which in turn cross-linked and metastasized into a new tyranny—an "army of officials." This army, as he later wrote in his autobiography, gradually decreases the freedom of citizens by the dictates and restrictions it enforces, while demanding that "more and more of their labor shall be devoted to maintaining it and paying for the work it superintends." The problem was people. Organic changes in government are not matched by an equal elevation of mass character. "The insidious growth of this organized and consolidated bureaucracy will go on," he wrote,

> because the electorate cannot conceive the general but distant evils it entails, in contrast with the special and immediate advantages to be gained by its action. For the masses can appreciate nothing but material boons—better homes, shorter hours, higher wages, more regular work. Hence they are in favor of those who vote for restricting time in mines, for forcing employers to contribute to men's insurance funds, for dictating railway fares and freights, for abolishing the so-called sweating system. It seems to them quite right that education, wholly paid for by rates, should be State-regulated; that the State should give technical instruction, that quarries should be inspected and regulated; that there should be sanitary registration of hotels. The power which local governments now have to supply gas, water and electric light, they think may fitly be extended to making tramways, buying and working adjacent canals, building homes for artisans and laborers, lending money for the purchase of freeholds, and otherwise adding to conveniences and giving employment.

In mid-June, Spencer received Youmans's next, somewhat less discouraging update—despite a continuing shortness of breath that made climbing stairs painful, he'd been able to travel to Mount Vernon. Foremost on Spencer's mind, as ever, was how to complete the next phase of his work. Now that he was exploring the development of social types, and applying Fiske's research in history, he felt impelled to study the United States and its people firsthand. America within five years had become the central proving ground of evolution, Marsh, Fiske, and Huxley having made it the decisive test case in the history of both nature and society. Bountiful wealth, science, steel, education, cheap power, social equality, and unprecedented immigration were combusting on her shores, forging a new variety of man. Troubled by Youmans's failing health, a priority now more pressing perhaps even than his own, Spencer set about laying the ground for a visit, cautiously hinting at his plans—being "shady," as Youmans would put it—in his reply from Bayswater:

My Dear Youmans: I got your last letter some three or four days ago, and regret to hear that you are not gaining strength more rapidly than appears. However, if you are avoiding relapses, that is something; and now that you have, I suppose, favourable weather, we will hope the progress will be more rapid. You ought to stay down in the country and bask in the sun; or, if too hot, then in the shade of a tree. Lounging about in the open air, doing nothing except, if you can, carrying on a lively conversation, is the best thing for you.

I am glad to see that you take the same view as I do with respect to the supreme importance of true political theory, especially for you in the United States. I do not believe that a true theory will do much good, but one may at any rate say, contrariwise, that an untrue one does a great deal of harm; and at present much mischief is going on among you as a result of untrue theories.

After my experience last year in going to and from Alexandria, on each of which occasions I had a three days' voyage, my fears of sea traveling in respect of entailed sleeplessness are somewhat diminished, and consequently, I have of late been entertaining the thought that I may possibly come over to see you. If so, it will be, I think, in the latter half of next year. At present I say this to yourself only, not having come to any positive decision.

IN WASHINGTON, Garfield hastened to get away from the office seekers, malaria, and extreme summer heat. It was announced that he would be traveling with his family and several cabinet members to attend the graduation ceremonies at his alma mater, Williams College, before going on vacation. Aligning with the Half-breeds, he had named Maine senator James Blaine secretary of state, and on Saturday, July 2, as Garfield's carriage arrived at the nearly deserted Baltimore and Potomac station for the 9:30 limited express to New York, Blaine climbed down with him, fancifully tossing his cane again and again in the air. They strolled together arm in arm chatting through the passenger rooms, trailed by a servant toting the president's bags, when a slight, sallow, dark-bearded man in scruffy dress whirled suddenly toward them, drew a .45-caliber revolver, and shot Garfield twice, in the arm and back. As Garfield collapsed to the floor—"his crushed top hat beside him, his gray traveling suit stained with blood," historian Charles Rosenberg wrote—the assassin was seized by an alert D.C. policeman.

He was Charles Guiteau, identified by the *Times* as "a half-crazed, pettifogging lawyer." Guiteau was a political and religious fanatic who never swore or drank and who subsisted by cadging small sums from family members who thought him dangerous, moving from city to city to dodge bill collectors, and theft. He had dreamed of becoming another Beecher, another Greeley, another Moody, until, after failing at every preaching and journalistic venture he tried, and beating and terrorizing his wife, who divorced him, he spiraled into insanity. Initially supporting Grant, he had switched to Garfield, hanging around the fringes of the campaign, then moved to Washington to propose himself for an ambassadorship and was snubbed at each office he visited: "a kind of butt, sent around from place to place, his own egotism sustaining him," an observer recalled.

Some time in the middle of May, Guiteau got the idea that Garfield needed to be "removed," and after praying for several weeks, decided that divine inspiration, not a tempting Satan, had selected him for the job. He bought a gun and practiced shooting in the marshlands along the Potomac. The previous night he had written a note addressed to the White House, and police now discovered it in his pocket. It read:

> The President's tragic death was a sad necessity, but it will unite the Republican Party and save the Republic. Life is a flimsy dream, and it matters little when one goes. A human life is of small value. During the war, thousands of brave boys went down without a tear. I presume the President was a Christian and will be happier in Paradise than here.
>
> I had no ill will towards the President. His death was a political necessity. I am a lawyer, a theologian, a politician. I am a Stalwart of the Stalwarts. I was with Gen. Grant and the rest of our men in New

York during the canvass. I have some papers for the press, which I shall leave with Byron Andrews and his co-journalists at No 1,420 New York Ave., where the reporters can see them. I am going to the jail.

Garfield was not dead. Several railroad men brought a coarse mattress from a worker's room and laid him on it; the first physician arrived shortly after. He gave Garfield brandy and spirits of ammonia, then, assuming the president was dying, plunged his unsterilized finger into a wound in his lower back, assuring Garfield that it wasn't serious. "I thank you, doctor," the president said, "but I am a dead man." Minutes later, he was evacuated to the White House, where throughout the day he was seen by teams of government and private doctors who concurred that his condition was too grave to permit probing for the bullet. "Most contented themselves," according to Rosenberg, "with introducing their fingers into the wound." Outside in the corridor, reporters swarmed those coming from the bedside. Extra editions were issued as huge, anxious crowds milled outside newspaper offices throughout the nation.

Americans quaked at the news, opinion quickly dividing over whether Guiteau was a lone madman, part of a larger conspiracy, or—because of his foreign-sounding name—a European-style nihilist, an imported consequence of uncurbed immigration. "If this is the outgrowth of Nihilism," Grant announced, "I am in favor of crushing it out immediately by the prompt execution of would-be assassins and their followers." The stock market dropped precipitously. Reformers like Schurz rushed to emphasize the connection to the spoils system, depicting Guiteau as the inevitable result of a political system predicated on self-promotion, and Garfield as a martyr to the cause of civil service reform.

Clergymen of all denominations led the national vigil, it being assumed, based partly on faith and partly on the primitive state of medical practice, that Garfield's fate was in God's hands. At Plymouth Church, Beecher, pausing over and over to wipe the tears from his cheeks, urged his weeping congregants to deliver "holy prayers, great prayers" that God in His mercy preserve Garfield's life. He assured his followers that the shooting had been the act of a lone gunman, not a conspiracy, and that in this the nation could find comfort. "It was a wanton stroke from without that struck our President down," he told them. "It was not from an army, not from a palace, not from any subterranean depth. It was from a lunatic asylum that this arrow of death was shot out."

Youmans, nurturing other concerns, neglected to mention the crisis in his next letter to Spencer on July 8. His bronchitis was disappearing, and he was getting out more, but he was troubled by the seeming indifference to Spencer's new work on the state. "In regard to the reception of the articles on Political Institutions, it has been of course far from what we could wish, but has been as much as we might have expected," he wrote to Spencer. "I am not aware that they have elicited intelligent discussion or criticism in any quarter. They have been noticed, with other articles by the newspapers—that is, simply referred to and generally with undiscriminating praise." The obstacles to success in trying to proselytize for a scientific political order in the face of a shocking tragedy provoked by a zealous madman appeared not to have occurred to him.

He used the rest of the letter—and his strength—to reassure Spencer that America still needed them both; that the nation, despite violent contradictions, remained more than ever the crowning reflection of Spencer's theory, and that Youmans's mission to promote Spencer as the guiding, inspirational light of the new age of science was winning adherents and would prevail. "I have, however, been perfectly satisfied to go on with the series because I know the papers are extensively read," Youmans continued.

Our circulation is not large, but the magazine is much read. It is the most worn of all in the clubs and libraries.

If we depended upon what the press says of the *Monthly* we should stop it tomorrow. It gets the least critical attention of all the magazines. There is the same commendatory mention of it every month where it is referred to at all. But there is a sort of dread of it, partly from incapacity to understand it, partly from religious prejudice, and very much because of its contrast to the light and lively journals that cater so skillfully to popular ignorance. I think our patronage is quite independent of anything the papers may or may not say. . . .

I think we could run the *Monthly* solely on the contributions that are sent us pro and con in relation to your ideas and works.

So I am delighted that your experiences at length make it possible to entertain the idea of coming to the United States. There will be much to interest you, and it is on every account desirable that you should pay this country a visit, if possible. Our fifty million people will soon be a hundred million, and they are developing a continent at a rate which must be seen to be understood. We are loose and getting wild on social matters, and the carpenter theory of government is predominant. Whatever the result may be, the experiment is a grand one, and you should not let it pass without some careful scrutiny. I hope that the project will look increasingly feasible, and as soon as it is fairly settled in your mind I wish you would let me know.

In Beecher's communion service while Garfield lay dying, he stressed that Americans had nothing to fear in losing one man, even their leader. "In the nature of free, intelligent government established by an educated common people the strength of the Government is not in the Government," he said. "The Nation is broad and strong. It stands as immovable as the mountains until it shall be rocked to its base by its own infidelity."

Now, in appealing to Spencer to visit, Youmans made much the same point: an evolutionary juggernaut, America could not be slowed by the acts of men, either great or small, but only by its own defiance of reason and truth. In the meantime, though Garfield's chances did not seem good, he rallied. Navy engineers began delivering an eventual half-million pounds of ice to cool the president's sickroom, and Alexander Graham Bell developed a metal detector and brought it to Washington to try to locate the bullet, the effort proving unsuccessful owing to interference from Garfield's bedsprings. Two weeks after the shooting, Garfield was sitting up and taking food; a doctor confidently predicted to a reporter from the *New York Tribune*, "ultimate recovery is beyond all reasonable doubt."

SUMNER WAITED until the overseers returned to Yale in June to respond to Porter's account of their discussion of his use of *The Study of Sociology*. In order to tell his side of the case, and vent his strong feelings, he sent an eighteen-page letter to each member of the faculty and Corporation under the heading "A private and personal communication." Troubled that it had taken six months for him to learn that Porter had told the trustees that he would drop the book from his curriculum, "suffering much annoyance from misrepresentation and public abuse," and faced with the unwanted prospect of resigning, Sumner, at age forty-one, lacking a secure offer elsewhere, wanted to clarify his position.

"Four or five years ago," he told them,

my studies led me to the conviction that sociology was about to do for the social sciences what scientific method has done for natural and physical science, viz.: rescue them from arbitrary dogmatism and confusion. It seemed to me that it belonged to me to give my students the advantage of the new standpoint and method just as fast as I could win command of it myself. . . . Sociology is so new that only three or four persons in the world have written upon it as an independent science.

When I looked about for using [a textbook], Spencer's *Study of Sociology* was the only one which could come into account. I considered it very faulty as a textbook, and I doubted if I could use it, but after considering the matter for more than a year I made up my mind that the right and interest of the students to learn something of sociology outweighed any faults or deficiencies in the book, and that, for want of something better, I could probably use this book as a means of giving the students the instruction to which they are entitled.

In this judgment I did not take into account the religious character or tone of the book, which is not, so far as I can see, open to any fair objection. Mr. Spencer's religious opinions seem to me of very little importance in this connection, and when I was looking for a book on sociology, the question whether it was a good or available book in a scientific point of view occupied my attention exclusively. Neither did I take into account the horror of Spencer's name, which, as I have since learned, is entertained by some people.

Sumner went on to elucidate, passionately, at length, how "Pres. Porter's statement of the issue does not agree at all with my understanding of it." He concluded:

I have always considered that the Corporation did me a great honor when they elected me, a young and untried man, to this important chair. I have tried to justify their confidence. I threw myself into the work of my department and of the college with all my might. I had no other interest or ambition. I have refused (until within six months) to entertain any proposition to go away or go into other work.

It is impossible, however, for me to submit to interference in my work. So long as I am interfered with, my relations to the college are constrained, unsatisfactory, and precarious. I have already lost ground with my work which I had won by great exertion, and I have been forced to suspend further plans on account of the interference to which I have been subjected. While my personal relations to the college are in this uncertain condition I cannot cooperate with my colleagues in planning about the institution as I have been accustomed to do. I seek no action and deprecate none. I simply seek to place myself on the same plane in regard to this matter on which Pres. Porter placed himself a year ago, and to correct any false impression which may exist as to my position in the minds of members of the Corporation who heard his paper.

By framing the dispute as a struggle over academic freedom, Sumner won strong support throughout the college community, and numerous other faculty members and alums urged him not to yield. His old friend Charles Grinnell, a Boston lawyer, counseled: "I hope that you will not allow yourself to be driven out, or frozen out, or shrewdly opposed so as to let yourself go out in disgust. You know we are comparatively young yet, and we shall bury most of the men who are fifteen years older than we are. Unless you have a mighty good and sure thing, not only in view, but in hand, I say, without further knowledge, stay and bury them." Prickly and independent, Sumner relished a good fight. But neither he nor Porter had the stomach for a showdown, and even those who didn't like him realized the college could hardly afford to lose him. Nor could it tolerate a replay of the previous year's publicity if he quit. "Either he found no other place to his liking, or the voices of his friends prevailed, for he stayed on at Yale," Harris Starr wrote.

As the fall term approached, the Spencer text controversy that had dominated Sumner's life for a year dissipated quietly in a fogbank of polite irresolution: Sumner stopped teaching the book, but not on Porter's orders. The evolutionary imperative of upending what Sumner called Yale's "closed canon of human learning" receded in the face of a mutual desire, which Spencer would say was uniquely and unsatisfactorily American, to make an unpleasant matter simply go away.

DARWIN TOILED AWAY at his newest research—with earthworms. Several nights in a row, after tossing in bed, he padded downstairs with his son Francis to observe them, by the light of a hurricane lantern, crawling around in his woods. He believed the effect of their activity in transforming the earth's surface was vastly underestimated, and, convinced that they had a germ of intelligence, he fed them leaves from many different plants, then recorded their dexterity in pulling irregularly shaped leaves into their burrows. "Each worm," his biographer Janet Browne wrote, "was capable of finding either the pointed end of a leaf or a stalk, or could locate the mid-point of a long thin leaf and pull it so that it folded into two halves." Encouraged, Darwin designed an experiment to determine whether this was a mechanical adaptation for pulling in food, carefully cutting out tiny paper triangles and diamonds and presenting them to worms in flowerpots in his laboratory.

The experiment failed. The worms "will do their worst work in such a slovenly manner when kept in pots," he wrote to his cousin Francis Galton, "and I am beyond measure perplexed to judge how far such observations are trustworthy." He also blew whistles at them, and asked Francis to play his bassoon close to them, to see whether they detected sound. They didn't. Darwin, endlessly curious, kept at it. Life's struggle underfoot, besides being an intriguing but undemanding project that he could investigate at home, absorbed him no doubt because he knew he'd soon become part of it.

At Downe, hunched over a garden spade, big white beard flowing over his chest, Darwin could almost forget his place in society. Darwinism, as Huxley aptly put it in a widely reported speech to the Royal Institute in April, had come of age—it was twenty-one years since the publication of *Origin*. Its author, despite his privately bleak religious views, was a venerated figure. He ventured out less and less in public, and went to fewer and fewer scientific meetings, having little enthusiasm or energy for public life.

In August, Darwin made an exception. He agreed to attend the opening of the Seventh International Congress on Medicine in London, the largest and most prestigious gathering of medical men up to that time. It was a ceremonial appearance. Darwin met the Prince of Wales and the "chieftains of Science," the renowned, mostly French and German researchers whose studies of cells and microbes had recently pushed medicine toward becoming a mature science and made health a major public issue. He delivered no speech and attended no sessions. At the reception, he shook hands like royalty, knowing many of the foreigners through correspondence. Huxley, amused, asked to be introduced to him, then bowed elaborately over his extended hand. Darwin sat at the head table.

"There was an immense crowd of all the greatest scientific swells and much delay and I was half-dead before luncheon began," Darwin wrote to his son William. "I sat down opposite the Prince and between Virchow and Donders who both spoke bad English incessantly and this completed the killing."

Rudolf Virchow was a German doctor, anthropologist, archaeologist, public health activist, author, and politician who launched the cell theory of disease and the study of it through microscopes—modern pathology. On the question of the unity of the races, he and Darwin agreed strongly. Assembling a collection that would total about four thousand skulls, ancient and modern, from all corners of the globe, Virchow conducted extensive cranial studies that showed that races could not be differentiated by their brains. More than a laboratory physician, he was a hard-charging advocate for political and social reform. Doctors, he believed, should be "natural attorneys for the poor."

The morning after Darwin left the conference, Virchow addressed the most contentious question facing medical investigators: the use of animals in experiments, which he favored. Darwin also supported vivisection despite his widely noted appreciation and respect for animal life. Animal tests in recent years had produced among the first modern cures. Millworkers who handled infected hides, animal hair, or wool contracted anthrax so often that it was called woolsorter's or ragpicker's disease; up to a hundred thousand cases were reported per year in Europe. In the audience were the young French fermentation biologist Louis Pasteur, who in the spring reported on the use of successful new vaccines for the disease, and the German bacteriologist who identified the bacillus that caused it, Robert Koch.

"Medicine can no longer be practiced in a rule of thumb fashion," Virchow told an audience of three thousand researchers and doctors. Anti-vivisectionism was a potent social movement, argued most passionately by religious humanists who warned that experimenting with God's creatures was a slippery slope: "First animals, then orphans, then the mentally retarded." But Virchow cited several examples of private malfeasance exploiting public ignorance: pulmonary consumption arising, for instance, from infected milk from cows with tuberculosis. "We drink the milk, the germ of the disease is planted, and we owe our death to an experiment made on us by the dairyman," Virchow said. "He knows that his cow is ill, but is it worthwhile for him to give up the sale of fluids coming from a diseased animal? He is not quite certain whether bad milk is or is not poison." He concluded, "In the experiments upon animals we are simply repeating in a scientific way the popular experiments which men daily make in blind ignorance upon men." Since mill owners and water company owners and cattlemen couldn't be expected or trusted to conduct proper experiments themselves, it was up to doctors and governments to do so.

Virchow's stab at chatting up Darwin notwithstanding, his relations with the "king" and "kingmaker" of evolution, Darwin and Huxley, were strained. Two years earlier, he had proposed restricting the teaching of science in Germany. Darwinism in the classroom had taken on political weight in the wake of Marx and Engels's efforts to meld it with "scientific socialism"—the argument that social equality and communitarian government were inevitable next steps in man's development—and Huxley, in the introduction to a German biology text, vigorously defended the principle of teaching evolution in school. Virchow recoiled, urging that its teaching be banned, ostensibly because of the uncertainties about it. Huxley fired back, writing how much greater were the uncertainties about "the linguistic accomplishments of Balaam's ass" that Christianity imposes. Finally, Virchow, taunted by Social Democrats, set out to make a text about Darwinism "look like a terrorists' manual," as Huxley's biographer Adrian Desmond wrote.

It was amid these tensions that Huxley rose to deliver the final address of the conference, to a large gathering of delegates at St. James Hall. He spoke on the connection between biological science and medicine. In fact, the Congress on Medicine was one place—perhaps the last place—where evolution notably had not reached maturity at all, as Huxley must have realized. It was one thing to discover, as Virchow had done, that cells originated from other cells just like them, thus disproving the age-old idea that organisms could arise from nonliving matter—for example, maggots from decaying meat; or to demonstrate, as Pasteur, son of a humble leather tanner, had done with sheep in June, the efficacy of an experimentally produced vaccine to prevent an infectious disease. It was quite another to see how evolution, a concept based on change through the inheritance of new traits, might be useful against illness, when no one understood the physical basis for heredity. Darwin's own theory was *pangenesis*, the abstract notion that every tissue, cell, and living part of an organism produced something called a gemmule, a germ that transmitted inheritable characteristics, but he had no proof that such life-seeds actually existed. Fifteen years earlier an obscure monk named Gregor Mendel had published research on peas that revealed how traits are passed from generation to generation; Mendel's work would not be recognized for another two decades. With no understanding of basic genetics, Huxley had little new science to contribute.

Within weeks, Darwin's anxieties about the results of his worm experiments crested. His doubts about the marketability of a dense volume on his newest discoveries on this subject drove him to deliver the manuscript in person to his longtime publisher, John Murray, who later recalled their exchange in his office:

"Here is a work which has occupied me for many years," Darwin said, "and interested me much. I fear the subject of it will not attract the public, but will you publish it for me?"

"It always gives me great pleasure and hope to hear an author speak of his work thus," Murray replied. "What is the subject?"

"Worms," Darwin said.

He needn't have worried. From the day it was released in October, his worm book sold wider and faster than even *The Expression of the Emotions*, becoming by far Darwin's most popular volume. The generous acceptance pierced his melancholy as he slowed down markedly during the next few months. A cartoon in *Punch* depicted him as the Creator, contemplating the evolutionary wheel of life from worm around again to worm, and a religious writer likened the worm to the Resurrection and the Life. If evolution was still too undeveloped as a science to help treat disease, it was now old enough to generate its own iconography.

In early December, Darwin felt too exhausted to travel to Cambridge to see his new grandchild. Days later, on a visit to London, he experienced a sudden spasm of heart pain. Dr. Clark was again called, and after examining him, declared "my heart is perfectly right," Darwin reported with relief. Returning to Downe, he continued devising experiments and purchased a strip of land to add to his garden, extend his orchard, and lay down a grass tennis court.

SEEKING HIS USUAL SEASONAL AMUSEMENTS, Spencer visited Braemar, a mountainside Scottish village west of Aberdeen where Catholicism reigned and two thirds of the population still spoke Gaelic. When a Free Church clergyman saw Spencer's name in the visitors' book, according to the London journal *The World*, "he was seen to shudder, and being asked, what was the matter, in tremulous accents said that the Anti-Christ was living under the same roof, and straightway convened a prayer meeting in the billiard room as a fumigatory measure." The "exorcism," as Spencer called it, entertained and astonished him.

He had packed and brought along, for final revision, the last chapter of *Political Institutions,* and in his next letter to Youmans, written aboard his friend Valentine Smith's resurrected steam yacht off the rocky coast of Ardtornish, he described its subject matter—the Industrial Type—as "of cardinal importance." Indeed, Spencer now viewed his work on the political necessities of the world's evolving business civilization as not only urgent but paramount: the "culminating chapter . . . of the Synthetic Philosophy, as far as practical applications are concerned," he told Youmans.

Having long and determinedly shunned political action—and with at least a decade of research and writing left in order to complete his multivolume synthesis—Spencer under normal circumstances would have been satisfied to limit himself to publication of his ideas. But working throughout August on the final chapter, he became "profoundly impressed with the belief that the possibility of a higher civilization depends wholly on the cessation of militancy and the growth of industrialism." During the past two years, the burdens of empire had polarized England. Prime Minister William Gladstone, serving a second time, had campaigned on checking the country's aggressive policies in Asia and Africa, and a year into his ministry he had ordered a force of forty thousand men to retreat from Afghanistan; an ignominious end to the country's second disastrous war there in four decades. Rumblings were growing in Parliament about the need to invade Egypt. Spencer had spoken with friends—Lord Leonard Hobhouse, several liberal MPs, professors, writers, politicians—about pressing the government to move harder to curtail the "colonial lobby." By the time he returned to London in early September, he had resolved, ignoring his own unceasing admonitions and "in direct contravention of a rule I had laid down for myself," to assert a leading role in the cause.

On arriving back in London, he found a letter waiting for him from Youmans: "The last installment of Industrialism has come. That and the preceding are two mighty chapters," he wrote. Youmans added that he was "latterly much better and more in the spirit of work." Now that Spencer had indicated that he hoped to visit America, Youmans pushed himself to ensure that he would be well enough to arrange a suitable itinerary, welcome Spencer over, and travel with him. He ended his note with a sweetener: "There are great fishing places on this continent in Canada and elsewhere, and I think you had better plan to give next August to the sport on this side."

Spencer replied two days later, "I am glad to hear that you are gaining strength, not so glad to hear that you are 'more in the spirit of work.' " Youmans had mentioned that he "hardly minded a single pair of stairs, but a second pair leaves me exhausted," and Spencer feared Youmans would abort his recovery by taking on too much, as always. "If instead of this you would write 'more in the spirit of play,' it would be very much better. The worst of you is, the moment you get a little extra strength you use it up too fast.

"I am glad," he went on, "that you like the two chapters on The Militant Type and The Industrial Type. They are, in fact, the culminating chapters of the part, and, indeed, of the whole work, in point of importance."

Fueled by an urgent new fervor that seemed, even to him, to flout his belief in gradualism and his stringent efforts to ensure that nothing interfered with his writing schedule, Spencer plunged into the antiwar campaign, writing the next day to, among others, Darwin. He enclosed a circular for the newly named Anti-Aggression League, an outgrowth of regular meetings started during the summer at Lord Hobhouse's home and which Spencer now agreed to lead, and he invited Darwin to add his name to the group. Darwin, anxious about his health and the impending appearance of his worm book, said he agreed with the league's "object" but declined to join until he saw how it worked.

AFTER REMAINING BEDRIDDEN in the White House with fevers and intense pain, his heart gored by infection, Garfield was relocated to the Jersey shore in early September, in the desperate hope that the sea air would do him some good. He died either of a massive heart attack or a ruptured artery, following bronchial pneumonia, blood poisoning, and a punctured liver from one of the digital examinations of his wound, on September 19—eighty days after being shot. Guiteau, acting as his own assistant counsel at trial, pleaded insanity: since Garfield's elimination was God's act and not his own, and since God in choosing him had stripped him of his moral faculty and intellectual judgment, there could be no criminal intent, no blame. He argued additionally, not without merit, that Garfield had been killed not by a bullet but by his doctors. His lawyer presented a medical expert who claimed Guiteau had inherited his madness from his father.

The jury deliberated less than an hour. Facing a large crowd of newspapermen, prison workers, and political hangers-on at his execution, Guiteau read a selection from the tenth chapter of Matthew. "And fear not them that kill the body but are not able to kill the soul."

CHAPTER TWELVE

NEW YORK, 1882

> *God is dead. God remains dead. And we have killed
> him.*
>
> —FRIEDRICH NIETZSCHE, *The Gay Science*

A T PLYMOUTH CHURCH ON JANUARY 2—inauguration day at City
Hall—the auctioning of church pews began just after seven o'clock
and continued till ten o'clock, when all the pews but seventeen in the
body of the church and thirteen in the gallery were sold at premiums
ranging from $425 down to $1. The auctioneer was surprised that no
larger bids were forthcoming, and altogether the sale realized about
$4,000 less than a year earlier—a notable falloff. "The past year has been
one of prosperity and peace in our church," Beecher remarked—neatly if
unintentionally affirming that as the depression, strikes, civic violence,
and conflict over the scandal all died out, local interest had declined in
what he had to say—"and I sincerely hope that the one we are now entering will be marked by the same zeal and activity on your part as has the
past, and that the same blessing of God will be upon us both for the edi-
fication and good of those who may need our services."

And yet if demand for his preaching was off in Brooklyn, it flourished
in the liberal newspapers and Christian periodicals that weekly carried
summaries of his sermons from coast to coast, and he felt more embold-
ened than ever to speak his mind on a wide range of subjects, especially
theology. "The Bible," he told his followers in early February, gesturing

with his arms, "is an eating book—it is the soul's refreshment table. . . . Some professed Christians would tear each other to pieces, like cannibals in private, and when asked if they were true Christians, would demand to be squared by the Catechism." Beecher renounced one by one the literalities of his father—the Fall, total depravity, the revelation of the scriptures—and replaced them with the idea that man is built from the bottom up, inside out, from an animal core, through moral training and guidance. He now came to identify himself, as he soon told a friend, as "a cordial Christian evolutionist."

A month later Beecher developed a severe cold, which grew worse during a train ride to Chicago, where an audience of three thousand turned out to listen to him lecture at the Central Music Hall on "The Moral Uses of Luxury and Beauty." About twenty-five minutes into his speech, he recalled later, he abruptly became so blind that he couldn't see his audience, although he kept on talking in the hope that the attack would pass and his eyesight would return. His feet and hands were ice-cold. He yawned wearily. Startled by seeing Beecher sway and stagger, a man in the audience shouted, "Catch him, he's going to fall!" and several men on the platform rushed forward and helped him to a seat. Intensely pale, his hands numb, he muttered, "I don't think I can go on." As the audience filed out toward home, he was put into a carriage and attended by a doctor, who found his head hot and pulse feeble. When Beecher started to recover, the doctor declared that the "trouble was caused by weakness and derangement of the physical functions" due to his cold and a bout of indigestion, the *Times* reported.

By the time he returned to Brooklyn in April, Beecher was moving decisively to expunge the last traces of his father's Calvinist theology from his own, as if recognizing suddenly that his fund of life was in short supply and that he might have little time left to do so. He was determined to state not only what he did not hold true but also what he did. And so, while he celebrated America one week as the pinnacle of human evolution, a school of fifty million hardworking students striving toward a higher state of mind and morality, he excoriated it the next for adding to "a path of blood around the globe." "As for ourselves," he bellowed, "what shall we say? Let the slaves speak; let the dispossessed Indians speak; let the Chinamen speak. Where is the Christianity of this country?"

He advocated liberty of thought in religious matters, returned to the theme of man-building, spoke again and again of the goal of an uplifted

Christian character. As his skepticism grew, he discarded old positions almost without a struggle. He now supported striking Italian, German, and Hebrew freight handlers: "When we were told of the evils of strikes and the stumblings of labor organizations, we should reply that every advance the world has made had been after stumblings upon stumblings. One thing was certain—our sympathy should be with the multitude, with the poor and weak as against the rich and strong." He challenged the mandarins of capital: "If he be a Christian man, the rich man ought to stand out and say it was an honor for him to bear his portion of the public burden." Parishioners who longed for the grandiose, ultracapitalist "Bread and Water" Beecher were disappointed.

In July, as the country drifted back to work after the spectacle of Guiteau's hanging, Beecher broached the final redoubt of dogmatic Christianity: Hell. He had dismissed the horrors of eternal damnation all his life, once explaining, "To tell me that back of Christ is a God who for unnumbered centuries has gone on creating men and sweeping them like dead flies—nay, like living ones—into Hell is to ask me to worship a being as much worse than the conception of any medieval devil as can be imagined." But now he felt fortified by scripture *and* science, and Beecher took his stance public.

Here was the ultimate conclusion of his evolutionary theology. Beecher told his parishioners that it was plain from Paul's writings in the Bible that in the final future there was to be a great change, and that that change was to be in the nature of an evolution. It was to be from the lower to the higher. At every step in the evolution of the race there was to be a gain for the law of benevolence. And so, how could God conceivably contravene all this by forever tormenting the souls of sinners?

Many people, Beecher said, were infidels simply from the force of their moral conviction and honesty—as lethal a threat to theism as it was to Christianity. "Do you ask me if at that time there will be a reserved place—a walled-in place—set apart for pain and suffering?" he concluded:

No! God is not God if that is so. I don't believe it! That pain and suffering go beyond the confines of this life I do believe, but not eternally. I don't know why, when persons who have not obeyed God's laws here drift over to the other world, pain should not have the same effect there as here—to drive them back to obedience. We can't prove it by the Scriptures, nor can we prove that it don't. . . . But in the grand hour of final victory there will be no undergroan of suffering that is eternal and knows no end but suffering. Such a thing would be barbaric, infernal, demonical. I can never worship any God but a just God. Take away the idea of eternal torment and you take away half the problems that prevent man's progress, and you throw light on God's justice.

AFTER SEVERAL MONTHS of intensifying strategy sessions at Lord Hobhouse's, a public meeting of the Anti-Aggression League convened in mid-February at London's Westminster Palace Hotel. "Being anxious to see a successful start made," Spencer recalled in his *Autobiography,*

I had allowed much work to devolve upon me which should have been undertaken by others. I agreed, contrary to my original intention, to take part in the meeting, move a resolution and make a speech. With my narrow margin of nervous power, it was an absurd thing to do; and still more so to persevere when, as my diary shows, I was for several days before, breaking down. But I had put my hand to the plough and would not turn back. There was here again illustrated a trait on which I have before commented—the liability to be terrorized over by a resolution once formed: consciousness becoming so possessed by the end in view that all thought of anything adverse is excluded.

Some thirty-six members of Parliament, including several future cabinet ministers, and more than forty professors, writers, and politicians formed the general council. Spencer hovered, fretting, at the center of the proceedings. He had been recruited by the jurist, historian, and religious teacher Frederic Harrison, president of the English Positivist Committee. In addition to delivering his own address, he now crusaded for Harrison's call for a government policy of nonbelligerence except to thwart direct aggression. Not pacifist, the league was pragmatic in its aims; its goal was to curb the urge to go to war, particularly imperialist war, in order to free England from militancy and allow it to advance to a more productive state of industrial harmony. As Harrison detailed the case in his speech:

The vast increase of the Empire in Asia and in Africa has been effected almost entirely by war. If we count up the years since 1832, and set against each year the wars in which we have been engaged, we should find that there have been more wars than there were years; that is, if now and then a year might be found free from war, the next gave us two, three, even four wars for one year.

Between 1850 and 1860, we were engaged in almost incessant war in every part of Asia, from the Black Sea to the Yellow Sea. The fact is that England is very rarely at peace, and has more wars than any other nation in Europe, not even excepting Russia. If we list the years of war we see a very significant fact: there *are* some years in which these Asiatic, African, and Colonial wars seem suddenly to lull. They ceased during the three years of the great Crimean War; they ceased after the great European revolutions of 1848 and 1849; they ceased during the great German war in 1866; and they ceased again during and after the great war in France of 1870–1871. During periods of great danger or watchfulness at home, they cease. That proves that they are under our own control. We can abstain from them when our safety and policy demands it.

Spencer believed the artisan class and the great mass of dissenters harbored strong antiwar feeling, but it soon became clear that the meeting's impact was to be short-lived and negligible. Exhausted by his efforts, frantic at the thought that he had not only wasted time but allowed himself to be diverted by a hopeless ideal, he concluded that he had made a grave and irreversible mistake—"the greatest disaster of my life," he wrote. All spring, usually his most productive season, he became increasingly obsessed with getting his health back. His writing ground to a dispiriting halt as he realized that a dominant feature of the average English national character was to injure others before they injure you, and that the league's work, however selfless and virtuous, was "absurd," "foolish," "irrational." A young woman friend, Beatrice Potter, whose family accompanied him on a brief trip to Holland, found him more consumed than ever with the prospect of never finishing his great opus. Harshly, he criticized the picture galleries at The Hague, observing that Rembrandt's celebrated *Lesson in Anatomy* failed "utterly in the essential point of dramatic truth." "There is something pathetic in the isolation of his mind," Potter wrote, "a sort of spider-like existence, sitting alone in the center of his theoretical web, catching facts, and weaving them again into theory."

Spencer sensed himself ebbing away, descending into infirmity, conscious that "there was slipping by that closing part of life during which [my work] should have been completed," and he blamed his low fires on an evolutionary paradox. While people commonly believe that the pleasurable feeling caused by doing right ought to suffice as inducement to moral behavior, in fact doing right often invites severe penalties and "no compensations whatever." Too well, his current crisis and withering insomnia told the point. He believed he had acted purely out of altruism, at a terrible price. "It is obvious that I had nothing to gain in this world by the implied expenditure of time, money and effort, and as I have no belief in anything to be gained in another world, it cannot be said that otherworldliness moved me," he wrote. "While no good came of our movement, great evil came to me."

"I AM FAIRLY WELL," Darwin wrote Alfred Russel Wallace, "but always feel half-dead with fatigue." Emma kept by him constantly: walking with him when he was able; supervising the servants who trundled him up and down stairs in a specially made chair when his doctors forbade all unnecessary exertion; reading aloud to him from Trollope, after deeming Henry James's *The Europeans* "rather too subtle"; playing backgammon, at which Darwin, listless and frail, nonetheless remained competitive; and in the evenings, "tootling" on the piano. He told his son Leonard that if he had his life to live over again he would make it a rule not to let a day go by without reading a few lines of poetry, and that he wished he had "not let his mind go to rot so."

Dr. Clark, summoned regularly, continued to tell him that his heart was sound, and three other doctors attended him on a daily basis, but after short walks in February and March, his chest pains recurred and he was forced to linger feebly on the veranda. He got to his study less and less often, though his mind remained clear, and he fretted when he couldn't find the strength to note the results of one of his and Francis's experiments. On April 18, he worked until after eight examining a plant, then was carried to his room. He read for a half hour before going to bed, slept uneasily, and was awakened at midnight by pains, faintness, and nausea—"a fatal attack," Emma called it. Darwin died the next afternoon in Francis's arms, at age seventy-three. "I am not the least afraid to die," he murmured to Emma. "Remember what a good wife you have been."

His exaltation doubtless would have mortified and pleased him. Huxley and others campaigned successfully to have Darwin laid to rest near Isaac Newton in Westminster Abbey, where the pallbearers included all but one of the X-Clubbers who'd become preeminent as scientific worthies; doubting he could induce Spencer to join them, Huxley decided not to try. In America, public attention was paid, but less than might have been imagined. Four weeks earlier, when Longfellow died, flags had flown at half-mast atop newspaper offices, and the *Times* article on his life and work started at the top of the front page and ran more than eighty densely packed inches. Darwin's passing was reported in a single paragraph, five days after he was laid out, under the lone headline: THE LATE CHARLES DARWIN. Asa Gray, bereft, wrote Darwin's niece to say that his death "was like the annihilation of a good bit of what is left of my own life."

A month later, the *Times* carried a short eulogy by Huxley. "Acute as were his reasoning powers, vast as was his knowledge, marvelous as was his tenacious industry, under physical difficulties which would have converted nine men out of ten into aimless invalids," Huxley wrote,

> it was not these qualities, great as they were, which impressed those who were admitted to his intimacy with involuntary veneration, but a certain intense and almost passionate honesty by which all his thoughts and actions were irradiated, as by a central fire. . . . He found a great truth, trodden under foot, reviled by bigots, and ridiculed by all the world: he lived long enough to see it, chiefly by his own efforts, irrefragably established in science, inseparably incorporated with the common thoughts of men, and only hated and feared by those who would revile, but dare not. What shall a man desire more than this?

IF DARWIN'S PASSING AFFECTED Spencer appreciably, he mentioned it in neither his letters to Youmans nor his autobiography, which, despite his deepening anguish over his health and work, eventually ran to four hundred thousand words in two volumes. Two days after Darwin died, he wrote Youmans a long letter clarifying his intentions regarding his up-coming visit, vowing to subordinate all other activities to "relaxation and enjoyment." "I have already given in the *Athenaeum* an authoritative con-tradiction to the rumour that I was about to lecture during my tour of America, and I do not propose to change my decision," he said.

> The reply I gave to one of the lecture bureaux which made an offer to me, was that neither the offer they made, nor any other offer, would induce me. . . . Were lecturing my habit, as in the case of Tyndall and Huxley, there would be nothing special in my undertaking to give lectures or a lecture; and the implication would be different. But as matters stand, the giving a lecture or reading a paper, would be nothing more than making myself a show; and I absolutely decline to make myself a show.

When Youmans wrote back proposing a dinner to honor him, Spencer grudgingly agreed: "I must, I assume, assent. To decline would be awk-ward; and as I propose to limit myself a good deal in the way of social in-tercourse and receptions I must, I conclude, yield to some arrangement which shall replace more detailed entertainments."

Youmans knew better than to exert any more pressure or advance any further suggestions regarding Spencer's stay. Each of their letters to the other now began with a detailed health report, and after nearly thirty years, Youmans recognized that Spencer was in an especially precarious way. "Though better," Spencer wrote on July 21, three weeks before he was booked to set sail aboard the *Servia*, "I am still not up to much work. I am looking forward to the voyage and my visit with you to raise me to a higher level of vigour." In fact, as he later recalled, the hope "was not a very rational one," and his decision to make the trip "decidedly impru-dent." He explained:

> But here was another case in which a plan once fixed upon becomes a tyrant over me, and dictates persistence regardless of consequences. Under the circumstance which has arisen I ought to have abandoned the projected voyage, and sacrificed my double passage money (I had taken a state-room all by myself, not daring to risk the additional hindrances to sleep entailed by the presence of a fellow passenger): at the same time reimbursing my friend Lott for his bootless outlay. But

such a course did not, I believe, even occur to me, and I unhesitatingly occupied the early part of August in completing my preparation.

Bumping over and over against the "tyranny" of having an idea, making a plan, then becoming so consumed with seeing it through that he ignored all else, Spencer lurched toward his departure from Liverpool. He took the train down from London on the tenth to spend a day or two with friends before embarking. Youmans, meantime, prepared to receive him, having won a single cherished concession—the public dinner in New York on the eve of Spencer's return voyage. Fearing that the least word about it in the newspapers would ignite a stampede among "a great number of the most intelligent people in the United States" besieging him with urgent requests to meet and welcome Spencer, Youmans took uncharacteristic pains to keep the planning for the banquet as secret as possible. Spencer's herald, his publicist, he now, in deference to his guest's condition, set about denying and squelching rumors about what the philosopher would and would not do while touring America.

IN PURSUING THE ROLE he had set out for himself as a baron both in America and England, Andrew Carnegie climbed to the top of both societies with alacrity and ease. Through his connections with the Nineteenth Century Club, he befriended Ingersoll and Beecher. Blaine kidded him about whether he should run for Congress or for Parliament: "If you take a seat in the House of Commons, you will be a greater man in the United States, but, if you enter the House in Washington, you will be a greater man in England." The previous year he had awkwardly begun courting a young woman in the face of his mother's stiff opposition, taking vigorous horse rides with her through Central Park; then, in February, he departed New York for several months in England, chiefly to launch a syndicate of workingmen's newspapers through which he planned to trumpet his positivism, antiroyalist leanings, and perhaps candidacy for high office. "Even Englishmen," he predicted, "will soon become satisfied that no man should be born to honors, but that these should be reserved for those who merit them. . . . The days of rank are numbered."

While other millionaires plundered Europe for art trophies and antiquities, Carnegie collected great men and intellectuals. On the strength of

Round the World, published by Scribner's in 1879, he had established himself as an author. Upon his arrival in England he published an article in *The Fortnightly Review,* edited by Jonathan Morley, who provided entrée to London's literary and Liberal circles. Morley introduced him to Gladstone, who became a frequent correspondent. Having long edited Spencer, Morley was all too aware of the restrictions he placed on his time and energy, but he was sufficiently intrigued by the sunny Scottish American steel man who boasted of being a "disciple" to write him a note of introduction to Spencer as well. When Carnegie learned that Spencer would sail to America aboard the *Servia,* he hurriedly booked a cabin. Armed with Morley's letter, he sped to Liverpool and presented himself to Spencer on the ship's tender.

"As an older traveler," Carnegie later wrote, "I took Mr. Lott and him in charge."

Averse to intrusions, strangers, and small talk, Spencer preferred his own company, relying on Lott, a lifelong friend, not to disturb his soliloquies. But he and Carnegie, irrepressibly voluble, dined together throughout the nine-day voyage, chatting exhaustively. During their first meal, Spencer groused about the cheese selection: "Waiter," he snapped, "I did not ask for Cheshire; I asked for Cheddar. *Cheddar.*" Constitutionally impatient, discovering too late that his choice of cabin placed him near the fog whistle, which kept him up half the night, Spencer grew steadily more out of sorts, writing in his journal on the fourth day: "Getting very much bored." Still, he and Carnegie—master and acolyte, theorizer and practitioner, Londoner and New Yorker—had much to discuss, and one day the conversation came around to "the impression made upon us by great men at first meeting," Carnegie recalled in his autobiography. "Did they, or did they not, prove to be as we imagined them?"

Carnegie suggested that "nothing could be more different than the being imagined and that being beheld in the flesh."

"Oh," Spencer asked, "in my case, for instance, was this so?"

"Yes," Carnegie said. "You more than any I had imagined my teacher, the great calm philosopher brooding, Buddha-like, over all things, unmoved; never did I dream of seeing him excited over the question of Cheshire or Cheddar cheese."

Spencer, a good laugher, roared his approval, though looking back in his autobiography he recalled Carnegie's remark as further evidence of prejudice against men of ideas. "To think that a philosopher should be so fastidious about his cheese!" he mocked. "The identification of philoso-phy with stoicism still prevails very generally, and continually crops up in unexpected ways and places."

Indeed, Spencer believed authors generally suffered under the weight of impossible expectations; specifically, that they be as erudite in person as they are in print, that everything they utter have precious meaning. "Most people frame very untrue, and often very absurd, conceptions of those who write books," he observed.

> One may say that as a rule no man is equal to his book; though there are, I believe, exceptions. All the best products of his mental activity he puts into his book; where they are separated from the mass of inferior products with which they are mingled in his daily talk. And yet the usual supposition is that the unselected thoughts will be as good as the selected thoughts. It would be about as reasonable to suppose that the fermented wort of the distiller will be found of like quality with the spirit distilled from it.

Other than meeting Carnegie, the voyage had proved worse than Spencer had feared, his ordinarily bad sleep more broken than ever. Not for the last time, he rebuked himself for agreeing to come, then for not backing out after his collapse in the spring. He imagined he could feel no worse, and expressed weary surprise when, entering New York harbor, he discovered that he could.

"A climax," he wrote, "was put to the mischief on the last night. We ar-rived too late to reach the wharf, and had to lie off Staten Island. Here the raising of the baggage and cargo, in preparation for landing in the morn-ing, gave me, as my diary says, 'a horrible night from the noises'; so that, when my friend Youmans came on board at 7 on the morning of the 21st to welcome me, he found me in an unusually dilapidated state."

WHATEVER SPENCER'S CONDITION—whatever benefit or harm ten weeks of travel would work upon his fragile nerves—Youmans focused keenly on the larger prize. Having Spencer in America presented not just an opportunity to establish his place in history and put his stamp on the nation, but a moment of exegesis, a final interpretation, the climax of a lonely, successful twenty-five-year campaign that had entailed sacrifice and suffering and, remarkably, left them both to outlive Darwin. Spencer, he intended to make clear, was man's most original thinker, the architect of a new system of truth. Moreover, his personal struggle and character were epic, inspiring, and still all but unappreciated—"the courage, the pluck, the heroism of this thinker in engaging upon his great task," as Youmans now wrote in preparing remarks for the testimonial dinner:

> Everything was against him. Single-handed, with no church or party behind him, backed by no university or scientific society, with but little means, in broken health, without even a publisher, and in the face of public prejudice and a hostile press, he nevertheless resolved to carry out a comprehensive system of thought that would require twenty years of his life. The moral intrepidity of the undertaking was as original as its intellectual character.

Youmans burned more than ever to clarify facts that "even interment in Westminster Abbey cannot change"—that is, that Darwin "will remain the illustrious Reformer of biology, and the most distinguished naturalist of the age, but with Mr. Spencer will abide the honor of complete originality in developing this greatest conception of modern times, if not, indeed, of all time." Youmans's "humble tribute" neglected to advertise his own invaluable contribution. As both knew, it was *he* who to a striking degree had been Spencer's church, party, university, scientific society, and publisher, also almost single-handedly, also with slender means and health, and yet with selfless loyalty and little complaint. Touting Spencer, Youmans couldn't help commending himself.

Youmans and his wife, the widow of a distinguished jurist, expected Spencer to be their guest and had made arrangements also for Lott, but "I was obliged to disappoint them," Spencer recalled. "In my shattered state I dared not undertake the social responsibilities which would have been entailed, even in the absence of visitors. And then the interviewers had to be avoided. These quickly made their appearance, and, though put off for a time by the statement that I was too unwell to see anyone, would have soon returned." Before the day was over, with Carnegie's assistance, he and Lott moved to the Windsor Hotel, where, he wrote, "my companion having a great faculty for silence when need was, I felt in his company safe against excitement."

Spencer ventured out, hesitant and dazed. Headlong business growth had turned downtown into a sprouting maze of soot-stained masonry and glass crisscrossed with privately owned utility poles up to 150 feet high. Flammable and vulnerable to rot, the poles were "mounted with festoons of barely insulated, drooping wires for all manners of telephones, stock tickers and burglar alarms, subject to the wear and tear of the elements, showering sparks, prey to heated arc street lighting below," as author Neil Baldwin wrote. For months Thomas Edison, under immense pressure to deliver by late summer the first great demonstration of several interlocking new technologies, had commanded construction of the First District system for supplying electric lighting to the financial center, his crews running conducting cables from the Pearl Street power station under cobblestone streets and up into the walls of buildings to lamps holding pear-shaped incandescent lightbulbs. Knocking off only for lunch and cigars at Delmonico's, Edison, all but deaf, supervised every aspect of connecting the "tree system" of cheap, clean, safe, and eye-pleasing illumination that he predicted would vanquish forever the "barbarous and wasteful gaslight . . . [the] nauseous, dim flicker of gas."

Uptown, meanwhile, was resplendent with gilded mansions, department stores, carriages, and restaurants, offset by the restorative natural splendor and elegant public walkways, fountains, and buildings of Central Park. "Am astonished by the grandeur of New York," Spencer recorded in his diary. Later, he explained the reasons for his surprise: "Thinking of it chiefly as a center of business-activity, and perhaps unduly influenced by much that I had read about ill-paved streets, I had conceived the place as having small pretensions to architectural beauty; and was consequently unprepared for the multitude of imposing edifices. . . . We have nothing to compare with 5th Ave."

After putting Spencer and Lott aboard a steamer for the first part of their journey up the Hudson, Youmans proceeded with plans for the banquet. Spencer's uncertainty about whether he would be able to take part left little time to prepare, and as the need for secrecy increased, so did Youmans's anxiety. "It was first intended," he recalled, "to take a large place that would accommodate five hundred persons, but there was not time for this, and Delmonico's Hall had to be accepted, with a convenient capacity of about two hundred seats." Rising luxuriously at the corner of Fifth Avenue and Twenty-sixth Street, a few steps from the hotels at

Madison Square—the Fifth Avenue, Albemarle, and Hoffman House—Delmonico's first-floor restaurant with its silver chandeliers hung from a frescoed ceiling, men's café, banquet hall, dining rooms, and retiring rooms were the latest, grandest incarnation of the fourth eating establishment in New York to bear the name of Giovanni and Pietro Delmonico, Swiss-born brothers who in 1827 had opened a small café and pastry shop on William Street and anglicized their names to John and Peter. It was a central gathering spot of the city's businessmen and politicians as well as visiting luminaries and culinary pilgrims. Charles Ranhofer, the most influential New York chef of the age, a master of classic French hotel cuisine, prepared popular American classics—Delmonico potatoes, Delmonico steaks, lobster à la Newberg—personally tasting and seasoning each course.

Youmans omitted the customary formal correspondence of invitation and acceptance: "wholly superfluous," he called it, since barring the most crippling circumstances, not one of the highly select group of men who were asked—there would be no women—could imagine refusing. He and his committee quietly wrote and wired prominent figures, many of them friends and self-avowed followers of Spencer's, from across the professional spectrum, comprising a guest list that Youmans described as "large, cultivated and brilliant." It consisted of an interlocking cadre from government (Schurz, Evarts, former Treasury secretary Benjamin Bristow, future senators Chauncey Depew and Elihu Root, Congressman Perry Belmont, New York mayor Abraham Hewitt); journalism (Godkin, Dana); industry (Carnegie; Cyrus Field, the financier behind the laying of the first transatlantic telegraph cable); science (Marsh, Sumner, Fiske, paleontologist and sociologist Lester Ward); publishing (Henry Holt, the Appletons); and ministry (Beecher and Lyman Abbott, his successor at Plymouth Church and biographer). Nineteenth Century Club impresario Courtlandt Palmer was high on the list, as was Mrs. Botta's husband, Vincent.

Sequestered in the *Monthly*'s cluttered offices on Bond Street, Youmans toiled over the arrangements, forced despite the luminous guest list to go begging for financial support. Betraying his promises to Spencer to employ a secretary, he handwrote repeated, scarcely legible appeals to six or eight wealthy patrons. He complained to Rhode Island industrialist and philosopher Rowland Hazard, an early subscriber of Spencer's, that

Spencer was in a "very bad way" and asked for help to defray $300 in extra expenses. Ever put upon, Youmans wrote to Hazard:

> We had to pay for the seats of our speakers and some of the expenses of those who came from a distance. Then there was engraving, printing, clerk work, and some cost of traveling entailed, and as Delmonico's demanded all the receipts from the sale of tickets, and in fact $12 for every plate whether tickets were sold or not, we have to meet the deficiency. I have worked like a slave on it for six weeks without remuneration of course, and now our friends who are better able to afford it can have their chance of filling up the gap. I don't know where it is coming from but it will no doubt come by sufficient exertion and I cannot see how we can let you off for less than $50. However, give us what you can afford and we will be satisfied. I do not wish to make it burdensome to anybody.

The process of selecting speakers fanned his underlying bitterness. Evarts was recognized as perhaps the nation's most felicitous toastmaster. Phrenology—the study of the skull's exterior, through the reading of shapes and bumps, to determine underlying character traits—was still deeply in vogue, and Evarts's large head, massive forehead, fullness across the brow, and elevated crown were believed to convey a brilliant mix of gravitas and humor. "On public occasions of moment," according to the *Phrenological Journal of Science and Health*, "Mr. Evarts is one of the few men who are looked to as capable of taking the leading place and performing its duties gracefully and efficiently." Youmans—"ready, as ever, to make capital of everything," as Spencer noted—planned to assemble the speeches into a book, and he and the event committee had selected the testimonials. They invited Sumner to discuss sociology; Schurz, the progress of science and international harmony; Marsh, the scientific world; and Fiske and Beecher, the most critical question: religion.

That left Youmans himself. He had borne Spencer to this triumphal occasion. But Evarts feared that even the ablest men had a limited tolerance for course after course of rich food, raucous toasts with wines of every description, pungent cigars, ponderous after-dinner speeches, drawn-out obsequious huzzahs, and philosophy, and he worried that the evening would go too long. It became distressingly clear to Youmans that there was no room for his lengthy remarks, which, as he told Hazard, "I would not make after Beecher and could not make before." Youmans later ensured that his speech was included in the official proceedings under the title "What Mr. Youmans Did Not Say," swiping in his introduction: "Had Mr. Evarts given the occasion a length proportional to its other magnitudes, and proceeded to offer the following toast, *'Spencer's Philosophy of Evolution: the most original achievement in the history of thought,'* and then called upon Mr. E. L. Youmans, he might have gotten in response what follows."

Youmans joined Spencer in Saratoga, seeing him on as far as the steamer quay at Lake George: "the most picturesque thing I saw in the United States," Spencer wrote. "Three of our English lakes placed end to end would be something like it in extent and scenery." Within days, the giant dynamos at Edison's central station rumbled to life, and a third of lower Manhattan, including the *Times* building, was lighted up. "The 27 electric lamps in the editorial rooms and the 25 lamps in the counting rooms made those departments as bright as day, but without any unpleasant glare," the paper reported. "It was a light that a man could sit down under and write for hours without the consciousness of having any artificial light about him." Spencer continued on through Montreal and the Thousand Islands to Niagara Falls, where Youmans and his sister traveled all night to join him for a couple of days, then detoured through Cleveland and Pittsburgh to Washington, which, to his delight, presented no official welcome.

"Whether the fact that the President (or rather the Vice-President, for Mr. Garfield was dead) was away at Newport, prompted the decision to go direct to Washington without stopping at Baltimore, I cannot remember," he recalled, "but I remember that this absence was a cause of satisfaction to me." Spencer hated ceremonial interviews, and he found the thought of having to meet with Chester Arthur disturbing and distasteful. "Partly this is due to a dislike of formalities, and partly to a disinclination to converse with strangers," he said. "Under ordinary circumstances, thinking is to me more pleasurable than talking; and hence, in the absence of an interlocutor in whom I feel interest, I am not tempted to talk." Spencer required "some sentiment of friendship or personal regard . . . to make conversation preferable." He also claimed not to enjoy compliments, unless they were indirect or disguised. How he or Youmans imagined he could gracefully endure the Delmonico's dinner defied the obvious fact that though both of them believed he deserved America's adulation, and that it was long overdue and sweeter now that it eclipsed Darwin's, Spencer found his fame cloyingly unpleasant and trying.

By LATE SEPTEMBER, with less than six weeks remaining, Youmans still didn't know whether Spencer's fragile condition would keep him from attending the public dinner, and he took the train to Baltimore to "see what was now my state and my decision," Spencer wrote. Some improvement had taken place. His diary refers frequently to "bad nights" and "wretched nights," but other nights he slept, and in the mornings felt invigorated. "Hence I thought I might venture," he told Youmans, who returned to New York to complete the preparations. When Spencer arrived in the city a week later and recounted to Youmans the annoying things that had been said about him in the newspapers, Youmans proposed that he interview Spencer instead. In fact, all but two of the questions were Spencer's own, with the result "that I practically interviewed myself."

"Of course my remarks, after my manner, were mainly critical," he wrote, "and while not failing to recognize the greatness of American achievements, consisted largely of adverse comments on their political life." Spencer enjoyed New York and Brooklyn, relished his visit with Marsh and his wondrous fossil mammals in New Haven, and was pleased to arrive in Newport well after the season, when the fashionables had gone and the scattered villas and natural attractions reminded him of Bournemouth, a cosmopolitan watering place south of London. Boston and Cambridge, with their "fine masses of gorgeous autumn foliage," felt familiar: the club dinner with Holmes, the visit to Gray's herbarium, Fiske's cluttered domestic life.

Then came the "disaster." Running full speed to catch the return train from Concord after visiting Emerson's grave proved too much for him, the effort doing, he believed, "great and permanent damage." If before it had been unrealistic to expect a man who normally didn't enjoy the company of strangers to sit through a public dinner in his honor and deliver what all assumed would be a kind of benediction—after eleven weeks in their country he would tell them what he thought of them—now Spencer felt himself perishing. "The night which followed was so wretched as to prompt the immediate resolution to leave Boston and its excitements," he wrote. Apologizing to Holmes, with whom he was to dine the following night, he and Lott returned to Newport in the hope that the quiet would restore him.

"I went wrong again at Boston," he wrote to Youmans on November 4, a Saturday. "I stay here until Wednesday, because it is *absolutely* needful to shun all excitements save that of the dinner itself." Youmans feared the worst. Beecher, after visiting his office to discuss his closing remarks and to see if Youmans could arrange a time for Beecher to feed and entertain Spencer at his home, wrote him dispiritedly the next day: "I learn that Spencer is on his back at Newport. That ends it. All viands and all wines are banished, and strict asceticism resumes its sway."

Spencer arrived back in New York on the afternoon of the eighth, the day before the banquet. The prospect before him alarmed him. "Wretched night; no sleep at all; kept in room all day," he wrote in his diary: "great fear I should collapse." Hours later, feeling worse than at any time since he broke down twenty-six years earlier after the commercial failure of *The Principles of Psychology,* he washed, shaved, dressed himself in evening clothes, left his room at the Windsor, went downstairs, and climbed into Carnegie's waiting carriage for the ride to Madison Square. He feared he was sinking. But Spencer saw life as a series of tough bargains, ordeals to be survived. "When the hour came for making my appearance at Delmonico's," he wrote, "I got my friends to secrete me in an ante-room until the last moment, so that I might avoid all excitements of introductions and congratulations; and as Mr. Evarts, who presided, handed me on to the dais, I begged him to limit his conversations with me as much as possible, and to expect very meager responses."

DINNER BEGAN at half past six with raw oysters on the half shell, "only . . . opened when ready to serve and sent to the table on finely broken ice," as Ranhofer, who considered raw oysters more digestible than cooked ones, and whose command of ingredients, preparation, service, and presentation was encyclopedic, instructed. The first wine most probably was an haut sauterne. With a new course arriving every ten minutes, the feast lasted two and a half hours, a band playing selected pieces throughout—"a little too much music for easy conversation," Youmans recalled. In deference to Spencer's "natural repugnance to any great display," the *Times* reported, no attempt had been made to decorate the hall;

there were no special tablecloths or cakes. The ornamentation, such as it was, was the company. On Spencer's right at the head table sat Sumner, Fiske, Bristow, Beecher, and Youmans; on his left Evarts, Schurz, Marsh, the British politician and colonial administrator Sir Richard Temple, Lott, and Mayor Hewitt. "It is seldom," the paper said, "that Delmonico's banquet hall is filled with a gathering of scholars and gentlemen so distinguished as those who assembled there last evening."

The menu, printed on an engraved seven-by-five card tatted with a silk bow to a red cloth backing, was written in French, Ranhofer's native tongue and the modern epicurean's lingua franca. Course after course cascaded from the kitchen, ferried by haughty French waiters—a consommé over sliced poached chicken pastries and boiled green peas that he'd named for a popular French noblewoman celebrated for her witty letters, followed by a Madeira; buttery scarlet kettle-drum-shaped pastry tufts stuffed with truffles, tongue, and pistachios; striped bass garnished with blanched oysters, mushroom heads, pike dumplings, and trussed crawfish, and washed down with a Rhine wine or Moselle; medallions of venison dressed with a tomato sauce with horseradish and lightly fried shallots and garnished with Spanish olives stuffed with anchovies; chateaubriand cutlets; sorbet for the palate; and then after a brief respite the second and third service—roast saddle-back duck in a buttered demi-glace sauce, salad, vegetables, sweets, and a dozen desserts, all matched to different champagnes and wines, which Ranhofer called the "intellectual" part of the meal. Rowland Hazard of Providence, like more than a few others, pocketed his card to take home.

By 9:30, cigars were lit, the waiters stopped clearing, everyone ceased talking. The band stopped playing. Evarts rose to his feet.

"We are here tonight, Gentlemen, to show the feeling of Americans towards our distinguished guest," he began. Since leaving government, Evarts had returned to practicing law and would in a few years make a successful run for a Senate seat from New York. "As no room or city can hold all his friends and admirers, it was necessary that a company should be made up by some method out of the mass," he said, "and what so good a method as natural selection?" Great peals of laughter filled the room.

"They say," he went on, "a continually stuffed body cannot see secret things. Now, from my personal knowledge of the men I see at these tables, they are owners of continually stuffed bodies." More laughter.

Evarts turned to Spencer, who cast his eyes downward, seeming to inspect his plate. "Now, Mr. Spencer, we are glad to meet you here. We are glad to see you, and we are glad to have you see us. We are glad to see you, for we recognize in the breadth of your knowledge, such knowledge as is useful to your race, a greater comprehension than any living man has presented to our generation." Thunderous applause interrupted him.

> We are glad to see you because in our judgment you have brought to the analysis and distribution of this vast knowledge a more penetrating intelligence and a more thorough insight than any living man has brought even to the minor topics of his special knowledge. In theology, in psychology, in natural science, in the knowledge of individual man and his exposition, and in the knowledge of the world, in the proper sense of society which makes up the world, the world worth knowing, the world worth speaking of, the world worth planning for, the world worth working for—we acknowledge your labors as surpassing those of any of our kind.

Again, there was great applause.

> You give us that knowledge of man which is practical and useful, and whatever the claims or the debates may be about your system or the system of those who agree with you, and however it may be compared with other competing systems that have preceded it, we must agree that it is practical, that it is benevolent, that it is serious, and that it is reverent; that it aims at the highest results in virtue; that it treats evil not as eternal but as evanescent, and it expects to arrive at what it sought through faith in the millennium—that condition of affairs in which there is the highest morality and the greatest happiness.

Evarts turned back to the audience. "Gentlemen, fill your glasses, and drink to the health of our guest, Herbert Spencer!" he said. Cheers and shouts flooded the room as Spencer rose wearily from his seat. Most assumed his downward gaze indicated modesty.

"MR. PRESIDENT AND GENTLEMEN," Spencer began, struggling to convey a hint of composure. With no gift for oratory, and what little talent he had for talking to large audiences having deserted him, he launched stolidly into a prepared speech.

> Along with your kindness there comes to me a great unkindness
> from Fate; for, now that, above all times in my life, I need full
> command of what powers of speech I possess, disturbed health so
> threatens to interfere with them that I fear I shall very inadequately
> express myself. Any failure in my response you must please ascribe,
> in part at least, to a greatly disordered nervous system. . . . I believe I
> may truly say that the better health which you have so cordially
> wished me, will be in a measure furthered by the wish; since all
> pleasurable emotion is conducive to health, and, as you will fully
> believe, the remembrance of this event will ever continue to be a
> source of pleasurable emotion, exceeded by few, if any, of my
> remembrances.

All Spencer's key precepts now merged—the evolution from militant to industrial man; the need for individuals, and societies, to take care of themselves lest they stop advancing and degrade; the crucial, if troublingly imbalanced, role of America in advancing the race; nature's awesome discipline; the democratic imperatives of criticism, assertiveness, and candor. He continued:

> And now that I have thanked you, sincerely though too briefly, I
> am going to find fault with you. . . . It seems to me in one respect
> Americans have diverged too widely from savages. I do not mean to
> say that they are in general unduly civilized. Throughout large parts of
> the population, even in long settled regions, there is no excess of those
> virtues needed for the maintenance of social harmony. Especially out
> in the West, men's dealings do not yet betray too much of the
> "sweetness and light" which we are told distinguish the cultured
> man from the barbarian.
> Nevertheless, there is a sense in which my assertion is true. You
> know that the primitive man lacks power of application. Spurred by
> hunger, by danger, by revenge, he can exert himself energetically for a
> time; but his energy is spasmodic. Monotonous daily toil is impossible
> to him. It is otherwise with the more developed man. The stern

discipline of social life has gradually increased the aptitude for persistent industry; until among us, and still more among you, work has become with many a passion. This contrast of nature has another aspect. The savage thinks only of present satisfaction, and leaves future satisfactions uncared for. Contrariwise, the American, eagerly pursuing a future good, almost ignores what good the passing day offers him; and, when the future good is gained, he neglects that while striving for some still remoter good.

What I have seen and heard during my stay among you, has forced on me the belief that this slow change from habitual inertness to persistent activity, has reached an extreme form from which there must begin a counterchange—a reaction. Everywhere I have been struck with the number of faces which told in strong lines of the burdens that had to be borne. I have been struck, too, with the large proportion of gray-haired men; and inquiries have brought out the fact that with you the hair commonly begins to turn some ten years earlier than with us. Moreover, in every circle I have met men who had themselves suffered from some nervous collapse due to stress of business, or named friends who had either killed themselves by overwork, or had been permanently incapacitated, or had wasted long periods in endeavors to recover health.

Beyond these immediate mischiefs, there are remoter mischiefs. Exclusive devotion to work has the result that amusements cease to please; and, when relaxation becomes imperative, life becomes dreary from lack of its sole interest—the interest in business. . . . Nor do the evils end here. There is the injury to posterity. Damaged constitutions reappear in children, and entail of them far more of ill than great fortunes yield them of good. When life has been duly rationalized by science, it will be seen that among a man's duties care of the body is imperative, not only out of regard for personal welfare, but also out of regard for descendants.

"The truth is," Spencer told them,

there needs a revised ideal of life. Look back through the past, or look abroad through the present, and we find that the ideal of life is variable, and depends on social conditions. Everyone knows that to be a successful warrior was the highest aim among all ancient peoples of note, and it is still among many barbarous peoples. . . . That is to say, when the chronic struggles of races necessitate perpetual wars, there is evolved an ideal of life adapted to the requirements. We have changed all that in modern civilized societies, especially in England, and still more in America. With the decline of militant activity, and the growth of industrial activity, the occupations once disgraceful have become honorable. The duty to work has taken the place of the duty to fight . . . business has been substituted for war as the purpose of existence.

"Is this modern ideal to survive throughout the future?" Spencer asked.

I think not. While all other things undergo continuous change, it is impossible that ideals should remain fixed. The ancient ideal was appropriate to the ages of conquest of man over man, and the spread of the strongest races. The modern ideal is appropriate to ages in which conquest of the Earth and subjection of the powers of Nature to human use, is the predominant need.

Hereafter, when this age of active material progress has yielded mankind its benefits, there will, I think, come a better adjustment of labor and enjoyment. . . . In brief, I may say that we have had somewhat too much of the "gospel of work." It is time to preach the "gospel of relaxation."

Spencer paused. His exhortation—extrapolated as much from his years of incessantly haranguing Youmans over his failure to rest as from his study of history and society, and coming this night from the most prized lectern in America—baffled most of those who heard it. Many were affronted. Unlike Evarts, he elicited neither applause nor laughter. Resplendent as they were as a group, many simply didn't know what to make of their English guest, though they agreed that his message was disappointing.

"This is a very unconventional after-dinner speech," Spencer acknowledged.

But I have thought I could not better convey my thanks than by the expression of a sympathy which issues in a fear. If, as I gather, this intemperance in work affects more especially the Anglo-American population—if there results an undermining of the physique not only in adults, but also in the young, who, as I learn from your daily journals, are also being injured by overwork—if the ultimate consequence should be a dwindling away of those among you who are the inheritors of free institutions and best adapted to them; then there will come a further difficulty in the working out of the great future which lies before the American nation. To my anxiety on this account, you must please ascribe the unusual character of my remarks.

WHEN THE POLITE BUT PROLONGED APPLAUSE that followed Spencer's remarks ended, Evarts read a letter of regrets from Holmes, too ill to attend. Holmes wrote that Spencer "has come nearer to the realization of Bacon's claim of all knowledge as his province than any philosopher of his time." Proposing the first regular toast of the evening, in honor of *The Study of Sociology,* Evarts then introduced Sumner, who in the aftermath of the Yale controversy was at pains to celebrate Spencer even as he distanced himself from much of his work. Having fitfully returned to his own studies, Sumner was beginning to reach beyond crude Social Darwinism to an understanding of the prevalence of mores—ruling ideas that influence social development as much as or more than competitive human nature.

"In the present state of the science of sociology the man who has studied it at all is very sure to feel great self-distrust in trying to talk about it," Sumner began.

The most that one of us can do at the present time is to appreciate the promise which the science offers to us, and to understand the lines of direction in which it seems about to open out. As for the philosophy of the subject, we still need the master to show us how to handle and apply its most fundamental doctrines.

Mr. Spencer addressed himself at the outset of his literary career to topics of sociology. In the pursuit of those topics he found himself forced, as I understand it, to seek constantly more fundamental and wider philosophical doctrines. He came at last to fundamental principles of the evolution philosophy. He then extended, tested, confirmed, and corrected those principles by inductions from other sciences, and so finally turned again to sociology, armed with the scientific method which he had acquired. To win a powerful and correct method is, as we all know, to win more than half the battle.

We now have acquired the method of studying sociology scientifically so as to attain assured results. We have acquired it none too soon. The need for a science of life in society is urgent, and it is increasing every year. . . . In the upheaval of society which is going on, classes and groups are thrown against each other in such a way as to produce class hatreds and hostilities. As the old national jealousies, which used to be the lines on which war was waged, lose their distinctness, class jealousies threaten to take their place. Political and social events which occur on one side of the globe now affect the interests of populations on the other side of the globe. Forces which come into action in one part of human society rest not until they have reached all human society. The brotherhood of man is coming to be a reality of such distinct and positive character that we find it a practical question of the greatest moment what kind of creatures some of these hitherto neglected brethren are.

It is plain that our social science is not on the level of the tasks which are thrown upon it by the vast and sudden changes in the whole mechanism by which man makes the resources of the globe available to satisfy his needs, and by the new human ideas which are born of the new aspects which human life bears to our eyes in consequence of the development of science and of the arts.

The last shadows of his years as a minister having vanished, Sumner discussed the impact of those new ideas on religion, but as a sorrowful abstraction, a thing apart:

Our traditions about the science and art of living are plainly inadequate. They break to pieces in our hands when we try to apply them to the new cases. A man of good faith may come to the conviction sadly, but he must come to the conviction honestly, that the traditional doctrines and explanations of human life are worthless.

I can see no boundaries to the scope of the philosophy of evolution. That philosophy is sure to embrace all the interests of Man on this Earth. It will be one of its crowning triumphs to bring light and order into the social problems which are of universal bearing on all mankind. Mr. Spencer is breaking the path for us into this domain. We stand eager to follow him into it, and we look upon his work on sociology as a grand step in the history of science.

NEXT CAME SCHURZ, none too soon for those in the crowd who expected after-dinner speakers not just to edify but to entertain. "Herbert Spencer never said a wiser word than when he said, 'The ultimate result of shielding men from the effects of their folly is to fill the world with fools,' " Schurz said, "but I will only say, 'with dyspeptic philosophers.' "

Rafts of nervous laughter gave way to solid applause, and Schurz proceeded to call up "some pleasant memories which this interesting occasion brings to my mind." Nineteen years earlier, after the battle of Missionary Ridge, he was with his command at a winter camp near Chattanooga. Many of the horses starved to death. Schurz carried a copy of Spencer's *Social Statics* that he read by candlelight in his tent, giving him assurance—here he quoted Spencer's first principle from the book, that "every man has freedom to do all that he wills, provided he infringes not the equal freedom of any other man"—that if southerners had read it "there would never have been any war for the preservation of slavery." Exalting science and the bloody shirt in a single anecdote, Schurz won a hearty ovation.

"There was a time," he went on,

> when the investigations of science and their results were kept in the possession of privileged orders and circles, and treated as profound mysteries which could not be exposed to the gaze and the understanding of the multitude without profanation and without endangering the fixed order of society. That time lies, fortunately, far behind us. But some of us can remember the day when philosophy and science were, by many at least, studiously clothed in the darkness of formidable terminologies and obscure forms of speech, which seemed to warn off all the uninitiated.

Here he offered a joking aside: "I know of works of that sort professedly written in German, but requiring translation into German as if they had been written in Sanskrit."

We may certainly congratulate ourselves upon the fact that in our days, among men of science and philosophers, a tendency has grown up to take the generality of intelligent mankind into their confidence by speaking to them in a human language; and also a tendency vastly to enlarge the range of their immediate usefulness by applying the truths discovered by them directly and practically to all the relations and problems of actual life. . . . For the greater the number of minds that are reached by new ideas, the greater will be the quantity and variety of new intellectual forces that will be inspired and stimulated into creative activity.

Schurz turned to Spencer. His cadences were now those of a politician climaxing a stem-winder, eliciting heightened applause at the end of every phrase, building momentum as he sought to rouse the assemblage to its feet:

I am confident, gentlemen, I express our sentiments as well as my own when I say that, in the man who to-night honors and delights us with his presence, we greet one of the greatest representatives of that democratic tendency; one of the boldest leaders of that philosophy that bursts the bonds of the closet; one of the foremost builders up of science in the largest sense by establishing the relations of facts; the apostle of the principle of evolution, which Darwin showed in the diversity of organic life, but which Spencer unfolded as a universal law governing all physiological, mental and social phenomena; a hero of thought, devoting his powers and his life to the vindication of the divine right of science against the intolerant authority of traditional belief; an indefatigable diver into the profoundest depths of ideas and things, who has also known how to bring the discovered treasures within the reach of every intelligent mind, and who has thus become one of the great teachers, not merely of a school, but of civilized humanity!

SCHURZ DROVE THE EVENT toward its culmination, the final question raised by Spencer's presence for a Christian nation: the relation of science to religion. Evarts announced the next toast— *"Evolution: once an Hypothesis, now the established Doctrine of the Scientific World"*—then introduced

Marsh, first of the three final speakers, who set out to characterize the question's natural history before establishing what he thought it foretold.

> Mr. President and Gentlemen: In meeting here to-night, to do honor to our distinguished guest, who is one of the great apostles of evolution, it seems especially fitting to the occasion that we should, for a moment at least, glance back to the past, and recall briefly the progress of a doctrine which has so rapidly brought about a revolution in scientific thought.
>
> Modern science and its methods may be said to date back only to the beginning of the present century. . . . The very recent appearance of man on the earth and his creation independent of the rest of the animal kingdom were scarcely questioned.

However cutthroat in his own investigations, Marsh generously apportioned credit.

> In the first decade of the present half-century, Darwin, Wallace, Huxley and our honored guest were all at the same time working at one problem, each in his own way, and their united efforts have firmly established the truth of organic evolution. Our guest tonight did not stop to solve the difficulties of organic evolution, but, with that profound philosophic insight which has made him read and honored by all intelligent men, he made the grand generalization that the law of organic progress is the law of all progress.
>
> The evolution of life and of the physical world are now supplemented by the evolution of philosophy, of history, of society, and of all else pertaining to human life, until we may say that evolution is the law of all progress, if not the key to all mysteries. These profounder departments of evolution I leave to others, for, in the few minutes allotted me, I cannot attempt to give even an outline of the progress of evolution in biology alone.
>
> If, however, I may venture to answer briefly the question, What of evolution today? I can only reply: the battle has been fought and won. A few stragglers on each side may still keep up a scattered fire, but the contest is over, and the victors have moved on to other fields.

"In this," he told the audience, which again had ceased laughing and clapping as a serious and respected Yale man asserted with supreme confidence that the war with the other side was over, its ideas defeated and worthless, "the doctrine of evolution has brought light out of darkness, and marks out the path of future progress. What the law of gravitation is to astronomy, the law of evolution is now to natural science. Evolution is no longer a theory but a demonstrated truth, accepted by naturalists throughout the world. The most encouraging feature in natural science, indeed, in all science, today, is the spirit in which the work is carried on."

His escalating bone wars with Cope notwithstanding—each now had competing mining interests and was running rapidly through his fortune—Marsh spoke for American science as much as anyone, and he foresaw a boundless future as universities, government, and business combined forces. Throughout the room, heads nodded appreciatively. In their lifetimes, the scientific spirit had overtaken the country's reigning institutions, its engine. No other country had such an arrangement, but all would soon have to reckon with its power.

Marsh ended with a prophecy: a revolutionary epoch in biology that would vastly enlarge its scope, penetrating to the heart of ultimate questions not long ago considered the exclusive territory of philosophy and religion.

> No authority is recognized which forbids the investigation of any question, however profound; and, with that confidence which success justly brings, no question within the domain of science is now believed to be insoluble; not even the grand problems now before us—the antiquity of the human race, the origin of man, or even the origin of life itself.

IT WAS AFTER ELEVEN by the time Evarts announced the last toast— *"Evolution and Religion: that which perfects humanity cannot destroy religion"*—and said that the dual topic required two final speakers. Spencer's baffling denunciation of the American work ethic and the dense, far-ranging subject matter of the later speeches had combined with the food, wine, and tobacco to make much of the assemblage logy and restless— potentially surly. Fiske, addressing theology, rose first to take the rostrum. A veteran of the lyceum, he decided nevertheless to read his essay, a dense treatise on how Spencer's work, far from atheistic, indeed went further than any other modern thinker's in verifying God's existence. He favorably compared Spencer's intellectual contribution to his era to those of Aristotle and Newton; "though coming in this latter age," he qualified, "it as far surpasses their work in its vastness of performance as the railway surpasses the sedan-chair, or as the telegraph surpasses the carrier pigeon.

"There are some people," Fiske noted,

who seem to think that it is not enough that Mr. Spencer should have made all these priceless contributions to knowledge, but actually complain of him for not giving us a complete and exhaustive system of theology into the bargain. What I wish, therefore, to point out is that Mr. Spencer's work on the side of religion will be seen to be no less important than his work on the side of science, when once its religious implications shall have been fully and consistently unfolded.

All religions agree in the two following assertions, one of which is of speculative and one of which is of ethical import. One of them serves to sustain and harmonize our thoughts about the world we live in and our place in that world; the other serves to uphold us in our efforts to do each what we can to make human life more sweet, more full of goodness and beauty, than we find it. The first of these assertions is the proposition that the things and events of the world do not exist or occur blindly or irrelevantly, but that all, from the beginning to the end of time, and throughout the furthest sweep of illimitable space, are connected together as the orderly manifestations of a divine Power, and that this divine Power is something outside of ourselves, and upon it our own existence from moment to moment depends. The second of these assertions is the proposition that men ought to do certain things, and ought to refrain from doing certain other things; and that the reason why some things are wrong to do and other things are right to do is in some mysterious but very real way connected with the existence and nature of this divine Power, which reveals itself in every great and every tiny thing, without which not a star courses in its mighty orbit, and not a sparrow falls to the ground.

This twofold assertion, that there is an eternal Power that is not ourselves, and that this Power makes for righteousness, is to be found, either in a rudimentary or in a highly developed state, in all known religions. . . . It is really of much more concern to us that there is an eternal Power, not ourselves, than that such a Power is onefold or threefold in its metaphysical nature, or that we ought not to play cards on Sunday, or to eat meat on Friday.

Fiske went on:

In spite of all this, however, it is true that in the mind of the
uncivilized man the great central truths of religion are so densely
overlaid with hundreds of trivial notions respecting dogma and ritual,
that his perception of the great central truths is obscure. These great
central truths, indeed, need to be clothed in a dress of little rites and
superstitions in order to take hold of his dull and untrained
intelligence. But in proportion as men become more civilized, and
learn to think more accurately, and to take wider views of life, just so
do they come to value the essential truths of religion more highly,
while they attach less and less importance to superficial details.

He stopped, clarifying just what he meant: "The doctrine of evolution
asserts, as the widest and deepest truth which the study of Nature can
disclose to us, that there exists a Power to which no limit in time or space
is conceivable, and that all the phenomena of the universe, whether they
be what we call material, or what we call spiritual phenomena, are manifestations of this infinite and eternal Power."

Fiske, having reconciled Darwin and Spencer with God, now discovered his—and the nation's—own true redemption in the marriage
between them. "And this brings me to the last and most important point
of all," he said.

What says the doctrine of evolution with regard to the ethical side of
this twofold assertion, that lies at the bottom of all religion? Though
we cannot fathom the nature of the inscrutable Power that animates
the world, we know, nevertheless, a great many things that it does.
Does this eternal Power, then work for righteousness? Is there a
divine sanction for holiness and a divine condemnation for sin? Are
the principles of right living really connected with the infinite
constitution of the universe?

Fiske approached his conclusion; he was emotional, lit up, inspired.
"Now," he professed,

science began to return a decisively affirmative answer to such
questions as these when it began, with Mr. Spencer, to explain moral

beliefs and moral sentiments as products of evolution. For clearly, when you say of a moral belief or a moral sentiment that it is a product of evolution, you imply that it is something which the universe through untold ages has been laboring to bring forth, and you ascribe to it a value proportionate to the enormous effort that it has cost to produce it. . . . The theoretical sanction thus given to right living is incomparably the most powerful that has ever been assigned in any philosophy of ethics. Human responsibility is made more strict and solemn than ever, when the eternal Power that lives in every event of the universe is thus seen to be in the deepest possible sense the author of the moral law that should guide our lives.

Here was the great cosmic synthesis that Darwin, Spencer, and Huxley had avoided and that Fiske alone had proudly pursued: the idea that evolution is the purest expression of the infinite power of the universe, both its method and its purpose, and that it finds its highest attainment in the moral sense. We behave rightly not because God tells us to, but because we have learned through the ages that survival favors it. Life makes who we are. *What Is Darwinism?* Hodge had asked. *What Is Spencerism?* It is the church of life itself, Fiske seemed to say in foretelling a new theology.

"I have here but barely touched upon a rich and suggestive topic," he declared, forty minutes, more or less, after he started. "When this subject shall once have been expounded and illustrated with due thoroughness— as I earnestly hope it will be within the next few years—then I am sure that it will be generally acknowledged that our great teacher's services to religion have been no less signal than his services to science, unparalleled as they have been in all the history of the world."

As Fiske concluded, Spencer rose partly from his chair and grasped his hand, evidently much moved. "Fiske," he said, "should you develop to the fullest what you have expressed here this evening, I should regard it as a fitting supplement to my life's work."

MIDNIGHT HOVERED when Beecher rose from his seat to make the final address. Everyone—Spencer most of all, having borne up uncomfortably long after he thought possible—was "weary and wanted to go home,"

Lyman Abbott recalled. A dense cirrus of tobacco smoke filled the hall. A few weeks earlier, Beecher, completing his final break with Puritan orthodoxy, had gone before the New York and Brooklyn Congregational Association and withdrawn his membership. He told his former brethren in the ministry that he still believed in some sort of Trinity and the inspiration of the Bible, and "without reserve" in the divinity of Christ, but beyond that he had left the impression that his fundamental belief was in the evolutionary hypothesis, to which all else now must yield. "It seemed to me as Mr. Beecher rose," Abbott observed, "that all he could do was to apologize for not speaking at that late hour and dismiss his audience."

"The old New England churches used to have two ministers," Beecher stated, gazing around. "One was considered as a doctor of theology, and the other a revivalist and pastor. The doctor has had his day"—Fiske—"and now you have the revivalist." Pulpit dynamics at such an hour called for a knowing jest, a promise of release. There was a smattering of laughter.

"Paul complained that Alexander the coppersmith did him much harm," Beecher said. "Mr. Spencer has done immense harm. I don't believe there is an active, thoughtful minister in the United States that has not been put in a peck of troubles, and a good deal more than that, by the intrusion of his views, and the comparison of them with the old views." His own troubles went unmentioned; no one needed to be reminded of them.

One thing is very certain—Mr. Spencer is coming; whether men want to have him or not, he is coming.

Now let me say, with a little more approach to sobriety, what I think about the doctrines of Mr. Spencer's philosophy. Not all his admirers or debtors or disciples need adopt his conclusions fully. . . . But let men come from where they will, or how they may have come, one thing is very certain, that the human race began at the bottom and not at the top, or else there is no truth in history or religion; and that the unfolding of the human race has been going on, if not from the absolute animal conditions, yet from the lowest possible savage conditions; and the Jewish legend that men were at the top, and then fell from the top to the bottom, and carried down all their posterity with them, and that God's business has been for eight, ten, twenty thousand years, and how many more I know not, the punishing of men for sins they never committed—well, that has to go.

Applause shot out from the crowd, and Beecher predicted: "It will not be twenty years before a man will be ashamed to stand up in any intelligent pulpit and mention it." Again the applause erupted. "In five minutes," Abbott wrote, "the more distant auditors had moved their chairs forward, the French waiters, who had paid no attention to anyone else, straightened themselves up against the walls to listen; Herbert Spencer on one side of him and Mr. Evarts on the other were looking up into his face to catch the utterance of his speaking countenance and of his words." Borrowing from the writings of Paul, Beecher proceeded to preach as evangelical a sermon as they had ever heard.

"Now, what is the theory that comes on the other hand, on the side of science?" he asked.

> It is the theory that man is first an animal, pure and simple, and that by the breathing of the breath of God into him there is the unfolding gradually of a rational soul, an intellectual capacity, a moral and spiritual nature, and that while he was an animal the exercise of selfishness, of plunder, was the law of his being; and then it was not only a necessity, but the act was a virtue; but by gradual development he has come to the possession of those higher qualities which should rule him. Sin lies in the conflict between animal nature and the dawning of the spiritual, moral and intellectual nature. It is the conflict in a man between his upper and lower nature.
>
> If you want to see that taught thoroughly, go to seventh Romans and see how Paul argues the matter. He says: "The things I would do, I do not; the things I would not do, I do. So, then it is not I," he says, "but sin that dwelleth in me. I find a law in my members." He was almost fit to be a minister to Darwin.

Like Methodist amens, cries of "That's so! That's so!" caromed across the room. Beecher continued to paraphrase Paul:

> I find a law in my members that compels me to sin, but that *I* in which my personal identity is, the *I* that thinks, the *I* that perceives,

that aspires, the flash of imagination (which he calls faith), the whole fruition of a great soul that approves the spiritual law, the manly law: whatever is right, pure, just, beautiful—I see that, but I am all the time doing the other. My under man, my physical man, is fighting against the upper man.

There isn't a man here but knows that is so. Every evening rebukes every morning among the whole of you. You go out in the morning with inspiration and noble feeling, and say, "This day I will cheat nobody," and you come back at night and you have cheated a dozen men.

A wave of laughter crested and broke.

And so on through the whole scale of conduct. Great light is thrown by this truly scientific and truly scriptural view, on the subject of the nature of sin. I might go on and show that in many other ways religious teaching is greatly benefited by the light that is coming on the world from the great thinkers of the day. Now men say, will you abandon revelation? No. We all believe, that believe in Moses, that God wrote on stone. I believe that was not the first time he wrote on stone. He made a record when he made the granite, and when he made all the successive strata in the periods of time. There is a record in geology that is as much a record of God as the record on paper in human language.

The applause mounted. "They are both true—where they are true." Laughter pealed through the hall.

"Gentlemen," Beecher said,

we have had a good time here to-night, too much of it, especially for a man like me, that can't eat because he has got a speech to make. We shall very soon break up. It is not our privilege to meet Mr. Spencer face-to-face as we all would be glad to do; I certainly would . . . I began to read Mr. Spencer's works more than twenty years ago. They have been meat and bread to me. They have helped me through a great many difficulties. I desire to own my obligation personally to him, and to say that if I had the fortune of a millionaire, and I should pour all my gold at his feet, it would be no sort of compensation compared with what I believe I owe him; for whoever gives me a thought that dispels the darkness that hangs over the most precious secrets of life, whoever gives me confidence in the destiny of my fellow-men, whoever gives me a clearer stand-point from which I can look to the great silent One, and hear him even in half, and believe in him, not by the tests of physical science, but by moral intuition— whoever gives that power is more to me than even my father and my mother; they gave me an outward and physical life, but these others emancipate that life from superstition, from fears, and from thralls, and make me a citizen of the universe.

Beecher turned to their esteemed guest, glass raised in honor. Spencer looked up into his boundless face.

May He who holds the storm in His hand be gracious to you, sir; may your voyage across the sea be prosperous and speedy; may you find on the other side all those conditions of health and of comfort which shall enable you to complete the great work, greater than any other man in this age has attempted; may you live to hear from this continent and from that other, an unbroken testimony to the service which you have done to humanity; and thus, if you are not outwardly crowned, you will wear an invisible crown on your heart that will carry comfort to death—and I will greet you beyond!

Beecher was shaking, tears streaking his face. His prayer that God would convey Spencer safely across the abyss resounded as emotions broke throughout Delmonico's hall. "The whole audience rose by a common impulse to their feet," Abbott wrote, "as if to make the prayer their own, cheering, clapping their hands, and waving their handkerchiefs." For several minutes, the Americans showed their guest their exaltation and esteem, and also the energy that sustained them past their endless exhaustion.

In his seat, unknown to all save perhaps Youmans, Spencer kept himself from wincing, immeasurably less moved or appreciative than his hosts could fathom. After the agony of delivering his own speech, the other addresses, he would write in his *Autobiography*, "were somewhat trying to sit through. . . . As may be imagined, unqualified eulogies uttered by one speaker after another before an audience to whose inquiring glances I was exposed on all sides, were not quite easy to bear—especially in my then state. However, they had to be borne, and by and by I became tolerably callous."

SPENCER WANTED ONLY to get away. Two days later, after lunching with Youmans, he and Lott boarded the *Germanic* for Liverpool. "Various friends and a sprinkling of strangers were there to see us off," he recalled. Someone expressed the hope that he would return. "Before I came it was a question with me whether I should make the trip," he said, "and I never expect to see the shores of America again." Amid the swirling goodbyes and last-minute exchanges, a reporter outmaneuvered him, eliciting an answer to a question about a recent election in which the "bosses" had been thrown out. "Thus I was, after all, interviewed at the last moment," Spencer remembered.

When the cry "All aboard" sounded throughout the ship, Spencer, in a rare burst of spontaneity and emotion, grabbed Youmans and Carnegie by the hand and said, "These are my two best American friends." If Fiske, who had returned to Cambridge, suffered disciple envy (Spencer had known Carnegie less than three months), he refrained from saying so publicly, and two weeks later Spencer wrote to him to reinforce the sentiment he'd expressed on the dais:

My dear Fiske: —
I regretted very much that I did not return to the Windsor in time to see you the day before sailing, but there were so many imperative matters to be settled that I found it impossible to get back in time. Had it not been that Youmans gave me the impression that I should again see you before starting, I should, notwithstanding my state of fatigue, have written you a letter on the Saturday morning.

I wanted to say how successful and how important I thought was your presentation of the dual aspect, theological and ethical, of the Evolution doctrine. It is above all things needful that the people should be impressed with the truth that the philosophy offered to them does not necessitate a divorce from their inherited conceptions concerning religion and morality, but merely a purification and exaltation of them.

THE SHIP CHURNED AWAY from the dock and into the river. Spencer stood on the forward deck wearing a dark suit with an overcoat of light material, a soft felt hat upon his head, waving. Flowers, fruit, wine, brandy, and oysters—"in quantities beyond the possibility of consumption," he wrote—filled his stateroom. "I was reminded by antithesis," he wrote, "of the title of a book published some time ago, *Plain Living and High Thinking;* for high living and plain thinking would fitly describe my regimen."

The ocean remained calm for much of the voyage, and Spencer, sleeping relatively well, rallied. As the ship approached Queenstown, however, a gale came up. By the next morning the *Germanic* was rolling so much that he had to hold his inkstand to keep it from sliding off the table. "I got no sleep until we were under the lee of the Irish Coast, about three or four in the morning," he recalled in his *Autobiography.*

> Then the third night was worse still. We were too late to pass the bar of the Mersey, and, anchoring outside, where I thought I was going to have a quiet night, I got literally no sleep, in consequence first of the riot kept up by some men who were having farewell convivialities in their cabin, and afterwards by the noises which went on nearly all through the night in preparation for landing in the morning—chiefly raising the baggage by machinery just over my head. The mischief was not simply the negative mischief of sleeplessness, but the positive mischief of nervous irritation and wear from the perpetual rattle. . . . It was an immense relief to get home, and I was so delighted I scarcely realized how much I was used up.

Spencer didn't "stir out" for three days, and it was ten days before he ventured out to the club or to call on friends. He believed he would never regain the margin of energy required to work, and he blamed himself, as always, for letting himself become overtaxed—and for his having to endure it in isolation. When he had first collapsed in 1856, he identified the reason to a friend: "You are doubtless perfectly right in attributing my present state to an exclusively intellectual life; and in prescribing exercise of the affections as the best remedy. No one is more thoroughly convinced than I am that bachelorhood is an unnatural and very injurious state." Huxley had long recommended that Spencer try what he facetiously called "gynoeopathy." But Spencer was long past having affections, much less exercising them. He had theorized that society was a superorganism, yet he was so interred in his own mind and thoughts that nearly his only outlet was in solitary work, an evolutionary cul-de-sac. Like Darwin, he had sacrificed a higher realm of human feeling to pursue his monumental calling, but unlike him, Spencer had come to lead a loveless and lonely life. What he would do now to recover he would do alone.

"Thus ended an expedition which I ought never to have undertaken," he would write. "Setting out with the ill-founded hope that the journey and change of scene would improve my health, I came back in a worse state than I went: having made another step downwards towards invalid life."

EPILOGUE

YOUMANS NEVER TRULY RECOVERED from his pneumonia, nor from what Spencer scoldingly called "this American mania in sacrificing yourself in trying to do more work." He believed Spencer had paved the way to a new, more scientific era that could only strengthen the morals and improve the lives of men, and that American evangelists would carry it forward. Nine months after the banquet, he apprised Spencer of their progress:

> Beecher has been lecturing this summer with great acceptance and to large audiences on the religious bearings of evolution; but his work is very crude, being of the same sort as his address at the dinner. It is no doubt better than that, and Beecher is rapidly improving; but he has taken up the subject very late in life, and has not had the time, as he never had the proper preparation, for mastering the philosophy.
>
> . . . I am not among the fortunate mortals who do work that is to survive. Yet the *Popular Science Monthly* is bound up in all the American public libraries, and it will hold its place there by sheer force of its bulk—it will hold over at least into the next century; and I am contented that it contains evidence that I knew a good thing when I saw it.
>
> Has Sumner sent you his new little book? It is quite well worth looking over. He presents the anti-philanthropic, anti-meddling side with considerable point and freshness.

Spencer, barely well enough himself to work, believed that "theological opposition to the doctrine is rapidly disappearing, and before the end of the century will be forgotten." But he now feared "a most disastrous movement" away from his social philosophy, having lost faith that evolution was ready to yield judicious and nonviolent governments. "We are on the highway to communism," he replied. (Fiske, more hopeful, thought Sumner's *What Social Classes Owe to Each Other*, a fierce laissez-faire tract that argued that the "rich, comfortable, prosperous, virtuous, respectable and healthy" owed nothing more than to be humane and charitable to those less fortunate or less fit, "a golden little book"—a manifesto to guide America ahead.)

Spencer was at the peak of his influence even as his nervous condition continued to plummet. Cued by Fiske, he started to give much thought to the evolution of religion, telling Youmans "the question [is] a burning one." In early 1884, Spencer published an article in which he asserted that, even though traditional dogmatic theism must now give way to agnosticism, some ecclesiastical practices such as ritual and music would survive. The vast unknown, he wrote, would forever inspire human curiosity and reverence; in other words, a real, scientific religion—the "religion of the future"—was at hand. "Amid the mysteries which become the more mysterious the more they are thought about," Spencer observed, "there will remain one absolute certainty, that [man] is ever in the presence of an Infinite and Eternal Energy, from which all things proceed."

Coming from a celebrated nonbeliever, Spencer's worshipful assertion of an all-giving universal power, if not exactly a benevolent and designing intelligence, garnered much favorable comment in England, though he expressed his usual annoyance when Youmans reported that the American press had shown scant interest. Then his friend and fellow agnostic and antiaggression leader, the positivist Frederic Harrison, rebutted him sharply in print, igniting the spectacle of two of Britain's leading infidels quarreling in public over the true nature of religious belief. Calling Spencer's formulation "A Ghost of a Religion," Harrison reproached Spencer for failing to appreciate the deeper meaning of a faith that is intensely anthropomorphic: that is, that there can be no religion without personal kinship and sympathy between the believer and the object of belief. Harrison wrote that religion cannot be based on mere metaphysical abstraction. It must have a "creed, doctrines, temples, priests, teaching, ritual, morality, beauty, hope, consolation."

Spencer was beside himself. For a year he and Harrison attacked each other in the pages of British journals—articles that Youmans reprinted in *Popular Science*. As ever, Youmans was eager to capitalize on the controversy with a book, and in early 1885 he sent Spencer an urgent appeal, telling him that Harrison's American friends were planning to bring Harrison to the United States to lecture and were going ahead with bringing out their own volume. Neither claim was true, but Spencer leaped, authorizing Youmans to publish his articles even as Youmans neglected to get Harrison's permission to reprint his. That spring, amid considerable interest, Appleton published *The Nature and Reality of Religion,* a summary of the Spencer/Harrison debate on the religion of the future, with a richly partisan introduction by Youmans.

Now it was Harrison's turn to erupt. "I regard this not only as an act of literary piracy," he told Spencer in a letter forwarded to the London *Times,* "but as a new and most unworthy form of literary piracy. May I ask if it is proposed to hand you the profits of a book of which I am (in part) the author, or are these to be retained by your American publishers and friend?" Demanding, in a fit of anger, an accounting of the profits, he impugned Spencer's honor. Startled by Youmans's unscrupulousness and stung by Harrison, "who has inflicted on me immeasurably more pain than has been inflicted by any other man," Spencer ordered Appleton in June to stop selling the book, destroy the stock on hand and the printing plates, and debit the loss to his account.

For Youmans, Spencer's bitter suppression of *The Nature and Reality of Religion* struck a final insufferable blow—"this catastrophe," he called it. He ceased going out and writing letters; he saw few visitors. Spencer and Fiske each wrote him with mounting alarm, despite hopeful reports from his family. Spencer's last letter to him reached Youmans on his deathbed:

7 MARINE SQUARE, BRIGHTON, *January 1, 1887*

MY DEAR YOUMANS: It is a long time since I heard anything about you, and I am getting anxious to have a report. Pray let me know how you have fared during the cold weather.

I cannot report favourably of myself. It is still the old story— improvement and then relapse. The last relapse was due to a cold, which, of course, in my present state, pulled me back considerably. "The malice of fate" from which I have suffered ever since last May has been almost incredible.

I have great difficulty in killing the time, especially now that I am kept wholly indoors by the weather, being unable to walk about or read or talk to any extent, or even to play games. I pass my hours on the sofa wearily enough, as you may imagine. What little work I do is at the Autobiography.

Though the day suggests it, it is absurd for me to wish you, or for you to wish me, a happy New Year. There is not much happiness remaining in store for either of us.

Pray dictate a few lines when you get this.

Ever yours,

HERBERT SPENCER

BEECHER'S 1883 SUMMER LECTURE TOUR, just as he turned seventy, took Eunice and him all the way to California. "I'm not afraid of seeing Christianity swept away," he repeated over and over again to the throngs who paid to see him. "Anything that can be swept away ought to be swept away. But I hold that the foundations of God stand sure, and in the near future this very doctrine of evolution that so alarms many of the churches and many ministers will prove to be a soil down into which the root of Christian doctrine will go."

In the presidential campaign the next year he first backed the incumbent, Chester A. Arthur, but the Republicans chose Blaine. Beecher, like Schurz, Godkin, and other liberals of the previous decade, broke with the party and supported Democrat Grover Cleveland, threatening the GOP's generation-long dominance in Washington and further straining Beecher's relations with his parishioners. Then, in midcampaign, allegations flared that Cleveland was an adulterer, the father of an illegitimate child. Cleveland admitted his transgression and took care of the boy financially, forcing Beecher yet again to confront the pain and embarrassment of the Tilton scandal.

Beecher hurled himself loyally into the fight for Cleveland, telling his congregation:

When in the gloomy night of my own suffering I sounded every depth of sorrow, I vowed that if God would bring the day-star of hope I would never suffer brother, friend or neighbor to go unfriended should a like serpent seek to crush him. . . . I will imitate the noble example set me by the Plymouth Church in the day of my calamity. They were not ashamed of my bonds. They stood by me with God-sent loyalty. It was a heroic deed. They have set my duty before me, and I will imitate their example.

Ten days before the election, he told young voters at the Brooklyn YMCA: "If every man in New York State to-night, who has broken the Seventh Commandment, voted for Cleveland, he would be elected by 200,000 majority." The *Tribune*, normally friendly, called it an appeal to adulterers.

Beecher, seeming to view Cleveland's election as a personal vindication, later commented on the inevitable outrage that followed his statements: "I had tasted blood. I had to go on tasting it." Yet thirteen years after Victoria Woodhull tried to get him to confess to adultery, he found vicarious deliverance as Cleveland, manfully confessing to his, won the White House. His service kept him connected to power through the downfall of Republican rule.

No longer caring what anyone thought, or whom he shocked with his religious and political apostasy, Beecher spent his last years excoriating "this whole theory of sin and its origin that lies at the base of the great evangelical systems of Christianity: I say it is hideous, it is horrible, it is turning creation into a shambles and God into a slaughterer, and the human race into a condition worse a thousandfold than that of beasts."

He died of a stroke in the spring of 1887. Of the forty thousand people who filed by to see him lie in state, nine out of ten were women. Neither Cleveland nor the governor sent a representative to the funeral.

AFTER JOHN WESLEY POWELL BECAME director of the U.S. Geological Survey in 1882, he appointed O. C. Marsh as the bureau's vertebrate paleontologist. Ten years later, opponents of the Survey, including Alexander Agassiz, who'd made a fortune in copper mining, singled Marsh out for attack. Alabama senator Hilary A. Herbert, pressing for budget cuts during a hearing, held up a copy of Marsh's monograph on toothed birds— bound in an expensive volume—and decried government spending on fanciful projects like "birds with teeth." As Cope, his long-aggrieved archfoe, exposed some of Marsh's discoveries as overzealous and unscrupulous, if not fraudulent, "birds with teeth" became a catchword in

Washington for bureaucratic waste and corruption. Marsh was fired, and his position as the government's bone collector abolished.

No longer able to maintain his beloved hilltop mansion on his dwindling inheritance—"the 'estate,'" he wrote a cousin, "is like a squeezed orange"—he mortgaged it to Yale, and at age sixty-four, Marsh's name appeared for the first time on faculty salary lists. With no money left for extensive collecting, he canceled several projects. Depressed, he arranged to donate his museum and collections to the university. In February 1899, under pressure to close out his Survey connections, he traveled to Washington, stopping off in New York on the return trip to attend a dinner for Schurz. The next morning, he walked home from the New Haven railway station through heavy rain, developing pneumonia, which killed him. Marsh's cash assets when he died totaled $186.

WITH THE PUBLICATION of *What Social Classes Owe to Each Other*, William Graham Sumner established himself as the nation's foremost social Darwinist, and as his views developed and matured, so did his output; between 1887 and 1890 he produced sixty papers and two or three books. In December 1890 he collapsed, shattered by overwork, illness, and relentless worries over money. "The bottom fact is my brain and nerves," he wrote his friend William Whitney, who—like Youmans with Spencer, and Darwin with Huxley—sought to resolve the crisis by taking up a purse. "What I need, however, beyond all question, is a year of rest. If any such thing as you mentioned could be carried out I am in no position to refuse it from my friends." A group made up primarily of Bones men established a fund to help pay for a teaching replacement at Yale and a year in Europe for Sumner, who, recovering slowly, sharply curtailed his writing and lecturing over most of the next decade.

IN THE 1890S, as industrial capitalism overtook American life and the nation emerged as a world power, the theory of evolution set the terms for the larger discourse over what America is. The wide popularity of Fiske's God-wrought evolutionary nationalism had helped give rise to a new sense of American racial superiority. Opponents and defenders of imperialism alike sought scientific justification for their causes in the natural world, relying obsessively on Darwin and Spencer to buttress their claims.

Josiah Strong, general secretary of the Evangelical Alliance, urged Protestant support for an expansionist foreign policy, arguing that the supreme Anglo-Saxon race had a responsibility to "civilize and Christianize" the world. Citing Darwin's *Descent,* Strong prophesied that as the unoccupied lands of the world became populated, those populations would begin impinging on the survival of the United States. "Then will the world enter upon a new stage of its history," he declared in 1885:

> *—the final competition of races for which the Anglo Saxon is being schooled.* If I do not read amiss, this powerful race will move down upon Mexico, down upon Central and South America, out upon the islands of the sea, over upon Africa and beyond. And can anyone doubt that the result of this competition of races will be the "survival of the fittest"?

Fiske himself was a minor voice in the ideological debate—he was busy, among other things, writing a biography of Youmans, helping Spencer with his work on religion, serving as titular head of the Immigration Restriction League of Boston, which sought to preserve Yankee stock in the blood of the nation, collecting honorary degrees from Harvard and the University of Pennsylvania, and moving to a better house, on Brattle Street. But expansionists invoked the law of progress and his historical arguments with equal zeal in making the case for increasing American influence around the world and asserting sea power in the Pacific and the Caribbean.

In 1896, following a dozen years during which the executive branch—and Carl Schurz's sympathies—swung back and forth between the political parties, Schurz campaigned vigorously for William McKinley, a Republican, who told him afterward in a private meeting, "You may be sure there will be no jingo nonsense under my administration." Schurz, now editor of *Harper's,* was outraged when McKinley tried the next year to annex Hawaii, but he remained hopeful when McKinley first resisted calls to invade Cuba, where rebels sought independence from genocidal Spanish rule. Schurz's "dread certainty that American imperialism would lead to a ruinous end for either American principles or the American constitutional system," as the historian Robert Beisner notes, compelled him to oppose aggression both there and in the Philippines. As the first modern president, with unprecedented power concentrated in the White House, McKinley in April 1898 signed a declaration of war against Spain, ostensibly to free Cuba but also as an opportunity to annex Hawaii and Puerto Rico and extend U.S. power across the Pacific.

Anti-imperialists mobilized as the country split deeply that summer over the implications of the war, which was won swiftly and decisively. Among them were those who thought the acquisition of foreign territory illegal and a violation of core American values (since the Constitution, drawn by fervid anticolonialists, lacked any provisions for acquiring colonies and could not be applied to distant territories, and fundamental Christian logic asserted that if no man was good enough to own another, neither was any nation) and those, like Carnegie, who thought the way to expand the country's economic and social influence was to sell goods to foreign markets by making them better and cheaper, not through the marshaling of gunboats. McKinley's negotiations with Spain—no Cubans or Filipinos were invited to attend—yielded a treaty, but it faced staunch opposition in Congress. Meanwhile, major public figures including Cleveland, Carnegie, Schurz, Sumner, E. L. Godkin, William James, Mark Twain, William Jennings Bryan, and Samuel Gompers united to form the Anti-Imperialist League to defeat it.

A week after the armistice, Schurz once again raised the specter that annexing foreign lands and taking responsibility for indigenous peoples was evolutionarily self-defeating. Fifty years after coming to America, which was now at the apex of the great European immigration, he told a conference in Saratoga that the annexation of the Philippines, populated as they were by a "large mass of more or less barbarous Asiatics," confronted America with an impossible choice: treat them either as first-class citizens with full civil rights, or as subject people with no rights. Writing a month later in *The Century Magazine,* he warned that McKinley's expansionist plans would soon relieve American worries about "a few thousand immigrants from Italy, Russia and Hungary" as it faced the larger task of assimilating "Spanish Americans, with all the mixture of Indian and negro blood, and Malays and other unspeakable Asiatics, by the tens of millions."

WHAT ARE YOU going to do with all these things? Huxley had asked twenty-two years earlier. With America now expanding overseas, the question held special urgency.

It was Carnegie whose often contradictory words and actions best reflected the limits of basing a liberal social and political program on the law of survival. A generation of Americans and Britons now knew him as an international business titan, an author on big subjects, and a scorching editorialist, and also as the embodiment of the democratic ideal of a self-made man, an archfoe of hereditary privilege. Yet throughout the early nineties, while promoting his *Gospel of Wealth*, which argued that the rich must be stewards for society and which transformed old-fashioned charity into modern philanthropy, and elsewhere in print going so far as to support socialism, he also famously allowed a strike at his Homestead Mill to be crushed by thousands of strikebreakers, Pinkerton agents, and state guardsmen. Carnegie strongly favored "keeping our empire within the continent, especially keeping it out of the vortex of militarism" even as he profited handsomely from supplying steel armor for the navy's new battleships.

After the armistice with Spain, Carnegie flooded newspapers, magazines, and elected officials with dire warnings against the perils of imperialism, claiming that it would divert resources away from domestic expansion, roil international stability, and dilute America's moral standing as the nation was drawn inevitably into suppressing local uprisings, especially in the Philippines. He donated heavily to the Anti-Imperialist League, and was elected the first vice president. Schurz, believing Carnegie's advocacy made him "the leader of the Anti-Imperialist Movement," urged him to "take active charge at once," while Godkin, now at the *Evening Post*, wrote him: "You are doing the best work of your life. God prosper you!" After Congress ratified the Treaty of Paris, authorizing $20 million to compensate Spain for losing the Philippines, Carnegie offered to buy the island chain's independence with a personal check for the same amount. Publicly admonishing McKinley, he threatened to oppose the Republican ticket in 1900.

SUMNER, TOO, SERVED as a vice president of the Anti-Imperialist League, laboring despite his weakened state to block U.S. expansion because he feared it was an evolutionary step backward toward militarism.

"The fathers of this republic created a peculiar form of confederated state formed on democratic republics," he wrote two years before the war with Spain. "They meant to secure us a chance to live in peace, happiness and prosperity, free from the social burdens which had cursed the civilized nations of the Old World. We were to be free from war, feudalism, state church, balance of power, heavy taxation and what Benjamin Franklin called the pest of glory." Like Spencer, Sumner associated militant societies with war, authoritarianism, and privilege and industrial ones with cooperation and reason, and in the last decade of his life he grew increasingly alarmed by the nation's lunge toward plutocracy and world power.

In January 1899, Sumner appeared in formal evening dress before the Phi Beta Kappa Society in New Haven to lecture—irony intended—on "The Conquest of the United States by Spain." "We have beaten Spain in a military conflict," he said, "but we are submitting to be conquered by her on the field of ideas and policies. Expansionism and imperialism are nothing but the old philosophies of national prosperity which have brought Spain to where she now is. . . . They are delusions, and they will lead us to ruin unless we are hard-headed enough to resist them." Contrarian as ever, he asserted that the price of America's victory would be a loss of democracy, since it foretold more "war, debt, taxation, diplomacy, a grand governmental system, pomp, glory, a big army and navy," and "political jobbery."

Sumner lived another ten years, during which the progressive reform movement overtook the niggardly social policies he advocated. As Social Darwinism declined, it yielded to the emergence of pragmatism, the philosophical current developed by William James and others, mostly Bostonians, who emphasized what was possible through human choice and endeavor over what was inevitable by nature. Though Sumner opposed to the end the rise of government activity to regulate economic and social conflicts, his last essay, in 1909—unpublished—indicated he was becoming more and more distressed by monopolization, economic inequality, and the concentration of power and opportunity within a favored social class.

IN THE SPRING of 1901, Fiske was invited to speak at the millennial celebration for King Alfred, also known as Alfred the Great, the self-styled "King of the Anglo-Saxons" famous for repulsing the Danish Vikings and integrating the Teutonic people inhabiting England into a distinct nationality with a common language, law, religion, and culture. Save Spencer, all his dearest English friends—Darwin, Huxley, Tyndall, and Lewes—were dead, but Fiske eagerly looked forward to making the voyage in September to present his views on the role of the English race in the new century.

He worked all through June on his lecture. He believed the expansion of the English people throughout the world constituted the greatest hope for man's moral and social well-being. But he foresaw two main obstacles: the awakening of China, which would upend the balance of power in the East, and the rise of militant Germany, which threatened Europe. He planned to argue that since England had vital interests in both Europe and Asia, and might well soon be forced to defend those interests on both continents, the United States could not remain on the sidelines. If England was to be a dominating influence in world affairs, the political sympathies and shared economic interests of Americans made Anglo-American solidarity—what Carnegie, with customary ambivalence, called "race imperialism"—evolutionarily imperative.

Fiske never delivered the lecture. Worn out by overwork, he was laid low by a beastly heat wave in early July and suffered heat prostration, then a stroke, killing him at age fifty-nine.

AFTER THE HARRISON FIASCO and Youmans's death, Spencer grew deeply pessimistic, about both his own fate and that of his ideas. Throughout the late eighties, as he finished his *Autobiography,* he "made a further great descent to confirmed ill-health and incapacity"—"my invalid life," he now called it. However much he had illuminated man's nature, most of what motivated the human heart still eluded him. In 1889, at age sixty-nine, tired of living alone in solitary rooms, he finally set up his own home, living with a pair of sisters who later wrote piquantly about the experience under the shared pseudonym "Two."

Only controversy revived him. Later that year, perturbed by a letter to the *Times* from Huxley criticizing him yet again for opposing government action—this time, to treat cholera—"by deductions from physiological principles," Spencer broke off all relations with his friend of thirty-five years. Huxley "was making me look like a fool to a hundred thousand readers," he complained to Joseph Hooker. The X-Club was "almost in xtremis," wrote Huxley, who told Hooker he didn't know how he'd put up so long with that "long-winded . . . pedant."

Spencer grew "dreadfully disturbed" when, in 1892, the German biologist August Weissman posited a new biological mechanism of inheritance. Like Darwin, Spencer believed that the acquired experience of one generation was passed on genetically to the next. But Weissman speculated that only germ cells—eggs and sperm—are agents of heredity, and that anything that the living cells of the body learn or any ability a body develops during its life cannot be passed along. If Weissman was correct—and most biologists supported him—Spencer feared his whole philosophy would be undermined. "Men could no longer hope to evolve an ideal race by gradual increments of knowledge and benevolence handed down to their children," Richard Hofstadter observed; "social evolution must be redrawn along stricter Darwinian lines; if there was to be any progress at all it must come from a severe reliance upon natural selection."

Shaken, his optimism collapsing, Spencer wrote three essays in 1893 and another in 1894 refuting Weissman and defending "use inheritance." Meanwhile, social theorists turned more aggressively critical of social Darwinism, many of them embracing a new, more "scientific" approach to human betterment by encouraging favored bloodlines through social, legal, and medical means—eugenics. Appealing to the emerging interest in preserving and extending America's "racial stock" in an era of dawning imperialism, nativist anxiety over rising poverty, disease, and immorality among immigrant groups, and a new zeal for government reforms, the eugenics movement swiftly took root across America. Beginning with Connecticut in 1896, which barred anyone who was "epileptic, imbecile or feeble-minded" from marrying, dozens of states adopted eugenics-based social policies. The rediscovery in 1900 of the Austrian monk Gregor Mendel's thirty-year-old plant studies, placing Weissman's germ-plasm theory on a firmer footing, introduced the modern era of biology and medicine while triggering, in the western states in particular, a eugenics craze.

Having outlived the era of competitive individualism he had helped define and inspire, Spencer withdrew deeper into his experiment with home life. He now worked no more than ten minutes at a stretch, dictating before resting or going for a short walk. He stopped going to the

Athenaeum Club and quit dining out. Public amusements, he wrote, were "rigorously excluded"—no theater or concerts. Carnegie bought him a piano, but after hiring a woman to play it for him, Spencer banished her after two sessions, having gotten no sleep afterward on either occasion. According to "Two," he inserted ear-stoppers when the domestic "conversation was too great a strain for him," and every evening punctually at ten, rose and said good night. In June 1893, he reflected dismally on the state of his diminished existence:

> Thus the waking hours have to be passed in an unexciting and, by implication, in an uninteresting way—lying on the sofa or lounging about, and when the weather and the place permit, as now, sitting very much in the open air, hearing and observing the birds, watching the drifting clouds, listening to the sighings of the wind through the trees, and letting my thoughts ramble in harmless ways, avoiding as much as possible exciting subjects. But of course, debarred, as I thus am, from bodily and mental exercise and most kinds of pleasures, no ingenuity can prevent weariness.
>
> When I speak of waking hours . . . I apparently imply that the hours of the night are not waking hours. But in large measure they are. If the day has been gone through with prudence, and I have taken my dose of opium (1 or 2 grains) at the right hour, then between half-past ten and perhaps one, perhaps two, perhaps half past two, broken sleep is obtained—never continuous sleep. After that comes hours of sleeplessness and tossing from side to side; mostly followed, but sometimes not followed, by more broken sleep before the servant comes with my breakfast in the morning, at 8. And then the dreams accompanying such sleep as I obtain, though not bad in the sense of being dreadful or horrible, are usually annoying.

According to "Two," one night in his drawing room, well into his seventies, he confessed "gravely and unimpassionedly" to having once been in love, more than fifty years earlier. "It seemed that he not only felt more deeply than he would admit," the sisters wrote, "but that he still cherished his illusions about her; for after he told us his one poor little romance he suggested rather sheepishly that he should write to her and propose exchanging photographs." When her letter arrived, Spencer opened it in private, then returned crestfallen. "It was clear that with the opening of that envelope the last of his illusions vanished."

"Why is everybody so interested in love affairs, Mr. Spencer?" one of the sisters asked, seeing him quite sad. "Is it because they are common to all?"

"Yes, that is one reason," Spencer replied; "but a greater reason is because love is the most interesting thing in life."

Spencer died in 1903, at age eighty-two. "After all my celibate life has probably been best for me," he reflected near the end of his autobiography, invoking one last time the Law of Equal Freedom: "as well as the best for some unknown other."

CARNEGIE AT AGE SIXTY-FIVE, with a wife of fourteen years and a four-year-old daughter named for his sainted mother, had become one of the world's richest men. By ruthlessly, though not as ruthlessly as some, buying up competitors and eliminating rivals, he had assembled Carnegie Steel, the largest, most integrated iron, coke, and steel operation in the country, which he sold in 1901 for $480 million (about $121 billion in 2007) to the financier J. P. Morgan, who then created United States Steel, the first billion-dollar company. Newly famous around the globe, the "Star-Spangled Scotchman" pledged to devote his retirement to putting all his energy and money toward advancing the gospels of wealth, anti-imperialism, and peace. By the time he was done, he had financed the construction of more than three thousand libraries in forty-seven states; endowed and lent his name to universities, research institutes, public baths, peace organizations, the restoration of seven hundred church organs, and pension funds for the Homestead strikers and college professors; and established "heroes' funds" in eleven countries.

He mended relations with the Republicans and, after McKinley was assassinated, with President Theodore Roosevelt, whom a year earlier he had regarded as "a dangerous man." He made himself a ubiquitous figure, relentlessly lobbying leaders in Washington, London, and Berlin for a League of Peace, treaty proposals that would submit disputes between countries to international arbitration, and disarmament. "Andrew Carnegie, Apostle of Peace," the *Times* called him in a flattering profile barely three years after he had been better known as a striving, avaricious steel man. Among his most imaginative projects was the Carnegie Institution in Washington, a national scientific institute devoted to pure research.

In 1904, the institution financed the founding of the Station for Experimental Evolution at Cold Spring Harbor, on Long Island, which promoted eugenic studies and preceded by two years the federal government's own entry into scientific breeding, the Department of Agriculture's Committee on Eugenics. Explaining that the purpose of both investigations was "to make a study of heredity in man with a view to racial improvement," the *Times* glowingly headlined a story about the federal project:

SCIENCE TO MAKE MEN
AND WOMEN BETTER

Committee Will Investigate Heredity in Man and Ways of Encouraging
Multiplication of Good Blood and Discouraging Vicious Blood of Human Family

Within a year, individual states began conducting forced sterilizations on those deemed unfit as parents because they were presumed mentally or morally inferior, a program that within a generation Nazi race scientists would cite as a successful technique for ethnic cleansing. As racial science reemerged as a rationale for state social policy a half century after Darwin tried to prove the unity of humankind in *Descent*, Spencer's theories and social Darwinism were frequently blamed, despite Spencer's lifelong abhorrence of all coercive state control of the individual. ("Spencer," Youmans had predicted, "will in time reap his greatest conquest in Germany.")

As the world edged closer to war, Carnegie "pressed inordinately" his reconciliation efforts, refusing to believe that the world's leaders would not ultimately step back from the brink and come to his side. When in 1914 they did not, he recovered from his initial shock at the outbreak of fighting in Europe to resume his crusade for a League of Peace, proposing that after the war was won, England, France, and Russia should invite Germany and Austria to join them in forming a collective body to mediate disputes and police its decisions with a combined naval force.

The following February, at age seventy-nine, he testified before Congress. Asked if he had lost faith in the peace impulse, he replied:

Certainly not. I verily believe that in this war exists the most impressive, perhaps the only argument which could induce humanity to abate forever the curse of military preparation and the inevitably resultant woe of conflict. . . . But don't imagine that I underestimate the horror of this conflict. This war staggers the imagination; it goes beyond the bounds of warfare as warfare has been known. I do not understand its horror, but I hope, and I believe that this very horrible, newly barbaric excess will so revolt human nature against all things of the kind that the reaction will be great enough to carry us into the realms of reason. And the realms of reason are the realms of peace.

It was Carnegie's last pronouncement. As the slaughter in Europe ground on, his Spencerian faith in reason and progress crumbled, and Carnegie, after a lifetime of voicing opinions and answers on every subject, descended into public silence. On his doctors' advice, his wife, Louise, bought a nine-hundred-acre hillside estate, Shadowbrook, overlooking Stockbridge Bowl in Lenox, Massachusetts—across from the small red wood-frame house where Nathaniel Hawthorne had retreated in 1850 after the nerve-racking success of *The Scarlet Letter*. He had been, Louise later told an interviewer, "the most vital, exuberant person imaginable—until August 4, 1914. Then he completely changed. He became an old man overnight. . . . He became thin, so that his clothes hung loosely around him; his face became deeply indented; his zest for mere existence had gone."

By the time he died in 1919 at age eighty-four, Carnegie had given away $350 million (about $5 billion, adjusted to 2007 values). Upon his death, the last $30 million of his fortune was also donated to charities, foundations, and pensioners.

ACKNOWLEDGMENTS

I could not have written this book without the generosity of Smith College, and especially the efforts of Dan Horowitz and Rick Millington, who arranged and abetted my status as a research associate. No freelance historian today can operate without an academic affiliation, and Smith took me in. This gave me the incalculable advantage of having access to the college's libraries, staff—especially Betsy Barone—and databases. Also at Smith, I am indebted to Helen Horowitz and Ernie Alleva, who each reviewed an early draft, and Brigitte Buettner, who helped with translation.

Many other libraries, organizations, librarians, and archivists patiently assisted as I—far more impatiently—pursued facts, clippings, quotes, artifacts, pictures, documents, letters, scholarly articles, and other material. I owe special thanks to Dana Fisher and Robert Young at the Harvard Museum of Comparative Zoology archives; Lisa DeCesare at Harvard's Gray Herbarium Botany Library; Allison Botelho at New Haven Public Library; Miranda Schwartz at New-York Historical Society; the Rhode Island Historical Society; the Library of Congress Prints and Photographs Reading Room; and the New York Public Library department of photographic services. I also greatly appreciate the assistance of editor Mark Jannot at *Popular Science*.

Dan Horowitz, Kathy Goos, Steven Shapin, Bob Nylen, Ed Hirsch, Evan Thomas, Jamie Shreve, and Dick Evans read early drafts and offered much-needed insight and encouragement. Hosea Baskin, Lisa Baskin, Chris Benfey, and Max Prior all provided friendly, and crucial, gestures of assistance.

I would be remiss if I did not acknowledge Nan Talese for her support, encouragement, grace, and wisdom. Amanda Urban, as always, has been a strong, smart, tenacious advocate. At Random House, my editor

Jonathan Jao provided astute guidance and vision, and a deft hand. Emily DeHuff and Vincent La Scala brought welcome clarity and discipline to the manuscript.

Kathy, Emily, and Alex are everywhere in this book, as they are in everything else I am, think, and try to do.

BIBLIOGRAPHY

Books

Abbott, Lyman. *Henry Ward Beecher: A Sketch of His Career.* New York: Chelsea House, 1980.

Ackroyd, Peter. *London: The Biography.* New York: Nan A. Talese / Doubleday, 2001.

Adams, Henry. *The Education of Henry Adams.* Boston: Houghton, Mifflin & Co., 1918.

Agassiz, Elizabeth Cary, ed. *Louis Agassiz: His Life and Correspondence.* Boston: Houghton Mifflin, 1885.

Agassiz, Louis. *Geological Sketches.* Reprint Services Corp. (January 1866).

Ahlstrom, Sydney E. *A Religious History of the American People.* New Haven: Yale University Press, 1972.

Alland, Alexander, Jr. *Human Nature: Darwin's View.* New York: Columbia University Press, 1985.

Applegate, Debby. *The Most Famous Man in America: The Biography of Henry Ward Beecher.* New York: Doubleday, 2006.

Ashton, Rosemary. *George Eliot: A Life.* New York: Penguin Books, 1996.

Baldwin, Neil. *Edison: Inventing the Century.* Chicago: University of Chicago Press, 1995.

Baltzell, E. Digby. *The Protestant Establishment.* New York: Vintage Books, 1966.

Bannister, Robert C. *Social Darwinism: Science and Myth in Anglo-American Social Thought.* Philadelphia: Temple University Press, 1979.

Beecher, Henry Ward. *Lectures on Preaching.* New Haven: Yale University Press, 1917.

Beisner, Robert L. *Twelve Against Empire: The Anti-Imperialists, 1898–1900.* New York: McGraw-Hill, 1968.

Benfey, Christopher. *The Great Wave: Gilded Age Misfits, Japanese Eccentrics, and the Opening of Old Japan.* New York: Random House, 2003.

Botta, Anne C. Lynch. *Memoirs.* New York: J. Selwin Tait & Sons, 1893.

Bowman, Sylvia E. *William Graham Sumner.* Boston: Twayne Publishers, 1981.

Bridge, James H. *The Carnegie Millions and the Men Who Made Them.* London: Limpus, Baker and Co., 1903.

Brockman, John, ed. *Intelligent Thought: Science Versus the Intelligent Design Movement.* New York: Vintage Books, 2006.

Brown, Dee. *The Year of the Century: 1876.* New York: Charles Scribner's Sons, 1966.

Browne, Janet. *Charles Darwin: Voyaging.* Princeton, New Jersey: Princeton University Press, 1995.

———. *Charles Darwin: The Power of Place.* Princeton, New Jersey: Princeton University Press, 2002.

Bruce, Robert V. *The Launching of Modern American Science, 1846–1876.* Ithaca, New York: Cornell University Press, 1987.

———. *1877: Year of Violence.* Chicago: Elephant Paperbacks, 1989.

Carnegie, Andrew. *Autobiography of Andrew Carnegie.* Boston: Northeastern University Press, 1986 (originally published 1920).

———. *Round the World.* Garden City, New York: Doubleday, Doran & Co., 1883.

Clark, John Spencer. *The Life and Letters of John Fiske.* Boston: Houghton Mifflin, 1917.

Cochran, Thomas C., and William Miller. *The Age of Enterprise.* New York: Harper & Row, 1942.

Colp, Ralph, Jr. *To Be an Invalid: The Illness of Charles Darwin.* Chicago: University of Chicago Press, 1977.

Commager, Henry Steele. *The American Mind.* New Haven: Yale University Press, 1950.

Coser, Lewis A. *Masters of Sociological Thought.* New York: Harcourt Brace Jovanovich, 1971.

Croce, Paul Jerome. *Science and Religion in the Era of William James.* Chapel Hill: University of North Carolina Press, 1995.

Curti, Merle. *The Growth of American Thought.* New York: Harper & Brothers, 1943.

Darwin, Charles. *Autobiography of Charles Darwin.* New York, W. W. Norton, 1958 (originally published 1887).

———. *The Descent of Man, and Selection in Relation to Sex.* London: Penguin Books, 2004 (originally published 1871).

———. *The Expression of the Emotions in Man and Animals.* Stillwell, Kansas: Digireads.com Publishing, 2005 (originally published 1872).

———. *The Origin of Species* and *The Voyage of the Beagle.* New York: Knopf Everyman's Library, 2003 (originally published 1859, 1839).

———. *The Variation of Plants and Animals Under Domestication.* New York: D. Appleton & Co., 1883.

Davison, Kenneth E. *The Presidency of Rutherford B. Hayes.* Westport, Connecticut: Greenwood Press, 1972.

Degler, Carl N. *In Search of Human Nature.* New York: Oxford University Press, 1991.

Desmond, Adrian. *Huxley.* Reading, Massachusetts: Perseus Books, 1994.

———, and James Moore. *Darwin.* New York: Warner Books, 1991.

Dulles, Foster Rhea. *America's Rise to World Power, 1898–1954.* New York: Harper & Row, 1954.

Dunn, Jacob Piatt. *Massacres of the Mountains: A History of the Indian Wars of the Far West.* New York: Harper, 1886.

Dupree, A. Hunter. *Asa Gray.* Baltimore: Johns Hopkins University Press, 1959.

Eiseley, Loren. *Darwin's Century.* Garden City, New York: Doubleday, 1958.

Emerson, Edward Waldo. *The Early Years of the Saturday Club, 1855–1870.* New York: Houghton Mifflin Co., 1918.

Farrington, Benjamin. *What Darwin Really Said.* New York: Schoken Books, 1966.

Feuer, Lewis S. *The Scientific Intellectual.* New Brunswick, New Jersey: Transaction Publishers, 1992.

Fiske, John. *Edward Livingston Youmans: Interpreter of Science for the People.* New York: D. Appleton & Co., 1894.

Foner, Eric. *A Short History of Reconstruction, 1863–1877.* New York: Harper & Row, 1990.

Fox, Richard Wightman. *Trials of Intimacy: Love and Loss in the Beecher-Tilton Scandal.* Chicago: University of Chicago Press, 1999.

Francis, Mark. *Herbert Spencer and the Invention of Modern Life.* Ithaca, New York: Cornell University Press, 2007.

Fuess, Claude. *Carl Schurz: Reformer.* Port Washington, New York: Kennikat Press, Inc., 1963.

Gabriel, Mary. *Notorious Victoria: The Life of Victoria Woodhull, Uncensored.* Chapel Hill, North Carolina: Algonquin Books, 1998.

Goldsmith, Barbara. *Other Powers: The Age of Suffrage, Spiritualism and the Scandalous Victoria Woodhull.* New York: HarperPerennial, 1998.

Gould, Lewis L. *Grand Old Party: A History of the Republicans.* New York: Random House, 2003.

Gray, Asa. *Darwiniana.* New York: D. Appleton & Co., 1876.

———. *Natural Science and Religion.* New York: Charles Scribner's Sons, 1880.

Harris, Marvin. *The Rise of Anthropological Theory.* New York: Thomas Y. Crowell, 1968.

Harrison, Frederic. *National and Social Problems.* New York: The Macmillan Co., 1908.

Hertz, Emmanuel. *Abraham Lincoln: A New Portrait.* New York: Horace Liveright, Inc., 1931.

Hibben, Paxton. *Henry Ward Beecher: An American Portrait.* New York: The Press of the Reader's Club, 1942.

Hillis, Newell Dwight, ed. *Lectures and Orations by Henry Ward Beecher.* New York: Fleming H. Revell Co., 1913.

Himmelfarb, Gertrude. *Darwin and the Darwinian Revolution.* New York: W. W. Norton, 1959.

Hodge, A. A. *The Life of Charles Hodge.* New York: Charles Scribner's Sons, 1880.

Hodge, Charles. *Systematic Theology.* New York: Charles Scribner and Co., 1873.

———. *What Is Darwinism?* Grand Rapids, Michigan: Baker Books, 1994.

Hoeveler, J. David, Jr. *James McCosh and the Scottish Intellectual Tradition.* Princeton, New Jersey: Princeton University Press, 1981.

Hofstadter, Richard. *Social Darwinism in American Thought.* New York: George Braziller, 1959.

Holt, Henry. *Garrulities of an Octogenarian Editor.* Boston: Houghton Mifflin Co., 1923.

Horowitz, Helen Lefkowitz. *Rereading Sex: Battles over Sexual Knowledge and Suppression in Nineteenth Century America.* New York: Alfred A. Knopf, 2002.

Howe, M. A. De Wolfe. *Later Years of the Saturday Club, 1870–1920.* Boston: Houghton Mifflin & Co., 1927.

Huxley, Thomas H. *American Addresses.* New York: D. Appleton & Co., 1888.

———. *Man's Place in Nature.* New York: Modern Library, 2001.

Irvine, William. *Apes, Angels and Victorians: The Story of Darwin, Huxley and Evolution.* New York: McGraw-Hill, 1955.

Jaffe, Mark. *The Gilded Dinosaur: The Fossil War Between E. D. Cope and O. C. Marsh and the Rise of American Science.* New York: Three Rivers Press, 2000.

Keller, A. G. *Reminiscences of William Graham Sumner.* New Haven: Yale University Press, 1933.

Kemeny, P. C. *Princeton in the Nation's Service.* New York: Oxford University Press, 1998.

Kennedy, James G. *Herbert Spencer.* Boston: Twayne Publishers, 1978.

Kessner, Thomas. *Capital City: New York City and the Men Behind America's Rise to Economic Dominance, 1860–1900.* New York: Simon & Schuster, 2003.

Krass, Peter. *Carnegie.* Hoboken, New Jersey: John Wiley & Sons, 2002.

Kuhn, Thomas S. *The Structure of Scientific Revolutions.* Chicago: University of Chicago Press, 1962.

Kurlansky, Mark. *The Big Oyster.* New York: Random House, 2007.

Laing, Samuel. *Problems of the Future, and Essays.* London: Chapman and Hall, 1900.

Larson, Edward J. *Evolution.* New York: Modern Library, 2006.

Livingstone, David N. *Darwin's Forgotten Defenders.* Grand Rapids, Michigan: William B. Eerdmans Publishing, 1987.

Lurie, Edward. *Louis Agassiz: A Life in Science.* Chicago: University of Chicago Press, 1960.

———. *Nature and the American Mind.* New York: Science History Publications, 1974.

Maier, Pauline, Merritt Roe Smith, Alexander Keyssar, and Daniel J. Kevles. *Inventing America: A History of the United States.* New York: W. W. Norton, 2003.

Marsden, George M. *Fundamentalism and American Culture.* New York: Oxford University Press, 1980.

———. *The Soul of the American University: From Protestant Establishment to Established Nonbelief.* New York: Oxford University Press, 1994.

Marsh, Othniel Charles. *Vertebrate Life in America.* Washington, D.C.: American Association for the Advancement of Science, 1877.

Marshall, Charles F. *The True History of the Brooklyn Scandal.* Philadelphia: National Publishing Co., 1874.

Mathes, Valerie Sherer, and Richard Lowitt. *The Standing Bear Controversy.* Chicago: University of Illinois Press, 2003.

McCloskey, Robert Green. *American Conservatism in the Age of Enterprise: 1865–1910.* New York: Harper & Row, 1951.

McCosh, James. *Christianity and Positivism.* New York: Robert Carter & Brothers, 1874.

McCullough, David. *Brave Companions: Portraits in History.* New York: Prentice Hall Press, 1992.

———. *The Great Bridge.* New York: Avon Books, 1972.

McFeely, William S. *Grant: A Biography.* New York: W. W. Norton, 1982.

McHugh, Jeanne. *Alexander Holley and the Makers of Steel.* Baltimore: Johns Hopkins University Press, 1980.

Menand, Louis. *The Metaphysical Club.* New York: Farrar, Straus and Giroux, 2001.

Miller, Kenneth. *Finding Darwin's God.* New York: HarperPerennial, 2002.

Miller, Perry, ed. *American Thought: Civil War to World War I.* New York: Holt, Rinehart and Winston, 1967.

Misa, Thomas. *A Nation of Steel: The Making of Modern America, 1865–1925.* Baltimore: Johns Hopkins University Press, 1998.

Morris, Charles R. *The Tycoons: How Andrew Carnegie, John D. Rockefeller, Jay Gould and J. P. Morgan Invented the American Supereconomy.* New York: Henry Holt, 2005.

Morris, Roy, Jr. *Fraud of the Century: Rutherford B. Hayes, Samuel Tilden and the Stolen Election of 1876.* New York: Simon & Schuster, 2003.

Nasaw, David. *Andrew Carnegie.* New York: Penguin Press, 2006.

Nichols, Peter. *Evolution's Captain: The Dark Fate of the Man Who Sailed Charles Darwin Around the World.* New York: HarperCollins, 2003.

Nott, J. C., and George R. Glidden. *Types of Mankind.* Philadelphia: J. B. Lippincott & Co., 1871.

Nugent, Walter T. K. *Money and American Society, 1865–1880.* New York: The Free Press, 1968.

Numbers, Ronald L. *Darwinism Comes to America.* Cambridge, Massachusetts: Harvard University Press, 1998.

Oppenheim, Janet. *Shattered Nerves: Doctors, Patients and Depression in Victorian England.* New York: Oxford University Press, 1991.

Ostrom, John H., and John S. McIntosh. *Marsh's Dinosaurs: The Collections from Como Bluff.* New Haven: Yale University Press, 1966.

Paley, William. *Natural Theology.* Oxford: Oxford University Press, 2006.

Pannill, H. Burnell. *The Religious Faith of John Fiske.* Durham, North Carolina: Duke University Press, 1957.

Parkes, Henry Bamford. *The American Experience.* New York: Vintage Books, 1959.

Persons, Stow, ed. *Evolutionary Thought in America.* New York: George Braziller, 1956.

Raby, Peter. *Alfred Russel Wallace: A Life.* Princeton, New Jersey: Princeton University Press, 2001.

Ranhofer, Charles. *The Epicurean.* New York: Charles Ranhofer Publisher, 1894.

Roberts, Jon H. *Darwinism and the Divine in America.* Madison: University of Wisconsin Press, 1988.

Rosenberg, Charles E. *The Trial of the Assassin Guiteau.* Chicago: University of Chicago Press, 1968.

Russett, Cynthia Eagle. *Darwin in America: The Intellectual Response, 1865–1912.* San Francisco: W. H. Freeman, 1976.

———. *Sexual Science: The Victorian Construction of Womanhood.* Cambridge, Massachusetts: Harvard University Press, 1989.

Schaff, Rev. Philip, and S. Irenaeus Prime, eds. *History, Essays, Orations, and Other Documents of the Sixth General Conference of the Evangelical Alliance, 1873.* New York: Harper & Brothers Publishers, 1874.

Schlereth, Thomas J. *Victorian America.* New York: HarperPerennial, 1991.

Schuchert, Charles, and Clara Mae LeVene. *O. C. Marsh: Pioneer in Paleontology.* New Haven: Yale University Press, 1940.

Schurz, Carl. *Reminiscences.* New York: McClure Co., 1907.

———. *Speeches, Correspondence and Political Papers, Vol. IV.* New York: G. P. Putnam's Sons, 1913.

Shipman, Pat. *The Evolution of Racism.* Cambridge, Massachusetts: Harvard University Press, 1994.

Slap, Andrew. *The Doom of Reconstruction.* New York: Fordham University Press, 2006.

Smith, Richard Norton. *The Harvard Century.* New York: Simon & Schuster, 1986.

Spencer, Herbert. *The Data of Ethics.* New York: D. Appleton & Co., 1880.

———. *Herbert Spencer: An Autobiography.* London: Williams and Norgate, 1904.

———. *The Principles of Sociology, 3 Volumes.* New York: D. Appleton & Co., 1876–1896.

———. *The Study of Sociology.* London: Routledge / Thoemmes Press, 1996 (originally published 1873).

Standiford, Les. *Meet You in Hell: Andrew Carnegie, Henry Clay Frick, and the Bitter Partnership That Transformed America.* New York: Crown Publishers, 2005.

Stanton, William. *The Leopard's Spots: Scientific Attitudes Towards Race in America.* Chicago: University of Chicago Press, 1960.

Starr, Harris E. *William Graham Sumner.* New York: Henry Holt, 1925.

Starr, Paul. *The Social Transformation of American Medicine.* New York: Basic Books, 1982.

Stewart, John W., and James H. Moorhead, eds. *Charles Hodge Revisited.* Grand Rapids, Michigan: William B. Eerdsmans Publishing, 2002.

Strong, Josiah. *Our Country: Its Possible Future and Its Present Crisis.* New York: American Home Missionary Society, 1885.

Sumner, Charles Burt. *The Story of Pomona College.* Boston: The Pilgrim Press, 1914.

Sumner, William Graham. *The Challenge of Facts and Other Essays.* New York: W. W. Norton, 1914.

———. *The Conquest of the United States by Spain.* Boston: Dana Estes and Co., 1899.

———. *A History of American Currency.* New York: Henry Holt, 1874.

———. *Social Darwinism.* Englewood Cliffs, New Jersey: Prentice-Hall, 1963.

———. *What Social Classes Owe to Each Other.* New York: Harper and Brothers, 1911.

Thompson, Noyes L. *The History of Plymouth Church: 1847–1872.* New York: G. W. Carleton & Co., 1873.

Townsend, Kim. *Manhood at Harvard.* Cambridge, Massachusetts: Harvard University Press, 1996.

Trachtenberg, Alan. *The Incorporation of America: Culture and Society in the Gilded Age.* New York: Hill and Wang, 1982.

Trefousse, Hans L. *Carl Schurz: A Biography.* Knoxville: University of Tennessee Press, 1982.

Turner, Frederick Jackson. *The Frontier in American History.* New York: Dover Publications, 1996.

Unger, Irwin. *The Greenback Era.* Princeton, New Jersey: Princeton University Press, 1964.

Vidal, Gore. *1876.* New York: Ballantine Books, 1976.

Wall, Joseph Frazier. *Andrew Carnegie.* Pittsburgh: University of Pittsburgh Press, 1989.

Webb, Beatrice. *My Apprenticeship.* New York: Longmans, Green and Co., 1926.

White, A. D. *A History of the Warfare of Science with Technology in Christendom.* New York: Dover Publications, 1960.

Winkler, John K. *Incredible Carnegie.* New York: Vanguard Press, 1931.

Winslow, John H. *Darwin's Victorian Malady.* Philadelphia: American Philosophical Society, 1971.

Woodward, C. Vann. *Reunion and Reaction.* Garden City, New York: Doubleday, 1951.

Wright, Robert. *The Moral Animal.* New York: Random House, 1994.

Youmans, Edward Livingston, ed. *Herbert Spencer on the Americans and the Americans on Herbert Spencer: Proceedings of the Farewell Banquet of Nov. 11, 1882.* New York: D. Appleton & Co., 1883.

Articles

Agassiz, Elizabeth C. "The Hassler Glacier in the Straits of Magellan," "In the Straits of Magellan," and "A Cruise Through the Galapagos." *The Atlantic Monthly*, October 1871 (pp. 472–78), January 1872 (pp. 89–95), May 1872 (pp. 579–84).

Agassiz, Louis. "Evolution and the Permanence of Type." *The Atlantic Monthly*, January 1874, pp. 92–101.

Ball, Terrence. "Marx and Darwin: A Reconsideration." *Political Theory*, November 1979, pp. 469–83.

Bannister, Robert C. "The Survival of the Fittest Is Our Doctrine: History or Histrionics?" *Journal of the History of Ideas*, July–September 1970, pp. 377–98.

Bledstein, Burton J. "Noah Porter Versus William Graham Sumner." *Church History*, September 1974, pp. 340–49.

Breslin, Jack. "American Press Coverage of Sociologist Herbert Spencer During His 1882 Visit to America." University of Minnesota School of Journalism graduate paper: http://msu.edu/cgi-bin/wa?A2=ind0101b&l=aejmc&P=13956.

Brilli, Michael. "The Native American Exhibit at the Centennial." http://www3.villanova.edu/centennial/paper.htm.

Cairnes, John E. "Social Evolution." *The Popular Science Monthly*, June 1875.

Carneiro, Robert L. "Herbert Spencer's 'The Study of Sociology' and the Rise of Social Science in America." *Proceedings of the American Philosophical Society*, December 27, 1974, pp. 540–54.

Caudill, Edward. "The Bishop-Eaters: The Publicity Campaign for Darwin and *On the Origin of Species*." *Journal of the History of Ideas*, July 1994, pp. 441–60.

Clark, Stanley. *"Ponca Publicity." The Mississippi Valley Historical Review*, March 1943, pp. 495–516.

Cornford, Daniel, ed. "To Save the Republic: The California Workingmen's Party in Humboldt County." *Working People of California*. Berkeley: University of California Press, 1995.

Croce, Paul Jerome. "Probabilistic Darwinism: Louis Agassiz vs. Asa Gray on Science, Religion and Certainty." *Journal of Religious History*, February 1998, pp. 35–58.

Curtis, Bruce. "William Graham Sumner 'On the Concentration of Wealth.' " *Journal of American History*, March 1969, pp. 823–32.

Dougherty, J. Hampden. "William M. Evarts: Lawyer and Statesman." *Law Department of the Brooklyn Institute*, October 28, 1901.

Downey, Matthew T. "Horace Greeley and the Politicians: The Liberal Republican Convention in 1872." *Journal of American History*, March 1967, pp. 727–50.

Eisen, Sydney. "Frederic Harrison and Herbert Spencer: Embattled Unbelievers." *Victorian Studies*, September 1968, pp. 33–56.

Freeman, Derek. "The Evolutionary Theories of Charles Darwin and Herbert Spencer." *Current Anthropology*, September 1974, pp. 211–37.

Gardner, Albert Ten Eyck. "The Arts and Mrs. Botta." *Metropolitan Museum of Art Bulletin*, November 1947, pp. 105–8.

Haar, Charles M. "E. L. Youmans: A Chapter in the Diffusion of Science in America." *Journal of the History of Ideas*, April 1948, pp. 193–213.

Hague, James. "A Reminiscence of Mr. Darwin." *Harper's Magazine*, April 1884, pp. 759–63.

Hardy, Osgood. "Ulysses S. Grant, President of the Mexican Southern Railroad." *The Pacific Historical Review,* May 1995, pp. 111–20.

Horowitz, Helen Lefkowitz. "Victoria Woodhull, Anthony Comstock, and Conflict over Sex in the United States in the 1870s." *Journal of American History,* September 2000, pp. 403–34.

Huxley, Thomas Henry. "Administrative Nihilism." *Collected Essays, I.* http://aleph0 .clarku.edu/huxley/CE1/AdNil.html.

Jensen, J. V. "Thomas Henry Huxley's Lecture Tour of the United States, 1876." *Notes and Records of the Royal Society of London,* July 1988, pp. 181–95.

Johnston, W. W. "The Ill Health of Charles Darwin: Its Nature and Its Relation to His Work." *American Anthropologist,* January–March 1901, pp. 139–58.

Ledger, Phila. "Written in Coal and Chalk." *The Friend,* October 6, 1887.

Leverette, William E., Jr. "E. L. Youmans' Crusade for Scientific Autonomy and Respectability." *American Quarterly,* Spring 1965, pp. 12–32.

Loewenberg, Bert James. "The Reaction of American Scientists to Darwinism." *American Historical Review,* July 1933, pp. 687–701.

Lowell, James Russell. "Agassiz." *The Atlantic Monthly,* May 1874.

Lurie, Edward. "Louis Agassiz and the Races of Man." *Isis,* September 1954, pp. 227–42.

Marsden, George M. "God and Man at Yale (1880)." *First Things,* April 1994, pp. 39–42.

Notestein, Robert B. "The Moralist Rigorism of W. G. Sumner." *Journal of the History of Ideas,* June 1955, pp. 389–400.

Peterson, Sven R. "Benjamin Peirce: Mathematician and Philosopher." *Journal of the History of Ideas,* January 1955, pp. 89–112.

Plochmann, George Kimball. "Darwin or Spencer?" *Science,* November 27, 1959, pp. 1452–56.

Porter, Noah. "Herbert Spencer's Theory of Sociology: A Critical Essay." *Princeton Review,* July–December 1880, pp. 268–96.

Randel, William Pierce. "Huxley in America." *Proceedings of the American Philosophical Society,* April 13, 1970, pp. 73–99.

Rogers, James Allen. "Darwinism and Social Darwinism." *Journal of the History of Ideas,* April–June 1972, pp. 265–80.

Schneider, Herbert W. "The Influence of Darwin and Spencer on American Philosophical Theology." *Journal of the History of Ideas,* January 1945, pp. 3–18.

Shapin, Steven. "Man with a Plan: Herbert Spencer's Theory of Everything." *The New Yorker,* August 13, 2007, pp. 75–79.

Smith, Henry Nash. "Clarence King, John Wesley Powell and the Establishment of the U.S. Geological Survey." *The Mississippi Valley Historical Review,* June 1947, pp. 37–58.

Spencer, Herbert. "Religion Retrospect and Prospect." *The Popular Science Monthly,* January 1884.

Sternstein, James L. "The Sickles Memorandum: Another Look at the Hayes-Tilden Election-Night Conspiracy." *Journal of Southern History,* August 1966, pp. 342–57.

Sumner, William Graham. "Sketch of William Graham Sumner." *Popular Science Monthly* 35, 1889, pp. 261–68.

Teller, James D. "Louis Agassiz and Men of Letters." *Scientific Monthly,* November 1947, pp. 428–32.

"Two." "Home Life with Herbert Spencer." *Harper's Magazine,* April 1906, pp. 755–60.

Weikart, Richard. "The Origins of Social Darwinism in Germany, 1859–1895." *Journal of the History of Ideas,* July 1993, pp. 469–88.

Wiener, Philip P. "Peirce's Metaphysical Club and the Genesis of Pragmatism." *Journal of the History of Ideas,* April 1946, pp. 218–33.

Woodhull, Victoria. "The Beecher-Tilton Scandal Case." *Woodhull and Claffin's Weekly,* November 2, 1872.

Wyllie, Irvin G. "Social Darwinism and the Businessman." *Proceedings of the American Philosophical Society,* October 15, 1959, pp. 629–35.

Youmans, E. L. "Can Christianity Stand the Assault of Science?" *Boston Journal,* September 5, 1874.

———. "The Literature of Evolution." *The Popular Science Monthly,* June 1875.

———. "Spencer's Evolution Philosophy." *North American Review,* October 1879, pp. 389–403.

NOTES

PROLOGUE: NEW YORK, NOVEMBER 8, 1882

xix "another step downwards" Herbert Spencer, *An Autobiography*, p. 409.

xix the most celebrated thinker of the day Richard Hofstadter, *Social Darwinism in American Thought*, pp. 31–50.

xx "The prospect before me" Spencer, *Autobiography*, p. 406.

xx "Our fifty million people" John Fiske, *Edward Livingston Youmans*, p. 373.

xx "I like to take my pleasure neat" Ibid., p. 374.

xx "I absolutely decline to make myself a show" Spencer, *Autobiography*, p. 385.

xx "Being one of the great thinkers" "Mr. Spencer Coming," *The Washington Post*, February 26, 1882.

xxi "To decline would be awkward" Spencer, *Autobiography*, p. 385.

xxi "Would that my boasted ability" Ibid.

xxi "in so low a nervous state" Edward Livingston Youmans, ed., *Herbert Spencer on the Americans and the Americans on Herbert Spencer*, p. 5.

xxii "The repulsiveness of Pittsburgh" Spencer, *Autobiography*, p. 397.

xxii "Avoidance of draught" Ibid., pp. 399–400.

xxii Reporters tailed him in every city Jack Breslin, "American Press Coverage of Sociologist Herbert Spencer During His 1882 Visit to America," University of Minnesota School of Journalism graduate paper.

xxiii "I remarked" Spencer, *Autobiography*, p. 403.

xxiii Youmans quizzed Spencer "Herbert Spencer Talks," *Times*, October 20, 1882.

xxvi "It was pleasant to meet" Spencer, *Autobiography*, p. 404.

xxvii "Doesn't it disturb you, Fiske" John Spencer Clark, *The Life and Letters of John Fiske, Vol. II*, p. 247.

xxvii Fiske believed America faced Ibid., pp. 249–50.

xxviii In England, he sometimes "borrowed" Mark Francis, *Herbert Spencer and the Invention of Modern Life*, p. 95.

xxix Late in returning from the graveyard Spencer, *Autobiography*, p. 405.

xxix a "cordial Christian Darwinist" E. Digby Baltzell, *The Protestant Establishment*, p. 101.

xxix "I will ride with him" Fiske, *Youmans*, p. 377.

xxx "I went wrong again at Boston" Youmans, *Spencer on the Americans*, pp. 6–7.

xxxi "Wretched night" Spencer, *Autobiography*, p. 406.

CHAPTER ONE: CAMBRIDGE, 1871

3 **or even to think** Elizabeth Cary Agassiz, *Louis Agassiz: His Life and Correspondence*, p. 34.

4 **"Their reign was over"** Louis Agassiz, *Geological Sketches*, p. 208.

4 **"Agassiz's Club"** Edward Waldo Emerson, *The Early Years of the Saturday Club, 1855–1870*, p. 30.

5 **"The year ends with a club dinner"** M. A. De Wolfe Howe, *Later Years of the Saturday Club, 1870–1920*, p. 483.

5 **"It is time to be old"** Ralph Waldo Emerson, "Terminus," 1867.

5 **"Now, my dear friend"** E. Agassiz, *Life and Correspondence*, p. 341.

6 **"My darling Ben"** Edward Lurie, *Nature and the American Mind*, p. 87.

7 **"I daresay I said that I thought"** Letter from Charles Darwin to Asa Gray, September 5, 1857.

7 **"one long argument"** Charles Darwin, *The Origin of Species*, p. 459.

8 **"My Dear Gray"** Letter from Darwin to Gray, February 5, 1871.

9 **Darwin had confessed to Gray** Letter from Darwin to Gray, March 15, 1870.

9 **"How so many absurd rules"** Charles Darwin, *The Descent of Man*, p. 122.

10 **"when the principles of evolution are generally accepted"** Ibid., p. 248.

10 **Gray apologized in his return letter** Letter from Gray to Darwin, April 14, 1871.

11 **"Things are going here furiously"** John Fiske, *Edward Livingston Youmans*, p. 266.

12 **He would breeze over these months** Herbert Spencer, *An Autobiography*, p. 226.

12 **Spencer's father was a quarrelsome** Mark Francis, *Herbert Spencer and the Invention of Modern Life*, p. 28.

12 **"My Dear Youmans"** Fiske, *Youmans*, p. 267.

13 **"For Darwin, evolution was directionless"** Steven Shapin, "Man with a Plan," *The New Yorker*, August 13, 2007, p. 79.

13 **Youmans despaired as a young man** Fiske, *Youmans*, p. 39.

13 **Youmans was a riveting public speaker** Ibid., pp. 79–80.

14 **"If you become attached to someone else"** Rosemary Ashton, *George Eliot: A Life*, p. 99.

15 **"a protracted meeting in full blast"** Fiske, *Youmans*, p. 244.

15 **Youmans found London to be no better** Ibid., pp. 269–83.

17 **Beecher had told Youmans in a letter** Ibid., p. 201.

18 **"Civilization is festering"** Barbara Goldsmith, *Other Powers*, p. 290.

19 **"Such a book is a tomb"** Ibid., p. 289.

19 **"You doubtless know that it is in my power"** Mary Gabriel, *Notorious Victoria*, p. 140.

20 **"Beecher preaches to seven or eight"** Debby Applegate, *The Most Famous Man in America*, p. 391.

20 **"polygamy is almost universally followed"** Darwin, *Descent*, p. 591.

20 **"Marriage is the grave of love"** Applegate, *Famous*, p. 416.

21 **"The basis of society is the relation of the sexes"** Gabriel, *Notorious Victoria*, pp. 143–48; Goldsmith, *Other Powers*, pp. 298–302.

NOTES 329

23 "the most astonishing doctrine" Gabriel, *Notorious Victoria,* p. 149.

23 "Drove over to the Navy Yard" James D. Teller, "Louis Agassiz and Men of Letters," *Scientific Monthly,* November 1947, p. 430.

24 "If there is, as I believe" E. Agassiz, *Life and Correspondence,* p. 342.

25 "Wild nonsense" Letter from Darwin to Charles Lyell, September 8, 1866.

25 "predetermined wish partly explains" Letter from Darwin to Gray, September 10, 1866.

25 "Pray give my most sincere respects" Letter from Darwin to Alexander Agassiz, June 1, 1871.

25 "As soon as we reached the Gulf Stream" E. Agassiz, *Life and Correspondence,* p. 345.

25 "I am back from Germany" Fiske, *Youmans,* p. 289.

26 "The State is simply a policeman" Thomas Henry Huxley, "Administrative Nihilism," 1871.

27 "Spencer couldn't stand it" Fiske, *Youmans,* p. 286.

27 "[Huxley] put his objection" Spencer, *Autobiography,* p. 232.

28 "Germany is not going to suit me" Fiske, *Youmans,* p. 287.

28 "I had a letter to one important man" Ibid., p. 288.

28 "The support which I receive from Germany" Richard Weikart, "The Origins of Social Darwinism in Germany, 1859-1895," *Journal of the History of Ideas,* July 1993, p. 471.

29 "Germany is more ripe" Fiske, *Youmans,* p. 290.

29 "I am bound to this enterprise" Ibid., p. 284.

29 "My Dear Sister" Ibid., pp. 292–93.

CHAPTER TWO: NEW HAVEN, 1872

31 "had a bad night, not feeling well" Lyman Abbott, *Henry Ward Beecher: A Sketch of His Career,* p. 210.

31 "I have been under the penumbra" Henry Ward Beecher, *Lectures on Preaching,* pp. 20–21.

33 "To *say* that I have a church" Debby Applegate, *The Most Famous Man in America,* p. 417.

33 "My dear Peirce" E. Cary Agassiz, *Louis Agassiz: His Life and Correspondence,* p. 348.

35 "The Fuegians twice came" Charles Darwin, *The Voyage of the Beagle,* p. 246.

36 "One could hardly believe" Elizabeth Agassiz, "In the Straits of Magellan," *The Atlantic Monthly,* January 1872, p. 90.

36 "As much as I try to feel pity" Louis Menand, *The Metaphysical Club,* p. 105.

37 "It shews that they graduated" Charles Darwin, *The Descent of Man,* p. 203.

38 "I had wished to have a near view of the Fuegians" E. Agassiz, "In the Straits," p. 94.

39 "the close connection there is" J. C. Nott and George R. Glidden, *Types of Mankind,* p. lviii.

39 "So we parted" E. Agassiz, "In the Straits," p. 95.

39 "neither anyone else's version" Herbert Spencer, *An Autobiography,* p. 243.

39 **Spencer suggested that Youmans approach a newspaper** John Fiske, *Edward Livingston Youmans,* pp. 298–300.

41 **"But if the *Tribune* prints the papers"** Ibid., pp. 300–302.

42 **("Being under great obligation")** Spencer, *Autobiography,* p. 242.

42 **"a genius for suicide"** William S. McFeely, *Grant,* p. 381.

43 **"Although I cannot become President"** Hans L. Trefousse, *Carl Schurz,* p. 203.

43 **"It became perfectly clear in my mind"** Edward Livingston Youmans, ed., *Herbert Spencer on the Americans and the Americans on Herbert Spencer,* p. 41.

44 **"The superstition that Grant"** McFeely, *Grant,* p. 381.

44 **"Suppose we annex the Dominican Republic"** Carl Schurz, Senatorial Address, January 11, 1871.

45 **"Sumner and Schurz"** Trefousse, *Schurz,* p. 198.

45 **"This is moving day!"** Claude Fuess, *Carl Schurz: Reformer,* p. 187.

46 **"stripped of its higher moral character"** Ibid., p. 206.

46 **"I would do anything"** Andrew Slap, *The Doom of Reconstruction,* p. 178.

46 **"The result of the Cincinnati Convention"** Trefousse, *Schurz,* p. 206.

47 **"the best woman that God ever made"** "Memoirs of Anne C. L. Botta," *The New York Times,* December 31, 1893.

47 **"house of the expanding doors"** Albert Ten Eyck Gardner, "The Arts and Mrs. Botta," *Metropolitan Museum of Art Bulletin,* November 1947, pp. 105–8.

48 **"One of her chief characteristics"** Anne C. Lynch Botta, *Memoirs,* p. 165.

49 **"Settle in Oxford"** Joseph Frazier Wall, *Andrew Carnegie,* pp. 224–25.

50 **"At the first opportunity"** Andrew Carnegie, *Autobiography,* p. 159.

50 **"the pages which explain how man"** Ibid., p. 327.

51 **"got the flash"** Peter Krass, *Carnegie,* p. 116.

52 **"I had not failed to notice the growth"** Carnegie, *Autobiography,* p. 177.

52 **After the *Hassler* came out of the strait** Edward Lurie, *Nature and the American Mind,* p. 91.

53 **"was a great loss for us all"** Letter from L. Agassiz to Peirce, July 29, 1872.

54 **Elizabeth retreated, bored and disappointed** Lurie, *Nature,* p. 114.

54 **"The distinction pleased me the more"** E. Agassiz, *Louis Agassiz: His Life and Correspondence,* p. 374.

55 **"what we might imagine"** Charles Darwin, *The Voyage of the Beagle,* pp. 384–413.

55 **"the merest *reconnaissances*"** Elizabeth Agassiz, "A Cruise Through the Galapagos," *The Atlantic Monthly,* May 1872, p. 583.

55 **"does not . . . go back to earlier geological periods"** E. Agassiz, *Life and Correspondence,* p. 376.

56 **"That is why I am on this voyage"** Letter from L. Agassiz to Karl Gegenbauer, July 28, 1872.

57 **Back in Cambridge, Agassiz wrote** Lurie, *Nature,* p. 95.

58 **"Mr. Beecher bowed and smiled"** Noyes L. Thompson, *The History of Plymouth Church: 1847–1872,* pp. 180–83.

58 **"See to it that she is to understand"** Applegate, *Famous,* p. 420.

59 **"That theology had put the emphasis"** Thompson, *History of Plymouth Church,* p. 212.

59 **"At its conclusion, Mr. Beecher"** Ibid., pp. 232–33.

60 "I will make it hotter on earth" Applegate, *Famous*, p. 422.

60 Woodhull's exposé Victoria Woodhull, "The Beecher-Tilton Scandal Case," *Woodhull & Claflin's Weekly*, November 2, 1872.

61 Beecher strode to the pulpit Gabriel, *Notorious Victoria*, p. 190.

62 Either Beecher was confessing Ibid., p. 191.

62 "Ultimately a highly complex sentiment" Darwin, *Descent*, pp. 119–51.

63 "That, two thousand years" Henry Adams, *The Education of Henry Adams*, p. 266.

63 "I wish I could say with what agony" Trefousse, *Schurz*, p. 215.

63 "he felt he was going" Applegate, *Famous*, p. 424.

CHAPTER THREE: NEW YORK, 1873

65 "The buildings were made to fit the transportation" Thomas Misa, *A Nation of Steel*, p. 24.

65 "We must be careful what class of men" James H. Bridge, *The Carnegie Millions and the Men Who Made Them*, p. 81.

66 "Well, what do you think now" Joseph Frazier Wall, *Andrew Carnegie*, p. 316.

66 "fire off my cracker" Letter from Gray to Darwin, February 25, 1873.

68 "much impressed by the general assent" James Hague, "A Reminiscence of Mr. Darwin," *Harper's Magazine*, April 1884.

68 "I can only rejoice that the discussion" Edward Lurie, *Louis Agassiz: A Life in Science*, p. 384.

69 "Pope Darwin" Janet Browne, *Charles Darwin: The Power of Place*, p. 384.

69 Huxley reeling from a combination Adrian Desmond, *Huxley*, pp. 428–30.

70 Spencer himself around this time Herbet Spencer, *An Autobiography*, p. 249.

71 "rejoicing if the post was a light one" Browne, *The Power of Place*, p. 389.

71 In August . . . Darwin suffered Ibid., p. 400.

72 "All was going well" Andrew Carnegie, *Autobiography*, pp. 182–83.

73 "It was one of the most trying moments" Peter Krass, *Carnegie*, p. 120.

73 He thought panics Wall, *Carnegie*, p. 318.

73 "Up to this time" Carnegie, *Autobiography*, p. 186.

74 "We are steadily outgrowing" Wall, *Carnegie*, p. 318.

74 "The man who has money" Ibid., p. 319.

75 "The banks have been departing" "The Panic," *The New York Times*, September 20, 1873.

75 As the time for the start of business "Resumption of Business," *Times*, October 1, 1873.

75 "intensely gloomy" "The Financial Outlook," *Times*, October 4, 1873.

76 "a broken and disordered front" "The Evangelical Alliance," *Times*, October 4, 1873.

76 "Who ever saw a face" A. A. Hodge, *The Life of Charles Hodge*, p. 547.

77 "Christ pervades his people" *History, Essays, Orations, and Other Documents of the Sixth General Conference of the Evangelical Alliance*, ed. by Rev. Philip Schaff and S. Irenaeus Prime, pp. 139–44.

77 "like a jewel to be worn" Ronald Numbers, "Charles Hodge and the Beauties

and Deformities of Science," in *Charles Hodge Revisited*, ed. by John W. Stewart and James H. Moorhead, p. 95.

77 **"We desire that the spirit of true religion"** J. David Hoeveler, Jr., *James McCosh and the Scottish Intellectual Tradition*, p. 230.

78 **McCosh used the term "development"** *Sixth General Conference*, ed. Schaff and Prime, pp. 264–71, 317–23.

80 **"I seem to have a double existence"** Debby Applegate, *The Most Famous Man in America*, p. 431.

80 **"I say the first power needed"** *Sixth General Conference*, ed. Schaff and Prime, pp. 392–96.

81 **"It is well, I think"** "Brooklyn's Welcome," *Times*, October 9, 1873.

81 **On the evening of Friday, October 31** Charles F. Marshall, *The True History of the Brooklyn Scandal*, pp. 32–35.

82 **"You must learn to look on fossil forms"** Elizabeth Agassiz, *Louis Agassiz: His Life and Correspondence*, p. 383.

82 **"He is a sort of demagogue"** Letter from Gray to Darwin, January 10, 1860.

82 **Agassiz now lauded Darwin** Louis Agassiz, "Evolution and the Permanance of Type," *The Atlantic Monthly*, January 1874.

84 **"I have already had this MS copied"** Lurie, *Agassiz*, p. 383.

84 **"Those who accompanied him"** E. Agassiz, *Life and Correspondence*, p. 385.

84 **"strangely asleep"** Lurie, *Agassiz*, p. 388.

85 **"Three tiny words grew lurid"** James Russell Lowell, "Agassiz," *The Atlantic Monthly*, May 1874.

85 **"Seldom, if ever, has the death"** "Louis Agassiz," *The Nation*, December 18, 1873.

85 **"It is becoming daily more apparent"** "Can Christianity Stand the Assault of Science?" Boston *Journal*, September 5, 1874.

CHAPTER FOUR: NEW HAVEN, 1874

88 **"My own judgment is that however much"** William S. McFeely, *Grant*, p. 394.

88 **But he soon grew disaffected** Harris E. Starr, *William Graham Sumner*, p. 169.

88 **"seems to be the only place where poverty"** Sylvia E. Bowman, *William Graham Sumner*, p. 43.

88 **Sumner would recall** William Graham Sumner, "Sketch of William Graham Sumner," *Popular Science Monthly* 35, 1889, p. 265.

89 **"rendered possible by consistent renunciation"** Robert B. Notestein, "The Moralist Rigorism of W. G. Sumner," *Journal of the History of Ideas*, June 1955, p. 393.

89 **"the bloom of a competitive civilization"** Richard Hofstadter, *Social Darwinism in American Thought*, p. 58.

89 **"The question whether it is necessary"** William Graham Sumner, *A History of American Currency*, p. 202.

90 **"the end of an ominous rifle barrel"** A. G. Keller, *Reminiscences of William Graham Sumner*, p. 6.

90 **Here was a new type of professor** H. E. Starr, *Sumner*, p. 177.

91 "I had arranged" Herbert Spencer, *An Autobiography*, p. 261.

91 "No. 2 of the *Des. Soc.* is out" Ibid., p. 268.

91 "It presents history as a social evolution" Bowman, *Sumner*, p. 62.

92 "a great evil" Charles Hodge, *What Is Darwinism?* ed. by Mark Knoll and David Livingstone, p. 63.

92 "visibly ripening for another life" A. A. Hodge, *The Life of Charles Hodge*, p. 531.

92 "It is obviously useless to discuss" C. Hodge, *What Is Darwinism?* p. 63.

92 "peculiar character and importance" Ibid., p. 92.

92 To ask Darwin "to give up his denial" Ibid., p. 121.

93 "This is the vital point" Ibid., pp. 156–57.

94 "However much we may wish it" Charles Darwin, *The Variation of Plants and Animals Under Domestication*, p. 428.

94 "I dare say I am much more orthodox" A. Hunter Dupree, *Asa Gray*, p. 359.

94 "The taint of atheism" Asa Gray, "What Is Darwinism?" *The Nation*, May 28, 1874.

94 "Having nearly despaired of converting scientists" Dupree, *Gray*, p. 360.

95 "We know of old that God" Gray, "What Is Darwinism?"

95 "You will see what uphill work I have" Letter from Gray to Darwin, June 16, 1874.

95 "I read with interest your semi-theological review" Letter from Darwin to Gray, June 30, 1874.

95 "in the course which the wind blows" Charles Darwin, *Autobiography*, p. 87.

95 "crept over me at a very slow rate" Ibid., p. 87.

96 "How can the generally beneficent arrangement" Ibid., p. 88.

96 Darwin, trellising his thoughts Ibid., pp. 88–90.

97 she and Lewes "left in disgust" Janet Browne, *Charles Darwin: The Power of Place*, p. 405.

97 "We had grand fun" Ibid., p. 405.

97 "Strange to say" Robert L. Carneiro, "Herbert Spencer's 'The Study of Sociology' and the Rise of Social Science in America," *Proceedings of the American Philosophical Society*, December 27, 1974, p. 550.

98 "I never believed in the reigning influence" Letter from Darwin to Spencer, June 10, 1872.

98 ("It comes to me like the air") Letter from Oliver Wendell Holmes to Youmans, May 3, 1874.

98 "adhere rigorously to this course of abstinence" Letter from Spencer to Youmans, August 26, 1873.

98 Youmans took the rostrum and launched a spirited defense John Fiske, *Edward Livingston Youmans*, pp. 502–51.

101 "Herbert Spencer's conversation" Darwin, *Autobiography*, pp. 108–9.

101 "With savages, the weak in body and mind" Charles Darwin, *The Descent of Man*, p. 159.

102 "Of course I cannot but rejoice" Letter from Spencer to Youmans, June 20, 1874.

102 "You have clearly enough stated" Ibid., July 12, 1874.

103 "There are many not only in Brooklyn" Charles F. Marshall, *The True History of the Brooklyn Scandal,* pp. 40–44.

103 "to inform you, on his word of honor" Ibid., p. 61.

103 "There is only one thing that I was born for" Richard Wightman Fox, *Trials of Intimacy,* p. 66.

103 "I rose quietly" Debby Applegate, *The Most Famous Man in America,* p. 435.

104 Bitter statements and counterstatements Ibid., pp. 433–34.

105 "A committee nominated by him" E. L. Godkin, "Trial by Newspaper," *The Nation,* July 30, 1874.

105 Beecher appeared before the panel Marshall, *True History,* pp. 286–302.

108 "If Mr. Beecher is innocent" Ibid., p. 608.

109 "My soul was on fire" Lewis S. Feuer, *The Scientific Intellectual,* p. 369.

109 "an atheist, an infidel, a blasphemer" H. Burnell Pannill, *The Religious Faith of John Fiske,* p. 10.

109 "a place where boys are made to recite" Ibid., p. 17.

109 "What we do not want" Ibid., p. 18.

111 his own early idea of God Ibid., pp. 5–6.

111 But under Cosmic Philosophy John Spencer Clark, *The Life and Letters of John Fiske, Vol. II,* pp. 33, 49–51.

112 It was Fiske's conclusion Ibid., p. 51.

112 "You must allow me to thank you" Letter from Darwin to Fiske, December 8, 1874.

113 "As yet, I have myself read but parts" Letter from Spencer to Fiske, December 11, 1874.

CHAPTER FIVE: BROOKLYN, 1875

114 "appeared in perfect health and spirits" "The Beecher-Tilton Suit," *The New York Times,* January 5, 1875.

115 "presents for the investigation of scientific men" Debby Applegate, *The Most Famous Man in America,* p. 444.

115 "Didn't you say that Mr. Beecher" Ibid., p. 445.

116 "Mr. Beecher was my man of all men" Richard Wightman Fox, *Trials of Intimacy,* p. 108.

116 "I think my wife loves everything good" Ibid., pp. 113–14.

116 When Emma Moulton took the stand Applegate, *Famous,* pp. 445–46.

117 "pinched Monsignor Beecher very hard" Ibid., p. 446.

117 "But then he evidently fails to see" "The Great Scandal," *The Nation,* August 20, 1874.

117 "swear in the New England custom" Applegate, *Famous,* p. 447.

117 But on cross-examination, he stumbled Fox, *Trials,* pp. 118–22.

120 Elizabeth abruptly stood up and addressed the judge Applegate, *Famous,* pp. 449–50.

120 "No, we have not" Ibid., p. 451.

121 "It can hardly be said" "Tilton against Beecher," *The Nation,* July 8, 1875.

121 "Is Mr. Beecher free from all blame?" "Henry Ward Beecher," New York *Evangelist,* August 5, 1875.

121 "I have no new course to take" "Beecher," *Chicago Tribune*, July 14, 1875.

122 "entirely unworthy of his name" Paxton Hibben, *Henry Ward Beecher*, p. 282.

122 "I will *not* worship cruelty" Ibid., p. 290.

122 "reef sailing" Andrew Carnegie, *Autobiography*, p. 185.

123 **Rockefeller reputedly trumpeted** Irvin G. Wyllie, "Social Darwinism and the Businessman," *Proceedings of the American Philisophical Society*, October 15, 1959, pp. 629–35.

123 "a mere morsel of two thousand tons of rails" Peter Krass, *Carnegie*, p. 133.

123 "Our competitors in steel" David Nasaw, *Andrew Carnegie*, p. 167.

124 "The liquid pig metal" James H. Bridge, *The Carnegie Millions and the Men Who Made Them*, p. 145.

124 **Carnegie anxiously told Shinn** Krass, *Carnegie*, pp. 133–34.

125 "iron voice" A. G. Keller, *Reminiscences of William Graham Sumner*, p. 4.

125 "The duty of the economist" William Graham Sumner, *The Challenge of Facts and Other Essays*, pp. 389–404.

126 "fixed in the order of the universe" Sylvia E. Bowman, *William Graham Sumner*, p. 59.

126 "I never consciously gave up" George M. Marsden, "God and Man at Yale (1880)," *First Things*, April 1994, p. 40.

127 "Professor, don't you believe" Richard Hofstadter, *Social Darwinism in American Thought*, p. 54.

127 "He broke upon us" Keller, *Reminiscences*, p. 3.

128 "I dislike to hear politicians sneered at" Sumner, *Challenge*, p. 396.

128 **Sumner opposed the project** Harris E. Starr, *William Graham Sumner*, pp. 182–83.

128 "the staples of Gilded Age liberalism" Robert C. Bannister, *Social Darwinism*, p. 70.

129 "Never before has the conception of a social science" John E. Cairnes, "Social Evolution," *The Popular Science Monthly*, June 1875, pp. 604–12.

130 "If the analogy of the body politic" Thomas Henry Huxley, "Administrative Nihilism," 1871.

130 **In an accompanying editorial** Bannister, *Social Darwinism*, p. 72.

130 "Professor Cairnes goes back" Ibid., p. 71.

130 "the only complete and systematic statement" E. L. Youmans, "The Literature of Evolution," *The Popular Science Monthly*, June 1875, pp. 745–48.

130 "But the *Nation* thinks differently" Ibid., p. 745.

131 **Usually when traveling by train** Mark Francis, *Herbert Spencer and the Invention of Modern Life*, p. 92.

131 "a discouraging account of himself" Herbert Spencer, *Autobiography*, p. 287.

131 "let me say first" Ibid., pp. 287–88.

CHAPTER SIX: WASHINGTON, 1876

133 "to devise means to prevent the campaign" Hans L. Trefousse, *Carl Schurz*, p. 226.

133 **Bruce said that the party could no longer be trusted** Dee Brown, *The Year of the Century: 1876*, pp. 199–201.

134 "The whole public are tired out" Eric Foner, *A Short History of Reconstruction, 1863–1867,* p. 236.

134 "The loss of the wife of one's youth" Trefousse, *Schurz,* p. 227.

135 "One hundred years ago our country" Brown, *Year,* p. 127.

136 "It is in these things of iron and steel" Ibid., p. 130.

137 "only the cleanest and finest looking" Michael Brilli, "The Native American Exhibit at the Centennial," http://www3.villanova.edu/centennial/paper.htm.

137 "The red man, as he appears in effigy" Ibid.

137 "Every true American" Brown, *Year,* pp. 203-4.

137 "I appeal to you as a soldier" Jacob Piatt Dunn, *Massacres of the Mountains,* p. 603.

138 "He knew that in a racial battle" William S. McFeely, *Grant,* p. 422.

138 "The indications point to the nomination of Blaine" Brown, *Year,* p. 208.

139 "Governor Hayes is a good selection" Ibid., p. 210.

139 THE REPUBLICAN PARTY Ibid.

139 "As the Indians closed in" "The Battle of Little Big Horn, 1876," http://www.eyewitnesstohistory.com/custer.html.

140 "without aid from the Federal Government" McFeely, *Grant,* p. 439.

140 "A German editor having written to me" Charles Darwin, *Autobiography,* p. 21.

141 "I can say in my own favour" Ibid., p. 26.

141 "I believe that I was considered" Ibid., p. 28.

141 "from various small circumstances" Ibid., p. 46.

141 Having read by then his grandfather Erasmus Darwin's *Zoonomia* Ibid., p. 49.

142 "Eheu!!" Janet Browne, *Charles Darwin: Voyaging,* p. 379.

142 "Being well prepared" Darwin, *Autobiography,* p. 120.

142 "was led to think much about religion" Ibid., pp. 85–96.

143 "Darwin lavished credit" Robert Wright, *The Moral Animal,* p. 276.

143 "My life goes on like Clockwork" Letter from Darwin to FitzRoy, October 1, 1846.

143 "the remains of the day" Janet Browne, *Charles Darwin: The Power of Place,* p. 434.

143 And yet if he had developed Darwin, *Autobiography,* pp. 136–41.

145 "I will take for lecture days" John Fiske, *Edward Livingston Youmans,* p. 334.

145 "shoved like a child's toys" Gore Vidal, *1876,* p. 3.

145 He asked an acquaintance Adrian Desmond, *Huxley,* p. 470.

145 "a new idea of the possibilities" William Randel, "Huxley in America," *Proceedings of the American Philosophical Society,* April 13, 1970, pp. 78–79.

146 "My own explorations led me" Mark Jaffe, *The Gilded Dinosaur,* p. 156.

146 Marsh had pieced together a sixty-million-year history Ibid., p. 157.

147 "It was not simply a story of specialization" Ibid.

147 "I believe you are a magician" Desmond, *Huxley,* p. 473.

147 "He then informed me" Jaffe, *Gilded,* p. 157.

148 "We may be rich yet" Desmond, *Huxley,* p. 471.

148 "Natural selection is not the wind" A. Hunter Dupree, *Asa Gray,* p. 367.

148 Gray and Huxley were cordial Ibid., pp. 367–68.

148   "killing me with kindness" Randel, "Huxley in America," p. 79.

149   Speaking without prepared remarks, Huxley Ibid., pp. 82–84.

150   The Right Reverend A. Cleveland Coxe Brown, *Year,* p. 294.

150   In Nashville Randel, "Huxley in America," pp. 86–87.

151   "Boom money" Desmond, *Huxley,* p. 477.

151   "I cannot say that I am . . . impressed" Randel, "Huxley in America," p. 91; Brown, *Year,* p. 295.

153   "tired and stupefied" Desmond, *Huxley,* p. 479.

153   "His tour has been a laborious ovation" Fiske, *Youmans,* p. 335.

153   "That Prof. Huxley will be heartily welcomed" "Professor Huxley's Lecture," *The New York Times,* September 17, 1876.

153   "When the Darwinian hypothesis was first put forth" "Darwinism and Atheism," *Times,* September 18, 1876.

154   "essentially a carnivorous swimming ostrich" Jaffe, *Gilded,* p. 88.

154   There was no indication, for instance "Prof. Huxley's Second Lecture," *Times,* September 21, 1876.

154   "I do not think, ladies and gentlemen" Ibid.

154   On Friday night, Huxley delivered "Prof. Huxley's Final Lecture," *Times,* September 23, 1876.

155   "Mr. HUXLEY himself stands on the baseless fabric" "Prof. Huxley's Lectures," *Times,* September 24, 1876.

156   "I am thinking of discoursing on the birds with teeth" Jaffe, *Gilded,* p. 163.

156   "I had him 'corralled' in the basement" Ibid., p. 164.

156   "Unless I am very much mistaken" Trefousse, *Schurz,* p. 230.

156   "I shall find many things to console me" Carl Schurz, *Speeches, Correspondence and Political Papers,* p. 339.

157   "I think we have undoubtedly been elected" Brown, *Year,* p. 318.

157   "stigmatized as a fraud" McFeely, *Grant,* p. 446.

157   "any suspicion of unfair dealing" Trefousse, *Schurz,* p. 232.

158   "I have no doubt that we are" Roy Morris, Jr., *Fraud of the Century,* p. 199.

158   "We must look the undeniable fact in the face" Ibid., p. 212.

158   "any demonstration or warlike concentration" McFeely, *Grant,* p. 447.

158   "Sixteen years after the secession crisis" Foner, *Short History,* p. 242.

159   "the sentiment of the country" Morris, *Fraud,* p. 217.

159   "What is left but war?" Brown, *Year,* p. 333.

160   "Mexicanized" C. Vann Woodward, *Reunion and Reaction,* p. 13.

160   "In effect the Southerners" Ibid., p. 7.

160   "A man whom the people rejected at the polls" Morris, *Fraud,* p. 241.

160   "The negro will disappear" Foner, *Short History,* p. 245.

161   "had not known the rules of the game" Harris E. Starr, *William Graham Sumner,* p. 193.

CHAPTER SEVEN: BALTIMORE, 1877

162   "No use coming" Lyman Abbott, *Henry Ward Beecher,* p. 305.

163   "the gallery is full of eggs" Ibid., p. 306.

163 "In the balmiest days of my life" Debby Applegate, *The Most Famous Man in America*, p. 457.

163 "as if nothing had happened" Ibid.

163 "glorious triumph" "Mr. Beecher's Triumph," *The American Socialist*, March 22, 1877.

164 "Still, there is a morbid curiosity" Ibid.

165 "The gravest danger" Peter Krass, *Carnegie*, p. 139.

165 With his competitors all under the same grueling pressure Ibid., pp. 143–46.

166 "The sixth and seventh days of the revolution" "The Great Strike," *Harper's Weekly*, August 11, 1877.

167 "the first uprising against the oligarchy" Alan Woods, "The Workers' Uprising of 1877," http://www.marxist.com/workers-uprising-marxism-usa1877-3.htm.

167 He sermonized at great length "The Pulpit on the Situation," *The New York Times*, July 23, 1877.

168 "Suicidal" Robert V. Bruce, *1877: Year of Violence*, p. 313.

168 Once again he consoled his followers "Communism Denounced," *Times*, July 30, 1877.

169 "I discovered in company with a friend" John H. Ostrom and John S. McIntosh, *Marsh's Dinosaurs*, p. 2.

169 "Please say to Prof." Mark Jaffe, *The Gilded Dinosaur*, p. 190.

170 "We would be pleased to hear from you" Ostrom and McIntosh, *Marsh's*, p. 7.

170 He lectured for an hour Phila Ledger, "Written in Coal and Chalk," *The Friend*, October 6, 1877.

171 The railroad men told him Ostrom and McIntosh, *Marsh's*, pp. 8–10.

172 "The opening of this museum" "New-York's New Museum," *Times*, December 23, 1877.

172 he now began "entertaining the thought" Herbert Spencer, *Autobiography*, p. 303.

173 "Why should not I give a picnic?" Ibid., p. 305.

174 "Have I, or have I not, named the fact" Ibid., p. 306.

174 "Mr. Spencer, I think, looks extremely well" John Fiske, *Edward Livingston Youmans*, p. 337.

175 and he, too, succumbed Ibid., pp. 338–40.

176 "So far as animals are concerned" Desmond, *Huxley*, p. 486.

176 "Why should I not treat myself" Spencer, *Autobiography*, p. 309.

CHAPTER EIGHT: BROOKLYN, 1878

177 "A few weeks since" "Mrs. Tilton Pleads Guilty," *The New York Times*, April 16, 1878.

178 "This weak and erring woman" "Editorial Article 2," Ibid.

178 "There is but one thing more" "Mr. Beecher Vindicated," *New York Times*, April 17, 1878.

178 "I believe Mr. Beecher is convinced" "What Mr. Beecher Thinks," Ibid.

178 "Poor woman!" Richard Wightman Fox, *Trials of Intimacy*, p. 41.

179 "They had to survive" Ibid., p. 42.

179 In Minneapolis in early August "Brains," *Times,* August 5, 1878.

181 Kearney was invited "Kearney in Brooklyn," *Times,* September 8, 1878.

181 "My Dear Youmans" John Fiske, *Edward Livingston Youmans,* p. 345.

182 Schurz had set the political struggle in motion Henry Nash Smith, "Clarence King, John Wesley Powell and the Establishment of the U.S. Geological Survey," *The Mississippi Valley Historical Review,* June 1947, pp. 37–58.

183 impeding the "big barbecue" Ibid., p. 39.

184 "and in less than two days got the approval" Charles Schuchert and Clara Mae LeVene, *O. C. Marsh: Pioneer in Paleontology,* p. 254.

184 "an effort of 'new-fledged collegiates' " Smith, "Clarence King," pp. 48–49.

185 "Now that the battle is won" Ibid., p. 55.

185 "If we do not believe in survival of the fittest" Sylvia E. Bowman, *William Graham Sumner,* p. 84.

185 "Nature's remedies against vice" Ibid.

185 Sumner counseled a severe hands-off approach "Yale Professor William Graham Sumner Prescribes Laissez-Faire for Depression Woes," http://history matters.gmu.edu/d/5729.

187 "the most miserable eleven days" Herbert Spencer, *Autobiography,* p. 309.

187 "More and more each winter" Ibid.

188 "Reluctant to sacrifice wholly" Ibid., p. 311.

188 "the gap left by the disappearance" Herbert Spencer, *Data of Ethics,* p. iv.

188 "I wish I could make you more fully realize" Fiske, *Youmans,* p. 347.

189 "Pray yield to my pressure" Ibid.

189 He warned Spencer to lower his expectations Ibid., p. 348.

189 Spencer was thrown off his routine Spencer, *Autobiography,* p. 318.

190 "I can but dimly perceive" Rosemary Ashton, *George Eliot,* p. 365.

190 "I got off at Liverpool" Fiske, *Youmans,* p. 350.

190 Now that he was in Spencer's protective care Ibid., pp. 351–54.

191 "What was most remarkable" David Nasaw, *Andrew Carnegie,* p. 184.

191 "What I do is to get good men" Ibid.

192 "Spencer and Darwin were then high" Andrew Carnegie, *Autobiography,* p. 199.

192 "two young lady missionaries in embryo" Joseph Frazier Wall, *Andrew Carnegie,* pp. 366–67.

192 Carnegie's disgust Ibid.

193 he had long ago concluded Ibid., pp. 368–69.

193 "In China I read Confucius" Carnegie, *Autobiography,* p. 199.

194 "How women can be induced" Andrew Carnegie, *Round the World,* p. 38.

194 "It is gorgeous in color" Ibid., p. 47.

195 "We had another opportunity" Ibid., p. 56.

195 "In America during the Civil War" Ibid., p. 71.

195 Happy, indeed Ibid., p. 63.

196 "all things Japanese" Christopher Benfey, *The Great Wave,* p. xi.

196 Carnegie tempered his estimation Carnegie, *Round the World,* p. 73.

197 "There is not a street or road" Ibid., p. 78.

197 "China's difficulty" Wall, *Carnegie,* p. 371.

197 "China is one vast cemetery" Carnegie, *Round the World*, p. 79.

198 "Do not mourn too much" Ibid., p. 92.

198 "China is, as far as I know" Ibid., p. 114.

198 "Really, three men kept at work" Ibid., p. 133.

199 "Here the 'survival of the fittest' " Ibid., p. 153.

CHAPTER NINE: FRENCH RIVIERA, 1879

200 "a rich, prosperous watering place" John Fiske, *Edward Livingston Youmans*, p. 355.

200 Submitting abjectly to his regimen Ibid., p. 356.

201 "Spencer pegs away at his revising" Ibid.

201 "This is a region of extremes" Herbert Spencer, *Autobiography*, p. 322.

201 "I am undergoing a sharp discipline" Fiske, *Youmans*, p. 357.

201 "Since Spencer has commenced" Ibid., p. 358.

202 "Remembering what the place had witnessed" Spencer, *Autobiography*, p. 323.

202 "I am getting up an appetite for exercise" Fiske, *Youmans*, p. 360.

202 "Of course we made expeditions" Spencer, *Autobiography*, p. 322.

202 "I have been bothered to snatch intervals" Fiske, *Youmans*, p. 361.

203 "the change was beneficial" Spencer, *Autobiography*, p. 323.

203 "At first every lady we took forward" Andrew Carnegie, *Round the World*, p. 164.

204 "colonizing craze" Ibid., p. 296.

204 "I gave up all hope of improvement" Ibid., pp. 201–2.

204 Invoking Spencer Ibid., pp. 177, 203.

204 "The claims which Mohammed has" Ibid., p. 214.

205 "Who can assure us" Ibid., p. 227.

205 "The absence of women" Ibid., p. 210.

205 Having read the tormented Ibid., p. 233.

206 "It is as warm and sympathetic as a woman" Ibid., p. 257.

206 "but there was no chance to get at him" Ibid., p. 265.

206 Carnegie grew agitated Joseph Frazier Wall, *Andrew Carnegie*, p. 356.

206 "I think Mr. Shinn might have spared me" Ibid.

206 "suffered a sea change" Ibid., p. 374.

207 "No nation has all that is best" Carnegie, *Round the World*, p. 353.

207 "Another advantage to be derived" Ibid., p. 356.

207 "I believe that you could do the work" John Spencer Clark, *The Life and Letters of John Fiske*, p. 72.

207 "more and more to sundry problems" Ibid., p. 71.

208 "The voyage of Columbus" Ibid., p. 106.

208 he attempted to show how the westward migration Ibid., pp. 106–7.

208 "The audience was the very cream of Boston" Ibid., p. 108.

208 "This was the worst of nasty March days" Ibid., p. 109.

209 Fiske culminated the series John Fiske, "American Political Ideals Viewed From the Standpoint of Universal History," http://www.streitcouncil.org/content/pdf_and_doc/John%20Fiske%20Political%20Ideals.pdf.

210 "Come" Clark, *Fiske,* p. III.

211 "nervous beyond my wont" Ibid., pp. 126–29.

211 "Huxley told me he thought" Ibid., p. 129.

211 "extremely jolly and friendly" Ibid., p. 130.

211 "The old man was as lovely" Ibid., p. 134.

211 "now and then lounging" Ibid., p. 135.

212 "Room jammed" Ibid., pp. 139–40.

212 "An evening of unrivalled glory" Ibid., p. 145.

213 "So you see your boy is in very good company" Ibid., p. 162.

213 "I am invited to address you" Asa Gray, *Natural Science and Religion,* p. 30.

213 He defended against the rise in secularism George M. Marsden, *The Soul of the American University,* pp. 125–31.

213 "Half a century ago" Gray, *Natural Science,* p. 35.

214 "It is a truth of the same kind" Ibid., p. 46.

214 "Darwinism does not so much explain" Ibid., p. 49.

214 "destroyed the argument from design" A. Hunter Dupree, *Asa Gray,* p. 375.

214 "There are perplexities enough" Gray, *Natural Science,* p. 64.

214 "lies hidden *the mystery of a beginning*" Ibid., p. 72.

214 Darwinism "is therefore a good hypothesis" Ibid., pp. 72–73.

215 "It must be reasonably clear" Ibid., p. 89.

215 Gray had long avoided commenting Ibid., p. 98.

215 "You are aware" Ibid., p. 99.

215 "the power of God working" Charles Hodge, *Systematic Theology,* p. 557.

215 "I do not allow myself to believe" Gray, *Natural Science,* p. 100.

215 "with all life goes duality" Ibid., p. 105.

216 "I accept Christianity on its own evidence" Ibid., p. 106.

216 "years before any such attempt" Sumner, "Sketch of W. G. Sumner," p. 265.

216 "brings errors into the estimates" Herbert Spencer, *The Study of Sociology,* p. 298.

216 "The ferocious Fijian" Ibid., p. 294.

217 "Speaking generally, then" Ibid.

217 "Here we have theologians" Ibid., p. 298.

217 "One who holds a creed as absolutely true" Ibid., p. 301.

218 On December 6, Porter wrote Robert L. Carneiro, "Herbert Spencer's 'The Study of Sociology' and the Rise of Social Science in America," *Proceedings of the American Philosophical Society,* December 27, 1974, p. 550.

218 "If there are defects in our system" Charles Burt Sumner, *The Story of Pomona College,* p. 24.

218 "a young gentleman of superior powers" Burton J. Bledstein, "Noah Porter Versus William Graham Sumner," *Church History,* September 1974, p. 341.

219 "The book, he thought" "Prof. Sumner's Statement," *The New York Times,* April 4, 1880.

219 Sumner, regretting the attempt at interference Ibid.

219 Porter vacillated Ibid.

219 "President Porter throughout acted" Ibid.

CHAPTER TEN: WASHINGTON, 1880

220 "Next to his love for his family" John Spencer Clark, *The Life and Letters of John Fiske,* p. 84.

220 "sadly disappointed" Ibid., p. 163.

221 "Got here to breakfast" Ibid., p. 166.

221 That night Fiske dined with Schurz Ibid., pp. 166–67.

222 "He received me very warmly" Ibid., p. 167.

222 "one of the most lucid and powerful peace arguments" Ibid., p. 172.

223 "I am unable to follow you in detail" Ibid., p. 173.

223 "Spencer is in better health" Ibid., p. 178.

223 he had adapted his range of topics Ibid., p. 191.

224 James launched a blistering attack Ibid., p. 192.

224 he felt compelled to rebut James Ibid., pp. 193–98.

224 "I have received your spanking" Ibid., pp. 198–99.

225 "In its full scope and significance" "Yale as Battle-ground," *The New York Times,* April 4, 1880.

225 "hated reformers and their emotionally charged 'causes' " Burton J. Bledstein, "Noah Porter Versus Sumner," *William Graham Church History,* September 1974, p. 342.

226 "Those men who think the classics will recover" Sylvia E. Bowman, *William Graham Sumner,* p. 45.

226 "With Mr. Spencer's individual opinions" "Prof. Sumner's Statement," *Times,* April 4, 1880.

227 "Very probably this local fight" John Fiske, *Edward Livingston Youmans,* p. 364.

227 "if the works of Herbert Spencer" Robert L. Carneiro, "Herbert Spencer's 'The Study of Sociology' and the Rise of Social Science in America," *Proceedings of the American Philosophical Society,* December 27, 1974, p. 125.

227 "The Yale College flurry" Fiske, *Youmans,* p. 364.

228 "I am getting sensibly stronger" Ibid.

228 "think of anything in the shape of a long holiday" Ibid., p. 365.

228 "substantially atheistic" Carneiro, "Herbert Spencer's 'The Study of Sociology,' " p. 550.

229 "I have never yielded the point" Harris E. Starr, *William Graham Sumner,* p. 362.

229 "Fellow citizens" "The People in Politics," *Times,* June 15, 1880.

230 Lincoln told his cabinet Emmanuel Hertz, *Abraham Lincoln: A New Portrait,* p. 106.

230 Beecher's Sunday sermons began to reveal Paxton Hibben, *Henry Ward Beecher,* pp. 297–98.

231 "Schurz and your mother" Hans L. Trefousse, *Carl Schurz,* p. 252.

231 "The country is to be congratulated" Ibid.

232 Chief Crazy Horse Ibid., p. 245.

232 "As a member of the present Administration" "Words from Carl Schurz," *Times,* July 21, 1880.

233 had drawn keen interest from Karl Marx Daniel Cornford, *To Save the Republic: The California Workingmen's Party in Humboldt County,* p. 288.

233 Schurz in his speech blamed "Carl Schurz in San Francisco," *Times*, August 9, 1880.

233 "wished to be to the Indian" Carl Schurz, *Reminiscences*, p. 389.

234 "His large wagon train" Trefousse, *Schurz*, p. 245.

234 the meeting gave Beecher an opportunity "Mr. Beecher to Young Men," *Times*, October 9, 1880.

235 Beecher presided over the largest meeting "Col. Ingersoll in Brooklyn," *Times*, October 31, 1880.

236 "If it would promote the cause" "Mr. Beecher and Col. Ingersoll," *Times*, November 1, 1880.

236 The second Sunday after the election "Weak Men and Strong," *Times*, November 15, 1880.

237 Grant, needing something to do Osgood Hardy, "Ulysses S. Grant, President of the Mexican Southern Railroad," *The Pacific Historical Review*, May 1955, p. 114.

237 Beecher, in his prayers "Mr. Beecher Attacks Calvinism," *Times*, November 29, 1880.

238 "When I took charge of this department" "Secretary Schurz's Work," *Times*, December 2, 1880.

239 "If these banished Indians" "Editorial Article 3–No Title," *Times*, December 7, 1880.

239 "I tell you the infamy of this business" Valerie Sherer Mathes and Richard Lowitt, *The Standing Bear Controversy*, p. 97.

239 "But more remains to be said" "Mr. Schurz and the Poncas," *Times*, December 13, 1880.

240 "the time has come when the policy should be" Mathes and Lowitt, *Standing Bear*, p. 153.

240 "I do not undertake to apportion the blame" Stanley Clark, "Ponca Publicity," *The Mississippi Valley Historical Review*, March 1943, p. 513.

240 The dispute was not over Mathes and Lowitt, *Standing Bear*, pp. 154–65.

241 "Still less would I justify" Ibid., pp. 165–66.

CHAPTER ELEVEN: NEW YORK, 1881

242 "My Dear Spencer" John Fiske, *Edward Livingston Youmans*, p. 367.

243 "As the soldier's will" Herbert Spencer, *The Principles of Sociology*, p. 564.

243 "I consider that [to be] the most interesting" Fiske, *Youmans*, p. 369.

243 To Spencer, as the old coercive arrangements Herbert Spencer, *Autobiography*, p. 368.

245 "My Dear Youmans" Fiske, *Youmans*, pp. 370–71.

246 "his crushed top hat beside him" Charles E. Rosenberg, *The Trial of the Assassin Guiteau*, p. 3.

246 "a half-crazed, pettifogging lawyer" "A Great Nation in Grief," *The New York Times*, July 3, 1881.

246 "The President's tragic death" Ibid.

247 "Most contented themselves" Rosenberg, *Trial*, p. 4.

247 "If this is the outgrowth of Nihilism" Ibid., p. 7.

247 "It was a wanton stroke from without" "What Mr. Beecher Said," *Times*, July 4, 1881.

248 "In regard to the reception of the articles" Fiske, *Youmans*, pp. 372–73.

248 "I have, however, been perfectly satisfied" Ibid.

249 "In the nature of free, intelligent government" "What Mr. Beecher Said," *Times*, July 4, 1881.

249 Sumner waited until the overseers returned Harris E. Starr, *William Graham Sumner*, pp. 357–66.

251 "I hope that you will not allow yourself to be driven out" Ibid., p. 368.

251 "Either he found no other place to his liking" Ibid., p. 369.

252 "Each worm was capable of finding" Janet Browne, *Charles Darwin: The Power of Place*, p. 479.

252 "will do their worst work" Ibid.

253 "chieftains of Science" Ibid., p. 486.

253 "There was an immense crowd" Ibid.

253 "Medicine can no longer be practiced" No Title, *Times*, September 8, 1881, p. 4.

254 Huxley fired back Adrian Desmond, *Huxley*, p. 498.

254 "look like a terrorists' manual" Ibid., p. 500.

255 "Here is a work which has occupied me" Browne, *Power of Place*, p. 490.

256 "my heart is perfectly right" Ibid., p. 491.

256 "he was seen to shudder" Spencer, *Autobiography*, p. 371.

256 "profoundly impressed with the belief" Ibid., pp. 375–76.

257 "in direct contravention of a rule" Ibid., p. 376.

257 "The last installment of Industrialism" Fiske, *Youmans*, p. 373.

257 "I am glad to hear" Ibid., pp. 373–74.

258 Darwin . . . said he agreed with the league's "object" Letter from Darwin to Spencer, after September 22, 1881.

258 "And fear not them that kill the body" Rosenberg, *Trial*, p. 336.

CHAPTER TWELVE: NEW YORK, 1882

259 "The past year has been one of prosperity" "The Sale of Plymouth Pews," *The New York Times*, January 4, 1882.

259 "The Bible is an eating book" "Immense Christianity," *Times*, February 6, 1882.

260 "a cordial Christian evolutionist" Debby Applegate, *The Most Famous Man in America*, p. 461.

260 Startled by seeing Beecher sway and stagger "Mr. Beecher Suddenly Ill," *Times*, March 7, 1882.

260 "a path of blood around the globe" "Mr. Beecher on Theology," *Times*, April 10, 1882.

261 "When we were told of the evils of strikes" "Capitalist and Workman," *Times*, June 26, 1882.

261 "To tell me that back of Christ" "Mr. Beecher's Skepticism," *Times*, July 10, 1882.

262 "Being anxious to see a successful start made" Herbert Spencer, *Autobiography*, p. 377.

263 "The vast increase of the Empire" Frederic Harrison, *National and Social Problems*, pp. 179–80.

263 "the greatest disaster of my life" Spencer, *Autobiography*, p. 375.

263 "absurd," "foolish," "irrational" Ibid., p. 377.

263 "There is something pathetic" Beatrice Webb, *My Apprenticeship*, p. 29.

264 Spencer sensed himself ebbing away Spencer, *Autobiography*, pp. 380–82.

264 "I am fairly well" Browne, *Power of Place*, p. 494.

265 "I am not the least afraid to die" Ibid., p. 495.

265 "was like the annihilation" Ibid., p. 497.

265 "Acute as were his reasoning powers" "Darwin," *Times*, May 21, 1882.

266 "I have already given in the *Athenaeum*" Spencer, *Autobiography*, pp. 384–85.

266 "I must, I assume, assent" Ibid., p. 385.

266 "Though better, I am still not up to much work" Ibid.

267 "a great number of the most intelligent people" Edward Livingston Youmans, ed., *Herbert Spencer on the Americans and the Americans on Herbert Spencer*, p. 21.

267 "If you take a seat in the House" Peter Krass, *Carnegie*, p. 183.

267 "Even Englishmen" Ibid., p. 182.

268 "As an older traveler" Andrew Carnegie, *Autobiography*, p. 321.

268 Spencer groused about the cheese selection Ibid.

268 "Getting very much bored" Spencer, *Autobiography*, p. 387.

268 "To think that a philosopher" Ibid., p. 424.

269 "Most people frame very untrue" Ibid., p. 423.

269 "A climax was put to the mischief" Ibid., p. 388.

270 "the courage, the pluck, the heroism" Youmans, *Spencer on the Americans*, pp. 73–74.

270 "I was obliged to disappoint them" Spencer, *Autobiography*, pp. 388–89.

271 "mounted with festoons" Neil Baldwin, *Edison: Inventing the Century*, p. 135.

271 "barbarous and wasteful gaslight" Ibid., p. 137.

271 "Thinking of it chiefly as a center" Spencer, *Autobiography*, p. 388.

271 "It was first intended" Youmans, *Spencer on the Americans*, pp. 21–22.

272 "wholly superfluous" Ibid.

273 "We had to pay for the seats" Letter from Youmans to Rowland Hazard, November 26, 1882.

273 "On public occasions of moment" "William M. Evarts," *Phrenological Journal of Science and Health*, January 1877.

274 "I would not make after Beecher" Letter from Youmans to Hazard, November 26, 1882.

274 Youmans later ensured that his speech Youmans, *Spencer on the Americans*, pp. 67–77.

274 "the most picturesque thing I saw" Spencer, *Autobiography*, p. 392.

274 "The 27 electric lamps" "Edison's Electric Light," *Times*, September 5, 1882.

274 "Whether the fact that the President" Spencer, *Autobiography*, p. 397.

275 Youmans still didn't know Ibid., p. 399.

275 "that I practically interviewed myself" Ibid., p. 403.

275 "Of course my remarks" Ibid.

275 Then came the "disaster" Ibid., p. 405.

276 "I went wrong again at Boston" Youmans, *Spencer on the Americans*, pp. 6–7.

276 "Wretched night" Spencer, *Autobiography*, p. 406.

276 "a little too much music" Youmans, *Spencer on the Americans*, p. 24.

277 "It is seldom that Delmonico's banquet hall" "Philosophy at Dinner," *Times*, November 10, 1882.

277 "We are here tonight, Gentlemen" Youmans, *Spencer on the Americans*, pp. 25–28.

278 "Mr. President and Gentlemen," Spencer began Ibid., pp. 28–35.

282 "has come nearer to the realization of Bacon's claim" Ibid., pp. 84–85.

282 "In the present state of the science of sociology" Ibid., pp. 35–40.

284 "Herbert Spencer never said a wiser word" Ibid., pp. 40–45.

286 "Mr. President and Gentlemen: In meeting here to-night" Ibid., pp. 45–50.

287 He favorably compared Spencer's intellectual contribution Ibid., pp. 50–58.

290 Spencer rose partly from his chair John Spencer Clark, *The Life and Letters of John Fiske*, p. 263.

290 "weary and wanted to go home" Lyman Abbott, *Henry Ward Beecher*, p. 404.

291 "The old New England churches" Youmans, *Spencer on the Americans*, pp. 58–67.

292 "In five minutes, the more distant auditors" Abbott, *Beecher*, p. 404.

292 Like Methodist amens Ibid., p. 405.

294 "The whole audience rose" Ibid.

294 "were somewhat trying to sit through" Spencer, *Autobiography*, p. 407.

295 "Various friends and a sprinkling of strangers" Ibid.

295 "These are my two best American friends" "Herbert Spencer's Departure," *Times*, November 12, 1882.

295 *"My dear Fiske"* Clark, *Fiske*, pp. 263–64.

296 "in quantities beyond the possibility of consumption" Spencer, *Autobiography*, p. 408.

296 "I got no sleep" Ibid.

297 "You are doubtless perfectly right" Ibid., p. 478.

297 "gynoeopathy" Ibid., p. 493.

297 "Thus ended an expedition" Ibid., p. 409.

EPILOGUE

298 "this American mania" John Fiske, *Edward Livingston Youmans*, p. 385.

298 "Beecher has been lecturing this summer" Ibid., p. 379.

298 "theological opposition to the doctrine" Ibid., p. 380.

299 "rich, comfortable, prosperous, virtuous" William Graham Sumner, *What Social Classes Owe to Each Other*, p. 8.

299 "a golden little book" Fiske, *Youmans*, p. 380.

299 "the question [is] a burning one" Sydney Eisen, "Frederic Harrison and Herbert Spencer: Embattled Unbelievers," *Victorian Studies*, September 1968, p. 41.

299 "religion of the future" Ibid., p. 34.

299 "Amid the mysteries which become the more mysterious" Herbert Spencer, "Religion Retrospect and Prospect," *The Popular Science Monthly*, January 1884, p. 351.

299 "creed, doctrines, temples, priests" Samuel Laing, *Problems of the Future, and Essays*, p. 213.

300 "I regard this not only as an act of literary piracy" Fiske, *Youmans*, p. 563.

300 "who has inflicted on me immeasurably more pain" Eisen, "Frederic Harrison," p. 51.

300 "this catastrophe" Fiske, *Youmans*, p. 562.

300 "My Dear Youmans" Ibid., pp. 394–95.

301 "I'm not afraid of seeing Christianity swept away" Paxton Hibben, *Henry Ward Beecher*, p. 302.

301 "When in the gloomy night" Ibid., p. 305.

302 "If every man in New York State" Ibid., p. 307.

302 "I had tasted blood" Ibid., p. 306.

302 "this whole theory of sin" Ibid., p. 310.

302 "birds with teeth" Charles Schuchert and Clara Mae LeVene, *O. C. Marsh: Pioneer in Paleontology*, p. 317.

303 "the 'estate' is like a squeezed orange" Ibid., p. 323.

303 "The bottom fact is my brain and nerves" Sylvia E. Bowman, *William Graham Sumner*, p. 56.

304 "Then will the world enter upon a new stage" Josiah Strong, *Our Country: Its Possible Future and Its Present Crisis*, p. 175.

304 "You may be sure there will be no jingo nonsense" Robert L. Beisner, *Twelve Against Empire: The Anti-Imperialists, 1898–1900*, p. 24.

305 "dread certainty that American imperialism" Ibid.

305 Schurz once again raised the specter Ibid., pp. 26–27.

306 "keeping our empire within the continent" Ibid., pp. 174–75.

306 "the leader of the Anti-Imperialist Movement" Ibid., p. 173.

306 "You are doing the best work of your life" Ibid.

307 "The fathers of this republic" Bowman, *Sumner*, p. 113.

307 "We have beaten Spain" W. G. Sumner, *The Conquest of the United States by Spain*, p. 3.

308 "race imperialism" Beisner, *Twelve*, p. 171.

308 "made a further great descent" Spencer, *Autobiography*, p. 411.

308 "was making me look like a fool" William Irvine, *Apes, Angels and Victorians*, p. 334.

309 "almost in xtremis" Adrian Desmond, *Huxley*, pp. 573–74.

309 "dreadfully disturbed" James G. Kennedy, *Herbert Spencer*, p. 83.

310 "rigorously excluded" Herbert Spencer, *Autobiography*, p. 453.

310 "conversation was too great a strain" "Two," "Home Life with Herbert Spencer," *Harper's Magazine*, April 1906, p. 756.

310 "Thus the waking hours" Spencer, *Autobiography*, pp. 453–54.

310 one night in his drawing room . . . he confessed "Two," "Home Life," p. 759.

311 "a dangerous man" David Nasaw, *Andrew Carnegie*, p. 611.

312 "to make a study of heredity in man" "Science to Make Men and Women Better," *Times*, May 18, 1906.

313 "Certainly not" Nasaw, *Carnegie*, pp. 788–89.

313 "the most vital, exuberant person imaginable" Ibid., p. 790.

INDEX

About the Author

BARRY WERTH is the author of *31 Days, The Scarlet Professor,* which was a finalist for the National Book Critics Circle Award, *Damages,* and *The Billion-Dollar Molecule.* He lives in Northampton, Massachusetts.

About the Type

This book was set in Caslon, a typeface first
designed in 1722 by William Caslon. Its widespread
use by most English printers in the early eighteenth
century soon supplanted the Dutch typefaces that
had formerly prevailed. The roman is considered a
"workhorse" typeface due to its pleasant, open
appearance, while the italic is exceedingly decorative.